SOFTWARE SYSTEMS CONSTRUCTION WITH EXAMPLES IN ADA

SOFTWARE SYSTEMS CONSTRUCTION WITH EXAMPLES IN ADA

Bo Sanden

George Mason University

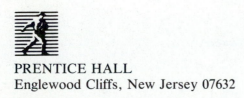

PRENTICE HALL
Englewood Cliffs, New Jersey 07632

Library of Congress Cataloging-in-Publication Data

SANDEN, BO.
   Software systems construction with examples in Ada / Bo Sanden.
      p.   cm.

   Includes bibliographical references and index.
   ISBN 0-13-030834-X
   1. Computer software—Development.   2. Ada (Computer program language)   I. Title.
QA76.76.D47S36   1994
005.13'3—dc20
                                                              93-2801
                                                              CIP

The author and publisher of this book have used their best efforts in preparing this book. These efforts include the development, research, and testing of the theories and programs to determine their effectiveness. The author and publisher make no warranty of any kind, expressed or implied, with regard to these programs or the documentation contained in this book. The author and publisher shall not be liable in any event for incidental or consequential damages in connection with, or arising out of, the furnishing, performance, or use of these programs.

Acquisitions Editor: Marcia Horton
Editorial Assistant: Dolores Mars
Cover: Carol Ceraldi
Supplements Editor: Alice Dworkin
Prepress Buyer: Linda Behrens
Manufacturing Buyer: Dave Dickey

Printed in the United States of America
10 9 8 7 6 5 4 3 2 1

ISBN   0-13-030834-X

Prentice-Hall International (UK) Limited, *London*
Prentice-Hall of Australia Pty. Limited, *Sydney*
Prentice-Hall Canada Inc., *Toronto*
Prentice-Hall Hispanoamericana, S.A., *Mexico*
Prentice-Hall of India Private Limited, *New Delhi*
Prentice-Hall of Japan, Inc., *Tokyo*
Simon & Schuster Asia Pte. Ltd., *Singapore*
Editora Prentice-Hall do Brasil, Ltda., *Rio de Janeiro*

To Elaine

Contents

3   Modularization ————————————————————— *86*

4   Object-Based Software Construction ———————————— *134*

8 Entity-Life Modeling ———————————————————— 304

9 Case Study: Flexible Manufacturing System ———————————————— 378

Preface

This book is about practical construction of software systems. It proposes an approach called *entity-life modeling*, where the software is patterned as closely as possible after structures found in the problem environment. With this approach, there is a seamless transition from problem analysis to design, leading to straight-forward software that is easy to understand and maintain. In this book, entity-life modeling is applied to an Ada programming environment.

Entity-life modeling has its roots in the *Jackson* approach to modeling soft-ware structures on threads of events in the reality, and the *object-based* approach, in which software objects are modeled on objects in the reality. The Jackson approach is modified to map directly onto concurrent tasks. This is an elegant fit that eliminates some awkward transformations often associated with that method. The object-based approach is inherent in the Ada syntax, with its pack-ages and provisions for user-defined ("abstract") types. The result is compelling software designs where the timing concerns are addressed with tasking and other concerns are separated by means of packaging.

The book is primarily intended for readers with practical experience in soft-ware construction. It targets graduate or upper-level undergraduate students of software engineering as well as practitioners who want to familiarize themselves with modern trends in software construction applied in a mainstream language environment. It complements general software-engineering texts by covering software construction in technical detail. The book contains a wealth of examples that are worked out from analysis to partial implementation in Ada. But the book is not a programming text and should be complemented with an Ada primer when appropriate. The contents have relevance beyond Ada, and experienced readers can easily transplant the concepts into other environments.

CONTENTS

The presentation of the subject matter is unconventional. No claim is made that software construction can be reduced to a neat series of steps. Instead, Chapters 2 to 7 each address a different aspect of software construction, such as control structuring, modularization, or concurrency, and discusses its use to express the problem structure in the software. Depending on the subject, the focus of each chapter shifts between problem description and a description of the means of expressing the problem in software. A reader familiar with any or all of these topics may skip ahead to the major case studies in Chapters 8 and 9. Here are the contents of each chapter:

> Chapter 1 introduces software construction principles and entity-life modeling in general and discusses the role of languages and notations.
>
> Chapter 2 is devoted to *control structuring*. The emphasis is on identifying and representing threads of events in the reality. Based on the Jackson technique, *sequence diagrams* are introduced as a notation both for such threads and for software control structures.
>
> Chapters 3 and 4 discuss *modularization* and emphasize information-hiding packages over traditional subprograms. Chapter 4 discusses the use of information-hiding packages and abstract data types to represent objects in the reality in an object-based design approach. These chapters emphasize the expressiveness of the software constructs. Identification of objects in the reality is also addressed.
>
> Software frequently deals with the changing states of objects in the reality. Chapter 5 reviews the basics of *finite automata* and their software representation. The behavior of various real-world objects is captured in *transition diagrams*, which are the counterpart of sequence diagrams. As in Chapter 2, the emphasis in this chapter is on capturing the properties of the reality.
>
> Chapter 6 introduces the Ada task syntax, which gives a good understanding of concurrent processing in general. The chapter focuses on the technicalities of tasks and task interactions. A temperature sensor is used as a small but real application example, based largely on simple, periodic tasks.

A concurrent program typically contains *shared* objects that must be accessed by one task at a time. Chapter 7 is a discussion of such *resource sharing*. The emphasis is on two practical issues: how to implement shared resources, and how to prevent *deadlocks* that occur when multiple tasks wait for each other to release resources.

Chapter 8 prevents *entity-life modeling*. Much of the earlier material serves as a buildup to this central chapter. In entity-life modeling, the problem environment is analyzed in terms of threads of events and objects. Some of the threads are modeled as *subject tasks* that "drive" the software. Each task is patterned after the behavior of some real-world entity in the manner introduced in Chapters 2 and 5 and operates on various objects in the manner discussed in Chapters 4 and 7. An elevator control system is used as a major case study.

Chapter 9 is a significant case study of a flexible manufacturing system developed with entity-life modeling. It is carried through from problem analysis to implementation with extensive excerpts of Ada text. This concrete, substantial, and realistic example brings together the various aspects of software construction discussed throughout the book and illustrates the close relationship between the final software product and the problem on which it is modeled.

The excerpts of program text used to illustrate the various topics are not necessarily complete, but the examples have been compiled and run with scaffolding simulating the actual working environments of the software. Irrelevant portions are left out, including trivial or hardware-dependent modules. For reasons of space, the excerpts have been kept terse, variable names short, and so on. The lack of comments in the program text is compensated by the accompanying narrative.

CLASS USE OF THE BOOK

The Software Engineering Master's program at George Mason University includes the mandatory courses *Software Construction*, *Software Design*, *Software Requirements*, *Software Project Management*, *Formal Methods and Models*, and *Software Project Laboratory*. Electives include *Quality Assurance*, *Object-Oriented Software Construction*, and *User Interface Design* in addition to many computer science courses. The prerequisites for the program are a block-structured programming language, data structures, assembly programming, and discrete mathematics.

This book has served as a text for Software Construction (Chapters 1 to 6) and Software Design (Chapters 6 to 9; with intended overlap). (The text can be covered in one course if the students know elementary Ada beforehand.) The

Crazy Eights project (Chapter 4) is used as a term project in Software Construction. The various projects at the end of Chapters 8 and 9 have been used as design projects for teams of three or four students in the Software Design course, leading up to a skeleton Ada program with package specifications and task outlines.

The projects are also used in the Software Project Laboratory course, where the final deliverables include a working, documented software product. Projects include a supermarket checkout system, an air-traffic control game, an automated vending machine, and a bottling plant. The project descriptions are open-ended, giving the students the freedom to partly define the problem environment. The book has been extensively class tested and successively expanded to cover all those topics that have proved to be stumbling blocks in the project work.

ACKNOWLEDGMENTS

This book is based on the experiences of a career of industrial software construction and academic teaching and methodology research. I am indebted to countless collaborators and students. I had the opportunity to spend a particularly momentous and formative year teaching at the now defunct Wang Institute in 1986–1987. I am grateful to the students of the *Software Engineering* class, spring 1987, and my *Real-Time Software Design* class, summer 1987. I have also received invaluable feedback from those Masters and Ph.D. students at George Mason University who have been subjected to this book in its various stages of development.

Anhtuan Dinh provided detailed technical comments as well as editorial suggestions regarding the entire book. Drs. David Rine, Carolyn Davis, and Jefferson Offutt used the manuscript in their offerings of the Software Construction course. Jeffrey Carter pointed out several subtle Ada errors. Dr. Richard Carver detected errors in the elevator example in Chapter 8 and Dr. Michal Young pointed out a flaw in an earlier version of the remote temperature sensor software in Chapter 6. Fatma Dandashi carefully produced the original illustrations.

The elevator example was introduced by Michael Jackson. The Crazy Eights project in Chapter 4 was suggested by Dr. Dana Eckhart. The VDU problem was originally suggested by Mats Sönnfors. The FMS problem in Chapter 9 was given by Dr. Hassan Gomaa. An entity-life modeling solution to that problem was first developed by Tony Bolt, Richard Rosenthal, and Dan Zuckerman while Masters students at the Wang Institute. My solutions to the VDU problem, the elevator problem, and the remote temperature sensor problem were earlier published in various articles in *Communications of the ACM*. Thank you to reviewers David A. Gustafson, Kansas State University, and William Decker, The University of Iowa. The work has been supported in part by the Center for Software Systems Engineering, George Mason University.

Bo Sanden
Stockholm, Sweden

SOFTWARE SYSTEMS CONSTRUCTION
WITH EXAMPLES IN ADA

1 Introduction

1.1 SOFTWARE MODELING PRINCIPLES

To construct software is to analyze a problem and establish the external require-ments of the software system and then synthesize software that exhibits the required properties. A software system may interact with physical devices in real time or manage a database about real phenomena. In either case, it exists in a problem environment in the real world. Its external properties reflect the struc-ture of things and relationships in that environment. Internally, the software has its own structure, consisting of modules, processes, data, and other elements. In general, a software designer is free to invent an internal structure that exhibits the required external properties.

In this book we propose a *modeling* principle of software construction. The principle imposes a discipline on the designer by requiring that the internal soft-ware structure be based on structures found in the problem environment. That way, the software itself becomes a *model* of a part of the reality. The modeling

1

principle restricts the freedom of the designer but also guides him or her toward a suitable internal software structure.

The purpose of the modeling is simplicity: There should be no more to the software than what is required. If the software is modeled on an intuitive view of the problem environment, it becomes easy to understand and maintain. Software that is easy to understand is open to inspection and is likely to become reliable and efficient. We will show that an intuitive and compelling description of the problem can lead to an efficient internal software structure.

Software cannot be modeled satisfactorily on any structure that an analyst may want to impose on a problem. Instead, the analyst must look for certain types of structures that both capture the problem and are useful for software design. In this book we are interested particularly in *objects* and *threads of events*. An object is an encapsulation of attributes and operations. The object structure is, in a sense, a *spatial* breakdown of the reality into objects related to each other. Threads of events capture the *temporal* aspects of the problem environment by describing the order of relevant events in time. To make the software resilient to future changes, the analyst must capture essential objects and essential threads of events that are unlikely to change dramatically over the software's lifetime.

The modeling is based on a philosophy of *conceptual economy*: The software should contain essentials only and nothing that does not contribute to its required purpose. It is possible to achieve this because of the abstract nature of software. Unlike a mechanical or electronic device, a software implementation suffers no physical constraints. It has no cogwheels, levers, or transistors that impose various practical limitations on the designer. Instead, the internal structure can be tailored to the structure of the problem environment. Each data structure should reflect the reality, each module correspond to an externally identifiable portion of the problem, and each process reflect an independent thread of real events.

Even if its structure is modeled closely on the structure of the problem environment, the software contains computational details and incidental hardware interfaces. To make the structure stand out, we need to abstract away such details. A modern programming language allows us to do this. In this book we rely on Ada, which allows us to represent single objects and object types as well as concurrent processes (tasks). To show that conceptual economy can be achieved in a practice, we carry several examples through to detailed design.

Modeling makes for a *seamless* development process starting with problem analysis and ending with a working software product. The process is seamless in that the same representation with objects and threads is used both in analysis of the problem and in the software. The highlight is on the relation between the problem and the software product developed to solve it. This contrasts with many traditional methods, where the emphasis is on a stepwise development process. This book proposes no such stepwise recipe leading the novice software engineer from analysis to implementation. Instead, it identifies the design issues and how they may be addressed. The book proposes no single solution, but presents a set of building blocks from which a solution may be formed.

The goal of this book is to demonstrate the modeling principle in a particular domain: the development of *reactive software*. In a reactive system, the relationship over time of input and output must be specified. (We discuss this further in Section 1.3.) Reactive software must typically operate in highly specialized environments under strict constraints on time and space. For this reason, it must be optimized and highly structured. This is more important for reactive software than for interactive software. Interactive software must typically serve a wide, unstructured variety of user needs, and this takes precedence over extreme efficiency. Historically, the need for efficiency has often made it necessary to sacrifice clarity and understandability in particularly time-critical portions of software. It is a challenge to give reactive software a clear and lucid structure without sacrificing efficiency. The approach to the design of reactive software developed in this book is referred to as *entity-life modeling*. With entity-life modeling, objects in the reality are represented as software objects and threads of events in the reality as concurrent tasks.

In this book we cover different aspects of software, such as control structuring, modularization, and tasking, and show how they can be used to model aspects of the problem. In the remainder of this chapter we develop the themes struck in the preceding paragraphs. In Sections 1.2 and 1.3 we discuss the development of software in general and of reactive software in particular. In Section 1.4 we expand on entity-life modeling, and in Section 1.5 we discuss the role of programming languages in modeling. The trade-off between heuristics and formalism in software development is discussed in Section 1.6.

1.2 SOFTWARE DEVELOPMENT

We have already distinguished between an *analytic* and a *synthetic* element in software development [Pfleeger]. We will now define each element somewhat further. The verb *to analyze* means "to decompose or examine." The analytical part of software development is the examination of the problem environment in which the software will operate, including the *external properties* of the software itself. Those external properties can be observed in the problem environment as the software interacts with elements of the reality. The purpose of analysis is to break down the problem into elements that can be represented in software. We will be concerned with a breakdown of both the *time dimension* and the *space dimension* of each problem. In the space dimension, we deal with *objects*, and in the time dimension with *behavior patterns*, which are sequential threads of events in time.

The verb *to synthesize* means "to compose or put together." During synthesis, a suitable software representation is found of each element identified in the analysis, and the representations are put together into a functioning system.

Synthesis is essentially a *constructive* activity that results in a program exhibiting the external properties defined in the analysis. In traditional software development, synthesis is often broken down into *architectural design*, *detailed design*, and *implementation*, where a level of detail is added in each phase. We will let the word *design* signify software synthesis in general and carry it through to whatever level is necessary to remove any vagueness in each case.

Analysis, design, and implementation are parts of a *software life cycle* covering all the activities associated with a software product from its conception until it is scrapped. This long-term view of software is important, but unfortunately, the life-cycle concept tends to carry with it the more controversial notion that the activities can be arranged in an orderly progression of steps, such as architectural and detailed design.

We may say that a *method* is a recipe for such stepwise software construction covering some part of the software life cycle. By a *principle* we mean, instead, a concept on which software is based, regardless of the steps necessary to develop it. Thus a method refers to the construction process, whereas a design principle is reflected in the structure of the completed product. For example, with the modeling principle, each entity in the software is justified by an entity in the reality. A method might prescribe that we identify all objects in the reality, then identify all operations, then model each object in software. With a method, it is assumed that quality is achieved through a certain development process. With a principle, quality is in the software artifact, the final product, and its relevance to the problem.

There is considerable commercial demand for stepwise methods. Each method is often narrow in scope and tends to present a somewhat monocular view, with the emphasis on a single aspect of software construction. A method that is helpful to the novice designer can often be a straightjacket for the more proficient software engineer.

A principle instead of a method allows the developer to see opportunities instead of restrictions. Rather than forcing a given problem into a form mandated by a method, he or she will then search the problem domain for properties that will fit into an elegant design. That way, the designer is given certain means of expression rather than a restrictive set of rules and regulations. Where a method claims to make software development into an orderly progression of steps, a principle opens for creativity.

A construction principle must be sufficiently broad to account for all relevant aspects of a problem. There is a danger in adopting a narrow principle and single-mindedly looking for ways to apply it. The software-engineering literature has examples of designs based exclusively on, say, functional decomposition and ignoring vital aspects of the problem that cannot be addressed by that particular principle. For a complete design, the software engineer must simultaneously apply different approaches to different aspects of a problem. Entity-life modeling forces the designer to look at each problem from all of these aspects.

Creative software construction calls for seamless continuity throughout development that ties the solution to the problem. But software development also has a managerial side, with a need for milestones, firm agreements on deliverables, and an organizational structure on which funding and personnel decisions can be based. The developer must recognize this managerial need. On the other hand, the administrator must understand the technical content of software development and recognize that planning and reporting must support the creative process. A managerial model that is alien to the developers may result in a series of token deliverables not contributing to the solution of a problem. The challenge is to strike a proper balance between the two conflicting interests and maintain conceptual integrity and continuity while still meeting legitimate deadlines and commitments.

1.3 DEVELOPMENT OF REACTIVE SOFTWARE

The term *reactive* has been introduced by Harel to describe systems with a "reactive behavior, whereby the system is not adequately described by specifying the output that results from a set of inputs, but, rather, requires specifying the relationship of inputs and outputs over time. Typically, such descriptions involve complex sequences of events, actions, conditions and information flow, often with explicit timing constraints, that combine to form the system's overall behavior" [Harel]. Such *sequences of events* and actions play a significant role in all the major examples in this book. We will use the term *reactive* when referring to software operating in real time and interacting with hardware or humans.

We will use *reactive* instead of widely used but rather vague terms such as *real time*. This term is often used in the expression *hard real time* when referring to a system where the timely response to external stimuli is crucial. "A timing constraint is hard if small violations of the constraint result in significant drops in a computation's value" [Payton]. The software *embedded* in a missile or a space craft is typically hard, while software interacting with humans is usually softer since the human operator can usually handle a variation in response times.

Some reactive software systems interact primarily with humans. We will distinguish such reactive systems from *interactive* systems. The interactive user is aware of running a program, be it a spreadsheet application, a word processor, a database query language, or a simulation. A reactive system is often embedded in a machine and the computing is *invisible* to the user, who instead has the notion of operating the machine. Examples of such systems are automatic teller machines (ATMs) and programmable cash registers. Typically, the options of the ATM customer and a checkout clerk are much more limited than those of the word processor user and are restricted to a fixed set of commands. The timing constraints in reactive systems are harder than in interactive systems, and the checkout clerk expects the electronic cash register to react as quickly and consistently as does an electromechanical device.

Efficiency is usually the overshadowing concern in reactive software. Typically, the more predictable the events are that a system has to deal with, the more efficient it can be. A large class of reactive systems can be characterized as *feedback systems*. A feedback system regulates the operation of a physical or chemical system, called the *plant*. It regularly senses the output from the plant and adjusts its inputs according to some rule called a *control law*. Applications that operate on a fixed schedule in this manner often rely on *cyclic executives*, simple schedulers that repeatedly execute software modules. In this book we are more concerned with problems where individual events occur at random times. This requires a more flexible handling of time, and that is where the task abstraction is suitable.

1.4 ENTITY-LIFE MODELING

In this section *entity-life modeling* is introduced as an approach to software construction. Before discussing its details, we will further justify the modeling principle. According to Fairley, "the software engineer creates models of physical situations in software. The mapping between the model and the reality being modeled has been called the intellectual distance between the problem and a computerized solution to the problem [Dijkstra]. A fundamental principle of software engineering is to design software products that minimize the intellectual distance . . ." [Fairley]. To minimize the intellectual distance, the software engineer builds software structures that resemble the physical structures closely with only a minimum of additional material. We will frequently let the terms *reality*, *real world*, and *problem environment* refer to the physical reality in which software operates.

Simulation software provides an intuitive example of modeling. A simulation program must behave as a modeled reality in certain important ways. It typically contains objects patterned on real-world objects and processes mimicking series of events that might take place in the reality. In a simulation language such as SIMULA, the software objects have behavior patterns that are modeled on the behaviors of the real objects. It makes good sense to model a simulation program on the problem environment since its entire purpose is to mimic the real world.

Entity-life modeling extends the idea of modeling to the construction of reactive software. We will construct reactive software systems that resemble the reality in a way similar to simulation systems. Where a process in a simulation program is separated from the modeled process in the physical reality, a process in a reactive system maintains an ongoing dialogue with its counterpart in the problem environment and is, in a sense, its mirror image.

Entity-life modeling has its roots in other modeling approaches to software construction. It combines the *object paradigm* and the *process paradigm* of software development. The object paradigm identifies objects and their relationships in the problem and recreates them in the software. The process paradigm identifies threads of events in the reality and models them as concurrently executing processes in the software. Entity-life modeling identifies both objects and threads and represents them in software.

Those language constructs that we will use to represent structures in the problem environment are primarily *software objects* and *control structures*. The control structure is the program logic with loops, if-statements, and so on. Software objects can be used to model real-world objects, and control structures can be used to model real-world *behavior patterns*. Armed with these constructs, we search the problem environment for suitable objects and patterns.

An *object* has certain attributes and can be operated on in certain well-defined ways. The operations query and/or change some of the attributes. For example, if the object is a bank account, the operations *deposit* and *withdraw* change its state by updating the balance of the account. Each relevant object in the real world is modeled as a software *object*, that is, a data structure describing the properties of the object. In Ada, this data structure is encapsulated in a *package* so that references to it can be controlled. This is possible since a data structure *hidden* inside a package cannot be directly manipulated by software outside the package, only via operations explicitly exported by the package. Object modeling is enhanced by means of data typing, and the modeler may define *abstract data types* corresponding to classes of real objects, and create instances of the types corresponding to individual objects.[1]

An object controls how it is manipulated by restricting the set of operations that it can suffer, but it cannot control the timing and ordering of the operations. The timing and ordering of operations on various objects can be described as a thread of events in the reality. We will sometimes refer to such a thread as a sequential *behavior pattern*. In the banking example, the succession of customers operating an automatic teller machine defines a behavior pattern by performing operations on various accounts. Just as the objects in the reality are modeled as software objects, behavior patterns generally form the basis for control structures. The control structure represents continuity and time ordering by indicating the sequence of operations on different software objects. Thus in the banking problem, the control structure includes a loop describing the repetitive steps followed by a customer operating an automatic teller machine. Control structure modeling has a natural extension to concurrent software where multiple *tasks* are used to model concurrent, asynchronous behavior patterns, as explained in the following.

The management of *time* is a difficult issue that is particularly important in reactive software. Programming languages that deal with time at all usually allow the programmer to define separate *threads of execution*. In Ada, such threads are called *tasks*. *Multitasking* allows many such threads to proceed concurrently and independently in one program. As a simple example, some systems may require some quantity to be sampled every 17 seconds and another every 29 seconds. This can be solved by means of two tasks, each of which samples with its own frequency. Similarly, in a software-controlled elevator system, elevators operat-

---

[1] We use an *object-based* approach supported by Ada. It is less ambitious than *object-oriented* approaches that emphasize the categorization of objects into *classes* that can *inherit* properties from each other.

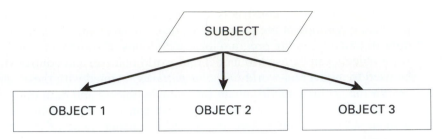

Figure 1-1 Subject–object structure of a sequential program with three objects.

ing in parallel shafts may be controlled by individual tasks. We will refer to a program with concurrent tasks as a *concurrent program*. The opposite is a *sequential* program, which has one single thread of execution.

In entity-life modeling, tasks that execute asynchronously and independently are referred to as *subjects* (or *subject tasks*) and the software is viewed in terms of *subjects operating on objects*. The word *subject* is used in the grammatical sense, as in the example "Adam eats the apple." Here the subject, Adam, carries the action forward by operating on the object, the apple.

In a sequential program, the main procedure is the only subject. It sets the pace for the execution of the program and accesses various objects. In a sense, it carries the story forward. Figure 1-1 shows the *subject–object structure* of a sequential program. The parallelogram represents the main procedure and the rectangles the objects. (We discuss this notation in detail later.) The boxes in Figure 1-1 are not subprograms but objects, which typically contain data as well as operations manipulating the data.

Figure 1-2 shows the situation in a concurrent program. Here the parallelograms are concurrent tasks. Each task in the figure is a subject operating at an individual pace on its own or shared objects. Like the main program in Figure 1-1,

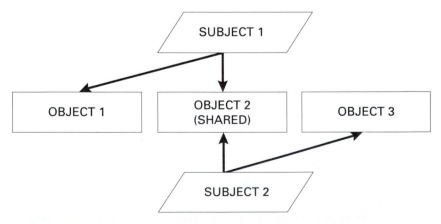

Figure 1-2 Subject–object structure of a concurrent program with two subjects and three objects, one of which is shared.

each task carries the story forward independently, while interacting with other tasks by accessing shared objects. The diagram shows two subject–object structures, which overlap in that both tasks operate on object 2.[2]

A thread of events in the reality can often intuitively be seen as the *life* of some *entity* in the problem environment. In a narrow sense, *entity-life modeling* refers to the representation of such threads as concurrent tasks in the software. We use the term in a wider sense as a name for an entire approach to software construction.

1.5 NOTATIONS AND LANGUAGES

The software engineer uses notations and languages as formal descriptions of structures in the problem environment and in the software. A notation used to capture the reality is sometimes referred to as a *domain language*. A *specification language* is used to define formally the properties of software modules without reference to their internal workings. A *pseudolanguage* or a graphical notation such as a flowchart is sometimes used to describe a design. Finally, a *programming language* describes the software itself and allows mechanical translation into executable code.

In the program domain we are interested primarily in threads of events and objects. We use *Jackson sequence diagrams* [Jackson 83] and *state transition diagrams* to describe threads. These notations provide effective graphical images of sequential structures and can be translated directly into text. Image and text are both important, since "[h]uman factors research seems to indicate that text contributes to processing accuracy, while graphics contributes speed" [Scanlan]. Lacking a satisfactory notation for the interaction of subjects and objects in the reality, we adapt for this purpose a notation used by Buhr to describe the structure of Ada programs [Buhr] (Figures 1-1 and 1-2).

Formal software specification languages, including *Z* [Spivey], [Potter] and *VDM* [Jones 86, 90], support module and object specification, and some programming languages, such as Eiffel [Meyer], incorporate formal module specifications. Structurally, a *Z* specification resembles a sequential program. Arguably, a formal notation such as *CSP* [Hoare] might serve to define the behavior of a concurrent program, and observable properties of communicating processes may be laid down in a CSP *specification*. But no formal language supports the interaction of processes and objects in entity-life modeling. For this reason we do not rely on a specification language. Interested readers may want to specify formally various modules used as examples by abstracting away the detailed design of each module. Such reverse engineering of Ada text into specifications may serve to highlight the generality of the solutions.

---

[2] The simple graphical notation in Figures 1-1 and 1-2 shows what subjects operate on what objects but fails to convey the true relationship between subjects and objects. In the diagrams, the subjects are physically separate from the objects. In reality, they are threads of execution passing through the objects.

A program written to a formal specification can be formally *verified* against the specification to prove its correctness. But the specification itself must also be *validated* against the reality to ensure the specifier has understood the problem. (This cannot be done formally.) In this book we do not include formal specifications against which the software may be verified. Instead we validate the software itself against the reality.

With or without formal specification and verification, all software construction always relies heavily on *programming languages* for the exact definition of software. We use graphical notations to illustrate designs but always let the program text define the software. The development of programming languages is one of the most important aspects of computing and software engineering, and language theory is a time-honored academic discipline. "At any particular point in time, the features provided by our programming languages reflect our understanding of software and programming" [Fairley]. Clearly, a language is not only a code understandable to a machine, but also a means to express algorithms and software structures. Early languages allowed programmers to abstract away immediate, machine-oriented concerns such as the allocation of variables in memory and the management of hardware registers. Modern languages allow a much higher level of abstraction, allowing the program structure to stand out against the computational details.

Languages such as ALGOL, Pascal, and Ada are called *algorithmic* since they allow algorithms to be expressed in a manner that is suitable for both human and computer consumption. For example, a procedure for computing the square root of a number is at the same time a suitable documentation of the algorithm involved. Before the advent of ALGOL, considerable effort was usually necessary to encode an algorithm expressed by a human being. This was particularly true if the algorithm was to be coded in assembler, but also with early versions of FORTRAN. Consequently, the algorithm would exist in two versions, one readable to a person, and one executable version, forbidding to a human reader. The readable version might be in the form of a flowchart or pseudolanguage and typically required manual translation into executable code. To a degree, this situation remains in the area of reactive software, where much programming is still performed either in assembler or in various special-purpose languages. This has been necessary to provide easy access to the hardware, and for bit manipulation. Since the code is forbidding, the designers' interest is often on the design rather than the code. The advent of language such as Ada has radically changed this situation by allowing systems programs to be expressed directly in an executable language. At the same time, such a modern language usually supports much more powerful software structures than those supported by any pseudolanguage or other design notation.[3]

---

[3] Proponents of *object-oriented* software construction often use separate design languages because of a lack of support in current production languages.

Ada has been chosen in this book more for its status as something of a standard in the reactive-systems area than necessarily as the best possible language. Using an established language has the advantage that its syntax need not be presented in full. Thus we discuss only those Ada features that are important to the modeling approach. The reader is referred to other literature for the complete language syntax [Barnes], [Booch], [Cohen], [Gonzalez], [LRM], [Naiditch], [Nyberg], [Skansholm], [Watt], [Young].

Even if it is expressed in an executable language, a good design is essentially language independent, at least within a given family of languages. The algorithmic languages form such a family with its own linguistic tradition. They contain constructs that have been accepted into the tradition, while other, unsatisfactory constructs have fallen by the wayside in the evolution. Constructs used to declare blocks, variables, types, and subprograms as well as those used to express control structure elements such as iterations, selections, and subprogram calls form a syntactic kernel, which future languages can be expected to preserve. A design built on the kernel syntax can be expected to remain useful in future languages.

1.6 HEURISTICS AND FORMALISM IN SOFTWARE CONSTRUCTION

Software construction can become a rigorous exercise if it is done to a specification that is assumed correct a priori. The program text precisely defines the behavior of the software and can be verified against the specification. There is sometimes a tendency, particularly in academia, to focus on this formal side of software construction. This is in a scientific tradition, where the official output has been the theorem and the proof, and the heuristic process through which the proof is reached is the private concern of the individual scientist. In a small community of theoreticians this is satisfactory, and the heuristics is perhaps studied through oral tradition from professor to doctoral candidate.

An approach in which software construction principles are communicated by oral tradition is unsuitable in a large professional community. Software engineers are not theoreticians who devote their time to studying each other's solutions to interesting problems. Instead, they spend most of their time finding reasonable solutions to fairly mundane but nontrivial practical tasks. They cannot do this by applying theory to each and every problem. Like other engineers, they need model solutions that easily adapt to their problems. Furthermore, it is insufficient to concentrate on the step from specification to design. In reality, "[t]he hardest part of the software task is arriving at a complete and consistent specification, and much of the essence of building a program is in fact the debugging of the specification" [Brooks].

Both analysis and synthesis rely on creativity, and the difference between a good solution and a bad one is a matter of style. The elegance of a design may also affect the development effort, which makes it an important money issue to software development organizations. It is interesting to compare software construction to another creative activity, such as writing. Both activities are characterized by the lack of physical constraints. In his book *The Sachertorte Algorithm*, John Shore devotes a chapter to "Programming as a literary activity" and a section to "The programmer as a writer" and says that "good programming is good writing" [Shore]. Correct spelling and grammer alone do not make a text readable. Similarly, "good" software is not synonymous with "provably correct" software. The software must express its intention as directly and clearly as possible, and an elegant solution may not only be more suitable but also more obviously correct than a clumsy set of formally well-defined modules complemented with an involved formal proof. "Mathematical equivalence is not a substitute for clarity and directness: we must say exactly what we mean, not something else that can be shown to have the same effect" [Jackson 84].

1.7 CHAPTER SUMMARY

More matter with less art

Shakespeare, Hamlet

The goal of the modeling approach to software construction is to pattern the structure of the software as closely as possible on the structure of the problem, with a minimum of material added for the sake of the software itself. This minimizes the intellectual distance between problem and solution and makes the software easy to understand based on an understanding of the problem environment.

Any abstraction of the reality can be modeled in software, more or less directly. If efficiency is a concern, as in reactive software, the abstractions used to describe the reality must be those most directly implementable in software. To achieve this, software concerns dictate how the requirements are expressed, and questions about the problem domain must be asked from a software point of view. The means of expression available to the software designer must be used to describe the reality. In entity-life modeling, we look for *objects* and *threads of events* in the reality that map directly onto software objects and tasks.

The issue is *conceptual economy*. The conceptual apparatus used in software design should be minimized and ideally, based totally on the reality of the problem environment. With a reference to the traditional separation of *what* and *how* in software development, where *what* refers to the externally visible function of the software and *how* refers to its internal structure, we can refer to structure and apparatus without basis in the reality as *how material*. Therefore, conceptual economy is about minimizing the amount of such material, ideally to zero. Clearly, the idea of conceptual economy reaches far beyond software construction and into philosophy. One famous proponent was the philosopher William of

Ockham, who said: "It is vain to do with more what can be done with less," or (for readers versed in medieval Latin): "*Frustra fit per plura quod potest fieri per pauciora*" [Wedberg].

REFERENCES

BARNES, J. G. P., *Programming in Ada*, 3rd ed., Addison-Wesley, Reading, Mass., 1989.

BOOCH, G., *Software Engineering with Ada*, 2nd ed., Benjamin-Cummings, Menlo Park, Calif., 1987.

BROOKS, F. P., JR., No silver bullet; essence and accidents of software engineering, *IEEE Computer*, April 1987, pp. 10–19.

BUHR, R. J. A., *Software Design with Ada*, Prentice Hall, Englewood Cliffs, N.J., 1984.

COHEN, N. H., *Ada as a Second Language*, McGraw-Hill, New York, 1986.

DIJKSTRA, E., Notes on structured programming, in *Structured Programming*, Academic Press, New York, 1972.

FAIRLEY, R. E., *Software Engineering Concepts*, McGraw-Hill, New York, 1985.

GONZALEZ, D. W., *Ada Programmer's Handbook*, Benjamin-Cummings, Menlo Park, Calif., 1990.

HAREL, D., LACHOVER, H., NAAMAD, A., PNUELI, A., PLITI, M., SHERMAN, R., SHTULL-TRAURING, A., and TRAKHTENBROT, M., STATEMATE: a working environment for the development of complex reactive systems, *IEEE Trans. Software Eng.*, 16:4, April 1990, pp. 403–414.

HOARE, C. A. R., *Communicating Sequential Processes*, Prentice Hall, Englewood Cliffs, N.J., 1985.

JACKSON, M. A., *System Development*, Prentice Hall, Englewood Cliffs, N.J., 1983.

JACKSON, M. A., *Contribution to Software Process Workshop*, Michael Jackson Systems Ltd., London, 1984.

JONES, C. B., *Systematic Software Development Using VDM*, Prentice Hall, Englewood Cliffs, N.J., 1986.

JONES, C. B., and SHAW, R. C., *Case Studies in Systematic Software Development*, Prentice Hall, Englewood Cliffs, N.J., 1990.

LRM, *The Ada Language Reference Manual*, MIL-STD-1815A, U.S. Government Printing Office, Washington, D.C., 1983.

MEYER, B., *Object-Oriented Software Construction*, Prentice Hall, Englewood Cliffs, N.J., 1988.

NAIDITCH, D. J., *Rendezvous with Ada: A Programmer's Introduction*, Wiley, New York, 1989.

NYBERG, K. A. (ed.), *The Annotated Ada Reference Manual*, Grebyn Corp., Vienna, Va., 1989.

PAYTON, D. W., and BIHARI, T. E., Intelligent real-time control of robotic vehicles, *Commun. ACM*, 34:8, August 1991, pp 48–63.

PFLEEGER, S. L., *Software Engineering: The Production of Quality Software*, 2nd ed., Macmillan, New York, 1991.

POTTER, B., SINCLAIR, J., and TILL, D., *An Introduction to Formal Specification and Z*, Prentice Hall International, Hemel Hempstead, Hertfordshire, England, 1991.

SCANLAN, D. A., Structured flowcharts outperform pseudocode: an experimental comparison, *IEEE Software*, September 1989, pp. 28–36.

SHORE, J., *The Sachertorte Algorithm and Other Antidotes to Computer Anxiety*, Viking Penguin, New York, 1985.

SKANSHOLM, J., *Ada from the Beginning*, Addison-Wesley, Reading, Mass., 1988.

SPIVEY, J. M., *The Z Notation: A Reference Manual*, Prentice Hall, Englewood Cliffs, N.J., 1989.

WATT, D., WICHMANN, B. A., and FINDLAY, W., *Ada Language and Methodology*, Prentice Hall, International, Hemel Hempstead, Hertfordshire, England, 1987.

WEDBERG, A., *A History of Philosophy: Antiquity and the Middle Ages*, Vol. 1, Oxford University Press, Oxford, 1982.

YOUNG, S. J., *An Introduction to Ada*, 2nd ed., Ellis Horwood, Chichester, West Sussex, England, 1985.

2 Control Structuring

In the switching software (written in C) there was a long do..while construct, which contained a switch statement, which contained an if clause, which contained a break, which was intended for the if clause, but instead broke from the switch statement.

Network message explaining the breakdown of the AT&T long-distance network on January 15, 1990

2.1 INTRODUCTION

The *control structure* of a program describes the order in which its statements are executed. The simplest control structure is a *sequence*, where statements are executed one after the other. Such a sequential *control flow* through the program text is broken by **loop** statements, which introduce *iterations* into the control flow, and **if** and **case** statements, which support *selections*. While the control structure of many simple programs is obvious and straightforward, control structure design or *control structuring* is a nontrivial and important issue in the construction of more complex software.

Control structuring is important because it is usually the key to execution efficiency. The execution efficiency reflects how long it takes for a program to process a certain input. This is important in batch programs that must process a voluminous input in reasonable time and where the total execution time is thus the primary concern. It is often equally or more important in reactive software, where the concern is the *response time* to a certain input.

Execution efficiency is not the only concern in software construction. Simplicity, clarity, and correctness are also important issues. With the modeling

15

approach introduced in Chapter 1, we achieve these goals by patterning software structures as closely as possible on structures in the problem environment. In this effort the control structure is used to model *sequential patterns* in the reality. A sequential pattern defines an *order* of things or events in time or space. Suppose, for example, that a simple program sequentially processes a string of characters forming words separated by intervals of blank spaces. The string of characters successively read by the program then represents a sequential pattern in the problem domain. We base the control structure of the program on this pattern in such a way that a reading of the program text from top to bottom immediately reveals the dynamics of program execution. In this case it will be obvious how the program alternates between word processing and interval processing, and how it processes words by iterating over letters and intervals by iterating over blanks.

A program processing a stream of input data provides a simple example of control structuring by modeling. Many other programs deal with sequential patterns of events occurring over time. In a program simulating a card game, the control structure may reflect how the turn shifts between the players and what steps each player takes during a turn. In reactive software, event streams often emanate from real entities in the environment, such as an elevator moving between floors in a building, or a train entering and leaving track segments. Events such as the elevator arriving at a floor or the train entering a segment are signaled to the controlling software. In such reactive software, the challenge is to build control structures that exhibit maximum efficiency and intuitive clarity at the same time. The efficiency and clarity goals may appear contradictory, but we shall see that they can be achieved without trade-off by means of careful control structuring.

Modeling control structures on threads events in the reality is one of two aspects of modeling discussed in Chapter 1. The other aspect is concerned with modeling software *objects* on objects in the reality. Each software object has a well-defined set of operations by which it is manipulated. In a card game program, for example, a pile of playing cards may be an important part of the problem, and the software may contain an object *pile* with operations such as *draw* and *discard*. In Ada, such object modeling is supported by the package syntax and is discussed at length in Chapters 3 and 4.

The card-game program example illustrates an important separation of concerns in software construction between object modeling and control structuring. Under that separation of concerns, the objects and their operations represent *what* the program does, while the control structure of the procedure operating on the objects decides *when* an operation is to be performed and the *order* of different operations. The simplest case is where one main procedure operates on a number of objects, but the same separation of *what* and *when* applies even if the main procedure calls several subprograms, which in turn operate on objects. It also applies when one object operates on another. This is so, since in a sequential program, the chain of subprogram calls and operations on objects must originate from a statement in the main procedure. Intuitively, we may think of the main procedure as a *subject* operating on the objects and thus carrying the action in the program forward.

A sequential program has one main procedure, that is, one subject. The subject–object metaphor becomes even more important in *concurrent* software, where multiple control structures are executed simultaneously by separate *tasks*. Tasks are independent subjects that carry the development forward by operating on objects. This is discussed in Chapter 6 and later chapters. Such *subject tasks* are typically built on asynchronous *behavior patterns* in the problem environment. (Some Ada tasks serve only to synchronize subject tasks, and are not subject tasks.)

The bulk of this chapter is devoted to *sequence diagramming* as a technique to build control structures on sequential patterns in the problem environment. The technique is first applied to control structures with pure sequences, iterations, and selections. Constructs such as exits from loops and exception handling present particular control structuring problems and are addressed in later subsections. The sequence diagramming technique is also compared to other programming styles.

2.2 STRUCTURED PROGRAMMING

The theoretical result that all program logic can be expressed by means of the three constructs *sequence*, *selection*, and *iteration* was first presented by Bohm and Jacopini in 1966 [Bohm]. The selection and iteration constructs are referred to as *control abstractions*, since they hide a hardware-oriented implementation based on *jump* instructions, which explicitly transfer control to given positions in the program text. While early versions of FORTRAN include simple loop constructs, early procedural languages, such as ALGOL, Pascal, and C, include full-fledged **if-then-else** and **do-while** constructs similar to those found in Ada. (Similar constructs have been incorporated in later versions of FORTRAN.)

A program based exclusively on loops and **if** constructs is often referred to as a *structured* program. Unfortunately, structured programs are not always very practical, and for that reason, most languages include various unstructured constructs, such as **exit** from loops and **return** statements that permit multiple exits from subprograms. These constructs violate the rules of orthodox structured programming, and so does the *exception handling* mechanism in modern languages such as Ada.

A recurring theme in the history of programming and software engineering has been the search for a single principle on which every software design could be based. (This has been called the "panacea syndrome" [Jackson 88].) Over the years, different principles have been proclaimed, and *structured programming*, based exclusively on the three control abstractions sequence, iteration, and selection, has been one. In a classic article from 1968, "Goto statement considered harmful" [Dijkstra], Dijkstra proposed that all control constructs other than the

```
    with TEXT_IO; use TEXT_IO;
procedure ZEROW1 is
package IIO is new INTEGER_IO(INTEGER); use IIO;
N: constant:=5;
ZEROROW: INTEGER:=0;
I, J: INTEGER;
REJECT: BOOLEAN;
type A is array (POSITIVE range <>, POSITIVE range <>) of INTEGER;
X: A(1..N,1..N);

procedure GET_ARRAY(Z: A) is separate;

begin
    GET_ARRAY(X); -- Enter array.
    -- Find first all-zero row.
    I:=X'FIRST(1);
    while I<=X'LAST(1) and ZEROROW=0 loop
        J:=X'FIRST(2);
        REJECT:=FALSE;
        while J<=X'LAST(2) and not REJECT loop
            REJECT:=X(I,J)/=0;
            J:=J+1;
        end loop;
            if not REJECT then ZEROROW:=I; end if;
            I:=I+1;
        end loop;
    if ZEROROW=0 then PUT("No all-zero row");
    else PUT("First all-zero row:"); PUT(ZEROROW);
    end if;
end ZEROW1;
```

Figure 2-1 Fragment of an Ada program that finds the first all-zero row in a two-dimensional array of integers. The program is in the traditional Pascal style with composite iteration conditions such as "I<=X'LAST(1) **and** ZEROROW = 0."

three control abstractions be banned. That became the spirit in which the languages of the era were usually taught. Figure 2-1 shows a fragment of an Ada program written in the style of standard Pascal, which was the primary educational language of the time. The program finds the first all-zero row in an integer array. Exits from the two **while** loops are avoided by means of composite iteration conditions such as

I<=X'LAST(1) **and** ZEROROW=0

Strict structured programming has been widely practiced for over 20 years, yet it has clearly not resulted in consistently reliable software. There is little doubt that

```
    with TEXT_IO; use TEXT_IO;
procedure ZEROW2 is
package IIO is new INTEGER_IO(INTEGER); use IIO;
N: constant:=5;
ZEROROW: INTEGER:=0;
REJECT: BOOLEAN;
type A is array (POSITIVE range <>, POSITIVE range <>) of INTEGER;
X: A(1..N,1..N);

procedure GET_ARRAY(Z: A) is separate;

begin
    GET_ARRAY(X); -- Enter array.
    -- Find first all-zero row.
    for I in X'RANGE(1) loop
        for J in X'RANGE(2) loop
            REJECT:=X(I,J)/=0;
            exit when REJECT;
        end loop;
        if not REJECT then ZEROROW:=I; exit; end if;
    end loop;
    if ZEROROW=0 then PUT("No all-zero row");
    else PUT("First all-zero row:"); PUT(ZEROROW);
    end if;
end ZEROW2;
```

Figure 2-2   This program finds the first all-zero row in a two-dimensional array of integers. It uses **exit** statements to transfer control out of a loop when a nonzero element or a zero row has been found.

the widespread use of **loop**, **if-then-else**, and **case** constructs promoted in languages from ALGOL to Ada has led to significantly improved program readability over that of FORTRAN-style programming. At the same time, the overzealous avoidance of such nonstructured constructs as **exit** and **return** may have had a negative net effect on the clarity and simplicity of the resulting software. A program with complete loops without exits is probably more easy to prove correct formally than an equivalent program with **exit** statements, but the latter may be significantly simpler and easier to understand.

It is noteworthy that Ada, as a representative of a modern programming style, includes restricted jump statements in the form of exits from loops, returns for subprograms, and exceptions, all of which go against orthodox structured programming rules. Figure 2-2 shows a modern rendering of the program that finds the first all-zero row in an integer array. The program is an example of the use of Ada **exit** statements. The statement

```
exit when REJECT;
```

transfers control to the end of the inner loop when a nonzero element has been found, and the compound statement

    if not REJECT **then** ZEROROW:=I; **exit**; **end if**;

transfers control to the end of the outer loop after a nonrejected row has been found. The exits simplify the loop conditions, so **for** loops can be used instead of **while** loops, and the explicit assignments

    I:=X'FIRST(1);

and

    I:=I+1;

which appear in ZEROW1 in Figure 2-1 can be eliminated. Furthermore, the loop parameters I and J are implicitly declared by appearing in the loop statements and take their types from the specified ranges, X'RANGE(1) and X'RANGE(2), respectively.

It is noteworthy also that in 1987, a letter to the editor of *Communications of the ACM* called "'Goto considered harmful' considered harmful" [Rubin] spurred one of the most lively debates in the history of that journal. The program shown in Figures 2-1 and 2-2 was the centerpiece of the debate, and the original letter proposed a solution similar to the one in Figure 2-2. The history of structured programming can thus be used as an example of classical dialectics: first, unrestricted use of **goto** statements, then a strong-felt reaction in the form of a fundamentalist structured-programming movement, and finally, a tolerant synthesis, where the structured programming is seasoned with the judicious use of restricted jump statements.

2.3 BASIC CONTROL STRUCTURING

In many cases the control structure of a program segment can be based in a very obvious way on the structure of the program data being manipulated. For example, the sequential processing of a one-dimensional array is routinely handled in a single **for** loop. That way, the loop will stop by default at the end of the array, while additional termination criteria, such as the occurrence of a certain element, translate into **exit** statements. In Ada, the loop parameter specification follows directly from the array declaration. For example,

    for I **in** A'RANGE **loop** .... **end loop**;

implicitly declares a *loop parameter* I constrained by the index range of the array A.

An *N*-dimensional array is handled similarly in an *N*-dimensional **for** loop. If, for example, B is a two-dimensional array, the following double loop declares an appropriate loop parameter for each dimension:

```
for I in B'RANGE(1) loop
for J in B'RANGE(2) loop .....
end loop; end loop;
```

One advantage of the program ZEROW2 in Figure 2-2 is that it relies on this well-known control structure.

The elements of the two-dimensional array B have the form B(I,J). If, instead, C is an array of arrays, its elements are denoted C(I)(J), and the corresponding loop construct is as follows:

```
for I in C'RANGE loop
for J in C(I)'RANGE loop ....
end loop; end loop;
```

For loops are suitable for arrays with their fixed number of elements. Other data structures have no given upper limit to the number of elements. A linked list, for example, is terminated by a null link. This is conveniently handled by means of a **while** loop. If PTR is an access variable that traverses the list and LIST is an access variable pointing at the first list element, the following statements apply:

```
PTR:=LIST;
while PTR/=null loop .... end loop;
```

In all of the foregoing cases, the control structure is based on an internal data structure such as an array or a linked list. Nevertheless, it is clear that a double loop is appropriate for handling input consisting of, say, a stream of words, each of which in turn consists of letters, even if there is no array, and the letters are processed as they are entered. As an example, the input of the program CHEER in Figure 2-3 consists of a text string, such as the following:

```
chEeR uP.tHe wORST is   YET To comE%
```

The program CHEER produces a cleaned-up string where the first letter in each word is upper case, and the rest are lower case, and where words are separated by exactly one blank, with no blanks preceding the first word, as follows:

```
Cheer Up. The Worst Is Yet To Come
```

In this program there is no array, but the problem is still two-dimensional: The input consists of words and each word consists of letters (and trailing blanks). Consequently, we can solve this problem by means of a loop over words, which in turn contains a loop over letters followed by a loop over blanks.

```
    with TEXT_IO; use TEXT_IO;
procedure CHEER is
NEXT: CHARACTER;
F: FILE_TYPE;
function UPPER(X: CHARACTER) return CHARACTER is
begin
    if X in 'a'..'z' then
        return CHARACTER'VAL(CHARACTER'POS(X)-CHARACTER'POS('a')+CHARACTER'POS('A'));
    else return X;
    end if;
end UPPER;
function LOWER(X: CHARACTER) return CHARACTER is
begin
    if X in 'A'..'Z' then
        return CHARACTER'VAL(CHARACTER'POS(X)-CHARACTER'POS('A')+CHARACTER'POS('a'));
    else return X;
    end if;
end LOWER;
begin
    PUT("Enter text ending in %"); NEW_LINE;
    OPEN(F,OUT_FILE,"CHEERS.DAT");
    -- Open an earlier-defined text file for output.
    SET_OUTPUT(F);    -- Redirect output to "CHEERS.DAT".
    ---------------------------------------------------
    GET(NEXT);
    while NEXT=' ' loop -- Over leading blanks
        GET(NEXT);
    end loop;
    while NEXT/='%' loop -- Over words
        PUT(UPPER(NEXT));
        GET(NEXT);
        while NEXT/=' ' and NEXT/='%' loop -- Over letters
            PUT(LOWER(NEXT));
            GET(NEXT);
        end loop;
        if NEXT=' ' then
            PUT(' ');                -- Put one blank.
            while NEXT=' ' loop -- Over input blanks
                GET(NEXT);        -- Skip blanks.
            end loop;
        end if;
    end loop;
    ---------------------------------------------------
    CLOSE(F);
end CHEER;
```

Figure 2-3 Simple program that processes a string of words and word intervals.

This example of control structuring is different from the examples of routine programming given earlier, since in the CHEER program, the control structure is used to remember the execution *mode*. CHEER has two basic modes: Either it is processing a word and waiting for a blank or the character '%', or it is processing a word interval, waiting for a nonblank character. The treatment of a given input character may be different in each mode. Thus a letter is converted to upper case if it is input in the word-interval mode, and to lower case if encountered in the word mode. In CHEER in Figure 2-3, different parts of the program text represent different modes, so that text processing and blanks processing go on at distinct places. This is referred to as *implicit mode representation*. An alternative way to keep track of the execution mode is by means of a *mode variable* whose value changes successively as a result of external inputs. This is referred to as *explicit mode representation*. The two mode representations are discussed and compared in Section 2.4.3.

When control structuring is used to represent modes it is an important modeling tool. This is discussed in detail in the following sections. At the same time, many other control structures, such as a loop over the elements of an array, are simple examples of routine programming that require no further discussion.

2.4 SEQUENCE DIAGRAMS

The CHEER program (Figure 2-3) shows how the control structure of a program is suggested by the sequential structure of its (input) data, that is, the order in which different input data elements are received by the program. This idea is conveniently introduced by means of simple input streams such as strings of characters, but it has far wider implications. For example, it is very useful in reactive software, where the input usually consists of signals reflecting events in the life of some real-world entity. Suppose that the software controls an elevator. When the elevator reaches a floor it triggers a sensor, which sends a signal to the software. Other signals might indicate that the elevator doors have been shut completely or that they are obstructed. The elevator software receives a series of such signals, reflecting various events, which taken together represent the *life history* or *behavior pattern* of the elevator. By building the control structure of a program on such a life history or behavior pattern, we make the program a model of the entity so that the mode of the external entity is maintained by the program at each point in time. (The elevator control structure is discussed further in Section 2.8.)

A single control structure can be used to reflect the mode with respect to one entity. Later we use concurrent tasks to model multiple entities, operating concurrently and asynchronously in the problem environment, such as multiple elevators traveling in parallel shafts. This is possible since each task represents an independently executed control structure. Concurrent tasks are discussed further in Chapters 6 through 9. (The complete elevator example with multiple elevators is discussed in Chapter 8.)

To model control structures systematically either on the structure of data streams or on the behavior of external entities, we need a uniform representation of data streams, entity behaviors, and control structures. For this, we can rely on the elements of structured programming: sequence, iteration, and selection, and use them not only in the program but also to describe the reality. This approach is introduced here based on a diagrammatical notation introduced by Jackson [Jackson 75].

2.4.1 JSP and JSD

Sequence diagramming was introduced as a programming method called *Jackson structured programming* (*JSP*) [Jackson 75], [Ingevaldsson 79], [Sanden 85a, 85b, 89], which basically covers the modeling of control structures on the sequential structures of the input and output data. In later works, the Jackson approach has been extended to *JSD* (Jackson system development) [Jackson 83], [Cameron 86, 89], [Ingevaldsson 90], which extends from requirements analysis to implementation and covers the modeling of control structures on the life histories of real-world entities. Program construction according to JSP should now be seen as a part of JSD rather than as a separate method. Nevertheless, the approach is best introduced as a programming method in which the control structure of a program is developed in a stepwise fashion from a sequential description of its input and output data. The approach is diagrammatic and built on *data* and *program sequence diagrams*. Further literature on JSP and JSD includes [Hughes], [King 88], [King 85], [Ratcliffe] and [Sutcliffe].

2.4.1.1 Data sequence diagrams

Figure 2-4 shows a data sequence diagram of the input to the CHEER program. A data sequence diagram is a graphical representation of a sequential structure, built on sequences, iterations, and selections. Figure 2-4 describes the input to the CHEER program as follows, reading largely from top to bottom and from left to right:

IN is the entire input stream of characters, consisting of zero or more leading blanks (LEAD_BLS) followed by TEXT, followed by '%'.

LEAD_BLS is an *iteration* of a blank character (L_BL). An asterisk in the L_BL box marks it as an iterated element; LEAD_BLS represents zero or more blank characters.

TEXT is an iteration of WORD, which, in turn, is a FIRST letter followed by the REST of the word, followed by a TAIL. (The first letter is singled out since it requires special treatment by the program.)

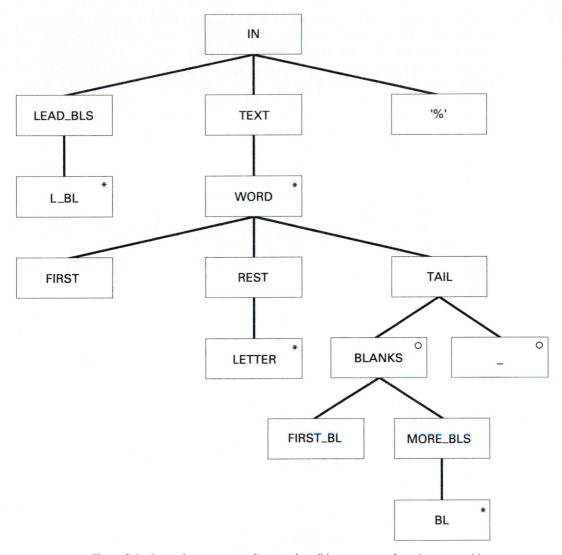

Figure 2-4 *Input data sequence diagram* describing a stream of words separated by one or more blanks.

TAIL either consists of one or more BLANKS or is empty, as indicated by a box containing only a dash. (The tail is empty when the terminating '%' immediately follows a word.) Rings in the box BLANKS and the empty box mark these as alternatives and makes TAIL a *selection* of BLANKS or nothing. BLANKS, in turn, is a sequence of FIRST_BL and the iteration MORE_BLS.

In the diagram, the *leaves* (i.e., the boxes without subordinates: L_BL, FIRST, LETTER, FIRST_BL, BL, and '%') represent data elements such as a blank character or a letter, while the other boxes represent abstractions such as the text, a word, or a set of blanks. Figure 2-4 shows the order in which data elements are read by the CHEER program, which processes the data sequentially. In JSP and JSD, a diagram such as the one in Figure 2-4 is called a *data structure diagram*, but the term *data structure* is unfortunate because of the confusion with internal data structures such as linked lists, records, and arrays. In that context, *structure* refers to a static arrangement of data. A program control structure is indeed sometimes based on internal data structures such as the arrays discussed in the preceding section. Such an internal data structure does not always have to be processed sequentially, however, but can be accessed randomly. The program CHEER does not rely on having all its input stored in internal memory. Instead, each data element is processed as it arrives, and that is exactly the situation where modeling of control structures on data sequences applies. The data sequence diagram describes a *sequence in time* with input data elements arriving one after the other.

While the data sequence diagram IN in Figure 2-4 shows the input of the CHEER program, the diagram OUT in Figure 2-5 shows the output. OUT does not

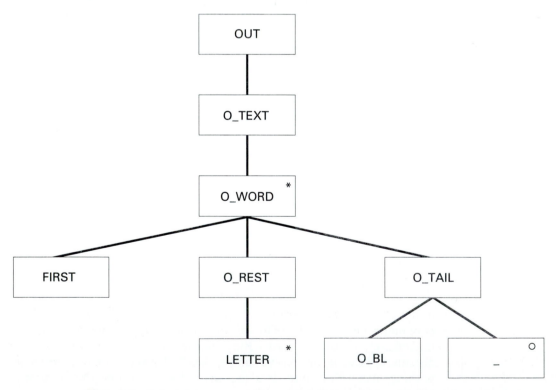

Figure 2-5 *Output data sequence diagram* describing a stream of words separated by one blank.

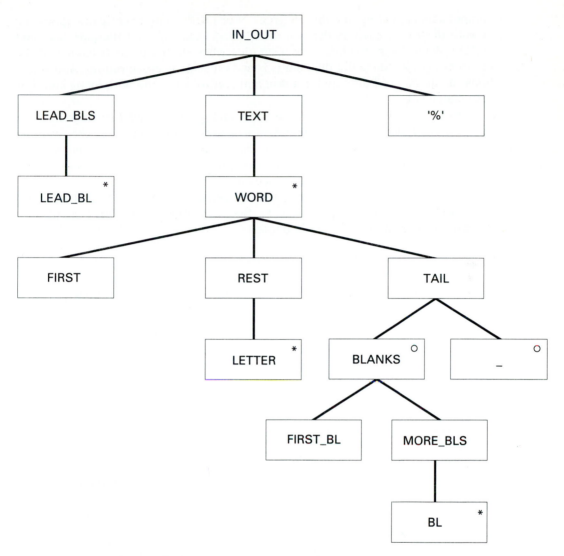

Figure 2-6 Combined input and output data sequence diagram IN_OUT based on the input diagram IN in Figure 2-4 and the output diagram OUT in Figure 2-5.

include leading blanks, since these are to be suppressed in the output, and it includes only one blank character between words. Also, the '%' is not shown, since it is not output. IN and OUT both include the nested iterations over words and letters.

Together, the two diagrams IN and OUT largely define the required behavior of the program CHEER, which must produce the output according to OUT while processing the input described by IN. The two sequence diagrams IN and OUT can easily be combined into one. The diagram IN_OUT in Figure 2-6 includes all components appearing in either diagram IN or OUT. Component pairs appearing in both diagrams, such as the pair WORD and O_WORD and the pair TEXT and O_TEXT, have been combined. IN_OUT describes the required behavior of the program CHEER. Since the diagram is based on sequences, iterations, and selections, it can be used directly for a program control structure with loops and **if** or **case** statements.

In this example the diagram IN_OUT in Figure 2-6 and the diagram IN in Figure 2-4 are identical, since the output is a subset of the input. In the resulting program control structure, the iteration REST, which appears in both diagrams IN and OUT, consumes input and produces output. The iteration MORE_BLS, which appears only in the diagram IN, produces no output.

The diagrams IN and OUT could have been combined even if OUT had contained subsequences not appearing in IN. Suppose, for example, that each word in the *output* were to be enclosed in quotes:

"Cheer" "Up." "The" "Worst" "Is" "Yet" "To" "Come"

In that case, the sequence O_WORD in Figure 2-5 would have contained two boxes, QUOTE1 and QUOTE2, say, each containing a quote. The sequence would have been as follows:

QUOTE1 FIRST O_REST QUOTE2 O_TAIL

The boxes would have reappeared in the sequence WORD in the combined diagram in Figure 2-6 as follows:

QUOTE1 FIRST REST QUOTE2 TAIL

In the program control structure based on the modified diagram IN_OUT, QUOTE1 and QUOTE2 would produce output without consuming any input data.

2.4.1.2 Program sequence diagrams

Figure 2-7 is a *program sequence diagram* in which the contents of each data element box (leaf) in Figure 2-6 has been replaced by program statements operating on the same data element. For example, the box FIRST in the diagram IN_OUT now contains the statement PUT(UPPER(NEXT)), which prints the first letter of each word in uppercase. This conversion of a data sequence diagram into a program sequence diagram affects the leaves while leaving the nonleaf boxes intact. GET statements have been inserted according to the *read-ahead* rule: One input data element is obtained first thing in the program, then as soon as the previous element has been processed. A leaf box in the already existing top-level sequence CHEER has been added to accommodate the initial, "priming" GET(NEXT) state-

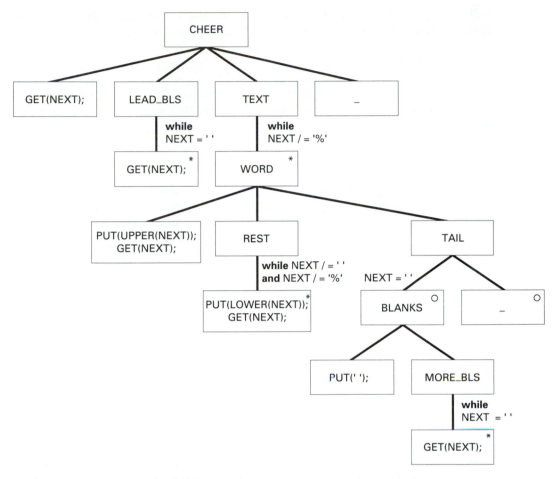

Figure 2-7 *Program sequence diagram* of the program CHEER based on the data sequence diagram IN_OUT in Figure 2-6.

ment. The box holding the symbol '%' in IN_OUT is empty in the program sequence diagram. This indicates that no processing is associated with that symbol, which is used only to mark the end of input. This empty box is included only as a reference back to the data sequence diagrams. While the leaves in the program sequence diagram contain program statements, the nonleaf boxes are inherited directly from the data sequence diagram in Figure 2-6.

Unlike the data sequence diagram in Figure 2-6, the program sequence diagram in Figure 2-7 indicates the conditions governing the iteration and selections. These conditions are normally derived from the input data sequence diagram. For example, in the diagram IN in Figure 2-4, the iteration LEAD_BLS is followed by FIRST, which by definition is a nonblank character. Based on the read-ahead rule,

NEXT always contains the next character in the input. Consequently, in the program sequence diagram, the condition on the iteration LEAD_BLS is

while NEXT=' '

In the data sequence diagram, REST is followed by either a blank or '%', which determines the condition on the iteration REST in the program sequence diagram:

while NEXT/=' ' **and** NEXT/='%'

It is important to note that the program sequence diagram represents the control structure of a program, not a decomposition into modules or subprograms. Each leaf box in a program sequence diagram represents a single, in-line statement or a segment of in-line program text. (That statement or segment may include a subprogram call, though.) For example, a box with an asterisk represents the iterated sequence of statements in a loop. A box with a ring represents either the statements between **then** and **else**, or between **elsif** and **end if**, and so on, or the statements following '=>' in a **case** statement.

2.4.1.3 Program text

The program sequence diagram in Figure 2-7 corresponds exactly to the control structure in Figure 2-8, which is the essential part of the program CHEER (Figure 2-3). The program sequence diagram contains named subsequences, such as LEAD_BLS, TEXT, WORD, REST, and TAIL, which are inherited from the data sequence diagram. These subsequences correspond to segments of the program, but it is rarely necessary to include the names in the program text. We make an exception in Figure 2-8, where the names are included as comments to facilitate the identification.

The program text in Figure 2-8 reflects the program sequence diagram, which, in turn, is based on data sequence diagrams. This means that we can recreate the structure of the data from the program text. From the text, we conclude that the entire data stream consists of a set of leading blanks followed by a set of words, followed by a terminating '%'. This is reflected in the top level of the program, where a loop over leading blanks is followed by a loop over words ending when the '%' is encountered. By examining the text at a more detailed level, we find that each word is decomposed into its FIRST character, the REST of the characters, and any TAIL of trailing blanks. This is shown by the structure of the loop over words where the handling of the first character is followed by a loop over any remaining characters and the handling of trailing blanks. In this way, the program text itself directly documents the sequential structure of the data it processes. This is indeed the objective of sequence diagramming.

```
-- Sequence CHEER:
GET(NEXT);

-- Iteration LEAD_BLS:
while NEXT=' ' loop -- Over leading blanks
   GET(NEXT);
end loop;

-- Iteration TEXT:
while NEXT/='%' loop -- Over words
   PUT(UPPER(NEXT));
   GET(NEXT);

   -- Iteration REST:
   while NEXT/=' ' and NEXT/='%' loop -- Over letters
      PUT(LOWER(NEXT));
      GET(NEXT);
   end loop;

   -- Selection TAIL:
   if NEXT=' ' then

      -- Sequence BLANKS:
      PUT(' '); -- Put one blank.

      -- Iteration MORE_BLS:
      while NEXT=' ' loop -- Over input blanks
         GET(NEXT); -- Skip blanks
      end loop;
   end if;
end loop;
```

Figure 2-8 Fragment of the program CHEER with references to the components of the program sequence diagram in Figure 2-7.

In JSP and JSD, the program sequence diagram is translated into *structure text* before being implemented in a *target language*, such as Ada. The structure text is written in a *pseudolanguage* designed as a textual equivalent of the sequence diagram notation. (Such a nonexecutable language is also called a *program definition language*.) In JSP and JSD, the structure text is considered the central document of program behavior, and the translation into the target language is viewed as a mechanical conversion. For this, the pseudolanguage must be defined precisely so that it can be translated unambiguously into a target language. In sequence diagramming as presented here, the target language Ada is used as the program definition language, and the separate structure text is eliminated. Rather than relying on a pseudolanguage, we rely on a well-publicized standard language, which is more likely to be defined unambiguously since it is the subject of scrutiny by a large community of users.

2.4.1.4 Wide and narrow sequence diagrams

An input data sequence diagram exactly describes the *valid* input, that is, all input that the program under construction must handle. But the analyst or designer may take a wide or narrow view of the input, which is expressed in a *wide* or *narrow* sequence diagram. These are relative concepts, where a wide diagram describes a greater variety of possible inputs than a narrow one. The diagram IN in Figure 2-4 faithfully reflects the verbal problem description. Suppose the reality is, instead, such that no leading blanks occur and there are never more than two blanks per word interval. Then Figure 2-4 is no longer the most faithful description of the input. But the analyst may still choose a wide view of the input and base the program on that diagram. A slightly wider view than necessary results in a program that is resilient in case the format of the input is changed later. Often, it can also make the program simpler. Note that the valid input includes any *error* data that may occur. A robust program should tolerate a wide variety of erroneous input. Of course, such input must be detected by the program and be handled properly.

Whether it is wide or narrow, the data sequence diagram must capture any sequential structure of the data that is important to the problem. CHEER, for example, relies on the concepts of words and word intervals. This is captured in the diagram IN in Figure 2-4, with its nested iterations (over words and over individual characters) and the sequence WORD consisting of a FIRST character, followed by REST and TAIL. Nested iterations such as the one in Figure 2-4 are found in almost all practically useful sequence diagrams.

Neither the nested iteration nor the sequential structure of an individual word is apparent in the diagram IN2 in Figure 2-9. This diagram describes an arbitrary mix of letters and blanks. IN2 does not represent a reasonable, wide view of the input to CHEER. Instead, it represents an incorrect view, ignoring important properties of the input. Even an extremely wide view of the input must distinguish between words and word intervals. Since this is not done, IN2 is of little help in constructing a program. A program based on IN2 would contain the following loop:

```
GET(NEXT);
while NEXT/='%'loop
   if NEXT=' 'then....
   else....
   end if;
   GET(NEXT);
end loop;
```

This program cannot rely on its control structure to distinguish, for example, the first letter in a word. (It must, instead, be based on *explicit mode representation*; see Section 2.4.3.) In general, very wide data sequence diagrams, such as

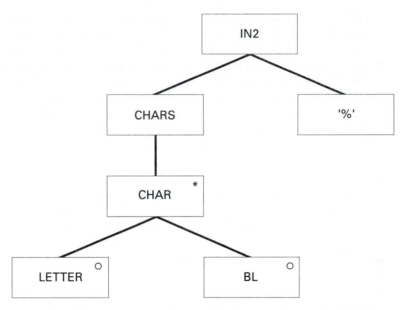

Figure 2-9   This data sequence diagram of the input to the program CHEER is too *wide* to be meaningful.

those which contain only an *iteration of a selection*, make only trivial statements about the data and should not be used. For all intents and purposes, the diagram in Figure 2-9 may be replaced by the statement: "The input consists of a stream of letters and blanks in any order." This needs no further illustration and need not be dressed up in a diagram. Diagrams that convey little or no information do more harm than good. It is important not to let important design information drown in a sea of trivialities, especially when large systems are constructed.

2.4.1.5 *Execution efficiency*

The *execution efficiency* of a program reflects how long it takes for the program to process certain input. In a batch program, the primary concern is usually the total execution time. In reactive software, the concern is usually the *response time* to certain inputs. In either case, the execution efficiency is often dependent on the structure of those often relatively small parts of the program where most of the execution time is spent. Since programs are often constructed with loops within loops, the sequences of statements in the *innermost loops* are usually executed the most often.

Efforts to improve the execution efficiency are usually directed at identifying and optimizing the innermost loops. *Optimizing compilers* automatically move statements from inside a loop and place them outside whenever possible. But the execution efficiency also depends on the overall program structure, and although some compilers do some global optimization in addition to the mere trimming of loops, they cannot entirely restructure the program.

Once a program has been constructed, the scope for optimization, whether automatic or manual, is limited. Instead, execution efficiency must be designed into the program from the start. While the primary goals of sequence diagramming are understandability and correctness, execution efficiency is an important side effect. Even though efficiency may not be a primary concern in the processing of simple text strings, the CHEER program can be used to illustrate the execution efficiency of programs developed from sequence diagrams.

If the input to the CHEER program contains words of reasonable lengths, the program spends most of its time either in the loop, REST, over letters, or in either one of the two loops over blanks, LEAD_BLS and MORE_BLS. As a result of the sequence diagramming technique, these are all tight loops containing only the necessary statements and the necessary conditions for termination. Later we shall see that other programs for the same problem, such as the one discussed in Section 2.4.1.4, tend to favor either blanks over letters, or vice versa. They also tend to incur additional overhead in each loop.

2.4.2 Sequence Diagram Elements

A sequence diagram such as those in Figures 2-4 through 2-7 represents the ordering of a set of elements represented by the *leaf* boxes. The diagram is a *tree* with the root at the top and the leaves at the bottom. The tree may consist of several named *subtrees*. In Figure 2-4, for example, IN is the root. Some of the subtrees are

> LEAD_BLS, which is an *iteration* of L_BL
>
> WORD, which is a *sequence* of FIRST, REST, and TAIL
>
> TAIL, which is a *selection* of BLANKS or nothing

A sequence diagram may also be discussed in genealogical terms. A *box* is then referred to as the *parent* of the boxes connected below it, and boxes with the same parent are called *siblings*. In Figure 2-10(a), WORD is the parent of FIRST, REST, and TAIL, which are siblings. In turn, FIRST, REST, and TAIL are the *children* of WORD.

While the foregoing terminology applies to any hierarchical structure, a sequence diagram is a representation of a *regular expression*. This means that it consists exclusively of sequences, iterations, and selections. The diagrammatic constructs representing a sequence, an iteration, and a selection are shown in Figure 2-10, and a discussion of each construct follows, including a discussion of a leaf. Regular expressions are discussed further in Chapter 5. In Sections 2.6 and 2.7 we discuss additional sequence diagrams constructs, which violate the rules of regular expressions.

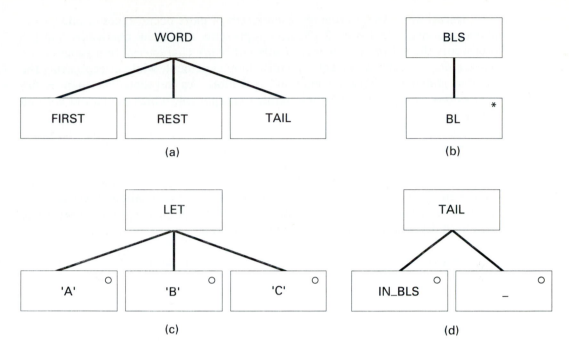

Figure 2-10 Sequence diagramming constructs. (a) WORD is a *sequence* of FIRST, followed by REST, followed by TAIL. (b) BLS is an *iteration* of BL. The iterated element, BL, is marked with an *asterisk*. (c) LET is a *selection* of either 'A', 'B', or 'C'. Each part of the selection is marked with a *ring*. (d) TAIL is a selection of IN_BLS or nothing. The box with a dash is an *empty* component.

Leaf.   In a data sequence diagram, a leaf represents a single data item.[1] (If the data sequence diagram represents the life of an entity, the leaf represents an event.) In a program sequence diagram, a leaf represents a single statement. Sometimes it is convenient to let a leaf in a program sequence diagram represent a small sequence of statements. In that case, the statements are executed sequentially, as they appear in the leaf box, and the construct should be seen as an abbreviation of a sequence.

Sequence.   A *sequence* consists of a number of ordered components, which are represented by unmarked boxes. In Figure 2-10(a), WORD consists of FIRST followed by REST followed by TAIL. (The order is important.) A sequence can have any number of components; that is, a box such as WORD can have any number of children. The children can be either leaves or composite components, which in turn may be decomposed into further components, and ultimately, into leaves.

---

[1] Sometimes a leaf is split in two parts, one describing an input data item and the other an output data item (see Exercise 2.2).

Iteration. An *iteration* represents zero or more occurrences of one particular component. In Figure 2-10(b), BL represents one blank character, and BLS represents the set of zero or more (ordered) blank characters. In a program sequence diagram, BLS represents an entire loop statement, while BL represents the iterated statements between **loop** and **end loop**. An iteration box such as BLS always has exactly one child, the iterated component, which is marked with an asterisk.

Selection. A *selection* contains a set of *parts* of which one must be selected. In Figure 2-10(c), LET is exactly one of 'A', 'B', and 'C'. Each part box is marked with a ring (○). In a program sequence diagram, the selection represents an **if-then-else** or a **case** construct. If a **case** statement with **when others** or an **if-then-else** construct is intended, the order of the selection parts is important, since the alternatives will be eliminated from left to right.

Empty component. A box with a dash is a *null* or *empty* component, which is particularly useful in selections. An empty component is always a leaf. Figure 2-10(d) shows TAIL as a selection of IN_BLS or nothing. In a program sequence diagram, a null component may represent a **null** statement. A selection with an empty box as its rightmost component may be implemented as an **if** statement without an **else** clause. A null component is also useful in a program sequence diagram if a box inherited from a data sequence contains no statements. It then indicates that the corresponding data element requires no processing. This is the case in the CHEER program, where the '%' character appears in the data sequence diagrams but needs no processing by the program.

The following rules guide the combination of constructs:

A box with an asterisk or a ring always has a parent. There can be no asterisk or ring in the top box.

A box with an asterisk has no siblings.

If a box has a ring, all its siblings have rings.

Figure 2-11 shows some correct and incorrect combinations of constructs, while the structures in Figures 2-12 and 2-13 are both correct.

2.4.3 Implicit and Explicit Mode Representation

A program whose control structure is modeled on the sequential structure of a data stream or the behavior of an external entity has the important property that the location in the program text reflects the current mode of execution. We refer to this as *implicit mode representation*. In this section we compare this type of program to one where the mode is, instead, remembered by means of mode variables. This is referred to as *explicit mode representation*.

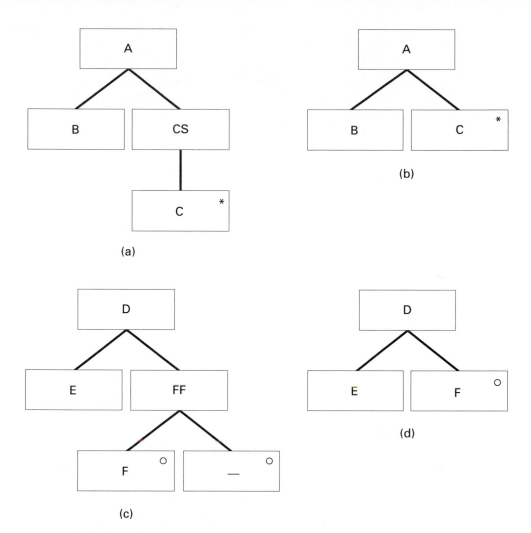

Figure 2-11 Correct and incorrect sequence diagrams. (a) *Correct*: The sequence A consists of B followed by CS. CS, in turn, is an iteration of C. (b) *Incorrect* sequence diagram. A box with an asterisk can have no siblings. (c) *Correct*: D is a sequence of E and FF, and FF is a selection of F or nothing. (d) *Incorrect* and *ambiguous* sequence diagram. Only one of the two siblings E and F has a ring.

To understand modes and mode representation, consider again the CHEER program and its stream of input characters. When the character stream is processed, the handling of each input character depends not only on the character itself but also on the current mode of execution as defined by the input that has gone before. In CHEER we may identify a word-processing mode and an interval-processing mode. To process an input data element properly, it is important to

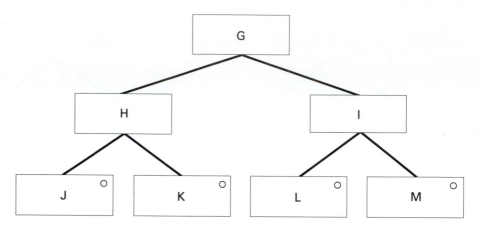

Figure 2-12 In this sequence diagram, G is a sequence of H and I. H, in turn, is a selection of J or K, while I is a selection of L or M. The diagram represents a stream G consisting of first either J or K and then either L or M.

know the current mode. As an illustration, suppose that a letter is encountered in the input stream. In the interval-processing mode, the letter represents the beginning of a new word and must be converted to uppercase, while in the word-processing mode, the letter is put in lowercase.

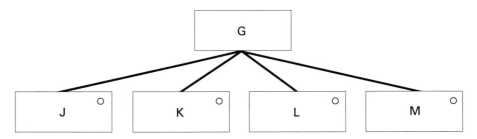

Figure 2-13 In this sequence diagram, G is a selection of J, K, L, or M. Here the component G is either J, K, L or M.

2.4.3.1 Implicit mode representation

Software design based on sequence diagrams is intended to produce programs with *implicit mode representation*. This means that in a program such as CHEER (Figure 2-8), the mode in which a certain statement is executed is always known from the location of the statement in the program text. We may say that each statement is always executed in a certain *mode context*. For example, whenever the loop over words is entered, NEXT contains the first character in a word, so the statement

```
PUT(UPPER(NEXT));
```

is relevant. Any other statement that must be executed once for each word can be put at this position. (For example, if we want to count the words, a counter variable could be incremented at this point in the program text.) This is the result of patterning the program control structure on the sequence of data or the sequence of events in the life of an external entity.

    With implicit mode representation, we can also say that the mode is reflected in the *program counter*. When a program is compiled and linked, it is ultimately converted into an executable program which is a file of hardware instructions, executed one by one by the hardware processor or CPU (central processing unit). Each instruction has a unique location in the file. The CPU keeps the location of the next instruction to execute in a hardware register known as the *program counter*. Normally, instructions are executed sequentially, and the program counter is incremented for each instruction. One exception is the jump instruction, which assigns a new value to the program counter, thereby forcing executing to continue at the corresponding location in the code.

    Since each Ada statement usually translates to a set of hardware instructions starting at a certain location in the executable program, we can also say that the program counter indicates which source statement is currently executed. For example, the program counter has a particular value when the loop over words is entered. This, in turn, happens only when the program is in the interval-processing mode. Consequently, when the sequence diagramming technique is used, we can say that the program counter remembers the mode.

    It should be noted that implicit mode representation is independent of sequence diagramming, so that programs with implicit mode representation can be developed without that technique. Such programs are common and often very straightforward, particularly if the problem involves a simple sequence of events occurring one after the other. It is often natural to solve such problems by means of a sequential program that deals with the events in the order of appearance. This can often be done without introducing sequence diagrams. Certainly, the CHEER program could have been developed that way.

2.4.3.2 Explicit mode representation

In programs with implicit mode representation, each statement is located in a specific mode context in the program text. Since such programs usually accept input in many different modes and rely on the read-ahead technique, this often means that a program with implicit mode representation contains many GET statements. Other programming styles do not rely on location for mode representation but instead use explicit *mode variables*. Such programs are often structured around one central GET statement, typically placed inside a loop. Each time the GET statement has been executed and an input data element has been obtained, the program branches on a condition based on the data element and the values of the mode variables in order to process the data element. After processing each element, it loops back to the GET statement. Just as programs with implicit mode representation can be developed systematically from data sequence diagrams, a program with explicit mode variables can be based on a description of the problem environment. This is discussed in Section 2.4.3.3.

Before discussing how programs with explicit mode representation can be systematically developed, we will briefly touch on a fairly common programming practice with ad hoc "history variables," which has significant drawbacks. The reason for mentioning this is that such history variables may otherwise be mistaken for mode variables. Identifying the disadvantages of history variables also helps us understand the importance of a more systematic approach to mode representation.

The program CHEER2 in Figure 2-14 uses two Boolean history variables, FIRST_WRITTEN and BLANK_WRITTEN, to remember whether the first letter in a word has been output and whether one blank has been output after a word, respectively. It is curious to note that CHEER2 spends its time reading little notes that it keeps writing to itself in order to remember its progress. The notes are the history variables, which the program uses to remember whether it has already written a blank or a letter. The approach is different in CHEER in Figure 2-8, which moves through the program text while dealing with different parts of the input. Incidentally, the control structure of CHEER2 is based on the wide data sequence diagram discussed in Section 2.4.1.4 and shown in Figure 2-9.

The programming style with history variables invites optimization and cleverness, and the resulting program can be made very compact as long as the number of history variables is limited. The approach scales up badly, however, and as the number of history variables grows, the conditions governing the processing often become very complex and incomprehensible. This makes the program difficult to understand and modify. The number of possible combinations that must be taken care of generally grows exponentially with the number of history variables, which tends to cause residual program errors. Furthermore, the repeated testing of history variables can make the program surprisingly inefficient.

2.4.3.3 *Explicit mode representation based on finite automata*

While history variables are not recommended, explicit mode variables may be introduced in an organized manner based on an analysis of the problem environment. This can be done by means of *finite automata*. Finite automata will be introduced rigorously in Chapter 5. For our current purposes, suffice it to say that a finite automation is a hypothetical machine that changes its internal mode as it accepts input symbols. For each input symbol, it may also produce an output symbol. Just as sequence diagrams can be used to define sequential patterns of symbols, so can finite automata.

```
    with TEXT_IO; use TEXT_IO;
procedure CHEER2 is
NEXT: CHARACTER;
F: FILE_TYPE;
FIRST_WRITTEN: BOOLEAN:=FALSE;  -- First letter written
BLANK_WRITTEN: BOOLEAN:=TRUE; -- One blank written

function UPPER(X: CHARACTER) return CHARACTER is
begin
    if X in 'a'..'z' then
        return CHARACTER'VAL(CHARACTER'POS(X)-CHARACTER'POS('a')+CHARACTER'POS('A'));
    else return X;
    end if;
end UPPER;
function LOWER(X: CHARACTER) return CHARACTER is
begin
    if X in 'A'..'Z' then
        return CHARACTER'VAL(CHARACTER'POS(X)-CHARACTER'POS('A')+CHARACTER'POS('a'));
    else return X;
    end if;
end LOWER;
begin
    PUT("Enter text ending in %"); NEW_LINE;
    OPEN(F,OUT_FILE,"CHEERS.DAT");
    SET_OUTPUT(F);
    loop
        GET(NEXT);
        case NEXT is
            when '%' => exit;
            when ' ' =>
                if not BLANK_WRITTEN then
                    PUT(' ');
                    BLANK_WRITTEN:=TRUE;
                end if;
                FIRST_WRITTEN:=FALSE;
            when others =>
                if not FIRST_WRITTEN then
                    BLANK_WRITTEN:=FALSE;
                    PUT(UPPER(NEXT));
                    FIRST_WRITTEN:=TRUE;
                else PUT(LOWER(NEXT));
                end if;
        end case;
    end loop;
    SET_OUTPUT(STANDARD_OUTPUT);
    CLOSE(F);
end CHEER2;
```

Figure 2-14 The program CHEER2 remembers its mode by means of *ad hoc* history variables. This programming style is error prone and not recommended.

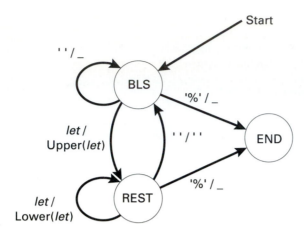

Figure 2-15 Transition diagram showing the input to the program CHEER with the modes BLS, REST, and END. The finite automation defined by this diagram moves from BLS to REST upon receiving a letter (let) and outputs the letter in upper case. When the program is in the mode REST and receives a letter, it remains in REST and outputs the letter in lowercase.

Figure 2-15 shows a *transition diagram* describing the input and output of the CHEER program. The circles represent the three modes BLS, REST, and END, and the arrows between circles represent mode transitions. An input element and an output element are associated with each transition and input/output appears with each arrow as in the following examples:

The arrow from REST to BLS is annotated with ' '/' '. This means that the transition from REST to BLS is triggered by a blank (' ') and produces a blank as output.

The arrow from BLS to REST is annotated with let/Upper(let). This means that the transition is triggered by a letter (let) and produces the uppercase variant of the same letter.

An arrow from REST back to REST carries the notation let/Lower(let). This means that let received in the mode REST causes no transition but causes the lowercase variant of let to be output.

This finite automation can easily be implemented by means of one mode variable, typically of an enumerated type, where each enumeration literal corresponds to a mode. The solution typically includes a nested **case** statement with an outer **case** statement over the mode variable, and an inner statement over the current input. Figure 2-16 shows a program CHEER3 with a mode variable M of type MODE_TYPE, which takes the values BLS and REST. The control structure of the program is similar to that of CHEER2 in Figure 2-14. It is not used for mode representation and corresponds to the wide data sequence diagram in Figure 2-9.

A transition diagram such as the one in Figure 2-15 shows the modes of a finite automaton, and for each mode, indicates the inputs that are accepted in that mode. There is a one-to-one correspondence between modes and circles, and a one-to-many correspondence between inputs and arrows. (For example, the input symbol ' ' appears on two arrows.) Consequently, CHEER3 contains an outer **case** statement with exactly one alternative for each mode. In each mode there is

```
      with TEXT_IO; use TEXT_IO;
   procedure CHEER3 is
   NEXT: CHARACTER;
   F: FILE_TYPE;
   type MODE_TYPE is (BLS, REST);
   M: MODE_TYPE:=BLS;

   function UPPER(X: CHARACTER) return CHARACTER is
   begin
      if X in 'a'..'z' then
         return CHARACTER'VAL(CHARACTER'POS(X)-CHARACTER'POS('a')+CHARACTER'POS('A'));
      else return X;
      end if;
   end UPPER;
   function LOWER(X: CHARACTER) return CHARACTER is
   begin
      if X in 'A'..'Z' then
         return CHARACTER'VAL(CHARACTER'POS(X)-CHARACTER'POS('A')+CHARACTER'POS('a'));
      else return X;
      end if;
   end LOWER;
   begin
      PUT("Enter text ending in %"); NEW_LINE;
      OPEN(F,OUT_FILE,"CHEERS.DAT");
      SET_OUTPUT(F);
      loop
         GET(NEXT);
         exit when NEXT='%';
         case M is
            when BLS =>
               case NEXT is
                  when ' ' => null;
                  when others =>
                     PUT(UPPER(NEXT));
                     M:=REST;
               end case;
            when REST =>
               case NEXT is
                  when ' ' =>
                     PUT(' ');
                     M:=BLS;
                  when others =>
                     PUT(LOWER(NEXT));
               end case;
         end case;
      end loop;
      SET_OUTPUT(STANDARD_OUTPUT);
      CLOSE(F);
   end CHEER3;
```

Figure 2-16 The program CHEER3 is based on the transition diagram in Figure 2-15. It works the same as CHEER in Figure 2-3.

an inner case statement over inputs, and each input may occur in more than one mode. Thus CHEER3 branches on mode before it branches on input symbol. In this respect it is similar to the original program CHEER, where the mode context of each GET statement is always known because of the implicit mode representation. With few exceptions, we will abide by *mode before input* as a programming rule of thumb. Notably, CHEER2 with its history variables branches first on input and then on mode, thus violating the rule.

2.4.3.4 *Comparison of mode representations*

The programs CHEER, CHEER2, and CHEER3 represent three different ways of solving the same problem. In CHEER (Figure 2-8), different parts of the text represent different mode contexts, and the program executes in different contexts depending on whether it is processing a word or a word interval. CHEER2 (Figure 2-14) keeps track of its mode by means of ad hoc history variables, while CHEER3 (Figure 2-16) is based on a mode variable derived from a transition diagram describing the input and output data.

   The systematic derivation of the modes from a finite automaton representing the problem makes CHEER3 easier than CHEER2 to understand. The original program, CHEER, which is based on sequence diagrams, has the advantage that all manipulation of mode and history variables is avoided, which makes the program more efficient. Nevertheless, the programming style used in CHEER3 is quite transparent and is often useful.

   As mentioned in Section 2.4.1.3, CHEER, which is based on implicit mode representation, spends most of its time in one of a few tight loops and is thus an efficient program. In general, a program with implicit mode representation is often more efficient than one with explicit mode representation, particularly if each mode has transitions to relatively few other modes. In that situation, the program text based on a sequence diagram tends to follow the main flow of mode transitions, and the mode context is changed automatically as execution progresses through the text. The program does not have to consult variables repeatedly to find out what mode it is in; this is implicit from the mode context. An equivalent program with an explicit mode variable incurs overhead for each mode transition. Like CHEER, CHEER3 spends most of its time iterating over letters inside words or blank characters in word intervals. For each letter or blank, it executes a **case** statement over mode to see whether it is currently in the word mode or the word-interval mode (Figure 2-16). Furthermore, either the word-interval mode or the word mode is favored, depending on the order of alternatives in the **case** statement. CHEER (Figure 2-8) does not have this problem, and all the three inner loops over letters and blanks are equally tight and efficient.

   A program with explicit mode representation has the additional disadvantage that the reader must deal with and understand the meaning of each of a possibly very large number of explicit modes. Explicit mode representation may

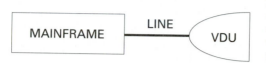

Figure 2-17 A video display unit (VDU) is connected to a mainframe. A control program in the VDU processes the stream of characters arriving over the line.

be preferable nevertheless, if there are relatively few modes and relatively many transitions back and forth between the modes rather than a main flow of mode transitions. An example of this (automobile cruise control) is discussed in Chapter 5.

2.4.4 Example: VDU Control Program

A video display unit (VDU) is equipped with a microprocessor that executes an embedded control program. The microprocessor receives a stream of characters from a mainframe host to which the VDU is connected via a communication line (Figure 2-17). The input consists of *text strings*, *commands*, and *error characters*, which are described as follows:

> A *text string* is an iteration of characters to be displayed on the VDU screen.
>
> A *command*, such as "position cursor" or "erase screen," is represented in the input by a character sequence bracketed by special, nondisplayable characters, which will be shown here as brackets, '[' and ']'.
>
> An *error character* is a nondisplayable character other than '['.

The data sequence diagram in Figure 2-18 shows the input to the VDU control program. The input is an iteration of FIELD, and each FIELD can be either a text string to be displayed (TEXT), a command (CMD), or an error character (ERR). A command consists of '[' followed by an iteration, CCS, of correct command characters. (C_CH represents a single command character.) A correct command ends with a closing bracket, but the input may also include erroneous commands without closing brackets. In practice, an erroneous command is detected when a maximum command size, C_MAX, is exceeded and no closing bracket has been received. In the diagram this is described by means of the data element following the CCS iteration. That element can either be a correct closing bracket or another character, called ERR. ERR signals an error situation, either because the maximum size has been exceeded or because an unacceptable character has been encountered in the command. The iteration CCS is thus taken to extend over at most C_MAX correct characters. Note again that the data sequence diagram in Figure 2-18 is a dynamic description of the input that shows the order in which the different data elements arrive over the line. It describes all *valid* data, that is, all data that we want to take into consideration, including error data.

In contrast to the CHEER program, where an input data stream must be

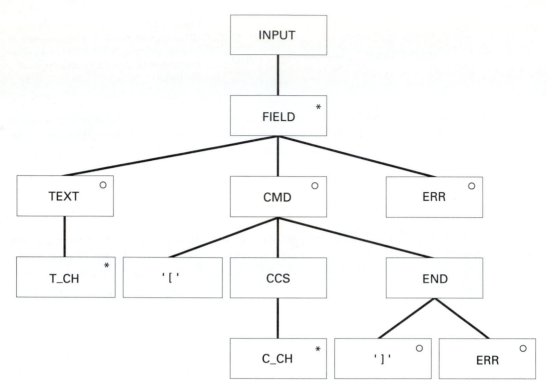

Figure 2-18 Data sequence diagram showing the stream of input characters to the VDU control program.

reconciled with an output data stream, only one data sequence diagram has to be taken into account by the VDU program, which can be patterned directly on the structure INPUT. The program uses the following procedures:

GET   Input one character.
PUT   Display one character on the screen.
EXEC   Execute a stored command.
ABT   Signal an error situation to the host.

PUT and EXEC are declared in a package SCREEN. We will return to the declaration of GET and ABT in Section 2.5.1. ABT sends a signal to the host, which then sends a command to reset the VDU. ABT is used when an error character is detected or the maximum command size (C_MAX) exceeded.

Figure 2-19 is the program sequence diagram. As before, an iteration condition is shown below the box representing the iteration, and selection conditions are shown above the boxes representing the alternatives. Note again that the box CCS represents the entire loop over command characters, including the loop state-

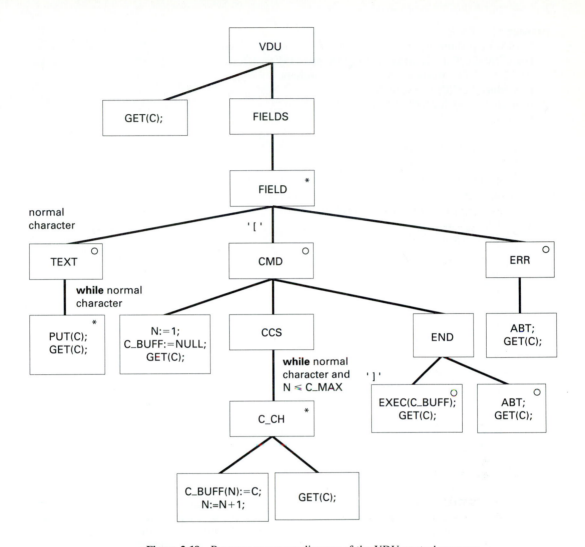

Figure 2-19   Program sequence diagram of the VDU control program.

ment itself, while C_CH represents the statements between **loop** and **end loop** (i.e., the processing of each individual command character). The program is shown in Figure 2-20.

```
package SCREEN is
    C_MAX: constant:=5;
    type CMND_BUFF is array (1..C_MAX) of CHARACTER;
    NULL_CMND: constant CMND_BUFF:=(others => ' ');
    procedure PUT(C: CHARACTER);
    procedure EXEC(CMND: CMND_BUFF);
end SCREEN;


    with INPUT_STREAM; use INPUT_STREAM;
    with SCREEN; use SCREEN;
procedure VDU is
C : CHARACTER;
subtype NORMAL is CHARACTER range 'A'..'Z';
C_BUFF: CMND_BUFF;
N: INTEGER range 1..C_MAX+1;
begin
    GET(C);
    FIELDS: loop
        if C in NORMAL then
            -- Text
            while C in NORMAL loop
                PUT(C); GET(C);
            end loop;
        elsif C = '[' then
            -- Prepare for command.
            N:=1; C_BUFF:=NULL_CMND; GET(C);
            -- Command characters
            while C in NORMAL and N<=C_MAX loop
                C_BUFF(N):=C; N:=N+1; GET(C);
            end loop;
            -- Command end
            if C=']' then
                EXEC(C_BUFF); GET(C);
            else -- Command string too long
                ABT; GET(C);
            end if;
        else -- Error character
            ABT; GET(C);
        end if;
    end loop FIELDS;
end VDU;
```

Figure 2-20 The VDU program built on the program sequence diagram in Figure 2-19. The package SCREEN contains subprograms operating on the VDU screen. (The package body is hardware dependent and has been left out.) The package INPUT_STREAM contains a subprogram GET, which receives one character at a time from the line. (It is discussed later.)

2.5 STRUCTURE CLASHES

In the CHEER program shown in Figures 2-4 through 2-8, one input and one output data sequence are easily merged into one combined data sequence, on which the program control structure is based. In the VDU example, only one data sequence has to be taken into account (Figures 2-18 through 2-20). A problem sometimes contains different data streams that cannot be reconciled, however, and this phenomenon is referred to as a *structure clash*. It is impossible to combine two or more clashing data sequence diagrams into one program sequence diagram; instead, the software solution must involve multiple, communicating program control structures, based on the different clashing data sequences. While such multiple, concurrent control structures can be managed as separate tasks, it is often possible to achieve a simpler solution by making each control structure into a separate procedure.

The JSP literature identifies different types of structure clashes, such as the *order clash*, where the two clashing data sequences contain the same data elements in different order. For example, a data stream containing the elements of a two-dimensional array ordered by row clashes with a data stream where the same elements are ordered by column. An order clash must be resolved by means of sorting. Another type of clash is the *interleaving clash*, where the data elements belonging to different sequences appear interleaved.

We deal exclusively with the *boundary clash*, which is the most common type of clash. A boundary clash is often the result of a physical, hardware constraint such as the line width or page size of a printer or a display unit, or a rigid software constraint such as a fixed block or buffer size. Assuming, for example, that the line or buffer holds MAX characters, this constraint can be expressed as a sequence diagram where an input data stream is seen as an iteration of blocks, each of which is an iteration of MAX characters. Whether the constraint is caused by hardware or software, we usually refer to such a data sequence diagram as *physical* or *hard*. At the same time, those data sequence diagrams that we have discussed so far, such as IN and OUT in the CHEER problem (Figures 2-4 and 2-5) and the INPUT of the VDU problem (Figure 2-18), are *logical* or *soft*.

As an illustration, assume that the data to the VDU arrive in fixed-size blocks of MAX characters. Each block also contains a *check sum* against which the sum of all the characters in the block must be verified to guard against communication errors (a so-called *cyclic redundancy* check). The blocking introduces the new, *hard* data sequence diagram shown in Figure 2-21. (The characters in each block are shown as an iteration CHARS, although there are always exactly MAX characters in a block. In this case, the iteration is an abbreviation of a sequence of MAX characters rather than as a representation of zero or more characters.)

To recognize the boundary clash, suppose first that we attempt to combine the diagram in Figure 2-21 with the sequence diagram based on fields in Figure 2-18 in the same way that we combined the IN and OUT sequence diagrams of the CHEER problem (Figures 2-4 and 2-5) into the diagram IN_OUT in Figure 2-6. For this we must find correspondences so that boxes can be pairwise combined (Figure 2-22). Indeed, the top boxes INPUT and BLOCKS correspond, since each top box represents all the input. It is also possible to find correspondences between boxes at the bottom level, since each character (CHAR) in the BLOCKS diagram corresponds to one element in the INPUT diagram, whether T_CH, '[', ']', C_CH, or

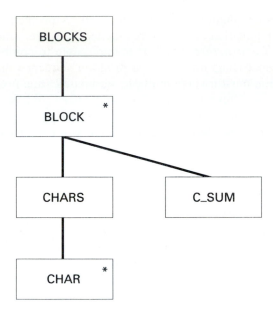

Figure 2-21 Input data sequence diagram showing the blocking of the input characters to the VDU program.

ERR. Although the INPUT diagram distinguishes between these different characters, there is no conflict, since the characters occur in both sequence diagrams in the same order.

The two sequence diagrams in Figure 2-22 correspond at the top and the bottom, but the iterations FIELD and BLOCK cause a problem. In the INPUT sequence, FIELD represents a field of characters, such as an entire text string or an entire command. At the same time, BLOCK represents a fixed-size block of MAX characters. For FIELDS and BLOCKS to be combined into one box, each FIELD and BLOCK would have to begin at the same time and end at the same time, so that fields and blocks might be processed at the same pace. This is impossible, however, since a new FIELD may start anywhere in a BLOCK and a new BLOCK may start anywhere in a FIELD. For example, one block may contain the beginning of a command, while the rest of it is in the following block. It is also impossible to subordinate FIELD to BLOCK and say that one BLOCK is an iteration of FIELD, or vice versa, since a FIELD does not necessarily span an integer number of whole BLOCKS, and a BLOCK does not contain an integer number of complete FIELDS.

The phenomenon described above, referred to as a *structure clash*, is very common in software design and programming. Many programs are unnecessarily convoluted because of unrecognized and unresolved structure clashes. Although programmers often try to deal with structure clashes by means of history variables, a better technique is to separate the control structures based on each of the conflicting data sequences in separate procedures or separate tasks. Tasking is introduced in Chapter 6, but a subprogram solution is discussed in Section 2.5.1.

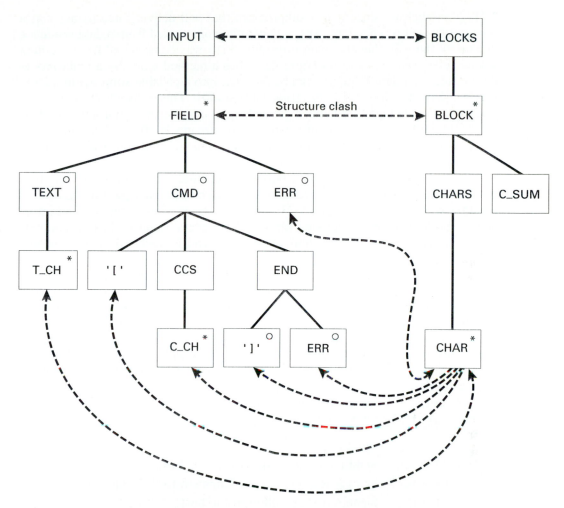

Figure 2-22   A boundary clash exists between the INPUT sequence diagram (Figure 2-18) and the BLOCKS diagram (Figure 2-21). The components BLOCK and FIELD cannot be reconciled.

2.5.1 Resolution of Structure Clashes

A structure clash can be resolved by program decomposition in such a way that each conflicting sequence diagram results in one procedure. In the VDU problem, a special-purpose subprogram GET is added to the earlier procedure, VDU (Figure 2-20), which is left unaltered. VDU is still built on the INPUT data sequence in Figure 2-18, but the GET calls in the program text now refer to the new subprogram.

In principle, GET is built on the data sequence diagram BLOCKS in Figure

2-21. Nonetheless, since it is a subprogram that will deliver one character at a time to VDU upon procedure calls, it cannot be constructed from a data sequence in exactly the way that the main procedure VDU was constructed from the data sequence FIELDS. The JSP literature describes a method whereby a main procedure based on a data sequence can be *inverted* into a callable subprogram [Jackson 75], [Sanden 85(a) and 85(b)], [Ingevaldsson 79]. This is also discussed briefly in Chapter 5. On the other hand, a deblocking or debuffering subprogram such as GET resulting from separation of clashing data streams is often fairly simple and can be constructed as a matter of routine programming. That approach is taken in the present case.

The subprogram GET needs a buffer accommodating a block arriving from the host. For separation of concerns, GET is placed in a package INPUT_STREAM together with the buffer (Figure 2-23). INPUT_STREAM is an example of an information-hiding package, discussed further in Chapters 3 and 4. In that context, GET is referred to as an operation subprogram and is declared in the package specification.

The introduction of blocks affects the treatment of error characters in the following way. While the VDU program still signals the host as soon as an error is detected, the host now responds by sending a new block starting with a command resetting the screen. Since an error character may occur in the middle of a block, the rest of that block is skipped. For that reason, the procedure ABT is included as an operation subprogram in INPUT_STREAM together with GET.

Internally, INPUT_STREAM uses another subprogram, SEND_ABT, to signal the error condition to the host. More generally, INPUT_STREAM relies on the following procedures for communication with the host. They are operation subprograms of the package HOST_COMM shown in Figure 2-23.

GET	Input one character.
SEND_ACK	Send an acknowledgment to the host.
SEND_NAK	Send a negative acknowledgment to the host.
SEND_ABT	Signal error condition to the host.

The implementation of SEND_ACK, SEND_NAK, and SEND_ABT is dependent on the communication hardware and hidden in the body of HOST_COMM. SEND_NAK and SEND_ABT both report error conditions. SEND_NAK signals a communication error and causes the host to resend the latest block. SEND_ABT, on the other hand, signals a more serious logical error in the sequence of texts and commands. It requires the host to abort the current output and send a new block with a suitable command to reset the screen.

2.6 LOOP EXITS

When a program is built on a data sequence diagram and the read-ahead rule, loop conditions are usually derived directly from the diagram. This is the case in the CHEER program in Figure 2-8 where the iteration LEAD_BLS over leading blanks is

```ada
package HOST_COMM is
   MAX: constant :=20; -- Number of characters per block
   procedure GET(C: out CHARACTER);
   procedure SEND_ABT;
   procedure SEND_NAK;
   procedure SEND_ACK;
end HOST_COMM;

package INPUT_STREAM is
   procedure GET(C: out CHARACTER);
   procedure ABT;
end INPUT_STREAM;

   with HOST_COMM; use HOST_COMM;
package body INPUT_STREAM is
type BUFF_TYPE is array (1..MAX) of CHARACTER;
BUFF:  BUFF_TYPE;
INDEX: INTEGER range 1..MAX+1:= MAX+1;
CHK_SUM: CHARACTER;

function CHECK return BOOLEAN is separate;
-- Suitable checksumming algorithm included as subunit

procedure GET_BLOCK is
begin
   for I in 1..MAX loop
      HOST_COMM.GET(BUFF(I));
   end loop;
   HOST_COMM.GET(CHK_SUM);
end GET_BLOCK;

procedure GET(C: out CHARACTER) is
begin
   if INDEX <= MAX then
      C:=BUFF(INDEX);
      INDEX:=INDEX+1;
   else
      GET_BLOCK;
      while not CHECK loop
         HOST_COMM.SEND_NAK;
         GET_BLOCK;
      end loop;
      SEND_ACK;
      C:=BUFF(1);
      INDEX:=2;
   end if;
end GET;

procedure ABT is
begin
   SEND_ABT;          -- Send abort to mainframe.
   INDEX:=MAX+1; -- Prepare to receive new block as
                      -- host recovers communication.
end ABT;
end INPUT_STREAM;
```

Figure 2-23 Package INPUT_STREAM, which resolves the boundary clash in the VDU problem. INPUT_STREAM relies on the package HOST_COMM for communication with the mainframe. (The body of HOST_COMM is not shown.)

    while NEXT=' ' **loop** ... **end loop**;

Similarly, the iteration TEXT over words is

    while NEXT/='%' **loop** ... **end loop**;

Here '%' is the terminating symbol following the text and appearing immediately after TEXT in the sequence diagram in Figures 2-4 and 2-6. Similarly, in the VDU program in Figure 2-20, the iteration TEXT is terminated by any nonnormal character:

    while C **in** NORMAL **loop** ... **end loop**;

This is adequate, since any nonnormal character marks the beginning of another FIELD. This follows from the data sequence diagram shown in Figure 2-18.

    In these three cases, the iteration condition is based on the first data element following the iteration. In the VDU program, the iteraction CCS over command characters is a slightly different example, with an additional condition N<=C_MAX:

    while C **in** NORMAL **and** N<=C_MAX **loop** ... **end loop**;

Also in this case, when the loop ends, C will contain the character immediately following the command characters, and the iteration is still terminated by a condition occurring immediately after the loop.

    In other cases, the termination of the loop is based on the last element in the iteration itself. This element must be processed inside the loop, which must then be terminated. In this case we cannot use a pure **while** or **for** loop, but must rely on an **exit** statement to terminate the loop from within. The **exit** statement is included in the program sequence diagram as any other statement.

    As a simple example, consider a program receiving messages over a communication line. Each message contains data to be processed and a status field with the two values LAST and OTHER, where LAST indicates that the message is the last one in a given communication session. Figure 2-24 is the input data sequence diagram, Figure 2-25 is the program sequence diagram, and Figure 2-26 is a program text fragment. The data sequence diagram shows a selection between LAST and OTHER. The data element that will be used as an exit criterion (LAST) is marked with an arrowhead. In the program sequence diagram and the program text, the selection is reduced to the construct

    exit when M.STATUS = LAST;

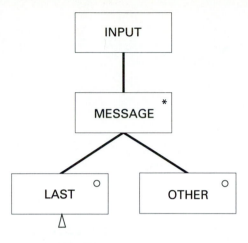

Figure 2-24 Data sequence diagram showing a simple stream of messages over a communication line. The last message carries the value LAST while all other messages carry the value OTHER.

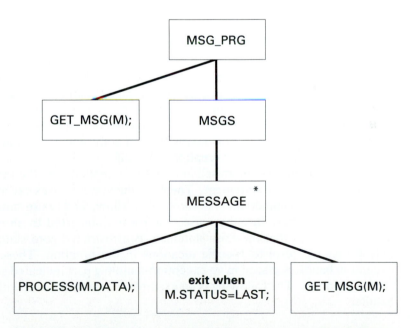

Figure 2-25 Program sequence diagram of the program MSG_PRG, which loops over messages arriving on a communication line and exits the loop when a message with the value LAST is received.

```
procedure MSG_PRG is
type STAT_TYPE is (LAST, OTHER);
subtype DATA_TYPE is STRING(1..100);
type MSG_TYPE is record
   DATA:    DATA_TYPE;
   STATUS: STAT_TYPE;
end record;
M: MSG_TYPE;
procedure GET_MSG(M: out MSG_TYPE) is separate;
procedure PROCESS(S: DATA_TYPE) is separate;
begin
   GET_MSG(M);
   loop
      PROCESS(M.DATA);
      exit when M.STATUS = LAST;
      GET_MSG(M);
   end loop;
end MSG_PRG;
```

Figure 2-26 The program MSG_PRG loops over messages arriving over a communication line and exits the loop when a message with STATUS = LAST has been received and processed.

2.7 EXCEPTIONS AND BACKTRACKING

2.7.1 Exception Syntax

The **exit** statement in Ada is not strictly in accordance with structured programming standards. Instead, it may be regarded as a restricted goto statement that transfers control from within a loop directly to the statement after the loop, bypassing any intermediate statements and the evaluation of a loop condition. In Ada, *exceptions* are handled by means of a similar construct that transfers control from anywhere inside a unit (a block, subprogram body, package body, or task body) to a particular *exception handler* placed at the end of the unit. This transfer of control occurs when the exception is *raised*.

An exception may be raised in two ways: implicitly by the run-time system, or explicitly by a **raise** statement. The run-time system raises exceptions in illegal situations such as numerical underflow or overflow, while **raise** statements appear in the program text. In either case, control is transferred to an exception handler. This means that the **raise** statement is a restricted goto statement that can only transfer control to specific locations in the program. These locations are exception handlers placed in an exception-handling part indicated by the reserved word **exception**. The following is an example of a program unit with an exception handler.

```
begin
   .....          -- Sequence of statements
   .....
   raise E;       -- Transfer control to
                  -- exception handler.
```

```
     .....
     .....
exception           -- Beginning of exception-handling part
    when E=> ... -- Exception handler
end;
```

2.7.1.1 Declaration of exceptions

The example above assumes that the identifier E has been declared as an exception and is in scope when raised. The declaration follows the usual format:

```
E: exception;
```

The Ada language also includes a set of predefined exception identifiers: CONSTRAINT_ERROR, NUMERIC_ERROR, PROGRAM_ERROR, STORAGE_ERROR, and TASKING_ERROR. These *built-in exceptions* are raised by the Ada run-time system. For an explanation of the error situations when these exceptions are raised, the reader is referred to any Ada primer. A built-in exception may also be raised explicitly by including one of the above-mentioned identifiers in a **raise** statement. (The identifier does not have to be declared.) Nevertheless, it is advisable to use other identifiers for exceptions detected by the program. It is easier to trace the error that has occurred if a different exception is declared for each error situation.

2.7.1.2 Handling of exceptions

When an exception is raised, control is transferred to the *exception handler* in the unit where the exception was raised. The exception handler is located in an exception-handling part preceded by the word **exception** at the end of a unit, whether the unit is a block, a subprogram body, a package body, or a task body. When a handler is included, each unit has the structure

```
begin
        ....    -- Normal processing
exception       -- Exception-handling part
        ....    -- Exception handlers
end;
```

When an exception has been raised and the exception handler has been executed, execution normally continues through the final **end** of the unit. If the unit is a procedure, this means that control is returned to the caller after the handler has been executed. If the unit is a main procedure, execution continues through the final end and terminates. (A similar situation occurs if the unit is a *task*; see Chapter 6.)

It is often undesirable to let an exception end the currently executed procedure, and for that reason, the exception handler is instead often placed in a block inside the unit. If we want normal processing to resume after the exception has been handled, we may put the block inside a loop. The following structure is often useful:

```
loop
   begin
         ....      -- Normal processing
   exception
         ...       -- Exception handling
   end;
end loop;
```

In other situations, the exception handler includes a statement that explicitly transfers control further. This may be an **exit** statement (if the exception handler is inside a loop) or **return** (if the exception handler is in a subprogram). We may also transfer control to another exception handler in certain ways. This is known as *exception propagation* and is explained in the following section.

2.7.1.3 Propagation of exceptions

If an exception is raised in a unit, U, that has no exception handler, U is terminated and the exception is *propagated* dynamically. If U is a block, the exception is raised in the surrounding block. If U is a subprogram, the exception is raised at the point of the call. If necessary, this propagation continues to the next-higher level until the exception can be handled.

An exception handler in a unit, V, say, may also propagate an exception explicitly, by means of a **raise** statement. This transfers control from the handler in V to the handler at the next-higher level, and so on, according to the propagation rules in the preceding paragraph. The statement

```
raise F;
```

inside a handler raises the exception F at the higher level. A **raise** statement without an exception identifier is permissible inside an exception handler. It propagates the exception that is currently being handled.

2.7.2 Exceptions in the VDU Problem

In Figure 2-27 the VDU procedure has been equipped with an exception handler. (This new version of the procedure is called VDU_EXC.) The exception ERR is raised if a nondisplayable character is encountered or if the maximum number of command characters (C_MAX) is exceeded. Both errors are now handled in the

```
package SCREEN_EXC is
   C_MAX: constant:=5;
   type CMND_BUFF is array (1..C_MAX) of CHARACTER;
   NULL_CMND: constant CMND_BUFF:=(others => ' ');
   ERR: exception;
   procedure PUT(C: CHARACTER);
   procedure EXEC(CMND: CMND_BUFF);
end SCREEN_EXC;


   with INPUT_STREAM; use INPUT_STREAM;
   with SCREEN_EXC; use SCREEN_EXC;
procedure VDU_EXC is
C: CHARACTER;
subtype NORMAL is CHARACTER range 'A'..'Z';
C_BUFF: CMND_BUFF;
N: INTEGER range 1..C_MAX+1;
begin
   GET(C);
   FIELDS: loop
      begin
         if C in NORMAL then
            -- Text
            while C in NORMAL loop
               PUT(C);
               GET(C);
            end loop;
         elsif C = '[' then
            -- Prepare for command.
            N:=1; C_BUFF:=NULL_CMND; GET(C);
            while C in NORMAL and N<=C_MAX loop
               C_BUFF(N):=C; N:=N+1; GET(C);
            end loop;
            -- Command end
            if C=']' then
               EXEC(C_BUFF); GET(C);
            else -- Command string too long
               raise ERR;
            end if;
         else -- Error character
            raise ERR;
         end if;
      exception -- Error in input stream
         when ERR => ABT; GET(C);
      end;
   end loop FIELDS;
end VDU_EXC;
```

Figure 2-27 VDU_EXC is the VDU
program provided with an exception
handler. The exception is declared in
the specification of the package
SCREEN_EXC.

59

exception-handling part. We want the exception handling to occur inside the infinite loop FIELDS, so that once an exception has been handled, the procedure will accept a new field. For this, the sequence of statements inside the loop is enclosed in a block. (The block is degenerate and lacks declarations.) Each time an exception has been handled, control passes through the final end of the block but stays within the loop.

The identifier ERR is declared in the specification of the package SCREEN_EXC, which is also shown in Figure 2-27. That way, the identifier is in scope both in SCREEN_EXC and in VDU_EXC. (This issue is discussed further in Chapter 3.) The package SCREEN_EXC also includes the subprogram EXEC, which is used to execute a command string. EXEC may have the following structure:

```
procedure EXEC (C: CMND_BUFF) is
begin
   .....
   if <condition> then
      raise ERR;  -- Error in command string
   end if;
   ....
end;
```

Assuming that EXEC contains no exception handler, the exception ERR is propagated to VDU_EXC, from where the call EXEC(C_BUFF) is made. The exception is handled as if it had been raised in the body of VDU_EXC itself.

2.7.3 Backtracking

Since Ada-style exception handling is incompatible with strict structured programming, a program with exceptions cannot be derived directly from a regular expression. Instead, a *backtracking* technique is used to derive such programs from sequence diagrams. The backtracking technique includes three steps: First, data and program sequence diagrams are constructed in the usual manner. Then normal processing and exception handling are separated and **raise** statements are inserted in the normal part. This conversion of the program sequence diagram from a regular expression into a diagrammatic representation of a program with exception handling may result in *backtracking side effects*. Such side effects include program text made redundant and errors introduced by the insertion of the **raise** statements. In a final step, the side effects are identified and dealt with. Each step is explained further below.

Step 1.   An input data sequence diagram is made with a *selection* between a normal input data stream and a data stream causing an exception to be raised. That way, the input is described correctly in terms of sequences, iterations, and selections. Some subsequences are usually shown in both parts of the selection,

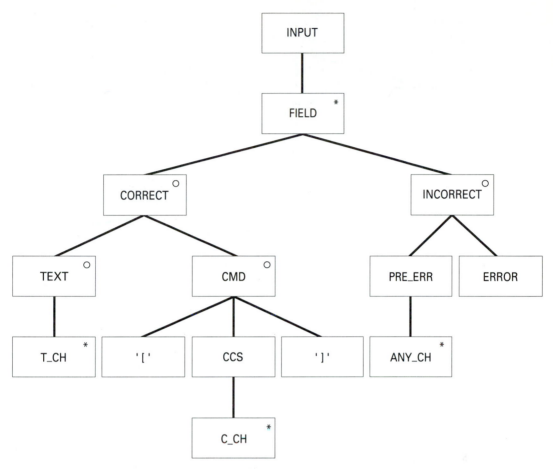

Figure 2-28   Input data sequence diagram for a backtracking solution of the VDU problem. The input is shown as a selection between a CORRECT case and INCORRECT case. INCORRECT consists of an error character and any characters preceding it.

since they occur in both correct and incorrect input data streams. A program sequence diagram is built on the data sequence diagram in the normal way. Figure 2-28 shows a data sequence diagram of the input to the VDU problem with a selection between a CORRECT field and an INCORRECT field. A program sequence diagram is built on this data sequence diagram in the usual way.

Step 2.   In the program sequence diagram, the selection between a normal and an erroneous data stream is converted into a *posit-admit* construct (Figure 2-29). 'P' and 'A' are used instead of the rings in the two parts of the selection. This indicates that the sequence diagram is no longer a formally correct regular expression. The posit-admit structure is translated directly into a unit with an

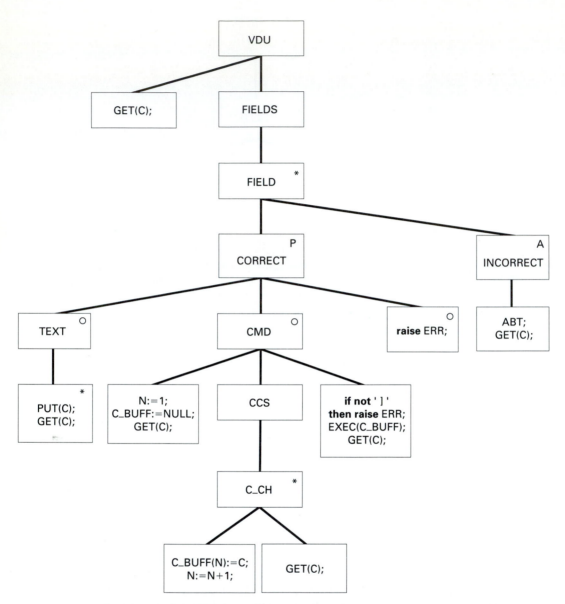

Figure 2-29 Program sequence diagram of a backtracking solution to the VDU problem. The iteration PRE_ERR in INCORRECT has been eliminated as a helpful backtracking side effect.

exception handler: the *posit* leg of the construct is the normal processing between **begin** and **exception**, and the *admit* leg is the exception-handling part. The statement **raise** ERR; is inserted as any other program statement. Since the selection

CORRECT in Figure 2-28 handles only TEXT and CMD, this forces us to add a third selection part dealing with incorrect input. That way, the component ERR in the earlier VDU input data sequence diagram in Figure 2-18 is rediscovered.

Step 3.   Finally, those *backtracking side effects* that may have been caused by the conversion in step 2 are found and dealt with as necessary. There are three types of backtracking side effects:

Harmful side effects, which must be eliminated

Neutral side effects, which may be ignored

Helpful side effects, which may be used for program simplification

In the program sequence diagram in Figure 2-29, a helpful side effect has been dealt with. This may be seen by comparing the program sequence diagram with the data sequence diagram in Figure 2-28, where the sequence INCORRECT consists of PRE_ERR followed by the erroneous character ERROR. In reality, when the admit sequence INCORRECT is entered, any characters in the incorrect field preceding the error character have already been dealt with. This is the helpful side effect, and as a consequence, the iteration PRE_ERR in the sequence INCORRECT has been eliminated in the program sequence diagram. The diagram in Figure 2-29 corresponds to the program text in Figure 2-27. Further examples of backtracking side effects and a complete description of backtracking can be found in the JSP literature [Jackson 75], [Ingevaldsson 79], [Sanden 85a].

2.7.3.1 Simplified backtracking

Complete backtracking as described above is sometimes considered unnecessarily cumbersome. For example, one may ask why we have to include the iteration PRE_ERR in the INCORRECT part when we know that it will be eliminated as a backtracking side effect later. The reason is a wish to base the backtracking solution soundly on a data sequence diagram describing the data in terms of sequences, selection, and iterations and make sure that all side effects are caught and dealt with.

Once the theory behind backtracking is understood, it is often possible to simplify the data sequence diagram at least in simple cases. The *admit* leg of such a simplified diagram then shows only the material remaining after the elimination of helpful side effects. Such a structure maps in an obvious way onto an Ada program unit with an exception-handling part. It must be noted that the simplified data sequence diagram is not a regular expression and may only be regarded as a diagrammatic prestage to the program text. Any reasoning about the correctness of the solution must rely on the program text itself.

2.7.4 Example: Buoy Problem

2.7.4.1 Problem description

Backtracking will be illustrated by means of an embedded software system, which is discussed fully in Chapter 8. The system is described as follows: A number of free-floating *buoys* provide navigation and weather data to air and ship traffic at sea. Each buoy collects air and water temperature, wind speed, and location data through various sensors. Each buoy is equipped with:

> A *radio transmitter* to broadcast *weather and location information* as well as an *SOS message*
>
> A *radio receiver* to receive requests from passing vessels

The transmission of SOS messages is initiated by a sailor in distress who reaches the buoy and flips an emergency switch [Booch].

For our present purposes we concentrate on the task REPORTER, which handles radio transmission from the buoy. The following rules define the transmission behavior of a buoy:

> *Periodic broadcast.* Under normal circumstances, current wind, temperature, and location information is broadcast periodically (every 60 seconds, say).
>
> *History transmission.* In response to a request from a passing vessel, accumulated information from the past 24 hours is broadcast. This transmission takes several minutes and preempts the periodic broadcast during that time.
>
> *Emergency transmission.* If a sailor engages the emergency switch, an SOS signal is transmitted continuously. The emergency transmission takes precedence over all other boradcasts, which are suppressed until the emergency condition is reset by a passing vessel.

2.7.4.2 Complete backtracking solution

The external reporter behavior of the buoy is described by the combined input-and-output sequence diagram in Figure 2-30. The diagram shows messages transmitted as well as radio messages and other signals received by the buoy, such as the engagement of the emergency switch. The repeated behavior REPORTER_BODY is shown as a selection between a normal case and an SOS case. The normal case is where no emergency transmission occurs, and shows regular

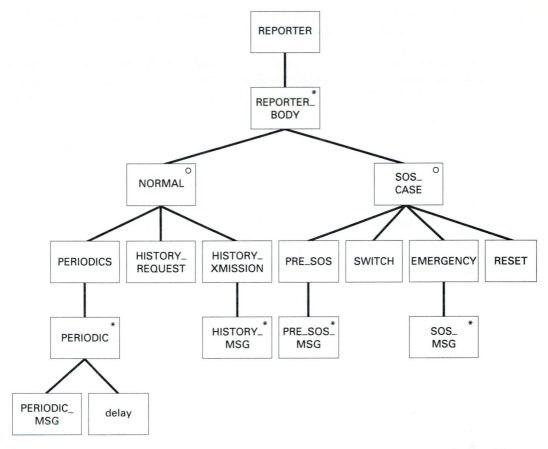

Figure 2-30 The REPORTER behavior of the buoy described in a sequence diagram. The behavior is an iteration of REPORTER_BODY, which is a selection of NORMAL and SOS_CASE. NORMAL is a sequence of PERIODICS, HISTORY_REQUEST, and HISTORY_XMISSION. PERIODICS is an iteration of PERIODIC, consisting of a PERIODIC_MSG and a delay. HISTORY_XMSSION is an iteration of HISTORY_MSG. SOS_CASE is a sequence of PRE_SOS, SWITCH, EMERGENCY, and RESET. In this case, PRE_SOS represents all messages preceding the flipping of the switch. EMERGENCY is an iteration of SOS_MSG.

and history transmissions only. The SOS case includes any number of regular and history transmissions followed by SWITCH, which indicates that the emergency switch is engaged. SWITCH is followed by multiple SOS messages and finally, an incoming RESET message from a passing vessel.

Figure 2-30 shows the REPORTER behavior as a regular expression over inputs and outputs. It has been made with a backtracking solution in mind, so the description of the message preceding the SOS messages (PRE_SOS) is vague. We know ahead of time that PRE_SOS will be eliminated when side effects are dealt with. Backtracking is carried out as follows:

Step 1. REPORTER is a regular expression over the events relevant to the reporting and consists of an iteration of REPORTER_BODY, which can be either NORMAL or SOS_CASE. Both are complete behaviors, including all occurring events. REPORTER in Figure 2-30 is a data sequence diagram of the reporter behavior. The same diagram becomes our first cut at a program sequence diagram.

Step 2. Figure 2-31 shows a program sequence diagram where REPORTER_BODY has been converted into a posit-admit construct. To guard against the possibility that the behavior is really an SOS case, the program must check for the emergency switch during periodic transmission and history transmission. A history request causes an exit out of the loop PERIODICS. When the emergency switch is engaged, control is transferred to SOS_CASE, which is the admit leg of REPORTER_BODY. This is done by means of the statement **raise** SOS, which occurs twice.

Step 3. When control is passed to the admit leg, parts of the posit leg (NORMAL) have been executed under an incorrect assumption: that the data sequence was a "correct" one, without emergencies. This assumption may have caused backtracking side effects that may have to be eliminated. In the case of REPORTER, the only side effect is the fact that periodic and history messages may have been transmitted. This is a *helpful* side effect, since they would have been transmitted anyway, even if SOS_CASE had been entered directly. This side effect allows us to simplify the admit leg by removing the iteration PRE_SOS.

2.7.4.3 Simplified backtracking
in the buoy problem

Complete backtracking is somewhat cumbersome, particularly in straightforward cases. Figure 2-32 illustrates a more pragmatic approach where the selection has been replaced by a posit-admit structure in the data sequence diagram. With this approach the sequence diagram is no longer a formal regular expression but rather, a working document leading up to the program text. This approach relies on the Ada program text itself to provide a formal description of the external behavior of the software. In Figure 2-32, upward-pointing arrowheads mark those places in the normal behavior pattern where an abnormal pattern may be detected. The engagement of the emergency switch can be detected on two occasions: during the delay between periodic broadcasts and during a history transmission. The program sequence diagram in Figure 2-31 can be built directly on the diagram in Figure 2-32.

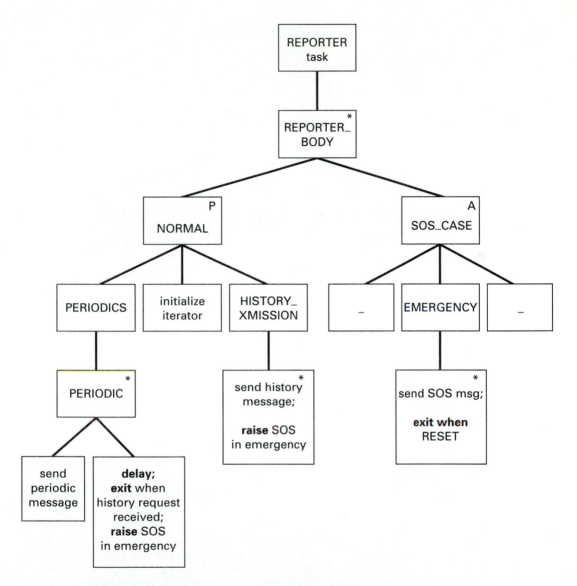

Figure 2-31 Program sequence diagram of the REPORTER task, based on the sequence diagram in Figure 2-30. Here the selection REPORTER_BODY has been replaced by a *posit-admit* construct. PRE_SOS has been eliminated as a helpful side effect. The boxes SWITCH and RESET in the earlier diagram appear as empty components since they cause no processing other than the starting and stopping of the EMERGENCY broadcast.

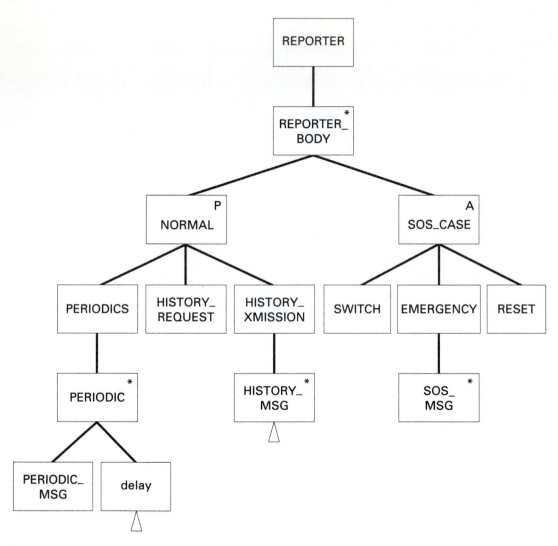

Figure 2-32 Pragmatic sequence diagram of the REPORTER behavior used for a simplified backtracking solution. REPORTER_BODY is immediately indicated as a posit-admit construct. The component PRE_SOS, which will be eliminated as a helpful side effect, has been left out. Arrowheads are used to indicate components where an abnormal behavior may be detected, causing a transfer of control to the admit branch. This sequence diagram leads immediately to the program sequence diagram in Figure 2-31.

2.7.4.4 Text of the REPORTER task

The program text of REPORTER (Figure 2-33) relies on some syntactical elements having to do with tasking, and is explained fully in Chapter 8. For our present purposes, we show only the close correspondence between the text and the pro-

```
task body REPORTER is
R_PERIOD: constant:=60.0;
SOS: exception;
IT: ITEM;
begin
   loop
      begin
         PERIODICS: loop
            -- Send periodic message.
            select accept EMERGENCY; raise SOS;
            or accept HISTORY; exit;
            or delay R_PERIOD;
            end select;
         end loop PERIODICS;

         -- History transmission
         ITER24;              -- Initialize iterator.
         IT:=GET_NEXT;
         while IT.ELEM/= NONE loop
            SEND(IT);     -- Transmit historic item.
            IT:=GET_NEXT;
            select accept EMERGENCY; raise SOS;
            else null;
            end select;
         end loop;
      exception
         when SOS =>
            -- Emergency transmission
            loop
               select accept RESET; exit;
               else SEND_SOS;
               end select;
            end loop;
      end;
   end loop;
end REPORTER;
```

Figure 2-33 Body of the task REPORTER based on the program sequence diagram in Figure 2-31.

gram sequence diagram in Figure 2-31. The normal processing and the exception handler in Figure 2-33 correspond to the posit leg NORMAL and the admit leg, SOS_CASE, respectively. Within NORMAL, the PERIODICS iteration contains transmission of the periodic message, followed by a **select** statement. In the **select** statement, the program receives signals that the emergency switch has been engaged or a history broadcast has been requested. This happens in the statements

```
accept EMERGENCY;
```

and

   accept HISTORY;

respectively. The emergency switch causes the program to raise the exception
SOS, while a request for a history broadcast causes an exit from the PERIODICS
iteration. The select construct also includes the statement

   delay R_PERIOD;

This means that if neither the emergency switch is engaged nor a history broadcast
requested, there will be a delay of R_PERIOD seconds until the next periodic
message.

   The history transmission involves retrieving successive items from the
buoy's database sensor readings. This is handled by means of an iterator, discussed in Chapter 4. The exception handler, finally, contains a loop that calls the
subprogram SEND_OS repeatedly until the emergency transmission is reset. The
REPORTER task is informed of this by means of the statement

   accept RESET;

2.7.5 Use of Exceptions and Backtracking

Exceptions and backtracking are necessary means of expression in certain situations. But they add complexity to the software and make it error prone, particularly because of the possible side effects. Exceptions and backtracking should be
used only where the regular control structure must be breached for a truly exceptional reason. Error handling is the most common case, as illustrated by the VDU
program, but many routine errors can actually be taken care of within the regular
structure. In the buoy program, backtracking is used only in the emergency case,
while the history request is integrated into the regular structure by means of a loop
exit.

   It is always wrong to use backtracking to resolve a structure clash [Sanden
85a]. As discussed in Section 2.5, the correct solution is, instead, program decomposition. In the VDU problem, a boundary clash exists between the INPUT
sequence of fields and the BLOCKS sequence of blocks (Figure 2-22). It might be
tempting to treat end-of-block as an exception, but this leads to a complex and
obscure program.

2.8 CONTROL STRUCTURING IN THE ELEVATOR PROBLEM

In most of the earlier examples in this chapter, program control structures have
been patterned on input and output data streams, processed sequentially. The
data sequence diagrams describing the input and output represent sequences in

time and show the order in which data items are read or produced by a program. Furthermore, an input data stream can be said to reflect the *behavior* of some entity outside the program, which produces the input successively. Meanwhile, the output data stream reflects the external behavior over time of the program itself, as the producer of output.

Reactive software often deals with concrete external entities such as various hardware devices. These entities produce input in the form of signals indicating changes of the state of each entity. Similarly, the output from the software consists of commands to the devices rather than data elements to be displayed or printed. The designer of reactive software focuses more on the behavior of the entities than on the structure of the input and output data series themselves. This makes it useful to pattern program control structures on the behavior or *life* of an entity with which the software interacts. We now study an example of an embedded elevator control program that is patterned on the behavior of an elevator.

2.8.1 Problem Description

The behavior of an elevator traveling upward and downward and stopping at various floors is shown in Figure 2-34. The diagram shows the elevator's vertical position as a function of time. In the particular example shown in the diagram, the elevator starts at the GROUND_FLOOR, stops at floor 4, continues to floor 5 (UPMOST_FLOOR), changes direction, stops again at floor 4, then stops and turns at floor 3 (BOTTOM_FLOOR), and so on.

The sequence diagram in Figure 2-35 shows the general elevator behavior. It is an input data sequence diagram where the input elements are the events ALERT and ARRIVED. The elevator behaves as follows:

> When there are no outstanding requests, the elevator sits idly at the ground floor.
>
> When a request is made, the elevator is alerted (ALERT) and sets out to serve the request by moving to the required floor.
>
> The elevator then continues moving up and down while there are requests outstanding. This activity is represented by the box OSCILLATE in Figure 2-35, which is an iteration of JOURNEY_PAIR.
>
> Each JOURNEY_PAIR consists of a journey UPWARD followed by a journey DOWNWARD.
>
> An UPWARD journey extends over one or more floors. It starts with an iteration UPBODY over UP_FLOOR and finally reaches an UPMOST_FLOOR, which is the highest floor that must be served in this journey and not necessarily the top floor of the building.
>
> A downward journey starts with an iteration DOWNBODY over DOWN_FLOOR and reaches a BOTTOM_FLOOR, which is not necessarily the ground floor.

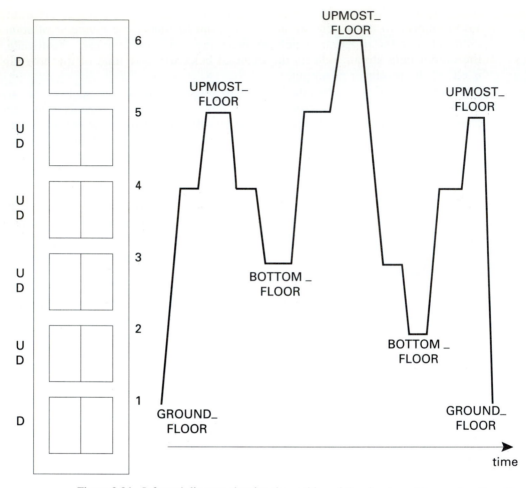

Figure 2-34 Informal diagram showing the position of the elevator cabin as a function of time. In this example, the elevator starts at floor 1 (GROUND_FLOOR), stops at floor 4, stops and turns at floor 5, stops again at floor 4, stops and turns at floor 3, and so on. The floor where the elevator turns on each journey are indicated as BOTTOM_FLOOR and UPMOST_FLOOR.

Figure 2-35 Sequence diagram of elevator behavior with the following inputs: ALERT: signal that a new request has arrived; ARRIVED: arrival at a floor sensor. The behavior of the elevator is an iteration of JOURNEY_GROUP, which is a sequence of GROUND_FLOOR and OSCILLATE. OSCILLATE is an iteration of JOURNEY_PAIR, which is a sequence of UPWARD and DOWNWARD. UPWARD is sequence of UPBODY and UPMOST_FLOOR. UPBODY is an iteration of UP_FLOOR with the event ARRIVED. DOWNWARD is analogous to UPWARD.

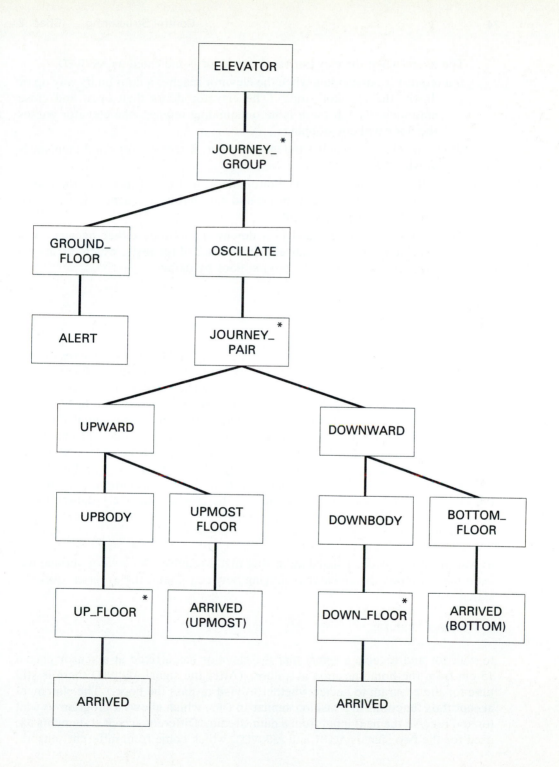

The event when the elevator reaches a floor is indicated as ARRIVED.

If a request is outstanding when the elevator reaches a floor on its way up or down, the elevator stops. (The elevator doors then open and close automatically.) If there is no outstanding request, the elevator passes the floor without stopping.

When the elevator reaches the upmost floor, it always stops and then starts downward.

When the elevator reaches the bottom floor, it stops. This marks the end of a JOURNEY_PAIR, and, if the ground floor has been reached, it is also the end of a JOURNEY_GROUP.

The ground floor is reached in a downward journey either because of a specific request or because of an absence of requests, which causes the elevator to return to the ground floor by default.

2.8.2 Sequence Diagramming

The sequence diagram ELEVATOR (Figure 2-35) is a regular expression over events in the life of the real elevator. The events appear in the leaves of the diagram. As before, the names in the nonleaf boxes refer to subsequences of the diagram.

The elevator control program receives information of events in the life of the elevator by means of signals from hardware sensors. How this is handled in Ada will be discussed further in later chapters. For the moment, suffice it to note that the program waits for and receives such signals by means of the statement **accept** followed by the signal name. (More precisely, ELEVATOR is a *task* and the name following accept is an *entry point* declared in the task specification; see Chapter 6.) Thus when the elevator is sitting idly at the ground floor the program uses

    accept ALERT;

to wait for and receive a signal indicating that a request for elevator service has been made. When the elevator is moving between floors, the program uses the statement

    accept ARRIVED;

to wait for and receive a signal that the elevator has arrived at a sensor placed 15 cm from the home position at a floor. (After the signal ARRIVED there is still time for the program to decide whether to visit or pass the floor.) The statement **accept** thus functions in a fashion similar to GET, which allows a program to wait for and receive the next input from a data stream. Different **accept** statements are used for the two signals ALERT and ARRIVED, which come from different sensors.

The program causes the elevator to stop and start in the proper direction by means of the following commands to the elevator motor:

START	Start motor.
STOP	Stop motor.
SET_UP	Set motor polarity for upward travel.
SET_DOWN	Set motor polarity for downward travel.

These commands appear as procedure calls in the program sequence diagram in Figure 2-36. The statement **accept** ARRIVED has been inserted according to the read-ahead principle. (As a matter of minor optimization, **accept** ALERT has been put in the beginning of the iterated sequence JOURNEY_GROUP rather than in two places: at the beginning of the program and at the end of the sequence JOURNEY_GROUP.) For simplicity, the separate boxes GROUND_FLOOR, UPMOST_FLOOR, and BOTTOM_FLOOR do not appear in this program sequence diagram.

In addition to the elevator program discussed here, the elevator system must also register travel requests made by persons pressing the elevator buttons at various floors and inside the elevator, and store the requests until they have been served. This is discussed in detail in Chapter 8. The elevator program itself accesses the set of outstanding requests by means of a set of subprograms which are called with the parameters

F:F_TYPE	A floor number
D:D_TYPE	A direction, UP or DOWN

Since there is an UP and a DOWN button at each floor (except the ground and top floors, which have only one button each), a direction may be associated with a request, in addition to a floor. The following subprogram calls are used:

function VISIT(F,D) **return** BOOLEAN;

The elevator inquires if it must stop at floor F when traveling in direction D.

function CONTINUE_DOWN(F) **return** BOOLEAN;

The elevator reports that it is approaching floor F from above and inquires whether to continue or change direction.

function CONTINUE_UP(F) **return** BOOLEAN;

The elevator reports that it is approaching floor F from below and inquires whether to continue or change direction.

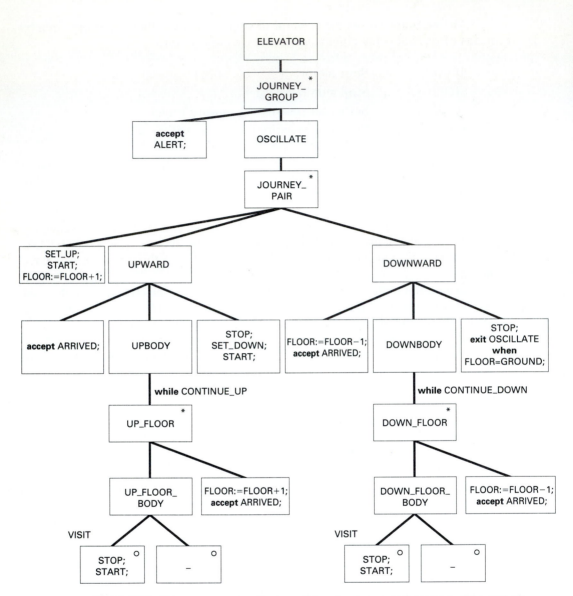

Figure 2-36 Program sequence diagram of the elevator control program. (The variable FLOOR of F_TYPE initially equals GROUND.)

In the program sequence diagram, the calls to CONTINUE_UP and CONTINUE_DOWN appear in the iteration conditions of UPBODY and DOWNBODY, respectively. The call to VISIT appears in the two selections UP_FLOOR_BODY and DOWN_FLOOR_BODY. These selections account for the elevator's stopping or not stopping at a floor, depending on whether there are any outstanding requests.

```
begin
    ELEV: loop    -- Over journey groups
        accept ALERT;
        OSCILLATE: loop  -- Over journey pairs
            SET_UP;
            START;
            FLOOR:=FLOOR+1;
            accept ARRIVED;
            UPBODY: while CONTINUE_UP(FLOOR) loop
                if VISIT(FLOOR, UP) then
                    STOP;
                    START;
                end if;
                FLOOR:=FLOOR+1;
                accept ARRIVED;
            end loop UPBODY;
            -- Upmost floor:
            STOP;
            SET_DOWN;
            START;
            FLOOR:=FLOOR-1;
            accept ARRIVED;
            DOWNBODY: while CONTINUE_DOWN(FLOOR) loop
                if VISIT(FLOOR,DOWN) then
                    STOP;
                    START;
                end if;
                FLOOR:=FLOOR-1;
                accept ARRIVED;
            end loop DOWNBODY;
            -- Bottom floor:
            STOP;
            exit OSCILLATE when FLOOR=GROUND;
        end loop OSCILLATE;
    end loop ELEV;
end;
```

Figure 2-37 Control structure of the task ELEVATOR based on the program sequence diagram in Figure 2-36.

While the box corresponding to a visit contains the calls STOP and START, the box corresponding to a nonvisit is empty.

The function calls appear in abbreviated form in this program sequence diagram. The complete calls are included in the Ada program text shown in Figure 2-37. The program faithfully follows the program sequence diagram. A more complete version of the elevator control program is discussed in Chapter 8.

2.9 CHAPTER SUMMARY

> *Total grandeur of a total edifice,*
> *Chosen by an inquisitor of*
> *Structures for himself.*
>
> *Wallace Stevens*, To an Old Philosopher in Rome

The *control structure* of a program describes the order in which its statements are executed. Whereas *structured programming* is based exclusively on the classical *control abstractions sequence*, *selection*, and *iteration*, a language such as Ada also allows nonstructured constructs, including **exit** and **return** statements and exception handling.

Control structuring is important for execution efficiency and for the clarity and understandability of the software. Control structures may be modeled on sequential patterns in the problem environment, which makes control structuring an important modeling tool. Such sequential patterns may reflect the order of data items in a sequential file or the sequence of events in a real-time environment. In either case, the pattern describes the *time sequence* in which the data items must be processed or the event occur. The control structure may be thought of as the *subject*, which moves processing forward by operating on software objects.

Sequence diagrams may be used in control structuring. A sequential pattern in the reality is represented as a *data sequence diagram*. Often, a program deals with one single sequential pattern. The sequence diagram may then be transformed into a *program sequence diagram*, which directly reflects the control structure of a program. This is done by replacing the data element in each leaf box with the operations on that data element and by adding iteration and selection conditions.

Sometimes, more than one diagram, such as an input data sequence diagram and an output sequence diagram, may have to be combined into one program sequence diagram. This is possible if there is no *structure clash*. Essentially, this is if the patterns described by each diagram can be handled at the same pace. Clashing data sequence diagrams cannot be combined and must result in separate program control structures.

Programs with exceptions may be developed from sequence diagrams by means of a *backtracking* technique, where a selection in the data sequence diagram becomes a *posit-admit* construct in the program sequence diagram. Normally, a sequence diagram represents a *regular expression*, but this is not true if it includes a posit-admit construct.

The way in which an input data item is processed by a program depends on the data item itself and the *mode* in which the program has been put by previous input. A program built on sequence diagrams exhibits *implicit mode representation*. This means that different modes are represented by different parts of the program. (In other words, the mode is reflected by the *program counter*, which keeps track of which statement to execute next.) Programs with implicit mode representation may also be developed without the sequence diagramming technique.

With *explicit mode representation*, the current mode of the program is kept in a *mode variable*. A program with explicit mode representation often consists of a loop with a GET statement followed by nested **case** statements, first over mode and then over different inputs. Programs with explicit mode representation may be based on a description of a sequential pattern in the reality as a *finite automaton*. There is a basic equivalence between finite automata and sequence diagrams, so that any sequential ordering of input items or events may be expressed either way.

With sequence diagramming, the program text shows a close resemblance to sequential structures in the problem environment. The diagrams are of primary importance during the design leading up to the program text. Once it exists, the text is the primary expression of the design, and any statements about the workings of the program must ultimately be validated directly against the text. Nevertheless, the diagrams may serve as important pieces of documentation, facilitating the understanding of the software.

REFERENCES

BOHM, C., and JACOPINI, A., Flow diagrams, Turing machines, and languages with only two formation rules, *Commun. ACM*, 9:5, May 1966, pp. 366–371.

BOOCH, G., Object-oriented software development, *IEEE Trans. Software Eng.*, 12:2, February 1986, pp. 211–221.

CAMERON, J. R., An overview of JSD, *IEEE Trans. Software Eng.*, 12:2, February 1986, pp. 222–240.

CAMERON, J. R., *JSP & JSD: The Jackson Approach to Software Development*, 2nd ed., IEEE Computer Society Press, Washington D.C., 1989.

DIJKSTRA, E., Go to statement considered harmful, *Commun. ACM*, 11:3, March 1968, pp. 147–148.

HUGHES, J. W., A formalization and explication of the Michael Jackson method of program design, University of Manchester Institute of Science and Technology, 1977.

INGEVALDSSON, L., *JSP: A Practical Method of Program Design*, Studentlitteratur, Lund, Sweden and Chartwell-Bratt, Brookfield, Vt., 1979.

INGEVALDSSON, L., *Software Engineering Fundamentals: The Jackson Approach*, Studentlitteratur, Lund, Sweden, and Chartwell-Bratt, Brookfield, Vt., 1990.

JACKSON, M. A., *Principles of Program Design*, Academic Press, New York, 1975.

JACKSON, M. A., *System Development*, Prentice Hall, Englewood Cliffs, N.J., 1983.

JACKSON, M. A., *Workshop Position Paper: The General and the Particular*, Michael Jackson Systems Ltd., London, 1988.

KING, D., *Creating Effective Software; Computer Program Design Using the Jackson Methodology*, Yourdon Press, Englewood Cliffs, N.J., 1988.

KING, M. J., and PARDOE, J. P., *Program Design Using JSP*, Wiley, New York, 1985.

RATCLIFFE, B., *Software Engineering: Principles and Methods*, Blackwell Scientific Publications, Cambridge, Mass., 1987.

RUBIN, F., 'Goto considered harmful' considered harmful, *Commun. ACM*, 30:3, March 1987, pp. 195–196.

SANDEN, B., *Systems Programming with JSP*, Studentlitteratur, Lund, Sweden and Chartwell-Bratt, Brookfield, Vt., 1985(a).

SANDEN, B., System programming with JSP: example—a VDU controller, *Commun. ACM*, 28:10 October 1985(b), pp. 1059–1067.

SANDEN, B., The case for eclectic design of real-time software, *IEEE Trans. Software Eng.*, 15:3, March 1989, pp. 360–362.

SUTCLIFFE, A., *Jackson System Development*, Prentice Hall International, Hemel Hempstead, Hertfordshire, England, 1988.

EXERCISES

2.1 Simple data sequence diagrams

Draw a data sequence diagram for each of the following cases.

(a) A *circus parade* is led by a *drum major* followed by his or her *band*. Then there are *animals*: *camels*, *elephants*, and *horses* in any order. The parade ends with either one or two *clowns*.

(b) A *goods train* consists of an *engine* followed by *cars*. Each car is either *refrigerated* or *nonrefrigerated*. After the cars comes a *caboose*. Finally, there may or may not be a *second engine*.

(c) The life of a *laser* is as follows: First it is *installed*. It then enters its *active life*, which consists of *cycles*. Each cycle starts with *laser on*. Then there are a number of *releases*. Each release has two steps: *open shutter* and *close shutter*. Each cycle ends with *shutdown*.

2.2 Automatic teller machine

In a sequence diagram of a dialogue such as between a human being and a computer, it is useful to include input and output in one diagram. To distinguish between input and output data, each leaf can be divided into two parts:

INPUT
OUTPUT

If a certain output follows a certain input unconditionally, the input and output are placed in each part of the same box. Otherwise, either part of the box is empty, marked by a dash. (This is quite common. For example, the very first data item in a human–computer dialogue is often a prompt output by the computer.)

Use the notation above to describe the following much simplified dialogue for an *automatic teller machine* (ATM):

ATM: "Please insert card."
User inserts ATM card.

If the card is accepted, then

> *ATM*: "Please enter personal identification number (PIN)."
> *User* enters an incorrect code zero or more times. *ATM*: "Please try again."
> *User* enters correct code.
> *ATM* repeatedly displays "Select Withdrawal, Balance, or End" until *End* is se-
> lected. One of the following subdialogues follows depending on the input:
> > *User*: "Withdraw." *ATM*: "Enter amount."
> > *User* enters amount. *ATM* outputs money.
> > *User* empties money compartment.
>
> > *User*: "Balance." *ATM* displays balance.
> *User*: "End." *ATM* issues receipt.
ATM returns card.

2.3 Keyboard input

An integer number is input as a series of *digits* from a keyboard. The number may be preceded by a *plus* or a *minus sign*. A special character, corresponding to a key marked 00 (*double zero*), may occur anywhere in the number. The number ends with a *space*.

(a) Draw a data sequence diagram of one number.

(b) Draw a data sequence diagram of an iteration of numbers, terminated by a '%' sign.

(c) Draw a program sequence diagram for a program processing the series of numbers. The program uses GET to read one digit at a time and transforms the digits into an integer number according to the following algorithm:

N:INTEGER:=0;
For each digit D read, multiply N by 10 and add D. When a double zero is read, multiply by 100.

For each complete integer, the program calls a procedure PROCESS(N). (You do not have to supply the procedure PROCESS.)

(d) Modify the data sequence diagram as follows: The program must be able to read either an integer number or a decimal number (i.e., an integer followed by a *decimal point* and zero or more *decimals*).

(e) Modify the data sequence diagram in part (d) to include *error input* and make a corresponding program sequence diagram. Assume that the procedure BEEP causes the keyboard to beep. Whenever an error character is encountered, call BEEP, ignore the error character, and GET a new character. (Error input includes plus or minus signs in the middle of the number, extra decimal points, a decimal point not followed by any digit, and so on.)

2.4 Currency transaction

A bank teller handles a currency transaction consisting of records in different currencies. Each record holds a currency field and an amount field. The records are grouped per currency, so that all D-Mark records are together, for example. The input is followed by an end-of-transaction (EOT) record.

(a) Draw an input data sequence diagram.
(b) Draw an output data sequence diagram as follows: One line is printed for each currency with the foreign amount and a converted dollar amount. At the end of the transaction, print a line with the dollar total.
(c) Combine the input and output data sequence diagrams. Transform the result into a program sequence diagram. Use the subprogram READ to read an entire record at a time, and CONVERT to convert foreign currency to dollars. Use variables for summation per currency group and for the total.

2.5 Polling program

A number of terminals are connected to a computer via a multi-dropped communication line. The computer *polls* each terminal regularly to see if it has any input for the computer. The computer also sends *output* messages to the different terminals. Make a sequence diagram of the traffic on the line, including the following: A POLL message is output to each terminal in turn. (A poll is a question: "Do you have any input data?")

   The terminal responds either with a DATA message or, if no input is available, with NO_DATA. If a terminal has been switched off, it will not answer and is timed-out. Use a leaf box TIME_OUT to mark the proper place of a time-out event in the sequence diagram. Each terminal is polled at most every R milliseconds. After all terminals have been polled once, the computer waits until the time R has expired before it again polls the first terminal. (This is shown as a TIME_OUT event in the sequence diagram.) In addition to the POLLs, the computer sends OUTPUT_BLOCKs of data to different terminals. This happens on two occasions: while the computer is waiting for the reply to a poll and after all terminals have been polled but the time R has not expired. At each occasion, zero or more blocks may be sent.

   Draw a *data sequence diagram* showing the behavior of the polling program. Let the leaves (data elements) in the sequence diagram be POLL, OUTPUT_BLOCK, DATA, NO_DATA, and TIME_OUT, each occurring at one or more places in the diagram.

2.6 VDU

In the VDU example, assume we require that each error character be followed by a command (rather than text). As before, once the maximum length (C_MAX) of a command has been reached, the following character is an error character unless it is a closing bracket. Modify the data sequence diagram, program sequence diagram, and program text accordingly.

2.7 Elevator doors

In the description of the elevator problem, we have assumed that the elevator doors are handled either manually or by the hardware. By introducing a number of appropriate subprograms and signals, we can integrate the handling of the doors into the program. The doors are managed by means of the subprogram OPEN_DOORS and the signal CLOSED as follows: OPEN_DOORS issues a command to the hardware to open the doors at the floor where the elevator is currently positioned. (If the doors are already open, the command has no effect.) The hardware uses door sensors to keep the doors open as long as necessary to allow passage. The doors close automatically when a certain time has elapsed since the doors were last blocked. When the doors are completely closed, a signal is given to the software. The program may wait for this signal by means of the statement

    accept CLOSED;

Modify the sequence diagrams in Figures 2-35 and 2-36 and the program text in Figure 2-37 so that OPEN_DOORS and **accept** CLOSED are used to allow the elevator program to operate the doors. The doors must open when the elevator has stopped at a floor if a request is outstanding for that floor. The doors must normally be closed while the elevator is waiting idly at the ground floor, but when a passenger presses the button at the ground floor, the doors must open.

2.8 Roman numeral[2]

The Roman numerals for 1 through 9 are as follows: 1: I, 2: II, 3: III, 4: IV, 5: V, 6: VI, 7: VII, 8: VIII, 9: IX. A program ROMAN must read a string of characters terminated by one blank and determine whether the string is a correct Roman numeral between 1 and 9. For a correct numeral, the program must determine the value of the numeral. The string may be preceded by any number of leading blanks.

(a) Describe the series of input to ROMAN by means of a data sequence diagram. The diagram must take the leading blanks into account and describe the input up to blank terminating a correct numeral and up to the first error character which determines that the input is not a correct numeral.

---

[2] This exercise was suggested by Steven Ferg (see also Exercise 3.1).

(b) Transform the data sequence diagram into a program sequence diagram for ROMAN.

Hint: The data sequence diagram may include one or more iterations of the character 'I', and the correctness of the numeral will depend on the number of 'I's. This constraint need not be expressed in the data sequence diagram but must appear in the program sequence diagram.

2.9 Traffic light

A traffic light serves an intersection of a major road in the east–west direction and a minor road in the north–south direction. The major road has separate left-turn lanes; the minor road does not. The traffic light has five different, mutually exclusive phases:

NS   Green for north–south traffic, red for east–west traffic

EW   Green for the forward lanes east and west, red for left-turning traffic and north–south traffic

LL   Green for both left-turn lanes on the major road, red for east–west forward traffic and north–south traffic

WL   Green for westbound traffic and for the left-turn lane parallel to the westbound lane in the major road

EL   Green for eastbound traffic and for the left-turn lane parallel to the eastbound lane

The traffic light steps through different phases in a cyclic pattern. A phase may be skipped if it is not necessary (i.e., there is no traffic in particular directions). Make a separate *data sequence diagram* to describe each of the following patterns.

(a) In each cycle, the north–south traffic first gets a green light, if necessary. Then, if any left-turning traffic is present on the major road, either the two left-turn lanes get green lights or one of the left-turn lanes gets a green light together with the forward traffic in the proper direction, east or west. Finally, the east–west traffic gets green lights.

(b) In each cycle, the north–south traffic first gets green lights, if necessary. Then, if there is traffic in both the left-turn lanes on the major road, both lanes get green lights. Then, if there is traffic in *one* of the left-turn lanes, it gets a green light together with forward traffic in the proper direction. Finally, the east–west traffic gets green lights.

Hint: The diagrams indicate only the *order* of the phases, not the conditions governing the choice of one phase over another or the extension in time of each phase. Each nonempty leaf in each diagram should contain one of the abbreviations EW, NS, LL, and so on, as given above.

2.10 Telegram problem[3]

A *ticker tape* contains a file, F, of *telegrams*. Each telegram consists of a number of words and ends with the word ZZZZ. The end of the file F is marked by an empty telegram containing ZZZZ as its only word. All words are separated by one or more blanks and the file may also contain leading blanks. A program, P, is required that must read the telegram file. For each telegram, print only a line stating the number of words and the number of over-length words (with more than 12 characters). The word ZZZZ is not counted.

(a) Draw an *input data sequence diagram* of F. Do not worry about error input; you may assume that the ticker tape is correct according to the description above.

(b) Draw an *output sequence diagram* of the printout.

(c) Based on the data sequence diagrams, draw a *program sequence diagram* of P. Assume that the following subprograms are available:

procedure T_LINE(N, W, O: INTEGER);
Print a line stating that telegram N has W words and O over-length words.

procedure F_LINE(N: INTEGER);
Print a line stating that N telegrams were found. (Do not worry about page breaks and other formatting.)
    The program *withs* the following package, which hides the interface to the physical ticker tape:

package TICKER_TAPE **is**
   subtype T_STRING **is** STRING(1..5);
   procedure READ(T: **out** T_STRING);
end;

The procedure READ allows *multiple read-ahead* as follows: Each call to READ returns the next five characters from the ticker tape and moves the tape one position forward. For example, if the tape contains the sequence

STOP ZZZZ START

consecutive calls to READ will return "STOP ", "TOP Z", "OP ZZ", "P ZZZ", " ZZZZ", "ZZZZ ", "ZZZ S", and so on. When the tape is positioned at the first 'Z', READ returns "ZZZZ ". This allows you to include conditions such as **if** T="ZZZZ " and **while** T/="ZZZZ " in your program, provided that the tape is carefully positioned. Conditions based on the next character alone, such as **while** T(1)='X', are also possible.

---

[3] A sequence diagram solution to the telegram problem was first given by Michael A. Jackson.

3 Modularization

Divide et impera

Louis XI

3.1 INTRODUCTION

A *module* is a program unit, such as a subprogram or a package. In Chapter 2 we used subprograms from standard libraries such as the *procedures* PUT and GET from the package TEXT_IO, as well as subprograms tailormade for various purposes. In the CHEER program (Figure 2-3), for example, we use the *functions* UPPER and LOWER to convert a letter to upper and lower case, respectively, and in the INPUT_STREAM package in the VDU example (Figure 2-23), a function CHECK returns a Boolean value indicating whether the sum of the input characters in the block is equal to a given check sum. In addition to the subprograms, we have also used *packages*, such as INPUT_STREAM and HOST_COMM in the VDU problem. Subprograms and packages are both used for software modularization, but they represent fundamentally different types of modules with different roots in programming tradition.

Subprograms have long played an important role in software design. *Structured design* [Yourdon], which is perhaps the best known software design method, is based on subprogram decomposition, and in languages from FORTRAN to Pascal and C, subprograms have been the most important means for decomposition. The emergence of other structuring means, such as the Ada *package* construct, have diminished the role of subprogram decomposition, however.

86

In this chapter we compare the syntactical features of subprograms and packages and discuss the role of subprograms in modern software construction.

Packages are important tools for modeling a problem environment in software. They allow us to create single *software objects*, representing single objects in the problem environment. A package modeled on a single object in that manner is referred to as an *information-hiding package*. In Ada, we also use the package construct to define *abstract data types (adt),* which allow us to create multiple *instances* of software objects. These instances can model multiple, similar objects in the environment. A package defining an abstract data type is called an *adt package*. These roles of packages will be studied in detail in Chapter 4.

The Ada specification of an information-hiding package or adt package contains subprogram declarations. For example, INPUT_STREAM contains the subprograms GET and ABT, and HOST_COMM contains GET, SEND_ABT, SEND_NAK, and SEND_ACK. These subprograms operate on the object represented by the information-hiding package or the instances of an abstract data type and are referred to as *operation subprograms*. TEXT_IO.PUT and TEXT_IO.GET are also operation subprograms. Other subprograms, such as UPPER, LOWER, and CHECK, that are not declared in a package specification will be referred to as *independent subprograms*.

3.1.1 Subprograms

The history of the subprogram goes back to the *subroutine*, which is called by means of the return-jump instruction. That instruction allows the processor to save the current value of the program counter, visit a sequence of statements starting at a given location, and return to the place of the call. When primary memory was scarce, the return-jump instruction and the subroutine were important inventions, and the possibility of supplying parameters with the calls made subroutines even more useful. In modern high-level languages, sophisticated subprograms have replaced the subroutines. Subroutines are still used extensively at the machine-language level, however. For example, the code produced by a compiler typically contains many calls to various built-in subroutines.

Block-structured languages from ALGOL to Ada provide a subprogram feature where invocation and parameter passing are based on a *stack* mechanism. This stack mechanism is managed by the *run-time system*, which is a set of built-in modules that the compiler automatically includes in the compiled program. When a subprogram is called, the *working environment*, including the program counter and parameters, is stored on a stack, from where it is retrieved upon return. A stack is a last-in-first-out data structure, so if the working environment is saved for a sequence of nested calls, the appropriate environment will always be on the *top* of the stack when each return is made. This allows *recursive* calls, with a function or procedure calling itself, either directly from within its own body, or indirectly, via another subprogram.

Primary storage has become cheaper over the years, but the use of subprograms also has conceptual advantages that remain important. Subprograms allow *procedural abstraction* and a separation of concerns between the subprogram and the *client* modules where the subprogram is called. For example, a programmer may invoke a procedure that calculates the square root of a number, X, say, by placing the call ''SQRT(X)'' in the program text. This *client programmer* deals with SQRT as an abstract function with an intuitive name and an *interface specification* that defines it completely. The client programmer need not know the sequence of statements necessary for calculation of the square root. How the root is calculated is the *secret* of the subprogram. Procedural abstraction is discussed further in Section 3.3.

A subprogram such as SQRT illustrates how close the subprogram concept is to the concept of a mathematical function. Indeed, the term *function* is kept in most programming languages for a subprogram that returns a single result. The function construct allows mathematical expressions to appear in the program text in a format that is very similar to mathematical notation, as, for example,

    SQRT(FACTORIAL(X))

This use of subprograms allows a close modeling in software of a problem expressed in mathematical terms. Similar modeling is also possible in nonmathematical problems, where clearly defined functions exist in the problem environment. In Section 3.5 we will see an example of a transaction system for banking where the tellers invoke such functions as *deposit* or *withdraw* from their terminals. These functions are modeled as functions or procedures in the software.

Throughout the history of programming, subprograms have often been considered the primary vehicles for software structuring. Design aiming at such a breakdown into independent subprograms is usually called *functional decomposition*. In traditional software development, the *architectural* or *preliminary* design phase is typically devoted to the functional decomposition of the software into a hierarchy of subprograms, which are then elaborated in the *detailed* design and implementation phases. In that development process, functional decomposition into subprograms is usually considered a higher-level activity, while control structuring is a lower-level activity and is handled within individual subprograms. This usually means that senior software engineers do the functional decomposition, while junior designers or programmers are responsible for the control structure.

This subprogram-centered design approach often results in artificial functions without natural counterparts in the problem environment. Although such procedures as ''*process all transactions*'' or ''*print instructions and read start balance*'' may make sense to the user, they are not established user concepts such as *insert* and *withdraw*, and they serve no modeling purpose in the software. The modern understanding of control structuring, packaging, and object-based approaches and the emergence of new, sophisticated programming languages have made contrived subprograms such as ''process all transactions'' unnecessary.

Although functional decomposition has lost its central role in software design, subprograms remain important pragmatic programming tools and are still used for separation of concerns and to avoid the duplication of program text. In that context it is interesting to study subprogram quality in terms of the *goodness criteria: cohesion*, *coupling*, and *fan-in*, introduced in structured design [Yourdon]. These concepts are discussed in Section 3.4 together with a justification of independent subprograms.

3.1.2 Separate Compilation; Information-Hiding Modules

3.1.2.1 Separate compilation units

In addition to subroutines or subprograms that are parts of the syntax of most programming languages, programmers have always relied on other means of software decomposition, which allows them to break a program into separately compiled source files. The compiler converts each source file into a *relocatable* program module, which a *linker* then combines into an *executable* program. The linker, which is a program separate from the compiler, can usually combine relocatable modules into an executable program regardless of the source language of each module.

The two-step process with compilation and linking and intermediate relocatable modules is necessary since the final executable machine code program must contain static references to locations in the code. For example, a return-jump instruction used to call a subprogram must contain the address of the subprogram. This address is not known until the executable is put together, since it depends on the place of each module in the complete executable code.

The linker matches the *external references* in each relocatable module to the *external definitions* of the other modules. The external definitions of a module are those constants, variables, subprogram names, and so on, that the module wants other modules to reference. The external references are those made by one module to constants, variables, and so on, of other modules. The linker matches external definitions with external references, and in the executable program, all external references are satisfied with external definitions.

3.1.2.2 Information-hiding modules

At a conceptual level, the term *information-hiding module* is used to describe a software module that has a *secret* and an *interface* to client modules. Different language environments support information-hiding modules to various degrees. Assembler programmers enjoy unlimited freedom to divide a program into modules and explicitly declare some quantities as external. Furthermore, information-hiding modules exist in the C language in the form of ''.c'' files. Various versions of FORTRAN allow separate compilation of modules with local data and externally accessible subprograms. Block-structured languages, such as ALGOL and standard Pascal, tend not to support separate compilation in principle, although practical language implementations often provide this feature.

In systems programming, *device drivers* are often implemented as information-hiding modules. For example, the physical interface to a secondary storage device such as a disk drive with its hardware-dependent details may be hidden in the module. The *client modules* of the device driver operate via a *logical* or *abstract* interface with operations such as "read," "write," and "search," which can remain the same even if the hardware interface is changed. (The clients of a module M are those modules that reference M and use its operations.)

Another typical example of an information-hiding module is one that hides a data structure and presents an interface consisting of a set of operations, by means of which the structure may be manipulated. The data structure is *persistent* in that it retains its value between calls. This makes such an information-hiding module different from a subprogram or set of subprograms. A subprogram operates on its input parameters and produces some output, which is returned to the caller. An operation on an information-hiding module operates on the input parameters plus the internal data structure and either produces output that is returned to the caller, or modifies the internal data, or both.

The packages HOST_COMM and INPUT_STREAM discussed in Section 2.5 and shown in Figure 2-23 are examples of information-hiding modules. INPUT_STREAM hides a block buffer and an index as internal data, while its interface consists of the subprograms GET and ABT. HOST_COMM hides the detailed communication interface with the host computer behind the abstract subprogram names GET, SEND_ABT, SEND_NAK, and SEND_ACK.

While information-hiding modules have long been used in systems programming, the concept *information hiding* was introduced into the computer science literature by Parnas [Parnas 76, 79, 84, 85]. Information hiding is a general principle of software construction and related to *separation of concerns* and *abstraction*. These concepts are discussed in Section 3.3 and in Chapter 4. We use the term *information-hiding module* (information-hiding *package* in Ada) in the specific sense discussed in the preceding paragraphs: An information-hiding module has a *secret*, such as a data structure or an interface to an external hardware device, and an *abstract interface* available to the *client* modules.

3.1.3 Ada Packages

Ada has incorporated the information-hiding module concept into the language syntax. An Ada *package* consists of two units, a *specification* and a *body*. The *specification* contains all external definitions, such as subprograms, types, and constants. It represents the interface that the package presents to the outside world. The body, on the other hand, represents the *secret* of the package. For example, a subprogram or a variable declared in the body (and not included in the specification) is not *visible* to the outside world. Other aspects of the package syntax are discussed in the following sections and in Chapter 4.

An Ada package is far more versatile than a separately compiled source program file. Although a package may be compiled separately, it can also be defined within a procedure or within another package. Furthermore, several separately compiled packages and procedures may exist in one source file. Indeed, separate source files have no syntactical significance in the Ada environment, and package specifications and package bodies, as well as procedure specifications and bodies, may exist in one file or in different files.

Packages, and particularly separately compiled package specifications and bodies, play a central role in Ada software development. A main procedure and a network of separate packages usually replace the traditional structure with a main program and a hierarchy of subprograms. This is one reason behind the limited role of functional decomposition in Ada. We distinguish among *information-hiding packages*, *abstract data type (adt) packages*, and *header packages* as described in the following sections.

3.1.3.1 Information-hiding packages

Figure 3-1 shows the Ada specification of an *information-hiding package*. The package STACK is an implementation of the well-known last-in-first-out data structure. It has two *operation subprograms*, PUSH and POP. By means of PUSH, a client program puts an item (an integer) on the stack, and by means of POP it retrieves the top item on the stack. A client program views the stack package as an *abstract object* that it can manipulate by means of the operations. This example is discussed further in Section 3.2.

We use the term *information-hiding package* only in a specific sense, where the package can be thought of as one object to be operated on. In a more general sense, information hiding applies to many different software constructs. For example, the body of a function SIN(X) hides the algorithm by which the sine of X is calculated. A package, MATH_PAC, say, may contain a set of mathematical subprograms, such as SIN, COS, and so on. The subprograms are logically related but normally do not share a particular secret. Although MATH_PAC may be very useful, it is not an information-hiding package in our limited sense.

3.1.3.2 Adt packages

An information-hiding package represents a single software object, and it is sometimes necessary to create more than one object of the same general description. We do this by first creating an *abstract data type (adt),* a general description of a

```
package STACK is
    procedure PUSH(X:INTEGER);
    function POP return INTEGER;
end STACK;
```

Figure 3-1 Specification of an information-hiding package STACK.

```
package STACKS is
   type STACK_TYPE is limited private;
   procedure PUSH(S: in out STACK_TYPE; X: INTEGER);
   procedure POP(S: in out STACK_TYPE; X: out INTEGER);
private
   type I_ARRAY is array (1..100) of INTEGER;
   type STACK_TYPE is record
      ST: I_ARRAY;
      TOP: INTEGER range 0..I_ARRAY'LAST:=0;
   end record;
end STACKS;
```

Figure 3-2 Specification of an adt package STACKS. The abstract data type STACK_TYPE is declared as **limited private**. The details of the declaration are hidden in the *private part* of the specification.

class of objects, which we then *instantiate*. Abstract data types represent an important and natural extension of the concept of abstract objects. Like any other type, an abstract data type is a template for a set of objects, all of which can be manipulated by means of a well-defined set of operations.

The package syntax includes features to support abstract data type declarations. An *adt package* exports a *type name* and a set of operations on instances of the type by including them in the package specification. Figure 3-2 shows the Ada specification of a package STACKS that defines a type STACK_TYPE and the operations PUSH and POP. The representation of the type is part of the secret of the package and is placed in the *private part* of the specification. On the other hand, the declarations of the operation subprograms appear in the package body. Adt packages are discussed further in Chapter 4.

3.1.3.3 Header packages

As we have seen earlier, the traditional hierarchy with a main program and subprograms is usually replaced in Ada by a main procedure and a network of packages, which are developed and compiled apart from the main procedure. While the goal is to separate concerns and hide information inside each package, the entire network often depends on a set of global constants, types, and subtypes. Typically, there will be array and integer subtypes with limited ranges as well as record types. These are often declared in a *global-definitions* or *header* package accessible to the main procedure and all the other compilation units specific to a certain Ada program. Such a package replaces the global type and constant declarations in a traditional program and is often a package specification without body. It is similar to an ".h" file in C.

Figure 3-3 shows a header package ELE_DEFS for the elevator system mentioned in Chapter 2 and discussed fully in Chapter 8. In the system, a number of elevators serve a building with several floors. The exact number of elevators and floors are defined as constants in the package ELE_DEFS. The integer subtypes F_TYPE and E_TYPE, which identify floors and elevators, respectively, are also declared. A variable of F_TYPE can take the values GROUND..TOP, where

```
package ELE_DEFS is
      -- Directions, up and down:
      type           EXT_D_TYPE is (NO_D, UP, DOWN);
      subtype        D_TYPE is EXT_D_TYPE range UP..DOWN;
      -- Floors:
      GROUND:        constant:=1;
      NO_F :         constant:=GROUND−1;
      TOP:           constant:=8;
      subtype        EXT_F_TYPE is INTEGER range NO_F..TOP+1;
      subtype        F_TYPE is EXT_F_TYPE range GROUND..TOP;
      -- Elevators:
      NO_E:          constant:=0;
      MAX_E:         constant:=5;
      subtype        EXT_E_TYPE is INTEGER range 0..MAX_E;
      subtype        E_TYPE is EXT_E_TYPE range 1..MAX_E;
      -- Button array:
      type           B_ARRAY is array (F_TYPE) of BOOLEAN;
end ELE_DEFS;
```

Figure 3-3 Header package ELE_DEFS belonging to the elevator program. Types, subtypes and constants are declared in the header package.

GROUND and TOP represent the ground and top floors in the building. An extended floor type, EXT_F_TYPE, takes the values GROUND−1..TOP+1, and F_TYPE, in turn, is a subtype of EXT_F_TYPE. The type EXT_E_TYPE is declared for the same reason.

While a header package is often necessary as a repository for truly global constants and types, it must be used with some care, especially in large projects. Typically, nearly all other packages and procedures will rely on the header package, and a change in that package, such as the inclusion of a new type, forces recompilation of all the other units. For this reason, the header package should be reserved for constants and types that can be expected to be reasonably stable throughout development.

In many cases the reason why a certain type is used in different modules is that it is used in an interface. For example, an operation subprogram may take parameters of a certain special type. Such types can often conveniently be declared in the package specification in conjunction with specification of the operation subprogram, and need not be in a header package.

3.2 MODULE SYNTAX

3.2.1 Subprogram Syntax

Like most procedural languages, Ada allows two categories of subprograms: *procedures* and *functions*. The specification of a procedure SWAP has the form

```
procedure SWAP(A, B: in out INTEGER);
```

```
procedure SWAP(A, B: in out INTEGER) is
X: INTEGER;
begin
    X:=A; A:=B; B:=X;
end SWAP;
```

Figure 3-4   Declaration of a procedure SWAP that swaps the values of the **in out** parameters A and B.

The procedure body is shown in Figure 3-4. The subprogram specification is repeated in the body, which thus alone fully defines the subprogram. Separate subprogram specifications are necessary only in special cases such as cross-referencing, where the specification is referenced by another unit, which in turn is referenced by the subprogram body. Separate subprogram specifications also appear in package specifications. The specification of a function FACTORIAL is

```
function FACTORIAL(N: NATURAL) return POSITIVE;
```

Figure 3-5 shows the (recursive) function body.

3.2.1.1 Parameter modes

The parameter mode indicates whether a parameter carries information in or out of a subprogram. The mode concept in Ada is different from similar concepts in many other languages. One of the following modes can be indicated between the parameter name and the type mark in the procedure specification:

in	The subprogram can only *read* the value of the actual parameter, not assign a value to it. (**in** is default.)
out	The subprogram can only assign a value to the actual parameter; it cannot read it.
in out	Both reading and updating are permitted.

To avoid side effects, *functions* have only **in** parameters, and since **in** is the default, parameter modes need not be indicated in function specifications.

```
function FACTORIAL(N: NATURAL) return POSITIVE is
begin
    if N=0 then return 1;
    else return N*FACTORIAL(N−1);
    end if;
end FACTORIAL;
```

Figure 3-5   The recursive function FACTORIAL returns the factorial of its parameter N. [If the factorial is greater than the INTEGER'LAST (i.e., the greatest positive integer that may be represented on a given machine), the exception NUMERIC_ERROR is raised.]

3.2.2 Library Units, Secondary Units, and Subunits

As explained in Section 3.1, an Ada program should be thought of as a network of units, such as subprograms and packages. These units are compiled separately but usually depend on each other in such a way that the compilation order becomes important. There are two basic composition–decomposition mechanisms: *bottom-up* and *top-down*.

In the *bottom-up* mechanism, a program is assembled from preexisting, perhaps reusable packages and subprograms found in libraries. A compiled subprogram or package specification is called a *library unit*, and the corresponding subprogram or package body is called a *secondary unit*. A subprogram without a separate specification is considered a library unit without associated secondary unit. A specification must be compiled before the associated secondary unit, and the specification of a package or subprogram (but not the body) must be compiled before any subprogram or package body that references it.

The *top-down* mechanism allows a package body or a subprogram body to be stubbed out for later compilation as a *subunit*. In the *parent* unit, the declaration of each subunit is replaced by a *body stub*, a specification followed by the word **separate** as follows:

```
procedure Y (P: INTEGER) is separate;
```

The subunit contains a reference to the parent unit. If the procedure Y is a subunit of the parent unit X, Y is declared as follows:

```
separate (X)
procedure Y (P: INTEGER) is...end Y;
```

Clearly, a program need not be developed exclusively according to the top-down or bottom-up mechanism. Often, library units and subunits coexist in one program. Furthermore, a secondary unit may itself have subunits. Subprograms and packages may also be compiled as integral parts of the program where they are referenced.

3.2.3 Package Syntax

A stack will be used to illustrate the various options of the package syntax. A stack is a software mechanism for last-in-first-out storage and is often used as a simple example of information hiding. A stack has the operations PUSH, which stores a new element on the top of the stack, and POP, which retrieves the top element from the stack and makes the second element, if any, the new top. For simplicity, we assume here that the stored elements are integers and use a simple-minded implementation with an array, S, containing the stacked elements, and an integer, TOP, equal to the number of positions in the stack that are currently

```
        with TEXT_IO; use TEXT_IO;
    procedure ST_0 is
    package IIO is new INTEGER_IO(INTEGER);
    use IIO;
    package STACK is
        procedure PUSH(X:INTEGER);
        function POP return INTEGER;
    end STACK;
    use STACK;

    package body STACK is
        MAX: constant:=100;
        S : array (1..MAX) of INTEGER;
        TOP: INTEGER range 0..MAX:=0;
        procedure PUSH(X : INTEGER) is
        begin
            TOP:=TOP+1;
            S(TOP):=X;
        end PUSH;
        function POP return INTEGER is
        begin
            TOP:=TOP-1;
            return S(TOP+1);
        end POP;
    end STACK;

    begin
        for I in 1..95 loop
            PUSH(I);
        end loop;
        for I in 1..95 loop
            PUT(POP);
        end loop;
    end ST_0;
```

Figure 3-6 Package STACK declared inside a procedure ST_0. The clause "**use** STACK;" permits the main program to reference the subprograms as PUSH and POP rather than STACK.PUSH and STACK.POP.

occupied. These variables are part of the secret of the package and declared in the package body. In the following sections we describe the three basic syntax options with internal packages, library units, and subunits.

3.2.3.1 Internal packages

Figure 3-6 shows a basic form of package syntax, where the package is declared inside the procedure ST_0, in which it is used. As mentioned earlier, the package has two parts: the specification,

    package STACK is....end STACK;

and the package body,

> **package body** STACK **is**....**end** STACK;

The package specification includes the specifications of the operations PUSH and POP, whose bodies appear in the package body. The objects S and TOP are declared in the package body and retain their values between calls but are not visible outside the package body; they are hidden.

3.2.3.2 Library units

Figure 3-7 illustrates the second syntax option. The specification, the package body, and the client procedure ST_1 that uses the package are all individual

```
package STACK is
   procedure PUSH(X:INTEGER);
   function POP return INTEGER;
end STACK;

package body STACK is
   MAX: constant:=100;
   S: array (1..MAX) of INTEGER;
   TOP: INTEGER range 0..MAX:=0;
   procedure PUSH(X : INTEGER) is
   begin
      TOP:=TOP+1;
      S(TOP):=X;
   end PUSH;
   function POP return INTEGER is
   begin
      TOP:=TOP-1;
      return S(TOP+1);
   end POP;
end STACK;

   with TEXT_IO; use TEXT_IO;
   with STACK; use STACK;
procedure ST_1 is
package IIO is new INTEGER_IO(INTEGER); use IIO;
begin
   for I in 1..95 loop
      PUSH(I);
   end loop;
   for I in 1..95 loop
      PUT(POP);
   end loop;
end ST_1;
```

Figure 3-7 Here the package STACK is a *library unit*. The procedure ST_1 *withs* STACK.

compilation units. The specification of STACK is a *library unit*, and the body is a *secondary unit*. (ST_1 is also a library unit.) The package specification STACK must be compiled first, followed by the package body of STACK and the procedure ST_1 in any order. ST_1 is preceded by the clause

> **with** STACK;

to indicate that the library unit STACK is referenced. In the informal terminology, *with* has become a verb, and we say that ST_1 *withs* STACK. (The clause "**use** STACK;" is discussed below.)

After its compilation, each library unit is inserted in the library, from where it is retrieved when the secondary unit is compiled. The same thing happens when a **with** clause is encountered. Library units support bottom-up hierarchical design, where a unit can build on a library of units compiled earlier.

Library units require a compilation order where the specification of a package, P, precedes both its body and any clients *withing* P. If H is a header package, P and Q are information-hiding or adt packages, and M is the main procedure. The compilation order is often as follows:

> **package** H **is** .... **end** H;
>
>   **with** H;
> **package** P **is** .... **end** P;
> **package body** P **is** .... **end** P;
>
>   **with** H;
> **package** Q **is** .... **end** Q;
> **package body** Q **is** .... **end** Q;
>
>   **with** H, P, Q;
> **procedure** M **is** .... **end** M;

Many variations are possible. In the following compilation order, P and Q cross-reference, in that the body of P *withs* Q while the body of Q *withs* P.

> **package** H **is** .... **end** H;
>
>   **with** H;
> **package** P **is** .... **end** P;
>
>   **with** H;
> **package** Q **is** .... **end** Q;
>
>   **with** Q;
> **package body** P **is** .... **end** P;

```
    with P;
package body Q is .... end Q;

    with H, P, Q;
procedure M is .... end M;
```

After successful compilation of all units involved, the Ada program can be linked. The linker requires that one procedure be designated as the *main procedure*. In the example above, M is the only possible main procedure, and the call to the linker will typically be "LINK M". Program execution starts at the beginning of the body of M.

The use clause

Whereas the **with** clause is necessary for ST_1 to reference the library unit STACK, the clause

```
    use STACK;
```

is used primarily for convenience and permits ST_1 to call PUSH and POP by those names rather than STACK.PUSH and STACK.POP. The scope of the **use** clause extends to the end of the block in which it appears.

With and **use** often appear together in the constellation

```
    with X; use X;
```

and are easily confused. Note that **with** references a library unit. **Use**, on the other hand, may refer to a *withed* library unit or an internal package. Consider the following example:

```
    package H is .... end H;

        with H; use H;
    package P is .... end P;

    package body P is
        package R is .... end R;
        use R;
        .....
    end P;
```

"**Use H**" here refers to a library package that is being *withed*, while **use** R refers to an internal package that has just been specified. The package R cannot be *withed*.

Some programmers avoid **use** and prefer complete names such as STACK.PUSH or STACK.POP. That way, it is always clear in which library unit a certain identifier is declared. The programming guidelines of some organizations explicitly prohibit **use**. On the other hand, the lengthy, dotted names are quite cumbersome, and even the strongest supporter of complete names might occasionally rely on **use** to avoid heavy constructs such as the following:

```
TEXT_IO.PUT(...);
TEXT_IO.PUT(...);
TEXT_IO.NEW_LINE;
...
```

In this case, **use** can be utilized without any loss of clarity:

```
use TEXT_IO;
PUT(...);
PUT(...);
NEW_LINE;
...
```

In this book, **use** is utilized freely. This is done to make the examples more manageable and easier to read. The reader who so prefers should be able to restate the examples with complete names. In organizations where **use** is prohibited, *renaming* is sometimes practiced to avoid the repetition of long, complete names. For example, it is possible to write

```
declare
    procedure PPUSH(I: INTEGER) renames STACK.PUSH;
    function PPOP return INTEGER renames STACK.POP;
begin
    PPUSH(3);
    ....
    i:=PPOP;
end;
```

The reader is referred to an Ada primer for complete renaming rules.

3.2.3.3 Subunits

In Figure 3-8, the operation subprograms PUSH and POP have been stubbed out as *subunits* of the package body STACK, which is a secondary unit. The subunits are compiled after the package body. It is particularly useful to stub out operation subprograms that are large and complex. They can then be developed and compiled separately from the rest of the package. (PUSH and POP are really too small and simple to be stubbed out meaningfully.)

Subunits represent a top-down design where a part of a program is deferred for separate, later design and compilation. A subunit logically exists in the environment from where it is separated, even though it is separately compiled. For

```
package body STACK is
    MAX: constant:=100;
    S: array (1..MAX) of INTEGER;
    TOP: INTEGER range 0..MAX:=0;
    procedure PUSH(X: INTEGER) is separate;
    function POP return INTEGER is separate;
end STACK;


    separate (STACK)
procedure PUSH(X: INTEGER) is
begin
    TOP:=TOP+1;
    S(TOP):=X;
end PUSH;


    separate (STACK)
function POP return INTEGER is
begin
    TOP:=TOP-1;
    return S(TOP+1);
end POP;
```

Figure 3-8   The package body of STACK with the operation subprograms PUSH and POP stubbed out as subunits. (POP and PUSH are really too small to justify their own subunits.) The package specification of STACK and the main procedure ST_1 can be used with this version of the body of STACK without recompilation.

example, the subunits PUSH and POP in Figure 3-8 directly reference MAX, S, and TOP, which are declared in the parent unit, the package body of STACK. It is important to note that the change of the body of STACK from the implementation in Figure 3-7 to that in Figure 3-8 can be made without affecting the package specification and the client program. Thus the specification and procedure ST_1 shown in Figure 3-7 work with the package body shown in Figure 3-8 without recompilation. (Relinking is necessary; see also Section 3.2.3.4.)

3.2.3.4 Changing the secret

The package syntax is designed to allow the secret of a package to be modified while the interface is left intact. Such modifications are particularly well supported by the library unit syntax. In the STACK example the implementation of a stack is a secret guarded in the body of the package. Figure 3-9 shows a new implementation of the body of STACK in Figure 3-7. The stack is now implemented not as an array but as a linked list. The package specification and a client program *withing* STACK, such as ST_1, are unaffected by the change of internal representation.

The change in the representation of the stack requires recompilation of the body of the package STACK. If the body resides on a separate source file that can be submitted for recompilation, this can be done without recompiling the package specification and any client programs *withing* STACK. Even though the package

```
package body STACK is
    type STACKABLE;
    type S_LINK is access STACKABLE;
    type STACKABLE is record
        VALUE: INTEGER;
        NEXT:  S_LINK;
    end record;
    TOP: S_LINK;
    procedure PUSH(X: INTEGER) is
    begin
        TOP:=new STACKABLE'(X, TOP);
    end PUSH;
    function POP return INTEGER is
    X: S_LINK;
    begin
        X:=TOP;
        TOP:=X.NEXT;
        return X.VALUE;
    end POP;
end STACK;
```

Figure 3-9   In this version of the package body STACK, the internal representation is based on a linked list. This change of implementation does not require recompilation of the specification and the client program ST_1 in Figure 3-7.

specification and the client program are not recompiled, recompilation of the body also requires *relinking* of all programs that include STACK.

We pointed out earlier that the placement of compilation units on different source files has no syntactical significance. In the present example it does have practical significance, however. For the body of STACK to be recompiled separately, it must reside in its own source file, different from those of the package specification and the client program, ST_1. One must take care not to recompile the specification of a package unless the specification is actually changed. The compiler and the filing system will take the recompilation itself as a signal that the specification has been changed and force recompilation of all client modules *withing* the package.

In the case of an internal package, such as in Figure 3-6, modification of the body of the package STACK obviously requires recompilation of the entire procedure ST_0. Here the distinction between secret and interface works only on a logical level, in the sense that a modification of the package body cannot affect the logic of the body of the procedure.

3.2.3.5 Scope and persistence of variables

An essential difference between packages and subprograms regards the scope of variables declared in the units. While local subprogram variables cease to exist upon return from the subprogram, variables declared in package specifications and package bodies are *persistent*. They remain defined and keep their values until they are explicitly modified. In the example in Figure 3-10, K1 is a variable in the procedure A1. A1 is the main procedure and K1 is global to A1; it remains

```
procedure A1 is
    K1: INTEGER:=1;
    procedure B is
        J: INTEGER:=0;
    begin
        J:=1; -- B statements
    end B;
begin
    B;
end A1;


procedure A2 is
    K2: INTEGER:=1;
    package C is
        L: INTEGER:=4;
        function F(I: INTEGER) return INTEGER;
    end C;
    package body C is
        X: INTEGER:=5;
        function F(I: INTEGER) return INTEGER is
        begin
            X:=X+I;
            return X;
        end F;
    end C;
begin
    C.L:=C.L + 2;    -- Reference to L
    C.L:=C.F(C.L);    -- Reference to F
end A2;
```

Figure 3-10   Procedure A1 contains a procedure B. J is a local variable in B. It is defined only while B is actually being executed. Procedure A2 contains a package C. L and F are declared in the specification of C and are in scope until **end** A2. X is declared in the body of C and is in scope until **end** C. Like L and F, X continues to exist until **end** A2 but cannot be referenced from outside its scope.

the procedure A1. A1 is the main procedure and K1 is global to A1; it remains defined until **end** A1. The variable J is a local variable in the procedure B. J is defined only while B is being called. It is allocated on the stack when the procedure B is entered and is deallocated when B is exited. Clearly, there is no way that J can be referenced from the body of A1, since it is not even defined outside the call to B.

A2 is also a main procedure, and K2 is a global variable that remains defined until **end** A2. The variable L is declared in the specification of the package C, while X is declared in the body of C. That L is encapsulated in C does not affect is scope, and L remains declared until **end** A2 just as K2. It can be referenced from the body of A2 with the dot notation, C.L, or by means of the statement **use** C. After **use** C, L can be referenced directly. Finally, the scope of X, which is declared in the body of C, also extends to **end** A2. Since X is hidden, it cannot be referenced from the body of A2. It nevertheless retains its value, which can be retrieved or changed by subprograms in C, such as the function F.

3.2.4 Generics

A generic is a template (a ''macro'') for a package or a subprogram: It is a package or subprogram text where the names of *types*, *variables*, *constants*, and *subprograms* are formal parameters. Once a generic has been declared, it can be *instantiated*. The formal parameters are then replaced by actual parameters, and the instantiation becomes an actual package or subprogram that can be integrated into the program or exist as a library unit.

While generics are generally useful for creating reusable software, they are necessary primarily because of Ada's strong typing, which limits the use of each subprogram or package to certain types that are hard-coded into the subprogram or package, even if the logic of the package or subprogram is general enough to apply to different types. For example, the procedure SWAP in Figure 3-4 is defined for integers only, although the simple algorithm works for characters, floating-point numbers, or almost any other type. With generics it is possible to create an algorithm that can be instantiated with suitable types as appropriate.

3.2.4.1 Generic subprograms

Figure 3-11 shows a generic subprogram, G_SWAP, which swaps the values of two variables of any one type. In the program S, the generic subprograms is instantiated for integers, characters, and an enumerated type, ENUM. The generic declaration is as follows:

```
generic
    type ANY_TYPE is private;
procedure G_SWAP (A, B: in out ANY_TYPE);
```

The word **generic** is followed by one or more *generic parameters* with given restrictions, such as **private** in the example above (see Section 3.2.4.3). Note that a subprogram specification is included in the generic specification and precedes the full subprogram declaration.

In the procedure S, the generic G_SWAP is instantiated for integers by means of the declaration

```
procedure SWAP is new G_SWAP(INTEGER);
```

An actual value for each generic parameter must follow in parentheses after the name of the generic procedure. Although this makes the instantiation look like a

```
generic
   type ANY_TYPE is private;
procedure G_SWAP(A, B: in out ANY_TYPE);

procedure G_SWAP(A, B: in out ANY_TYPE) is
X: ANY_TYPE;
begin
   X:=A; A:=B; B:=X;
end G_SWAP;

   with G_SWAP;
procedure S is
   procedure SWAP is new G_SWAP(INTEGER);
   procedure SWAP is new G_SWAP(CHARACTER);
   type ENUM is (HUEY, DEWEY);
   procedure SWAP is new G_SWAP(ENUM);
   I: INTEGER:=1;
   J: INTEGER:=2;
   C: CHARACTER:='C';
   D: CHARACTER:='D';
   E: ENUM:=HUEY;
   F: ENUM:=DEWEY;
begin
   SWAP(I, J);
   SWAP(C, D);
   SWAP(E, F);
end S;
```

Figure 3-11   Generic procedure G_SWAP and a procedure S where G_SWAP is instantiated for integers, characters, and an enumerated type, ENUM. All the instantiations are called SWAP by overloading, creating the illusion that SWAP is a type-independent swapping procedure. Note that S *withs* G_SWAP.

subprogram call, it must be distinguished from call to the instantiated procedure, which occurs in the body of S:

```
   SWAP(I,J);
```

In this call, I and J are the parameters of the instantiated procedure SWAP. In the figure, G_SWAP is also instantiated for characters and for an enumerated type. The Ada rules for overloading allow us to call all three instantiations SWAP and distinguish the various procedures by the types of their parameters.

Figure 3-12 shows a more elaborate example of a generic subprogram. SORT is a generic procedure that sorts an array of items of a ITEM_TYPE by comparing the items pairwise using the function ">". The array is of type TABLE, and ITEM_TYPE, TABLE, and ">" are all formal, generic parameters. The sort procedure in the figure uses a simple sorting algorithm known as *selection sort* [Knuth]. Figure 3-13 shows an instantiation I_SORT that is used to sort a table of type I_TABLE of integers in ascending order. For this, SORT is instantiated with the parameters INTEGER, I_TABLE, and ">", where ">" is the built-in operator for integers. The skeleton program in Figure 3-13 also shows a call to the instantiation I_SORT(I), where I is an object of the type I_TABLE.

```
generic
    type ITEM_TYPE is private;
    type TABLE is array (INTEGER range <>) of ITEM_TYPE;
    with function ">" (X, Y: ITEM_TYPE) return BOOLEAN;
procedure SORT(A: in out TABLE);

procedure SORT(A: in out TABLE) is
BIG: ITEM_TYPE;  -- Largest item found so far
INDEX: INTEGER; -- Index of BIG
begin
    if A'LENGTH<=1 then return; end if;
    -- Analyze successive subarrays, index 1..J
    -- with J ranging from A'RANGE to 1.
    for J in A'RANGE loop
        -- Find greatest element in subarray.
        BIG:=A(1); INDEX:=1;
        for K in 2..(A'LAST − J+1) loop
            if A(K)>BIG then BIG:=A(K); INDEX:=K; end if;
        end loop;
        -- Swap greatest and last element in subarray.
        A(INDEX):=A(A'LAST − J+1);
        A(A'LAST − J+1):=BIG;
    end loop;
end SORT;
```

Figure 3-12   Generic sorting procedure based on selection sort. The procedure sorts an array, TABLE, of ITEM_TYPE by using the function ">" to compare elements pairwise. ITEM_TYPE, TABLE and ">" are all generic parameters.

Figure 3-14 shows a more elaborate instantiation of SORT. Here R_TABLE is an array of R_TYPE. R_TYPE is a record with the fields NAME and NUMBER. NAME is the primary sort key and NUMBER is the secondary key. The intention is to sort the records alphabetically in ascending order according to NAME. If more than one record has the same NAME, they are sorted in ascending order according to NUMBER. SORT is instantiated with the parameters R_TYPE, R_TABLE, and

```
with SORT;
procedure SORTING1 is
type I_TABLE is array (INTEGER range <>) of INTEGER;
procedure I_SORT is new SORT(INTEGER, I_TABLE, ">");
I: I_TABLE(1..20);
begin
    I_SORT(I);
end;
```

Figure 3-13   Skeleton program illustrating the instantiation of SORT for the type I_TABLE, which is an array of 20 integers. The built-in operator ">" is used for the pairwise comparison of elements. The call I_SORT(I) sorts the integers in the array I in ascending order.

```
      with SORT;
procedure SORTING2 is
type R_TYPE is record
   NAME: CHARACTER;
   NUMBER: INTEGER;
end record;
type R_TABLE is array (INTEGER range <>) of R_TYPE;
RT: R_TABLE(1..10);
function R_COMPARE(X, Y: R_TYPE) return BOOLEAN is
begin
   if X.NAME = Y.NAME then return X.NUMBER > Y.NUMBER;
   else return X.NAME > Y.NAME;
   end if;
end;
procedure R_SORT is new SORT(R_TYPE, R_TABLE, R_COMPARE);
begin
   R_SORT(RT);
end;
```

Figure 3-14   In this skeleton program, the array to be sorted consists of records of R_TYPE. Each record has a NAME field and a NUMBER field. Sorting is done with the NAME field as the primary key and NUMBER as the secondary key. In the instantiation of SORT, the third generic parameter is R_COMPARE, a function that compares two objects of R_TYPE first according to NAME and then according to NUMBER.

R_COMPARE, where R_COMPARE is a special-purpose function that compares two R_TYPE records first according to NAME and then according to NUMBER.

3.2.4.2 Generic packages

Earlier we saw various versions of a package STACK, all of which have the limitation that the stack can only accommodate integers. By means of generics, we can define a general-purpose stack such that each instantiation can accommodate objects of any one type, to be specified at programming time, when the generic stack is instantiated.

Figure 3-15 shows a generic information-hiding package G_STACK and some instantiations. The generic declaration is as follows:

```
generic
   MAX: POSITIVE;
   type ITEM is private;
package G_STACK is
   procedure PUSH(X:ITEM);
   function POP return ITEM;
end G_STACK;
```

```
generic
    MAX: POSITIVE;
    type ITEM is private;
package G_STACK is
    procedure PUSH(X:ITEM);
    function POP return ITEM;
end G_STACK;

package body G_STACK is
    S: array (1..MAX) of ITEM;
    TOP: INTEGER range 0..MAX := 0;
    procedure PUSH(X: ITEM) is
    begin
        TOP:=TOP+1;
        S(TOP):=X;
    end PUSH;
    function POP return ITEM is
    begin
        TOP:=TOP-1;
        return S(TOP+1);
    end POP;
begin null;
end G_STACK;

    with TEXT_IO; use TEXT_IO;
    with G_STACK;
procedure G_ST is
-- Stack accommodating 100 integers:
package INT_STACK is new G_STACK(100, INTEGER);
-- Stack accommodating 25 characters:
package CH_STACK is new G_STACK(25, CHARACTER);
R_MAX: constant:=30;
type REC is record
    A, B, C: INTEGER;
    D: STRING(1..5);
end record;
-- Stack accommodating R_MAX records of type REC:
package REC_STACK is new G_STACK(R_MAX, REC);
R1, R2: REC;
begin
    CH_STACK.PUSH('A');
    REC_STACK.PUSH(R1);
    R2:=REC_STACK.POP;
    for I in 'B'..'X' loop
        CH_STACK.PUSH(I);
    end loop;
    for I in 'a'..'x' loop
        PUT(CH_STACK.POP);
    end loop;
end G_ST;
```

Figure 3-15 Generic information-hiding package, G_STACK. In the procedure G_ST, G_STACK is instantiated as a stack INT_STACK for up to 100 integers, as a stack CH_STACK for up to 25 characters and as a stack REC_STACK for up to R_MAX records of type REC.

108

The declaration includes two generic parameters, the variable MAX and the type ITEM, which is the type of the stackable objects. MAX is the maximum size of the stack. The generic declaration also includes the package specification. References to the generic parameters may occur in the package specification as well as the body.

In G_ST, G_STACK is instantiated in three ways. Thus INT_STACK accommodates 100 integers and is identical to the information-hiding package STACK discussed earlier. The instantiation, CH_STACK, accommodates 25 characters, while REC_STACK accommodates REC_MAX records of type REC. While INT_STACK and CH_STACK depend on built-in types, REC_STACK depends on REC and is declared after the declaration of REC.

The package TEXT_IO, which has been used in various examples, contains several generic packages, such as INTEGER_IO and ENUMERATION_IO. These are instantiated as in the following example:

```
package IIO is new INTEGER_IO(INTEGER);
package PIO is new INTEGER_IO(POSITIVE);
type ENUM is (HUEY, DEWEY);
package EIO is new ENUMERATION_IO(ENUM);
```

3.2.4.3 Restrictions on generic type parameters

The declaration of a generic type parameter may include a restriction such as **private** or **limited private**. (For further restrictions, see any Ada primer.) We discuss these terms in conjunction with abstract data types in Section 4.3.2. For now, suffice it to say that an object of a **limited private** type may not be assigned a value or tested for equality. When the restrictions are used for generic type parameters, they restrict the implementer of the generic rather than the client. Thus if a type parameter is declared as **limited private**, any type may be used as actual generic parameter, including a **limited private** type. This means that objects of the type are not assigned values or tested for equality inside the generic.

The restriction **private** limits the user of the generic more than **limited private** but puts fewer restrictions on the implementer of the generic. G_SWAP in Figure 3-11 has a type parameter ANY_TYPE declared as follows:

```
type ANY_TYPE is private;
```

The restriction **private** instead of **limited private** suggests that objects of ANY_TYPE are either assigned values or tested for equality inside G_SWAP. The actual type parameter must allow these operations and cannot be **limited private**. The same restriction, **private**, holds for the type ITEM in the generic G_STACK in Figure 3-15. This is because an object of type ITEM is returned by the function POP and cannot be a **limited private** type. (The return of a value by a function is regarded as an assignment.)

3.3 PROCEDURAL ABSTRACTION AND SPECIFICATION

Abstraction is "[t]he principle of ignoring those aspects of a subject that are not relevant to the current purpose in order to concentrate more fully on those that are" [Oxford]. Functionally cohesive subprograms support the concept of *procedural abstraction*. For example, once the calculation of the factorial of N has been implemented as the function FACTORIAL(N), we can forget (for most purposes) about the steps involved in the calculation and treat FACTORIAL(N) like a built-in operation provided by Ada. This is what procedural abstraction means; we abstract from the details involved in computing the factorial and think of the computation as one operation.

When we read a program text and encounter a subprogram call such as FACTORIAL(N), we expect the subprogram name to convey the meaning of the call. It would be counterproductive if we had to look up and read the subprogram text. Further information is provided in the *interface specification* of the subprogram. This information is sufficient for a client programmer who inserts the call in a program. The interface specification includes all the client programmer must know about the subprogram and can be viewed as a *contract* or agreement that limits the responsibility of the maker of the subprogram. For example, the maker of FACTORIAL(N) may guarantee that the function returns a correct result if N is less than 10. Similarly, the maker of a function SQRT(X) may guarantee only that the subprogram produces a correct result if X is greater than or equal to zero. In Ada, the word *specification* is used in a more limited sense. For example, the Ada specification of FACTORIAL is as follows:

function FACTORIAL(N: NATURAL) **return** POSITIVE;

The Ada specification is one part of the interface specification. The additional information necessary in an interface specification is often expressed as a *precondition* (or a "*requires*" assertion [Liskov]) and a *postcondition* (or "*effects*" assertion). The precondition must be sufficient to ensure proper operation of the subprogram. It is the responsibility of the caller to ensure that the precondition is met; otherwise, the effect of the subprogram is undefined. The postcondition specifies something that is true at the return from any invocation of the subprogram made under the precondition. If Y is the value returned by SQRT(X), a postcondition guaranteeing a certain precision in the result might be stated as follows:

$$X - e \leq Y * Y \leq X + e$$

In this expression, *e* is the maximum error.

An interface specification defines the effect of a subprogram under certain conditions without describing how the effect is achieved. That way, the algorithm remains the secret of the subprogram. The *interface specification* is a *definitional* specification based on assertions and conveys the meaning of the subprogram call. This means that it explicitly lists properties that the subprogram must exhibit. A definitional specification specifies *what* a module must do without suggesting any design [Liskov]. The finished module can be verified against the specification to see that it exhibits the required properties.

The opposite of a definitional specification is an *operational* one. "An operational specification, instead of describing the properties of the specificands, gives a recipe for constructing them" [Liskov p. 153]. For example, any program is a complete operational specification of itself. In principle, the specificand set of an operational specification includes all programs that exhibit the same external properties as one constructed according to the recipe. But the only practical way to demonstrate that a program satisfies an operational specification is to construct the program according to the given recipe.

According to Liskov and Guttag, "any portion of a specification that is operational rather than definitional should be viewed with suspicion" [Liskov p. 153]. Consequently, we will not use operational *interface* specifications but only use subsystems with definitionally specifiable interfaces. Nevertheless, operational specifications are sometimes necessary. The interface specification allows a client programmer to use a subprogram without being aware of how it works. This is often insufficient for someone who is tasked with implementing the subprogram. In addition to the interface, the implementer of FACTORIAL must also comply with a given algorithm for the calculation. This algorithm is an operational specification that describes the steps through which the result is computed. A numerical algorithm for the calculation of a factorial or a square root can be directly implemented in an algorithmic language.

The effect of a subprogram such as FACTORIAL or SQRT is limited to the values delivered to the calling program. Such a subprogram is said to have no *side effects*. Some subprograms, such as TEXT_IO.PUT and GET, have important and useful side effects. When a client program calls PUT(X) to produce output to a terminal screen or a printer, the postcondition will include a statement that X has been output. This describes the effect at a level of abstraction suitable for the client program. The maker of the TEXT_IO.PUT also has responsibilities to parties other than the caller of the procedure, however, and must make sure that it interfaces correctly with external hardware. The external behavior pattern of the software may be restricted by the device with which it interfaces. Like the square-root algorithm, such a behavior pattern should be specified in a way allowing the internal structure of the software to be modeled on it directly. This leads back to the discussion of control structuring in Chapter 2, and the device behavior pattern can be captured in terms of a sequence diagram. (Note also that the subprogram side effects discussed here and the backtracking side effects discussed in Chapter 2 are different concepts.)

3.4 USE OF INDEPENDENT SUBPROGRAMS

In this section we review the classical subprogram quality concepts and discuss the use of independent subprograms in modern software design. As mentioned above, a subprogram is *independent* if it is not an operation on an information-hiding package or an abstract data type. While the abstraction facilities of a language such as Ada drastically reduce the need for such subprograms, they remain important vehicles for the breakdown of control structures into manageable pieces. Such a breakdown may be useful to avoid the duplication of program text and localize an algorithm that is used at various places in a program. It is also useful for separation of concerns to facilitate the understanding of the software.

3.4.1 Traditional Quality Concepts for Subprograms

As mentioned in the introduction, the concepts of cohesion, coupling, and fan-in introduced in structured design are useful to describe subprogram quality. Each concept is discussed in the following sections.

3.4.1.1 Cohesion

Cohesion is the trade word for the conceptual or semantic coherence of a module. It reflects the unity of the module in terms of one module–one thought. Generally, *strong* cohesion is better than *weak* cohesion. Structured design introduces degrees of cohesion ranging from *coincidental* (very weak) to *functional* (very strong). A good description of each of these can be found in [Page-Jones].

   The evolution of programming languages and practices have made most of these degrees of subprogram cohesion obsolete. It is now reasonable to require virtually every subprogram to be *functionally cohesive*. A functionally cohesive subprogram does one thing only, and what it does should be obvious from its name. Mathematical functions such as SQRT(X) and standard input/output procedures such as PUT(Z) are good examples of functional cohesion. The earlier-mentioned subprograms UPPER, LOWER, and CHECK are also functionally cohesive. The cohesion concept extends to other modules than subprogram. An information-hiding module (Section 3.1) exhibits *informational cohesion*: It includes a set of operation subprograms operating on the same, internal data structure.

3.4.1.2 Coupling

Coupling generally refers to the dependence of modules on one another. In a narrow sense, it refers to the way data is exchanged between a subprogram and the calling (sub)program. *Loose* coupling is generally better than *tight* coupling. According to structured design, the loosest, and therefore preferred, kind of coupling is *data coupling*, where data is transferred as parameters in subprogram calls. In the tightest kind of coupling, on the other hand, subprograms directly reference global variables declared in a main program. Various forms of coupling are described in the structured design literature [Page-Jones]. Many of them are prohibited by the syntax of modern languages such as Ada.

Data coupling is not always the best solution, although it is favored by conventional wisdom. Lengthy parameter lists where the same variables are shuffled from one subprogram to the other are often counterproductive. Subprograms defined within a close context, such as a package or a small program, should be freely allowed to reference variables that are local to that context. We will refer to this as *context coupling*. The operation subprograms of an information-hiding module are context coupled in that they reference the internal structure directly. On the other hand, a general-purpose, independent subprogram must be loosely coupled, and ideally rely on parameters only (data coupling).

In a wider sense the coupling of modules depends not only on the way data is exchanged but also on other practical assumptions made by the implementers. In a strongly typed language such as Ada, coupling may result from the use of common type declarations. This may be referred to as *type coupling*. The modules in a large program may all depend on a set of global types, constants, and ranges, which are referenced directly throughout the program. Such constants and ranges are often declared in a *header package* (see Section 3.1.3.3).

Types cannot be passed as parameters to subprograms, so a truly general-purpose, independent subprogram must rely on built-in Ada types only. If types are necessary in the interface, the subprogram can be declared in package, whose specification also includes the specification of any such *interface types*. To a degree, the problem with type coupling may also be solved with *generics*. In this solution we first develop a type-independent, generic subprogram and then instantiate it for a specific type (see Section 3.2.4).

3.4.1.3 Fan-in

The *fan-in* of a module reflects how often it is used in different situations. Structured design defines the fan-in of a subprogram S as the number of other (sub)programs that call S. We will instead define fan-in as the number of places from which S is called. Usually, we are only interested in whether a subprogram is called from more than one place, and we will refer to fan-in greater than one as *high fan-in*. Sometimes, a subprogram that is used only once in the current configuration fulfills the criterion of high (potential) fan-in. This happens if the subprogram is functionally cohesive and loosely coupled and has true potential for reusability. For example, the subprogram may be used more than once if the current program is expanded, or it may be reused in another, similar program.

3.4.2 Justification of Independent Subprograms

Cohesion and coupling are goodness criteria for subprograms, and all subprograms should be cohesive and loosely coupled (usually *data* or *context* coupled). Structured design also places heavy weight on fan-in and refers to it as "the *raison d'être* of modularization" [Yourdon]. In actual practice, however, the method often produces vast hierarchies of subprograms, many of which are called only once. Practitioners of structured design sometimes seem to regard subprogram decomposition as a goal in itself and consider a subprogram with weak cohesion or low fan-in as better than no subprogram at all.

The goodness criteria have been developed in an environment where subprogram decomposition is the primary tool for software structuring. In an environment where other aspects of software design, such as control structuring, have become equally or more important, it is insufficient to strive for an optimum subprogram decomposition according to the criteria. The apparent objective of structure design is to find the best subprogram decomposition. In a modern environment, we must also ask whether we need a subprogram decomposition at all, since one undecomposed procedure may be the clearest solution. A subprogram may be introduced for one (or both) of the following reasons:

1. To avoid duplication of program text. Such subprograms (potentially) have fan-in greater than 1. They will be referred to as subprograms with high fan-in.
2. For separation of concerns within the program.

It should be noted that the discussion here applies to independent subprograms and not the operation subprograms introduced with information-hiding or adt packages. If an information-hiding or adt package is justified, necessary operation subprograms may be introduced without individual justification.

3.4.2.1 Subprograms with high fan-in

Duplicated program text is avoided if a subprogram can be called from many different places. Such a subprogram contributes to reliability as well as memory efficiency, since the algorithm implemented by the subprogram will exist in one copy only. A subprogram is justified when the duplication of any reasonable portion of program text is avoided. It is also justified if it is *potentially* useful. It is reasonable to require that the subprogram be *functionally cohesive*, which makes it easy and safe to use.

Since high-fan-in subprograms often have the potential to be used in different places in the overall program, they shoud be loosely coupled and rely primarily on parameters. (If general reuse is not an explicit goal, a subprogram S may directly reference types, constants, and other subprograms that are declared in the same scope as S.) High-fan-in subprograms should be declared within a wide scope (i.e., at a high level in a procedure or in a separate package). The more general purpose the subprogram, the wider the scope and the higher the level. Repetitive subpatterns may often be identified in the analysis of behavior patterns in the reality. When a control structure is modeled on the behavior pattern, such a subpattern gives rise to a subprogram in the software. Subprograms can also be identified during control structuring when repetitive patterns are discovered.

3.4.2.2 Subprograms for separation of concerns

Subprograms with fan-in = 1 are sometimes justified as a means to separate concerns within the program. To be justified, such subprograms must make the software easier to understand, develop, and/or maintain. Sometimes, the decomposition may be justified by a practical need to keep modules on separate files or as separate compilation units. In contrast to high-fan-in subprograms that should often be *data coupled* and designed with potential reuse in mind, subprograms for separation of concerns are special-purpose and may often be *context coupled*. As with all subprograms, these subprograms should be functionally cohesive. An example of subprogram decomposition for separation of concerns is given in Section 3.5. As we shall see in Chapter 4, packaging is often a better tool than subprograms for the separation of concerns.

3.4.3 Program Fragmentation

Subprogram decomposition seen as the primary means for software structuring often results in excessive modularization or *program fragmentation*. The criteria of structured design and similar methods have been interpreted simplemindedly as "the more modules the better." Unfortunately, this tendency has penetrated textbooks on programming and programming languages, and software construction by subprogram decomposition is often promoted. In the following subsections, we discuss the problem of fragmentation by means of an example originally taken from a Pascal text [Koffman]. (It is also discussed in [Feldman].)

3.4.3.1 Example: checkbook problem

Consider a simple personal-computer program that reads the initial balance of a checking account and then accepts check and deposit transactions entered by the user from the PC keyboard. The program prints a balance after each transaction and a warning message if the balance becomes negative. At the end of the session, the starting and final balances and the number of checks and deposits are printed. Figure 3-16 is a *structure chart* according to structured design. It shows the breakdown of the program FRAGMENT into subprograms. Figure 3-17 shows the program text. The procedure FRAGMENT is first broken down into three procedures: INSTRUCT, PROCESS, and REPORT. In turn, PROCESS is broken down into READ_TRANS and UPDATE that are declared inside PROCESS. The body of the main procedure FRAGMENT is reduced to the following statements:

```
INSTRUCT(STARTBAL);
PROCESS(STARTBAL, CURBAL, NUMCHECK, NUMDEP);
REPORT(STARTBAL, CURBAL, NUMCHECK, NUMDEP);
```

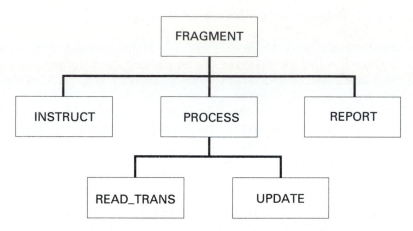

Figure 3-16 Structure chart of the program FRAGMENT. FRAGMENT consists of the subprograms INSTRUCT, PROCESS, and REPORT. In turn, PROCESS consists of READ_TRANS and UPDATE. [From E. B. Koffman, *Problem Solving and Structured Programming in Pascal*, © 1989 by Addison-Wesley Publishing Company, Inc. Reprinted (with adaptation) with permission of the publisher.]

```
    with TEXT_IO; use TEXT_IO;
procedure FRAGMENT is
    type REAL is new FLOAT;
    package FIO is new FLOAT_IO(REAL); use FIO;
    STARTBAL, CURBAL: REAL;
    NUMCHECK, NUMDEP: INTEGER;
    procedure INSTRUCT(STARTBAL: out REAL) is
    begin
            -- Display instructions.
            -- Get start balance.
    end INSTRUCT;
    procedure PROCESS(STARTBAL: REAL; CURBAL: in out REAL; NUMCHECK, NUMDEP: in out
    INTEGER) is
        SENTINEL: constant CHARACTER:='Q';
        TRANTYPE: CHARACTER;
        AMOUNT: REAL;
        procedure READ_TRANS(TRANTYPE: out CHARACTER; AMOUNT: out REAL) is
        T: CHARACTER;
        begin
            NEW_LINE;
            PUT("C, D, or Q: ");
```

Figure 3-17 The program FRAGMENT reads inputs corresponding to deposits and checks, and balances a checkbook. FRAGMENT is an example of a fragmented program.

```
    GET(T); TRANTYPE:=T;
    if T/=SENTINEL then
       PUT("AMOUNT $ "); GET(AMOUNT);
    end if;
 end READ_TRANS;
 procedure UPDATE(TRANTYPE: CHARACTER; AMOUNT: REAL; CURBAL: in out REAL;
 NUMCHECK, NUMDEP: in out INTEGER) is
 begin
    case TRANTYPE is
       when 'D' =>
          CURBAL:=CURBAL + AMOUNT;
          NUMDEP:=NUMDEP + 1;
          PUT("Deposit $"); PUT(AMOUNT);
          PUT(" Balance of $");
          PUT(CURBAL); NEW_LINE;
       when 'C' =>
          CURBAL:=CURBAL-AMOUNT;
          NUMCHECK:=NUMCHECK + 1;
          PUT("Check $"); PUT(AMOUNT);
          PUT(" Balance of $"); PUT(CURBAL);
          if CURBAL < 0.0 then
             PUT("Account overdrawn");
          end if;
          NEW_LINE;
       when others =>
          PUT_LINE("Invalid trans");
    end case;
 end UPDATE;
 begin -- Process
    NUMCHECK:=0; NUMDEP:=0; CURBAL:=STARTBAL;
    READ_TRANS(TRANTYPE, AMOUNT);
    while TRANTYPE/=SENTINEL loop
       UPDATE(TRANTYPE, AMOUNT, CURBAL, NUMCHECK, NUMDEP);
       READ_TRANS(TRANTYPE, AMOUNT);
    end loop;
 end PROCESS;
 procedure REPORT(STARTBAL, CURBAL : REAL; NUMCHECK, NUMDEP: INTEGER) is
 begin
       -- Print report.
 end REPORT;
 begin  -- Fragment
    INSTRUCT(STARTBAL);
    PROCESS(STARTBAL, CURBAL, NUMCHECK, NUMDEP);
    REPORT (STARTBAL, CURBAL, NUMCHECK, NUMDEP);
 end FRAGMENT;
```

Figure 3-17   (*continued*)

The program FRAGMENT has several problems, which have been introduced by the decomposition. In the next few sections, we discuss the problems one by one.

a. Understandability.   The first problem is a violation of the programming style rule that says: "Make your programs read from top to bottom" [Kernighan]. Although the breakdown is surely intended to make the program text easier to understand, the result is really the opposite. A reader starting at "**procedure** FRAGMENT **is** ..." must commit the purpose of various procedures to memory before reaching the main procedure body. A reader who starts at the beginning of the body must refer back to the text of each procedure as the calls are encountered, since the names INSTRUCT, PROCESS, and REPORT give insufficient information about the purpose of each subprogram.

This is particularly true for PROCESS, and for this reason, its text should have been included in the main procedure. As it stands, the text of the main procedure provides only a kind of index to the major parts of the program. The modules are unbalanced, with the main procedure almost content-free and addressing almost no concern at all.

From the point of view of understandability and resilience to future changes, a case can be made for making DEPOSIT and CHECK into subprograms. They represent well-defined, intuitively understandable functions in the problem environment. They are small and simple in the present program, but might conceivably be expanded if the program is modified.

b. Chinese-Box Structure of Nested Declarations.   The second problem has to do with what we will call the *Chinese-box* structure of the program. A Chinese box is the well-known toy consisting of a set of lacquered boxes neatly fitting in one another. We will use this term for modules declared within one another in this manner. The syntax of such nested declarations presents a problem that is inherent in Ada as well as similar languages, such as Pascal and ALGOL. In our example, UPDATE is declared inside PROCESS. The declaration of UPDATE, including its entire, potentially complex text, then appears in the declaration part of PROCESS, among the declarations of other local objects. After the declarations of READ_TRANS and UPDATE, an anonymous **begin** marks the beginning of the body of PROCESS itself, whose specification appears far earlier. This syntactical disadvantage may be offset by commenting and indentation, but it still limits the usefulness of nested procedure declarations. It would have been even worse if UPDATE in turn had contained local subprograms.

There are ways to keep the subprograms while avoiding the Chinese-box structure. UPDATE and READ_TRANS could be declared at the top level of the program (i.e., in the main procedure). This has the drawback that the procedures cannot reference any data or any types declared in PROCESS. Another disadvantage with this approach is that a large program may contain a large unorganized mass of unrelated subprogram declarations.

The subprograms can also be stubbed out as subunits, but that solution has drawbacks, too. With this approach, the main procedure of a fragmented, large program will always be followed by a tail of subunits. While the programmer is free to organize the subunits in some appropriate way, perhaps alphabetically, this approach is not particularly conducive to understanding.

In a third solution, the subprograms could be made into individual library units. This has the drawback that the library would be filled with the special-purpose pieces of various programs rather than reusable components. Global naming conventions might be required to avoid conflicts between procedures belonging to different programs. In yet another solution, the subprograms belonging to a particular main program could be collected in a package. For many practical purposes, such a package is similar to a collection of subunits in one source file. In conclusion, the subprograms resulting from excessive fragmentation seem to make a nuisance of themselves wherever they are, and the best solution is not to create them in the first place.

c. Excessive Data Coupling.   The program FRAGMENT also shows that loose coupling, particularly data coupling, is not always helpful. Except READ_TRANS, which is called twice, no subprogram in FRAGMENT can be justified by high fan-in or even potential usefulness. Instead, PROCESS and REPORT are introduced for separation of concerns in the particular context of the program FRAGMENT. They are *data coupled* in that all data is transferred to and from the procedures in long parameter lists. Since the procedures are not reusable, this transfer back and forth of several global variables is meaningless. The presence of such ''tramp data'' is a recognized problem that follows from program fragmentation and the encouragement of data coupling. Since PROCESS and REPORT cannnot exist oustide the context of the program FRAGMENT anyway, they might be *context coupled* and reference the variables directly.

d. Simpler Solution for the Checkbook Problem.   Figure 3-18 shows a simplified program CHKBOOK, where a strict justification of subprograms has been enforced. CHKBOOK functions exactly as FRAGMENT; the only difference is the modularization. Since subprograms for the separation of concerns are unjustified in this small program, READ_TRANS is the only subprogram. It is functionally cohesive and called twice. The control structure is contained in the main procedure and readable from top to bottom. The detailed statements necessary to display instructions and print the final report have been left out both in CHKBOOK in Figure 3-18 and in FRAGMENT in Figure 3-17. In FRAGMENT, they are contained in two subprograms, INSTRUCT and REPORT. In CHKBOOK, the intention is to insert them at the indicated positions in the main procedure. Since the statements are localized at the beginning and end of the main procedure, concerns can be sufficiently separated by means of comments and blank lines.

```
with TEXT_IO; use TEXT_IO;
procedure CHKBOOK is
   type REAL is new FLOAT;
   package FIO is new FLOAT_IO(REAL); use FIO;
   SENTINEL: constant CHARACTER:='Q';
   STARTBAL, CURBAL: REAL:=0.0;
   NUMCHECK, NUMDEP: INTEGER:=0;
   TRANTYPE: CHARACTER;
   AMOUNT: REAL;
   procedure READ_TRANS(TRANTYPE: out CHARACTER; AMOUNT: out REAL) is
   T: CHARACTER;
   begin
      NEW_LINE;
      PUT("C, D, or Q: ");
      GET(T); TRANTYPE:=T;
      if T/=SENTINEL then
         PUT("Amount $"); GET(AMOUNT);
      end if;
   end READ_TRANS;

begin
   -- Display instructions and read starting balance.
   -- Initialize counters.
   READ_TRANS(TRANTYPE, AMOUNT);
   while TRANTYPE/=SENTINEL loop
      case TRANTYPE is
         when 'D' =>
            CURBAL:=CURBAL + AMOUNT;
            NUMDEP:=NUMDEP + 1;
            PUT("Deposit $"); PUT(AMOUNT);
            PUT(" Balance of $");
            PUT(CURBAL); NEW_LINE;
         when 'C' =>
            CURBAL:=CURBAL-AMOUNT;
            NUMCHECK:=NUMCHECK + 1;
            PUT("Check $"); PUT(AMOUNT);
            PUT(" Balance of $"); PUT(CURBAL);
            if CURBAL < 0.0 then
               PUT("Account overdrawn");
            end if;
            NEW_LINE;
         when others =>
            PUT_LINE("Invalid trans");
      end case;
      READ_TRANS(TRANTYPE, AMOUNT);
   end loop;
   -- Print balances, check and deposit counts.
end CHKBOOK;
```

Figure 3-18 Simplified checkbook program with one single subprogram, READ_TRANS, which is justified since it is called twice in the text of the main program, CHKBOOK.

120

3.4.3.2 Programming practices leading to fragmentation

Programming techniques that are reasonable enough in themselves are sometimes misused in such a way as to cause program fragmentation. In this subsection we discuss briefly how this problem can be addressed in stepwise refinement and structured design.

a. Stepwise Refinement.   Stepwise refinement [Wirth] is a technique to implement an already known algorithm. The algorithm is broken down into steps that are successively refined. As an example, consider the "game of life" problem (Exercise 3.2), which is played on an array representing a game board. The game board symbolizes a habitat with organisms reproducing according to certain rules. The "game of life" is not really a competitive game but a simulation of primitive life, and in the course of the game, successive generations of organisms are created. Some of the steps in the refinement of a software solution of the game of life problem follow.

Step 1

```
Initialize game array
Print game board
Process generations
```

Step 2.   Further refinement of "Process generations":

```
for X in GENERATIONS loop
    Compute next generation
    Print game board
end loop;
```

Step 3.   Further refinement of "Compute next generation":

```
for I in G'RANGE(1) loop
    for J in G'RANGE(2) loop
        Count neighbors
        Determine birth, survival, or death
    end loop;
end loop;
```

Although stepwise refinement is reasonable enough in the game-of-life problem, it is a misunderstanding that units such as "Process generation" and "Compute next generation" must necessarily be implemented as modules. The final subprogram structure does not have to reflect the successive steps in which it has been developed. Instead, the successive refinements can be edited into a successively evolving program text. In a sense, the units are props in the stepwise refinement process and need not clutter the final product. On the other hand, generally useful sequences of actions such as "Print game board" can be identified during the refinement process and made into subprograms.

b. Structured Design.   Structured analysis and design [Yourdon] is a popular approach to functional decomposition. It is primarily a data processing approach with its roots in the 1960s, when a major issue in software engineering was the breakdown of huge monolithic programs into manageable modules. In structured analysis, a program is likened to a factory with material flows entering and leaving processing stations, and it is appealing to programmers to regard data records as *flowing* in a similar way between *transforms* that successively convert them from input to output [Heller]. Sometimes, an analogy with a human, bureaucratic organization is used instead, where the transforms exchanging data correspond to specialized clerks and their supervisors, shuffling papers to each other.

In structured design, the transforms identified during structured analysis are implemented as a hierarchy of subprograms. The data flow is realized by means of parameters passed between the subprograms. The promoters of structured analysis and design address the danger of fragmentation and potential inefficiency and include goodness criteria that can be used to eliminate unwanted subprograms. These are the cohesion, coupling, and fan-in criteria discussed earlier. The approach also allows small subprograms to be incorporated into the calling subprograms. Nevertheless, these provisions are often disregarded, leading instead to vast hierarchies of subprograms, many of which may be unjustified. Program fragmentation in connection with the promotion of data coupling also leads to "tramp data" passed between many different subprograms.

3.5 JUSTIFICATION OF GENERIC SUBPROGRAMS

In Section 3.2.4 the procedure G_SWAP was introduced as a small example of a generic subprogram. G_SWAP takes one generic parameter,

    type ANY_TYPE **is private**;

and produces a procedure that takes two parameters, A and B of ANY_TYPE. The procedure swaps the values of A and B. While very small, G_SWAP is a justifiable generic in principle. Its secret, how the values of two variables are swapped, applies to any type. A client program can rely on G_SWAP to produce the required result without knowing how it is achieved. The generic sort procedure in Figure 3-12 is a more elaborate example of the same idea. The sorting algorithm can be made a secret that is independent of the types of the records being sorted. While the generic in Figure 3-12 is based on the simple selection-sort algorithm, a more sophisticated algorithm can be substituted without affecting the client programs.

Both the G_SWAP and the SORT generic allow us to use the same algorithm on objects of different types, and thereby alleviate Ada's strong typing rules. They both have secrets that can be changed without affecting the client. It is important that a generic subprogram have a secret, and that generics not be used for convenience only, in order to catch some arbitrary similarity between different subprograms. If the subprograms that result from instantiating the generic are not fundamentally similar, the generic will have no secret that can be changed without affecting the client. Such a generic may lead to a design where a change has disastrous ripple effects. We introduce an example from a transaction system to show this. The example also illustrates the use of subprogram decomposition for separation of concerns.

3.5.1 Example: Teller Terminal System

3.5.1.1 Problem description

In a particular bank, each teller has a special-purpose PC on which customer transactions are entered. The teller selects transactions by means of function keys and numeric keys. Once selected, each transaction follows a given pattern defined by prompts, for example:

> Account number:
> Check number:
> Amount:
> etc.

Each prompt is displayed separately and the field is filled before the following prompt is displayed. (In user interface design, this is sometimes referred to as *progressive disclosure*.)

An amount field is entered left-justified ending with a $ sign. As soon as the complete field has been entered, it is redisplayed right-justified. The check and account number fields are fixed-format. As soon as a complete field has been entered, it is validated by means of a check digit. If the field is incorrect, the teller is alerted by means of a beep and must reenter the field before continuing.

The system includes a number of transaction types belonging to different *subsystems*, such as Savings, Checking, and Certificate of deposit (CD), as follows:

> Savings transactions
> > Deposit
> > Deposit without book
> > Update book
> > Withdraw

Checking transactions
    Deposit
    Withdraw

CD transactions
    Open
    Close
    Renew

Payment of bills

Currency exchange

Each transaction is selected in two steps: a function key corresponding to the subsystem is entered, and then a number corresponding to a transaction type within the subsystem.

A bank customer may use a number of different checks and other documents to make a single deposit or payment. The deposit or payment transaction then includes *subtransactions* of the following types:

This bank's check
Other bank's check
Document (certified check, government check)
Cash

3.5.1.2 Software design

The behavior of the teller (or, conversely, the required behavior of the software) is conveniently described as a sequence diagram. At the top level, there is an iteration of a selection, first over subsystem and then, within each subsystem, over transaction type. Figure 3-19 is a top level description of teller behavior with an iteration over transactions and a selection of subsystem. Figure 3-19 also shows the control structure of the main procedure TELLER. (A CLOSE operation performed by the teller at the end of the day is included.)

For separation of concerns, each subsystem, SAVINGS, CHECKING, and so on, is implemented as a procedure. The sequence diagram in Figure 3-20 shows the control structure of the subprogram SAVINGS. For further separation of concerns, each transaction in each subsystem is a procedure declared in the subsystem procedure. Figure 3-21 shows the steps involved in a savings deposit transaction. The figure also serves as a program sequence diagram of a subprogram DEPOSIT declared locally in SAVINGS.

Figure 3-22 shows the handling of subtransactions in any subsystem. There is an iteration over subtransaction and a selection of subtransaction type. At the same time, the diagram shows the control structure of a global function SUBS, which is called from each of the transaction subprograms DEPOSIT (in SAVINGS),

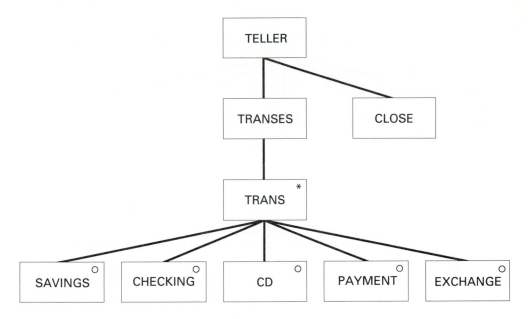

Figure 3-19 Top-level sequence diagram of teller behavior with an iteration over transactions and a selection of subsystem. The diagram can also be read as a program sequence diagram and shows the control structure of the main program TELLER.

DEPOSIT (in CHECKING), PAYMENT, and so on. Other global subprograms are the functions ACCOUNT, which obtains an account number, and AMOUNT, which obtains an amount. Like SUBS, the subprograms ACCOUNT and AMOUNT have high fan-in since they are used for different transaction types.

In the design of the teller terminal system, both control structure and subprograms can be justified based on the reality. The control structure with loops and **if** or **case** statements is based on teller behavior and includes:

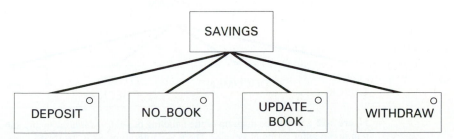

Figure 3-20 Sequence diagram of the teller behavior within the Savings subsystem with a selection of transaction type. The diagram also shows the control structure of the subprogram SAVINGS.

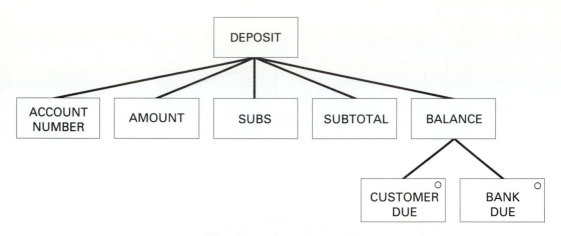

Figure 3-21 Sequence diagram showing the steps involved in a deposit transaction in the Savings subsystem. The diagram also shows the control structure of the subprogram DEPOSIT, declared locally in SAVINGS.

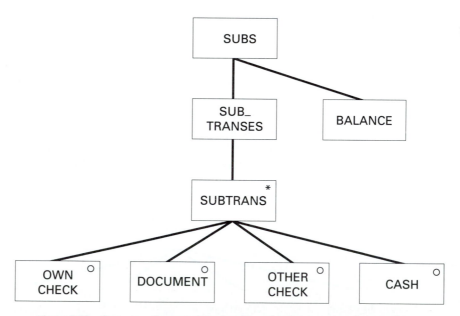

Figure 3-22 Sequence diagram of the handling of *subtransactions* in any subsystem in the teller terminal system. There is an iteration, SUB_TRANSES over subtransactions, which in turn is a selection of subtransaction type. The diagram is also a program sequence diagram of the subprogram SUBS, which is called from each of the subprograms DEPOSIT (Savings or Checking), PAYMENT, and so on.

A top-level loop over transactions and a selection of subsystem

Within each subsystem, a selection of transaction type

A loop over subtransactions and a selection of subtransaction type

The subsystem subprograms SAVINGS, CHECKING, and so on, are likely to be suitable design/programming assignments. Within each subsystem, each transaction type becomes a subprogram. DEPOSIT, WITHDRAW, and so on, are declared in SAVINGS, for example. The savings subsystem contains two additional transaction subprograms: NO_BOOK, which is used when the customer does not bring the passbook, and UPDATE_BOOK, which enters earlier NO_BOOK transactions in the passbook.

3.5.1.3 *Misuse of generics in the teller example*

Many transaction subprograms in the Teller system exhibit a superficial similarity, as the DEPOSIT procedures for savings and checking in Figure 3-23. It is tempting to use these superficial similarities as the basis for generic subprograms. The generic procedure MISUSE in Figure 3-24 covers both DEPOSIT transactions. Since the procedure PRINT_BOOK occurring in savings has no counterpart in checking, a dummy procedure, NULL_PROC, is introduced just to supply the necessary generic parameter.

If enough subprograms are sufficiently similar, the introduction of generics may reduce the programming effort somewhat. Nevertheless, a generic such as MISUSE is unfortunate. As any other module, a generic should have an interface and a secret. The advantage of using the module is that the client need only deal with the interface. For the module to be justified, there must be an important piece of knowledge that the client need not possess in order to use the module. It is the "trade secret" of the maker of the module, and may be changed without affecting the client.

In the case of MISUSE, there is no secret that may be changed without affecting the generic instantiations. The specification of the generic contains a set of subprograms. (In Figure 3-24 the formal subprogram parameters are FUNC and PROC, and the actual parameters are PASSBOOK and PRINT_BOOK, and CHECKNO and NULL_PROC.) The client must know in which order these subprograms are called from within the generic, since that directly reflects the order in which different prompts will appear on the teller's screen. If that order is changed within the generic, all its clients will be affected.

The order in which fields are entered today may be similar in different transactions, but there is no reason to believe that they will necessarily always remain that way. The fields are transaction dependent, and new fields may be added to one transaction without affecting another. If one deposit transaction is changed, the generic MISUSE must be changed, affecting all other transactions based on MISUSE. Thus the modularization attempted by means of MISUSE is **coun-**

```
procedure DEPOSIT is
-- Deposit, savings
T_ACCOUNT, T_BOOK_NO, T_AMOUNT: INTEGER;
T_REC: ACCOUNT_REC_PTR;
begin
    T_ACCOUNT:=ACCOUNT;      -- Get account.
    T_REC:=RETRIEVE(T_ACCOUNT);
    if T_REC=null then raise NO_ACCOUNT; end if;
    T_BOOK_NO:=PASSBOOK; -- Get passbook no.
    T_AMOUNT:=AMOUNT;
    SUBS(T_AMOUNT);
    PRINT_BOOK(T_AMOUNT);
    END_TRANS(T_REC);
end DEPOSIT;
```

```
procedure DEPOSIT is
-- Deposit, checking
T_ACCOUNT, T_CHKNO, T_AMOUNT: INTEGER;
T_REC: ACCOUNT_REC_PTR;
begin
    T_ACCOUNT:=ACCOUNT;      -- Get account.
    T_REC:=RETRIEVE(T_ACCOUNT);
    if T_REC=null then raise NO_ACCOUNT; end if;
    T_CHKNO:=CHECKNO;        -- Get check no.
    T_AMOUNT:=AMOUNT;
    SUBS(T_AMOUNT);
    --
    END_TRANS(T_REC);
end DEPOSIT;
```

Figure 3-23 The procedures DEPOSIT (Savings) and DEPOSIT (Checking).

terproductive: Rather than localizing changes, it spreads them. MISUSE illustrates a misguided attempt to use generics in order to save the minor duplication of effort involved in making these individual procedures. Instead, the result is a tightly coupled solution where the different transactions have become highly interdependent. Another result is an unfortunately complicated generic interface, revealing the internals of the generic procedure since the client must know how the subprograms are called. Rather than a help, the generic has become a straitjacket forced upon the designers and implementers of the different transactions.

The simple solution with individual procedures as in Figure 3-23 is much more flexible, even if it appears repetitive. In that solution, the handling of each transaction is clearly localized and easily changed. At the same time, the common properties of the different transactions have been exploited. Thus, all transactions obtain account numbers and amounts in the same manner, by calling ACCOUNT and AMOUNT.

```
generic
    T_DUMMY: in out INTEGER;
    with function FUNC return INTEGER;
    with procedure PROC(X: INTEGER);
procedure MISUSE;

procedure MISUSE is
T_ACCOUNT, T_AMOUNT: INTEGER;
T_REC: ACCOUNT_REC_PTR;
begin
    T_ACCOUNT:=ACCOUNT;
    T_REC:=RETRIEVE(T_ACCOUNT);
    if T_REC=null then raise NO_ACCOUNT; end if;
    T_DUMMY:=FUNC;    -- Generic statement
    T_AMOUNT:=AMOUNT;
    SUBS(T_AMOUNT);
    PROC(T_AMOUNT);    -- Generic statement
    END_TRANS(T_REC);
end MISUSE;

    with MISUSE;
procedure SAVINGS is
T_BOOK: INTEGER;
function PASSBOOK return INTEGER is separate;
procedure PRINT_BOOK(X: INTEGER) is separate;
procedure DEPOSIT is new MISUSE(T_BOOK,PASSBOOK,PRINT_BOOK);
begin
    ....
end SAVINGS;

    with MISUSE;
procedure CHECKING is
T_CHKNO: INTEGER;
function CHECKNO return INTEGER is separate;
procedure NULL_PROC(X: INTEGER) is
begin null;
end NULL_PROC;
procedure DEPOSIT is new MISUSE(T_CHKNO,CHECKNO,NULL_PROC);
begin
    ....
end CHECKING;
```

Figure 3-24   Generic procedure MISUSE with instantiations in the subprograms SAVINGS and CHECKING. The generic is based on a superficial similarity between the DEPOSIT procedures and may become an impediment if the procedures are later changed in different ways.

In conclusion, a generic subprogram can be used to circumvent Ada's strong typing requirements by providing a reusable implementation of an algorithm. This is justified if the algorithm is reasonably complex. The implementation of the algorithm is the secret of the generic subprogram and may, at least in principle, be changed without affecting the client. Generic subprograms should not be used based on superficial and arbitrary similarities between subprograms. In that case the generic is counterproductive and hampers the individual modification of the subprograms.

3.6 CHAPTER SUMMARY

There are two primary means for program modularization: *independent subprograms* and *packages*. (Independent subprograms are so called to distinguish them from the *operation subprograms* of packages.) Independent subprograms allow *procedural abstraction*; that is, we can abstract away from the details of an algorithm, think of it as one operation, and refer to it by a name.

Packages allow *data abstraction* and *information hiding*. An information-hiding package has an *interface* and a *secret*. The secret can be a data structure hidden in the body of the package, accessible via external *operation subprograms*. That way we may think of the data structure as one *software object* that can be operated on in certain well-defined ways. The secret may also be a physical hardware interface. Then the operations provide an abstract, logical interface to a particular hardware device.

Every subprogram should be *functionally cohesive*. A functionally cohesive subprogram does one thing only, as described by its name. Excessive decomposition of a control structure into independent subprograms may lead to *program fragmentation*. To avoid this, independent subprograms must be justified. A subprogram with *high fan-in* is always justified, provided that it is functionally cohesive. A subprogram has high fan-in if it is either frequently used within one program or reusable in different programs.

Subprograms should rely on a combination of *data coupling* and *context coupling*. Data coupling relies on parameters, while context coupling implies direct access to variables that are global to the environment of the subprogram.

REFERENCES

FELDMAN, M. B. and KOFFMAN, E. B., *Ada: Problem Solving and Program Design*, Addison-Wesley, Reading, Mass., 1992.

GARDNER, M., Mathematical games: the fantastic combinations of John Conway's new solitaire game "life," *Sci. Am.*, October 1970, pp. 120–123.

GARDNER, M., Mathematical games: on cellular automata, self-reproduction, the Garden of Eden and the game "life," *Sci. Am.*, February 1971, pp. 112–117.

HELLER, P., *Real-Time Software Design*, Birkhauser, Boston, 1987.

KERNIGHAN, B. W., and PLAUGER, P. J., *The Elements of Programming Style*, 2nd ed., McGraw-Hill, New York, 1978.

KNUTH, D. E., *The Art of Computer Programming*, Vol. 3, *Sorting and Searching*, Addison-Wesley, Reading, Mass., 1973.

KOFFMAN, E. B., *Problem Solving and Structured Programming in Pascal*, 2nd ed., Addison-Wesley, Reading, Mass., 1985.

LISKOV, B., and GUTTAG, J., *Abstraction and Specification in Program Development*, MIT Press, Cambridge, Mass., 1986.

Oxford Dictionary of Computing, 3rd ed., Oxford University Press, Oxford, 1991.

PAGE-JONES, M., *The Practical Guide to Structured Systems Design*, Yourdon Press, Englewood Cliffs, N.J., 1980.

PARNAS, D. L., On the design and development of program families, *IEEE Trans. Software Eng.*, 2:1, March 1976, pp. 1–9.

PARNAS, D. L., Designing software for ease of extension and contraction, *IEEE Trans. Software Eng.*, 5:2, March 1979, pp. 128–137.

PARNAS, D. L., Software engineering principles, *INFOR Can. J. Oper. Res. Inf. Process.*, 22:4, November 1984, pp. 303–316.

PARNAS, D. L., CLEMENTS, P. C., and WEISS, D. M., The modular structure of complex systems, *IEEE Trans. Software Eng.*, 11:3, March 1985, pp. 259–266.

WIRTH, N., Program development by stepwise refinement, *Commun. ACM*, 14:4, April 1971, pp. 221–227.

YOURDON, E., and CONSTANTINE, L., *Structured Design*, Prentice Hall, Englewood Cliffs, N.J., 1979.

EXERCISES

3.1 Roman numeral

A Roman numeral between 1 and 3999 consists of four consecutive groups of characters as follows:

M-group   C-group   X-group   I-group

Although the groups always appear in this order, each group may or may not be present in any given numeral. Each group has the following structure:

    The M-group consists of one, two, or three M's representing the following values: 1000: M, 2000: MM, 3000: MMM.

    The C-group is one of the following combinations of the letters C, D, and M: 100: C, 200: CC, 300: CCC, 400: CD, 500: D, 600: DC, 700: DCC, 800: DCCC, 900: CM.

    The X-group is one of the following combinations of the letters X, L, and C: 10: X, 20: XX, 30: XXX, 40: XL, 50: L, 60: LX, 70: LXX, 80: LXXX, 90: XC.

    The I-group is one of the following combinations of the letters I, V, and X: 1: I, 2: II, 3: III, 4: IV, 5: V, 6: VI, 7: VII, 8: VIII, 9: IX.

The value of a numeral is computed by adding the value of the M-group, the C-group, the X-group, and the I-group. In Exercise 2.8 a program is constructed that recognizes a correct I-group and determines its value. Now construct a program that recognizes a correct numeral between 1 and 3999.

Hint: The C-group, X-group, and I-group each have the same structure. Construct a subprogram that takes three parameters P, Q, and R, and recognizes a partial numeral consisting of the combinations P, PP, PPP, PQ, Q, QP, QPP, QPPP, and PR. Then call that subprogram three times with the following actual parameters for each group:

	P	Q	R
C-group	C	D	M
X-group	X	L	C
I-group	I	V	X

3.2 Game of life

The *game of life* invented by John H. Conway [Gardner 70, 71] is supposed to model the genetic laws for birth, survival, and death. We will play it on a board of 15×15 squares that will be represented by an array.[1] Each square can contain zero or one organism. Each square (except the border squares) has *eight* neighboring squares. The borders of the game are infertile regions where organisms can neither survive nor be born. (The borders consist of rows 1 and 15 and columns 1 and 15.) The next generation of organisms is determined according to the following criteria:

1. *Birth*. An organism will be born in each empty location that has *exactly three neighbors* (i.e., exactly three of the neighboring squares are inhabited).
2. *Death*. An organism with *four or more neighbors* will die from overcrowding. An organism with *fewer than two neighbors* will die from loneliness.
3. *Survival*. An organism with *two or three neighbors* will survive to the next generation.

Write a procedure PRINT_GAME that takes a game array as parameter and prints it, indicating the inhabited squares by '*' and the uninhabited ones by '.', as in the configuration below. Include row and column numbers. In the main **procedure** GAME_OF_LIFE, initialize the game array either by reading from a file or by prompting the user. Prompt the user for the number of generations desired. Call PRINT_GAME to print the original game array. Then repeat the following the required number of times:

1. Calculate the next generation of organisms. Note that all the calculations must be based on the old generation, which must be saved intact until the entire new generation has been calculated. Do not process the border squares.

---

[1] This variation on the game of life was suggested in [Koffman].

2. Print the new game array using PRINT_GAME.

3. Copy the new array into the original array.

Sample initial configuration:

```
       123456789012345
 1..............
 2.**...........
 3.**......*****.
 4.........*****.
 5.******..*****.
 6.******..*****.
 7.******..*****.
 8.******........
 9.******........
10.************..
11........*****..
12........*****..
13........*****..
14........*****..
15..............
```

3.3 Generic sort

Instantiate and test the generic SORT procedure in Figure 3-12 for various purposes: Sort an array of integers in *descending* order. Declare a record INDIVIDUAL with the fields LAST_NAME, FIRST_NAME, and SALARY. Declare instantiations that sort a table of INDIVIDUAL records in various ways:

(a) With LAST_NAME as the primary key and FIRST_NAME as the secondary key.

(b) According to increasing SALARY.

(c) According to decreasing SALARY.

4 Object-Based Software Construction

The noblest function of an object is to be contemplated.

Unamuno, Mist

4.1 INTRODUCTION

The topic of this chapter is the modeling of software objects on objects in the problem environment. This will be referred to as *object-based* software construction.[1] In this section we discuss what we will mean by "object" and how objects are identified in the problem environment. The elevator problem introduced in Chapter 2 is used as an example. In the following sections we shall see how information-hiding packages and abstract data types may be modeled on such objects. Information-hiding modules are modeled on single, static objects in the reality that do not begin or cease to exist during program execution. This is discussed in Section 4.2. Objects with multiple instances and objects that are dynamically created during execution are modeled by means of abstract data types. An abstract data type represents a class of objects and can be instantiated as necessary when individual objects come into existence. This and object-based software in general is discussed in Section 4.3, which also includes the Ada syntax supporting abstract data types. In Section 4.4 we discuss the choice between information-hiding and adt packages for modeling.

---

[1] The distinction between the *object-based* and *object-oriented* software construction is discussed birefly in Section 4.3.1.

134

The breakdown of a program into packages raises other, more practical concerns than modeling. There may be different, justifiable ways to break down a given problem. A trade-off between such concerns as maintenance, reuse, and configuration may be necessary. Packages are also a good basis for the division of labor during design and implementation, due to the separation of interface and secret. These aspects of packaging are discussed in Section 4.5.

4.1.1 Software Objects and Real-World Objects

In Ada, an *object* is an instantiation of a type. An integer variable and an integer constant are simple examples of objects. An instantiation of a record type is a more complex example. We define a *software object* as either an Ada object in this sense or an information-hiding package.[2] A software object has *attributes* and *operations*, where the operations retrieve and/or change the value of the attributes. If the object is an instance of a record type, its attributes are represented by its fields. Operations on the object return and/or change these values.

With the modeling approach, we justify software objects by relating them to *objects in the problem environment* or *real-world objects*. (These terms will be used synonymously.) Unfortunately, these concepts are notoriously hard to define. One definition is as follows: "An object represents an individual, identifiable item, unit or entity, either real or abstract, with a well-defined role in the problem domain" [Smith]. According to another definition, an object is anything (whether concrete or abstract) with a crisply defined boundary [Cox]. A discussion of these and other definitions of object can be found in [Booch].

Early books on object-based software design have sometimes supplied rules of thumb for the choice of objects. For example, the designer may be advised to identify the *nouns* in a problem description and make them the objects. It is now recognized that this kind of rule is too simplistic. It may help a novice designer to distinguish potential objects from, say, functions, but may easily lead to a mass of objects of little value. Instead the proficient analyst or designer uses the object paradigm selectively to achieve a compelling model of the problem that leads smoothly to a software design and also takes into account the relationship between the objects and a *subject,* responsible for the timing and ordering of the operations on objects. In the next section we discuss the choice of objects in the elevator problem.

4.1.2 Choice of Objects in the Elevator Example

The elevator program introduced in Chapter 2 operates in a familiar problem environment, which is suitable for a discussion of the choice of objects. We list a number of objects in the problem domain and then discuss the usefulness of each

---

[2] A task not encapsulated in a package is sometimes an object (see Chapters 6 and 8).

for the construction of the elevator control software. Here are some objects of varying character:

The elevator

The elevator motor

A button

A request for service

A passenger

Various elevator parts, found in a parts explosion of the elevator assembly

The elevator schedule

A scheduler

A dispatcher

We discuss each of these possible objects:

The *elevator* itself is an important entity in the problem environment. In the solution in Chapter 2, the elevator is the subject rather than an object. In the software it is represented by the main procedure. An interesting variation occurs when multiple elevators are introduced, and in later chapters we shall see how this problem is solved by means of concurrent tasks. In that situation the elevator behavior remains the subject, but with multiple elevators, the solution contains multiple subjects, each implemented as a task (Chapter 8).

The *motor* is an intuitive, concrete object with the operations SET_UP, SET_DOWN, START, and STOP. It is conveniently represented as an information-hiding package in the software. A *button* has a Boolean attribute *pressed* indicating whether it is currently being held pressed. There are buttons on each floor and inside the elevator. The management of the buttons introduces asynchrony into the elevator problem, since buttons are pressed independent of the movements of the elevator. We postpone further discussion of the buttons until the complete solution of the elevator problem is discussed in Chapter 8.

A *request* is an abstract object with the attributes *floor* and *direction*. A request exists from the moment a button is pressed and until it has been served by the elevator. This makes it a short-lived object. Since the set of all possible requests is limited, it is also possible to model each *potential* request. Each potential-request object includes an attribute indicating whether the request is currently outstanding. The advantage is that a potential request is a persistent object. Even if individual potential requests are modeled, it is also convenient to consider the *set of all requests* as an object, since the elevator needs to query several requests at a time. We base the solution to the elevator problem on such *set* objects. In the software the set of requests is represented as a package containing a data structure of potential requests.

A *passenger* may appear to be an important object in the elevator environment. Potentially, a passenger has a behavior pattern: call elevator at floor X, enter, press button for floor Y, exit. But this behavior is irrelevant to the elevator. We lose no important information by abstracting away the passengers and dealing only with their requests for elevator service.

A *parts explosion* of the elevator assembly would yield an almost endless number of potential objects, such as the elevator cabin with its floor, roof, walls, button panels, and so on, as well as the parts of the elevator motor and other machinery. Most of these details are irrelevant to the software design. It would be a detour to start with a complete inventory and then pare it down to a set of useful objects. Some of the parts of the physical elevator system will indeed play a role in the software. The buttons used to generate requests are examples of this. But trivial, concrete objects such as the buttons usually give the designer little leverage for structuring the software. It is better to start with more abstract objects, such as the set of requests, and deal with the nitty-gritty later. A mass of mostly insignificant, trivial objects can easily cloud the picture.

The *schedule* of elevator travel is an abstract object. Clearly, it must be embodied in the elevator system somehow, but it is difficult to treat it as an object with a meaningful set of operations. In the solution chosen, we express the schedule as the behavior of the elevator, which in turn, is modeled in the control structure.

A *functional decomposition* of the elevator software might include a *scheduler* or a *dispatcher* module. These modules should not be confused with objects modeled on the reality, since there is no scheduler or dispatcher in the problem environment. Instead, the scheduler and the dispatcher are functional modules commonly found in software systems similar to the elevator controller. A functional decomposition with a scheduler or a dispatcher may be suitable in the elevator controller, too. But the object-based approach requires that the solution be based on the realities of the problem at hand. We cannot make a functional decomposition into an object-based design just by calling software modules "objects."

The literature on object-oriented analysis and design has further guidelines as to the choice of objects [Coad], [Booch], [Rumbaugh]. The choice of objects for the construction of concurrent software is discussed further in Chapter 8.

4.2 INFORMATION-HIDING MODULES IN MODELING

As mentioned in Chapter 3, a module such as an Ada package has an *interface* and a *secret*. The interface contains what the outside world, or more exactly the programmers of other modules, need to know about a module. In other words, it includes all *connections* between the modules. The connections are both syntactical, such as various forms of coupling (Chapter 3) and semantic, such as the meaning of the different operations. They are "the assumptions that the programmers implementing a module make about other modules" [Parnas]. We will consider a module M a *model* of a real-world object O if the assumptions made about

M could be made about O. This means that writers of other modules can think of M as they might think of the object O, and expect that M behave like O to a reasonable degree. On the other hand, M must be designed to meet these expectations.

Modeling is a design heuristic allowing us to identify and conceptualize appropriate modules. It is intended to ensure that the modules are reasonable and intuitive, not free inventions by a software developer. Modeling does not replace the exact definition of the interface of the module but is intended to encourage consistent interfaces that are not the arbitrary result of implementation preferences.

As a simple example, the interface to a printer driver may include the operations PUT_LINE and NEW_LINE. By calling PUT_LINE, a client program makes a line of text appear in the output, and by calling NEW_LINE, skips a line in the output. The printer driver hides the hardware interface to the physical printer and creates the illusion of a device with these (and other) operations. In that sense, the driver models a printer. In other common cases, the secret of a package is a data model of some real-world object. In the elevator example (Section 4.2.4), a package represents the set of all outstanding requests for elevator service. Operations on that package answer questions such as: "Is there any request for upward travel from floor 4?" This example shows that the object on which a package is modeled does not have to be concrete.

The operations PUT_LINE and NEW_LINE are parts of an *abstract* interface in the sense that they express the essential operations from a client's point of view, while the technical details of how they are accomplished on a given hardware device are hidden. Such an abstract interface allows us to *design for change* in that it remains the same even if the physical printer interface changes. In general, we strive toward a design that is adaptable to future changes in the problem environment. Although any part of the environment may change, we assume that the things that may change independently can often be attributed to independent objects. If each such object is modeled by a module with an abstract interface, the change in the real-world object will affect only the secret of that module.

4.2.1 Diagrammatic Notation
for Information-Hiding Packages

As discussed earlier, we use a diagrammatic representation to give a quick overview of a design and reveal its structure. Diagrams are used as complements to the detailed textual representation, which ultimately defines the design. Figure 4-1 shows a diagrammatic notation for information-hiding packages, introduced by Buhr [Buhr 84]. Buhr calls such a diagram a *structure graph*, but instead, we will use the word *buhrgraph* to avoid the often used word "structure." The buhrgraph notation includes the following elements:

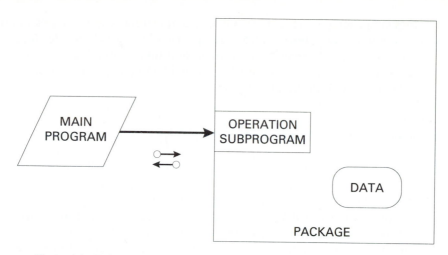

Figure 4-1 Buhrgraph showing a main program operating on a package. The parallelogram represents a main program (more exactly a task; see Chapter 6). The rectangle represents a package; the small rectangles inside its borders are operations. (The little arrows represent **in** and **out** parameters.)

A package is shown as a rectangle.

An operation subprogram is represented by a smaller rectangle attached to the inside of the border of a rectangle representing a package. Such a small rectangle is referred to as a *socket*.

An arrow pointing to a socket represents a call. If call parameters are shown, they are represented by separate little arrows with rings on their tails. (**In** parameters are pointed toward the package and **out** parameters away from it.)

The main procedure is shown as a parallelogram. (Strictly speaking, the parallelogram represents the *subject* operating on the package. It includes the main procedure and any independent subprograms. In multitasking software, each diagram may contain several parallelograms, each representing a task; compare Chapters 6 through 9.)

Data hidden inside a package may be shown as a so-called *bubtangle* (a rounded rectangle).

A full description of the buhrgraph notation with graphical representation of all relevant Ada constructs can be found in [Buhr 89, 90]. We will use buhrgraphs as informal illustrations of software designs, as a complement to program text, not as a rigorous notation. We usually use the diagrams to provide an overview of a design. Some details of the design will often be suppressed. For example, we occasionally suppress the sockets or let a single socket represent several operation subprograms. Note that only operation subprograms included in the package *specification* are shown. Subprograms used exclusively inside the package body are not shown. References to an operation subprogram from the package where it is declared are not shown. Furthermore, independent subprograms are not represented in our Buhrgraphs.

4.2.2 Levels of Abstraction

The software representations of real-world objects may have varying degrees of abstraction. Sometimes it is useful and necessary to model one and the same real-world object at multiple *levels of abstraction*. A module that closely models a hardware device is at a low abstraction level. The simple printer driver mentioned earlier is an example. Operations such as PUT_LINE can be carried out fairly directly on the physical printer. But the real power of software lies in the ability to model much more abstract and versatile objects. Software objects at such high levels of abstraction are powerful tools for the client modules. Data communication is a good example. An application program typically operates on a high-level communications module that hides the details of how the communication is accomplished. The application program may have an interactive user who operates on a sophisticated network allowing direct addressing of other users or application program nodes.

The high-level software communication module used by an interactive program relies on lower-level abstractions and ultimately on a communication line driver. Various standards exist for such a *layered* architecture. The ISO standard, ''Open Systems Interconnection'' (OSI), for example, has seven layers [Black]. A low OSI layer manages the transmission of single packages of data between two directly connected computers according to a relatively simple protocol. Software at that level models the capabilities of the physical line fairly closely. Higher OSI layers provide more sophisticated services and end-to-end connection via intermediate computers. Each layer communicates with the same layer in another computer according to a specific protocol. Each layer is an information-hiding module presenting a well-defined interface to the layer immediately above and hiding the protocol of its own layer. The communication protocol is part of the module specification but not its *interface* specification (see Section 4.3.1).

Levels of abstraction create a practical packaging problem. From the point of view of the application software, the top-layer module M_N inside M_N, say, in an N-layer architecture models the entire network, and the lower layer packages M_{N-1}, and so on, are part of the secret. Consequently, we might want to hide the module M_{N-1} inside M_N. With multiple layers, this would lead to a *Chinese-box* structure similar to that occurring in some subprogram structures (Section 3.4.3). Instead of creating a Chinese-box structure, we usually build a hierarchy of Ada packages, each of which is typically a library unit. The most primitive module is placed at the bottom, and each higher layer of packages *withs* the one below. This way, the packages at a certain level L can be said to be hidden *below* the packages at the next higher level, L + 1, from the packages at level L + 2. This hierarchical discipline is upheld by agreement only and cannot be enforced by means of the Ada syntax. A malicious programmer may bypass a layer and give his package direct access to a lower layer simply by including the proper **with** clause.

The layered architecture is sometimes referred to as a *virtual machine* structure in the following sense: The bottom layer depends exclusively on facilities in the hardware (or provided with the programming language). The next-higher layer relies not on a physical machine, but on a refined, virtual machine that provides the bottom-layer functions, and so on. It is sometimes not necessary to maintain a strict discipline where modules at level L exclusively access objects at the next lower level, L − 1. Instead, it is often reasonable to make level L − 1 partially transparent and give the units at level L selective access to objects at lower levels.

4.2.3 Packaging in the VDU Example

In the VDU example in Chapter 2, a video display unit is equipped with a micro-processor that executes an embedded control program. The microprocessor receives a stream of characters from a mainframe host to which the unit is connected. It displays characters on a screen. The buhrgraph in Figure 4-2 shows the

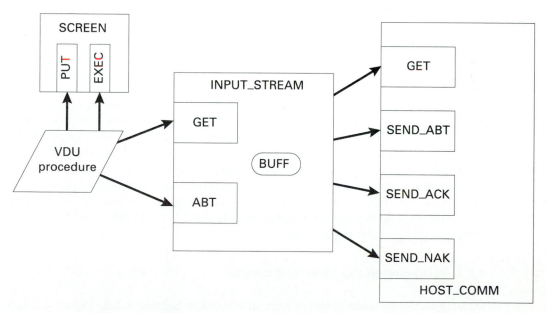

Figure 4-2 Buhrgraph of the VDU procedure and the package SCREEN, INPUT_STREAM, and HOST_COMM.

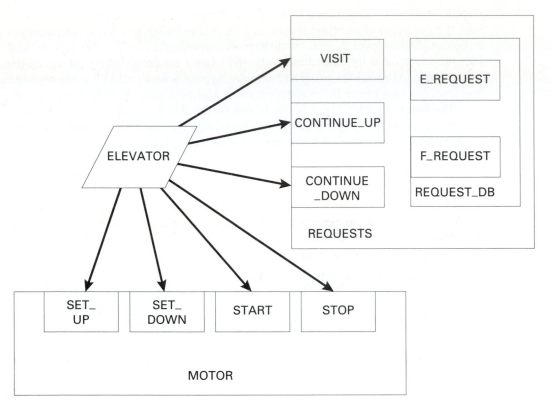

Figure 4-3   Buhrgraph of the elevator program with the packages MOTOR, REQUESTS, and REQUEST_DB.

main procedure VDU and the information-hiding packages SCREEN, INPUT_STREAM, and HOST_COMM. (The specifications of SCREEN is shown in Figure 2-20 and those of INPUT_STREAM and HOST_COMM in Figure 2-23.) INPUT_STREAM is the top-level model of the communication interface with the mainframe. HOST_COMM, which is a lower-level model, is hidden below INPUT_STREAM in the sense that it is operated on exclusively from within INPUT_STREAM. Recall that INPUT_STREAM came about because of a structure clash identified during control structuring (Section 2.5.1). In this case, the control structure dictated the object structure.

4.2.4 Packaging in the Elevator Example

Objects in the elevator problem were discussed in Section 4.1.2. Figure 4-3 is a buhrgraph of the elevator program operating on the packages, MOTOR and REQUESTS. The MOTOR package hides the physical interface to the elevator motor and provides the operation subprograms SET_UP, SET_DOWN, START, and STOP, which control the elevator motor as discussed in Chapter 2. MOTOR is a simple package that converts abstract software operations into concrete hardware commands. Its usefulness appears when the physical interface to the elevator motor is changed. Such a change is localized to the body of the MOTOR package, which contains all affected subprograms.

The package REQUESTS models the set of outstanding requests. It hides a data structure and the hardware interface through which new requests are captured. It provides the following set of operation subprograms:

CONTINUE_UP(F)	Is it necessary to go above floor F?
CONTINUE_DOWN(F)	Is it necessary to go below floor F?
VISIT(F,D)	Is there any request at floor F, direction D?

CONTINUE_UP and CONTINUE_DOWN are clearly special-purpose operations tailored to the exact needs of the elevator program. Each subprogram corresponds to a complex query the elevator program must make in order to proceed. Thus REQUESTS is modeled on the set of requests from the point of view of the elevator.

In the solution shown in Figure 4-3, REQUESTS is based on a more straightforward, lower-level model of the set of requests, called REQUEST_DB. REQUEST_DB has two Boolean operation subprograms, E_REQUEST(F) and F_REQUEST(F,D), which answer the questions: "Is an elevator request for floor F outstanding?" and "Is a floor request for floor F, direction D outstanding?", respectively. In turn, CONTINUE_UP and CONTINUE_DOWN call E_REQUEST and F_REQUEST. If REQUEST_DB is used only by REQUESTS, it may be hidden in the body of REQUESTS in the Chinese-box fashion. The solution in Figure 4-3 is simplified. The complete elevator program discussed in Chapter 8 is based on concurrent tasks representing multiple elevators traveling in parallel shafts. It also takes into account the capturing of new requests.

4.3 ABSTRACT DATA TYPES AND OBJECT-BASED SOFTWARE

Whereas an information-hiding module represents a single, static object, the declaration of an *abstract data type (adt)* allows us to model more than one object of the same general description, and to create and destroy objects dynamically during execution. To do this, we define a data structure (often a record) that represents the object and make it a *type* so that it can be *instantiated*. The type is called an *abstract data type (adt)*. Any number of individual objects can be created by instantiation of the type. An instance can be manipulated only by means of a set of well-defined operations.

When working with abstract data types we separate the type name and the operations, on the one hand, from the representation of the abstract data type and the implementation of the operation subprograms, on the other. The specification of the *abstract-data-type (adt) module* contains the name of the abstract type and a set of suitable operations on parameters of the abstract data type. Representation of the type and implementation of the operation subprograms is kept secret. Thus client modules can create multiple instances of the type, organize them in arrays or other data structures, and use them as the basis for other types. At the same time, the client modules cannot rely on any knowledge of the *internal* representation. This means that the internal representation may be changed without affecting the logic of the client modules. It also means that the data structures are protected against unintended manipulation by client modules.

Abstract data types support modeling in the same sense as information-hiding modules. Thus the designer of a client module is permitted to make certain assumptions about the instances of the abstract data type, A, and if these assumptions could also be made about some class, C, of objects in the reality we will say that A models C. Like an information-hiding package, an abstract data type may model a class of objects by hiding either a physical interface or a data structure. Sometimes the type is tailor-made for a particular application. Later we will use an adt SPACE_TYPE as a data model of a class of secondary storage devices (Section 4.4) and an adt WINDOW_TYPE whose instantiations represent the windows on a VDU screen (Chapter 5). WINDOW_TYPE hides both the physical interface to the windows and data about them.

At other times, the abstract type is a natural generalization of the built-in type set. For example, if a program must manipulate complex numbers, we may define a COMPLEX type and declare constants and objects of that type. Since a complex number consists of a real and an imaginary part, each of which is a floating-point number, the type COMPLEX may be a record with two fields, REAL and IMAGINARY. The type COMPLEX is declared in the adt module together with such functions as "+" and "∗" operating on COMPLEX objects.

A client program may include declarations of COMPLEX objects and statements with complex numbers as follows:

```
A, B, C, D: COMPLEX;
A := B + C ∗ D;
```

The client programs are unaffected if the internal representation of a complex number is changed. For example, COMPLEX can be defined as a record with the fields RADIUS_VECTOR and POLAR_ANGLE rather than the fields REAL and IMAGINARY.

The Ada syntax allows us to create an *adt package* such as COMPLEX_PAC, where type names and operations appear overtly in the specification while the internal representation of the type is placed in a private portion. As with information-hiding packages, the implementations of the operation subprograms are in the package body. Client programs *with* COMPLEX_PAC and may utilize the **use** clause to make direct references to COMPLEX and the operations "+" and "∗" as shown above. We will return to the Ada syntax for abstract data types in Section 4.3.2.

4.3.1 Software Construction
by Data Abstraction

As we have seen, an instance of an abstract data type often hides a data structure, which may be nontrivial. Each operation defined for the type may then perform a complex manipulation of that structure and be implemented as a multitude of operations on individual data items. The abstract data type allows us to abstract away the details of the data structure and think of it as one whole object. This is referred to a *data abstraction*. Like the procedural abstraction discussed in Section 3.3, this reduces the amount of detail the client module must deal with.

Earlier software development methods such as structured design have sought to separate concerns by splitting a program into functional modules implemented primarily as subprograms. Data abstraction allows us to separate overall program algorithms from implementation details by raising the complexity level of the data objects. Where a traditional program operates on individual instances of built-in types by means of built-in operations, a program utilizing abstract data types operates on instances of these with fewer and more powerful operations. We can refer to the operations on built-in types as *micro-operations* and those on an abstract data type as *macro-operations*. The set of such macro-operations and any protocol governing their use is the *interface specification* of the abstract data type.

Like procedural abstraction, data abstraction can be backed up by formal specifications. Such specifications include *pre-* and *postconditions* governing each operation, and *invariants* (or *axioms*), which are universal assumptions that a client program may make about an abstract object. An invariant holds throughout the program except in *critical sections*, where the object is changed. The critical sections are hidden inside the operation subprograms. As with procedural abstraction, the specification serves as a contract between maker and user of the information-hiding or adt module. The client programmer must rely on the specification and may not assume anything further about the way the abstract object has been implemented. The maker is bound by the specification of the interface to the client, but may implement the abstract type in any suitable way as long as the specification is met. (An information-hiding package can be regarded as a single instantiation of an anonymous abstract data type.)

Software construction with abstract data types is sometimes referred to as *object-based*. *Object-oriented* software construction relies on *classes*, *inheritance*, *polymorphism* and *dynamic binding*. The reader is referred to the object-oriented literature for a definition of these facilities, which are supported by *object-oriented languages*, such as SIMULA [Dahl], CLU [Liskov], Smalltalk [Goldberg], C++ [Stroustrup 91], and EIFFEL [Meyer]. The facilities are not readily available in Ada, which is instead referred to as an *object-based* language. With the package construct and the syntactical provisions for abstract data types, Ada supports the modeling of real-world objects in software quite nicely.

The term *abstract data type* is a misnomer, and *user-defined* or *programmer-defined type* captures the idea better. As Stroustrup points out, a user-defined type is no more abstract than a built-in type [Stroustrup 88]. We will continue to use the widely accepted term *abstract data type* and the abbreviation *adt* when referring to a type whose representation is hidden. Of course, Ada also allows the user to declare other, user-defined types in ordinary type declarations.

4.3.2 Object-Based Software Construction in Ada

Ada provides for abstract data types by means of a syntactical feature that allows us to make the name of a type public but keep its definition hidden. The specification of an adt package contains a *public* and a *private* part. In the public part, an abstract data type is declared only as **private** or **limited private**. This private-type declaration appears where the ordinary type declaration would normally be. The public part also includes operation subprogram specifications and the declarations of *deferred constants*. The complete type and constant declarations appear in the private part of the specification. The following subsections discuss the syntax in more detail and make a distinction between private and limited private types.

4.3.2.1 *Private types*

The specification of an adt package P for an abstract data type T is schematically as follows:

```
package P is
    type T is private;
    .....           --
private
    .....
    type T is... --
    .....          --
end P;
```

The public part belongs to the interface of the package, while the private part belongs to the secret. For technical reasons, it appears in the specification rather than the package body.

As an example of an abstract data type and an adt package, assume that in some problem it is necessary to deal with exact integers greater than the maximum, built-in integer. The data representation of such integers, which may rely on arrays or linked lists of digits, is irrelevant to an application program. Instead, the application program needs to be able to declare and operate on variables and constants of an abstract data type, LONG_INT.

The adt package LONG in Figure 4-4 provides an abstract data type, LONG_INT, that accommodates integers of up to MAX digits. The public part of the

```
package LONG is
   type LONG_INT is private;
   ZERO: constant LONG_INT;
   OVERFLOW: exception;
   function "+" (X,Y: LONG_INT) return LONG_INT;
   procedure GET(X: out LONG_INT);
   procedure PUT(X: LONG_INT);
private
   MAX: constant INTEGER:=8;
   subtype DGT is INTEGER range 0..9;
   type LONG_INT is array (1..MAX) of DGT;
   ZERO: constant LONG_INT:=(others => 0);
end LONG;

   with TEXT_IO; use TEXT_IO;
package body LONG is
package IIO is new INTEGER_IO(INTEGER); use IIO;
   function "+" (X,Y: LONG_INT) return LONG_INT is
   Z: LONG_INT:= ZERO;
   Z1: INTEGER;
   begin
      for I in reverse 2..MAX loop
         Z(I-1):=(X(I)+Y(I)+Z(I))/10;
         Z(I):=(X(I)+Y(I)+Z(I)) mod 10;
      end loop;
      Z1:=Z(1)+X(1)+Y(1);
      if Z1>9 then raise OVERFLOW; end if;
      Z(1):=Z1;
      return Z;
   end "+";
   procedure GET(X: out LONG_INT) is
   C: CHARACTER;
   I: INTEGER range 0..MAX:=0;
   T: LONG_INT:=ZERO;
   begin
      GET(C);
      while I<MAX and C in '0'..'9' loop
         I:=I+1;
         T(I):=CHARACTER'POS(C) - CHARACTER'POS('0');
         GET(C);
      end loop;
      if C in '0'..'9' then raise OVERFLOW; end if;
```

Figure 4-4 Adt package LONG with the **private** type LONG_INT. LONG_INT represents an exact integer of MAX digits. The function "+", the procedures GET and PUT, and the constant ZERO are defined for instances of LONG_INT. A client program PVT *withs* LONG_INT.

```
        for J in 0..I−1 loop
            X(MAX−J):=T(I−J);
        end loop;
        for J in 1..MAX−I loop
            X(J):=0;
        end loop;
    end GET;
    procedure PUT(X: LONG_INT) is
    I: INTEGER range 1..MAX:= 1;
    begin
        while X(I) = 0 and I < MAX loop
            PUT(' ');
            I:=I+1;
        end loop;
        for J in I..MAX loop
            PUT(X(J),1);
        end loop;
    end PUT;
end LONG;

    with TEXT_IO; use TEXT_IO;
    with LONG; use LONG;
procedure PVT is
A, B, C: LONG_INT:=ZERO;
begin
    loop
        begin
            PUT("Enter number:  ");
            GET(A); SKIP_LINE;
            PUT("Enter number:  ");
            GET(B); SKIP_LINE;
            C:=A+B;
            PUT("SUM:  ");
            if B=ZERO then PUT(A); else PUT(A+B); end if;
            NEW_LINE;
            PUT("SUM:  "); PUT(C);
        exception
            when OVERFLOW=>SKIP_LINE; PUT_LINE("Overflow  ");
        end;
    end loop;
end PVT;
```

Figure 4-4 (*continued*)

package specification includes a type specification, LONG_INT; a number of operations ("+", GET, and PUT); a deferred constant, ZERO; and an exception. The operations all have parameters of type LONG_INT. The operation "+" has been *overloaded* on the built-in addition operator (+).

The actual type declaration is placed in the private part of the specification together with other declarations on which it relies. Note that the declaration of the constant ZERO is split in a public and a private portion just as the declaration of the type LONG_INT.

With this package specification, a client module may operate on objects of type LONG_INT by means of the subprograms declared in the public part. In addition, the objects may be tested for equality and inequality and appear in assignment statements. In Figure 4-4, the procedure PVT *withs* the package LONG and includes the declarations of various LONG_INT variables:

    A, B, C: LONG_INT;

The procedure body contains explicit calls to operation subprograms, such as GET(A) and PUT(C), and expressions based on LONG_INT objects, such as A + B. This expression is an implied call to the operation procedure "+". The procedure body PVT also includes statements where these variables are assigned values, and conditions where they are tested for equality. These statements do not imply calls to the operation subprograms. Instead, Ada allows instances of private types to be assigned values and tested for equality and inequality.

4.3.2.2 Limited private types

In addition to private types, Ada also allows types to be designated as **limited private**. Except for the word **limited**, the declaration is the same as for a **private** type, and the complete type declaration appears in the private part of the package specification. A limited private type is more restrictive than a private one and client modules may operate on objects of the limited private type only by means of the explicitly declared operation subprograms. Objects of a limited private type may not be tested for equality or inequality unless the operator "=" is overloaded by an operation subprogram in the specification. They may not appear in assignment statements.

Figure 4-5 shows the specification of a package LONG2, where LONG_INT is declared **limited private**, and a client procedure *withing* LONG2. The public part of the specification contains the additional operations ASSIGN and "=". The implementation of ASSIGN and "=" are in the body of the package LONG2. Inside the body, variables of type LONG_INT are not treated as **limited private**, and the implementation of ASSIGN is very simple:

```
procedure ASSIGN(X: out LONG_INT; Z: LONG_INT) is
begin
   X:=Z;
end ASSIGN;
```

Unfortunately, "=" cannot be implemented in the same convenient manner, since the expression X = Y appearing inside the body of the function "=" would be a

```
package LONG2 is
   type LONG_INT is limited private;
   ZERO: constant LONG_INT;
   OVERFLOW: exception;
   procedure ASSIGN(X: out LONG_INT; Z: LONG_INT);
   function "+"(X,Y: LONG_INT) return LONG_INT;
   procedure GET(X: out LONG_INT);
   procedure PUT(X: LONG_INT);
   function "="(X,Y: LONG_INT) return BOOLEAN;
private
   MAX: constant INTEGER:=8;
   subtype DGT is INTEGER range 0..9;
   type LONG_INT is array (1..MAX) of DGT;
   ZERO: constant LONG_INT:=(others => 0);
end LONG2;


   with LONG2; use LONG2;
   with TEXT_IO; use TEXT_IO;
procedure LPVT is
package IIO is new INTEGER_IO(INTEGER); use IIO;
A, B, C: LONG_INT;
begin
   ASSIGN(C, ZERO);
   loop
      begin
         PUT_LINE("Enter number followed by nondigit");
         GET(A); SKIP_LINE;
         PUT_LINE("Enter number followed by nondigit");
         GET(B); SKIP_LINE;
         PUT("SUM: ");
         if A = ZERO then PUT(B);
         else ASSIGN(C, A+B); PUT(C); NEW_LINE; PUT(A+B);
         end if;
      exception
         when OVERFLOW=> NEW_LINE; PUT_LINE("Overflow "); SKIP_LINE;
      end;
   end loop;
end LPVT;
```

Figure 4-5   The specification of an adt package LONG2 with LONG_INT declared
as a **limited private** type, and a client program, LPVT. The body of LONG2 is not
shown.

recursive call and cause an infinite loop. One way to avoid this is to rely explicitly
on the internal representation of a LONG_INT object as an array of digits, and
implement the function "=" as follows:

```
function "=" (X, Y: LONG_INT) return BOOLEAN is
begin
    for I in X'RANGE loop
        if X(I)/=Y(I) then
            return FALSE;
        end if;
    end loop;
    return TRUE;
end "=";
```

In the procedure LPVT *withing* LONG2, the assignment statements appearing in PVT have been replaced by explicit calls to the ASSIGN operation subprogram:

ASSIGN (C, A+B);

This statement assigns the sum of A and B to C. Furthermore, the expression A+B now implies a call to the overloaded equals operation declared in LONG2. (The operator ''/='' is automatically declared with ''=''.)

While **limited private** types provide more complete information hiding than do private types, it is awkward to make a type such as LONG_INT **limited private** since that makes the assignment statements look different for LONG_INT objects than for objects of built-in types such as INTEGER. A more suitable example of a limited private type is given in the following section.

4.3.2.3 Stack example

As another example of a **limited private** abstract data type, consider again the stack discussed in Chapter 3. In Figures 3-7 and 3-8, where a STACK is an information-hiding package, it is assumed that our problem needs exactly one stack. The package is a single, abstract object on which the user program may operate by means of the operations PUSH and POP. The storage area for the stacked integers is inside the package body.

Assume instead that we need (or may need, potentially) more than one stack in a given problem. It is then reasonable to define an abstract data type STACK_TYPE thay may be instantiated as necessary. Figure 4-6 shows this implementation. The type STACK_TYPE is declared in the specification of a package STACKS (a library unit). Like the information-hiding package STACK discussed earlier, the specification of STACKS also includes the subprograms PUSH and POP. Here PUSH and POP each has a parameter of STACK_TYPE that identifies a specific stack object.

Unlike the package STACK in Chapter 3, the package body STACKS in Figure 4-6 contains no data declarations. Instead, the subprograms operate on parameters only; the actual stack object is passed as a parameter together with the integer

```
package STACKS is
   type STACK_TYPE is limited private;
   procedure PUSH(S: in out STACK_TYPE; X: INTEGER);
   procedure POP(S: in out STACK_TYPE; X: out INTEGER);
private
   type I_ARRAY is array (1..100) of INTEGER;
   type STACK_TYPE is record
      ST: I_ARRAY;
      TOP: INTEGER range 0..I_ARRAY'LAST:=0;
   end record;
end STACKS;

package body STACKS is
   procedure PUSH(S: in out STACK_TYPE; X: INTEGER) is
   begin
      S.TOP:=S.TOP+1;
      S.ST(S.TOP):=X;
   end PUSH;

   procedure POP(S: in out STACK_TYPE; X: out INTEGER) is
   begin
      X:=S.ST(S.TOP);
      S.TOP:=S.TOP-1;
   end POP;
end STACKS;

   with STACKS; use STACKS;
   with TEXT_IO; use TEXT_IO;
procedure ST_4 is
package IIO is new INTEGER_IO(INTEGER); use IIO;
FREE_KEYS, USED_KEYS: STACK_TYPE;  -- Stack objects
type A_T is array (1..3) of STACK_TYPE; -- Array of stacks
A: A_T;
Y, Z: INTEGER:=1;
begin
   PUSH(A(1), 3); POP(A(1), Y); PUT(Y);
   PUSH(FREE_KEYS, 7);
   POP(FREE_KEYS, Y); PUT(Y);
   for I in 101..200 loop PUSH(FREE_KEYS, I); end loop;
   for I in 1..100 loop
      POP(FREE_KEYS, Y); PUSH(USED_KEYS, Y);
   end loop;
   for I in 1..100 loop
      POP(USED_KEYS, Z); PUT(Z);
   end loop;
end ST_4;
```

Figure 4-6 Adt package with the **limited private** type STACK_TYPE and a client program, ST_4.

that is to be pushed or popped. Thus, while the information-hiding package STACK discussed earlier actually represents the stack and any data stacked in it at each point in time, the adt package STACKS is only a template defining a type and the operations on objects of that type. The objects themselves are declared in the client program.

The need to pass the stack object as a parameter has a technical consequence: While POP is a function in the information-hiding package STACK in Figures 3-7 and 3-8, it must be a procedure in STACKS in Figure 4-6. This is because the STACK_TYPE parameter S is an **in out** parameter. Note also that STACK has been declared **limited private** since there is no reasonable need to operate on STACK_TYPE objects with anything but the explicitly declared operations. No explicit "=" and assignment operations are included, since we do not expect a client program to need them.

Like the package STACK discussed in Chapter 3, STACKS provides client programs with an interface that is independent of the actual implementation of the stack data type. In Figure 4-7, the private part of the specification of STACKS and

```
package STACKS is
    type STACK_TYPE is limited private;
    procedure PUSH(S: in out STACK_TYPE; X: INTEGER);
    procedure POP(S: in out STACK_TYPE; X: out INTEGER);
private
    type STACKABLE;
    type STACK_TYPE is access STACKABLE;
end STACKS;

package body STACKS is
    type STACKABLE is record
        VALUE: INTEGER;
        NEXT:  STACK_TYPE;
    end record;
    procedure PUSH(S: in out STACK_TYPE; X: INTEGER) is
    begin
        S:=new STACKABLE'(X, S);
    end PUSH;
    procedure POP(S: in out STACK_TYPE; X: out INTEGER) is
    L: STACK_TYPE;
    begin
        L:=S;
        S:=S.NEXT;
        X:=L.VALUE;
    end POP;
end STACKS;
```

Figure 4-7 Adt package STACKS with the type STACK_TYPE implemented as a linked list. The change from the earlier implementation (Figure 4-6) requires a change of the private part of the specification.

the body of the package have been changed so that the stack type is implemented not by means of an array but as a linked list. A client program declaring and using STACK_TYPE objects is unaffected by the change of representation. (Re-linking is necessary when the package specification has been changed, however.) In the private part, STACK_TYPE is now declared as an access type, pointing to objects of type STACKABLE. Note that the full record declaration of STACKABLE has been placed in the package body. With this arrangement, the layout of the record may be changed without affecting the specification or the clients.

4.4 ADT PACKAGES AND INFORMATION-HIDING PACKAGES

The technical difference between an information-hiding package and an adt package is similar to that between an array declaration and an array type declaration: The declaration of a single array with certain characteristics is tantamount to the declaration of an anonymous array type followed by the declaration of one object of that type. A similar distinction exists between the declaration of a task and a task type in Ada, where again, the declaration of a single task can be seen as the declaration of an anonymous task type followed by one instantiation (Chapter 6). Similarly, an information-hiding package can always be thought of as an adt package followed by one instantiation. Nevertheless, there are frequent cases where the oneness of the object is important, and the introduction of a type would be counterintuitive. For that reason we continue to distinguish between information-hiding packages corresponding to single abstract objects, and adt packages. In this section we discuss the choice of information-hiding packages and abstract data types in various examples.

4.4.1 Hybrid Packages

Some Ada packages are both adt packages and information-hiding packages. Such a package defines abstract data types at the same time as it hides data or a physical interface in the body. For example, TEXT_IO exports the types FILE_TYPE and FILE_MODE, which are abstract types manipulated by several operation subprograms. TEXT_IO also interfaces to the hardware I/O devices and maintains internal data, such as the identity of the current default file. It is often reasonable for an information-hiding package to export such *interface types*. The database package discussed in Section 4.4.3 is another example.

In later chapters we will also see examples where an adt package not only serves as a template but also represents the set of all instantiations. This kind of hybrid package is particularly useful in environments with concurrent tasks where the set of instances must be protected from conflicting access by different tasks (Chapter 7).

4.4.2 Example:
Space Allocation Module

A space allocation module keeps track of free and occupied sections of some common area, such as a disk. A generic implementation of a space allocation module as an information-hiding package is shown in Figure 4-8. The maximum space size is the only generic parameter. The package has two operations, specified as follows:

procedure ALLOCATE(SIZE: INTEGER; ADDRESS: **out** INTEGER; GRANTED: **out** BOOLEAN);

procedure RELEASE(ADDRESS: INTEGER);

ALLOCATE allocates an area of a certain size and returns its starting address, while RELEASE deallocates an area starting at a given address.

```
generic
    MAX_SPACE: INTEGER;  -- Space size
package DISK_SPACE is
    procedure ALLOCATE(SIZE: INTEGER; ADDRESS: out INTEGER; GRANTED: out BOOLEAN);
    procedure RELEASE(ADDRESS: INTEGER);
    ALREADY_RELEASED: exception;
end DISK_SPACE;

package body DISK_SPACE is
type BITMAP is array (1..MAX_SPACE) of BOOLEAN;
ALLOCATED: BITMAP:=(others => FALSE);
type BLOCK;         -- Incomplete declaration of BLOCK
type BLOCK_PTR is access BLOCK; -- BLOCK_PTR declaration references BLOCK
type BLOCK is record
    ADDRESS: INTEGER;
    SIZE: INTEGER;
    NEXT: BLOCK_PTR;
end record;         -- Complete declaration of BLOCK
BLOCKS: BLOCK_PTR;
procedure ALLOCATE(SIZE: INTEGER; ADDRESS: out INTEGER; GRANTED: out BOOLEAN) is
I, J: INTEGER;
begin
    GRANTED:=FALSE;
    if SIZE = 0 then return; end if;
    I:=1; -- I is index of next bit to look at. I−1 bits have been looked at.
    loop
        while ALLOCATED'LAST − (I − 1) >= SIZE and then ALLOCATED(I) loop
            I:=I+1;
        end loop;
```

Figure 4-8   Generic space-allocation package DISK_SPACE.

```
      exit when ALLOCATED'LAST − (I − 1) < SIZE;
      J:=0; -- J is number of allocated bits.
      while J<SIZE and then not ALLOCATED(I+J) loop
         J:=J+1;
      end loop;
      if J=SIZE then
         GRANTED:=TRUE;
         ADDRESS:=I;
         BLOCKS:=new BLOCK'(I, SIZE, BLOCKS);
         for J in I..I+SIZE−1 loop
            ALLOCATED(J):=TRUE;
         end loop;
         exit;
      end if;
      I:=I+J;
   end loop;
end ALLOCATE;
procedure RELEASE(ADDRESS: INTEGER) is
P, Q: BLOCK_PTR:=BLOCKS;
begin
   while P/= null loop
      exit when P.ADDRESS = ADDRESS;
      Q:=P;
      P:=P.NEXT;
   end loop;
   if P=null then raise ALREADY_RELEASED; end if;
   for J in ADDRESS..ADDRESS+P.SIZE−1 loop
      ALLOCATED(J):=FALSE;
   end loop;
   if BLOCKS=P then BLOCKS:=P.NEXT;
   else Q.NEXT:=P.NEXT;
   end if;
end RELEASE;

end DISK_SPACE;
```

Figure 4-8   (*continued*)

In this example, an information-hiding package and an adt package are both reasonable solutions depending on whether there are (or may be) more than one space resource that can be allocated in the same way. This is the case if there are multiple disk drives, particularly if the number of drives is variable.

If more than one space must be controlled, the generic information-hiding package is replaced by an adt package. This is illustrated in Figure 4-9. The package DISK_SPACES exports a discriminated, limited private type, SPACE_TYPE, where the discriminant is the maximum size of the allocatable space. (For a description of discriminated types, refer to an Ada primer.) In the client program,

```
package DISK_SPACES is
    type SPACE_TYPE(MAX_SPACE: POSITIVE) is limited private;
    procedure ALLOCATE(S: in out SPACE_TYPE; SIZE: INTEGER;
    ADDRESS: out INTEGER; GRANTED: out BOOLEAN);
    procedure RELEASE(S: in out SPACE_TYPE; ADDRESS: INTEGER);
    ALREADY_RELEASED: exception;
private
    type BITMAP is array (POSITIVE range <>) of BOOLEAN;
    type BLOCK;
    type BLOCK_PTR is access BLOCK;
    -- Complete declaration of BLOCK is in package body.
    type SPACE_TYPE(MAX_SPACE: POSITIVE) is record
        ALLOCATED: BITMAP(1..MAX_SPACE):=(others => FALSE);
        BLOCKS: BLOCK_PTR;
    end record;
end DISK_SPACES;
```

Figure 4-9   The specification of an adt package DISK_SPACES, including the discriminated, **limited private** type SPACE_TYPE and the operation procedures ALLOCATE and RELEASE. Each instance of SPACE_TYPE represents one contiguous, allocatable area, such as a disk. The discriminant MAX_SPACE defines the number of allocatable sections in each such area. The complete declaration of BLOCK, which is in the package body, is the same as in Figure 4-8.

an instance of SPACE_TYPE can be declared for each space resource, as needed. The discriminated type eliminates the need for a generic, since the instances of SPACE_TYPE may include the desired size as a parameter, as in the following examples:

```
DISK1: SPACE_TYPE(80);                              -- One space resource with
                                                       80 sections
type DISK_ARRAY is array (1..5) of SPACE_TYPE(100); -- A set of five disks with
                                                       100 sections each
D: DISK_ARRAY;
```

4.4.3 Hybrid Package in the Buoy Example

The buoy problem was introduced in Chapter 2 and is treated in detail in Chapter 8. The task REPORTER periodically broadcasts current wind, temperature, and location information. On request from a passing vessel, accumulated information from the past 24 hours is broadcast in a history transmission. REPORTER gets all its data from a package DATABASE. (Another task puts the data there; this is discussed in Chapter 8.)

Figure 4-10 shows the specification of the information-hiding package DATABASE. The types ELEMENT and REAL_ELT are primarily interface types. REAL_ELT contains the elements WIND, AIR, WATER, and LOC (for location) and is

```
            with CALENDAR; use CALENDAR;
         package DATABASE is
            type ITERATOR is limited private;
            type ELEMENT is (WIND, AIR, WATER, LOC, NONE);
            subtype REAL_ELT is ELEMENT range WIND..LOC;
            type ITEM is record
               ELEM: ELEMENT:=NONE;
               TIME_STAMP: TIME:=TIME_OF(1901,1,1);
               VALUE: INTEGER:=0;
               NO: INTEGER:=0;
            end record;
            function GET_CURRENT(E:ELEMENT) return ITEM;
            procedure PUT_VALUE(T:TIME;E:ELEMENT;V:INTEGER);
            procedure ITER24(ITER: out ITERATOR);
               -- Initialize iterator to return each item starting 24 hours ago.
            procedure GET_NEXT(ITER: in out ITERATOR; IT: out ITEM);
               -- Return next item, provided that iterator has been initialized.
            NO_ITERATOR: exception;    -- Iterator not initialized
         private
            type ITERA is record
               PTR: INTEGER;
            end record;
            type ITERATOR is access ITERA;
         end DATABASE;
```

Figure 4-10   Specification of the package DATABASE in the buoy problem.

used to identify the data records. ELEMENT includes the same enumeration literals plus an additional neutral element, NONE. A record with the element equal to NONE is used as an end-of-file marker in the interface. GET_CURRENT and PUT_VALUE are straightforward subprograms providing read and write access to the database. GET_CURRENT is used during the periodic broadcast of the most recent reading of each element, and PUT_VALUE is used to add a new reading for a certain element to the database.

   The **limited private** type ITERATOR and the two procedures ITER24 and GET_NEXT together represent an *iterator* operation which allows a user to obtain the data from the last 24 hours, one record at a time in chronological order. ITER24 finds the appropriate starting record and saves it in a field PTR in the ITERA record. GET_NEXT returns successive records beginning with the starting record and ending with the most current record. It keeps track of its progress by updating the PTR field. Figure 4-11 shows how the iterator is used in the body of the task REPORTER. After all relevant records have been delivered, GET_NEXT returns a record with ELEM = NONE. The limited private type ITERATOR is not modeled on an external object. Instead, it is an implementation facility that allows us to hide the iteration index from the client program. The body of DATABASE is not shown. The database itself must be implemented as a circular buffer that allows 24 hours' worth of records to be stored (see Chapter 8).

```
task body REPORTER is
IT: ITEM;
begin
   -- ....
   ITER24(ITER);
   GET_NEXT(ITER, IT);
   while IT.ELEM/=NONE loop
      SEND(IT);
      GET_NEXT(ITER, IT);
      -- ....
   end loop;
   -- ....
end REPORTER;
```

Figure 4-11 Outline of the control structure of REPORTER.

4.5 PRACTICAL ASPECTS OF PACKAGING

In addition to modeling, the breakdown of a program into packages raises other, more practical issues. A given problem can often be broken down in different ways, which are all justifiable. The breakdown is often a trade-off of different concerns. Some of these concerns are testing, maintenance, reuse, and configuration, which are discussed in this section. The separation of interface and secret makes packages a good basis for the division of labor during design and implementation. This aspect is discussed in Section 4.5.1. *Testing* is facilitated if each test module is self-contained, cohesive and well specified with minimal connections to other modules. This reduces the need to build extensive test harnesses or scaffolding to simulate the module's working environment.

Maintenance is facilitated if the software is designed for change. This can be achieved if likely future changes are contained in single modules. To identify such modules, ''an experienced software designer studies the system and identifies things that are likely to change. . . . One then designs a module . . . that 'hides' or 'makes a secret of' each of the aspects identified earlier'' [Parnas]. That way, things that may change independently are isolated in separate packages. Although this approach is general and often useful, it relies on the designer's ability to foresee future changes. With the approach taken in this book, we attempt to design for unforeseen changes by modeling the software on real-world objects. If the objects are central to the problem, the assumption is that they and their fundamental relations to each other will remain even after a change. Thus, even if the change cannot be limited to the body of a module, it will not upset the general structure of the software.

Software reuse is an issue that relies on well-defined interfaces. A module designed for reuse must have a clear interface and be loosely coupled and clearly specified so that it can be plugged into various systems. Reuse is supported by the library philosophy of Ada, since reusable packages are conveniently handled as library units. Device drivers, mentioned earlier as a typical example of information-hiding packages, also provide a time-honored example of reuse.

Software configuration is a related issue. Many a large software system is intended to be executed on different hardware constellations. (An operating system is a good example.) Such a system often comes as a set of basic modules, from which each particular configuration can be assembled. Moreover, each basic module is often parameterized, so that quantities such as the maximum number of users, the number of devices of a certain kind, and so on, can be specified at configuration time. Software configuration is conveniently based on packaging, and a package is a suitable unit to be included or excluded in a given version. Furthermore, the generics capability in Ada, which allows parameterization at compilation time, is usually based on packages as generic units.

4.5.1 Division of Labor in Software Development

As mentioned earlier, an interface specification may be seen as a *contract* between the user and the producer of the module. With the contract concept, the design and implementation of different packages can be treated as separate, self-contained efforts. Work assignments based on this can be identified during the total design process and carried out either in parallel with the total design effort (*co-projects*), or after the general design is complete.

An arrangement with work assignments based on contracts between suppliers and users of modules intuitively seems to make for efficient software development, especially if the amount of information that must be included in the contract is kept to a minimum. It is interesting to compare this with the situation in many traditional, functional software development organizations. There, the division of labor is often based on the *waterfall model*, where analysis, design, and implementation are distinct steps. Consequently, the development organization often has separate analysis, design, and implementation groups. The results of the analysis, which covers the entire system, is communicated from the analysis group to the designers, who in turn communicate the entire design to the implementation group. This makes the interface between the groups extremely information-rich and often error-prone.

The secret of a module may be thought of as the *trade secret* of its producer. If the contract requires a subprogram to deliver the square root of a number under certain preconditions, the client must assume that it is done correctly without knowing the algorithm. The idea of a trade secret is part of the contract metaphor, which applies to the relationship between the producer of a module and the clients. It is important not to make too much of this metaphor. It applies only to the knowledge that the producer and client encode in their respective modules. There are many reasons why people other than the maker of a module may know about its secret. The design of the secret may well have to be addressed in the total design, and the suppliers of client modules may be part of the design effort. For example, a particular, time-critical algorithm may be a crucial and difficult design issue. At the same time, it may be entirely localized to a single module, and the rest of the software may be independent of how it is implemented. The secret of such a module may thus be the topic of much general discussion. Furthermore, the secret of a module is not immune to inspection by superiors and fellow team members. Information hiding is not a licence to conceal shoddy programming practices, and making something a secret does not mean hiding it so that no one will ever find it.

4.5.2 Pragmatic Packaging

In Chapter 3 we saw that subprograms can often be used pragmatically. For example, a subprogram can be introduced to eliminate duplication of program text without further justification or analysis. Simple information-hiding packages can often be used in the same pragmatic manner in order to encapsulate a data structure or an interface to some external device. The STACK package is an example of this. It represents a data structure that is operated on exclusively by means of PUSH and POP and can thus easily be encapsulated in a package with a simple interface. Just as a subprogram, a pragmatic package must meet certain quality criteria and also be justified either by high fan-in or separation of concerns.

4.5.2.1 Traditional quality criteria for pragmatic packages

In the parlance of structured design, a suitably defined information-hiding module consisting of a hidden data structure and a set of public operation subprograms exhibits *informational cohesion*, which is considered a strong form of cohesion. Strong cohesion has to do with conceptual integrity: one module–one thought. Thus to be cohesive, a package should have an intuitive "personality," preferably related to the problem domain. We often express this by saying, for example, that package A "knows" about commands, while B "knows" the hardware interface to the elevator motor. This is an informal way of saying that the knowledge about commands has been encoded in A and so on. As any other subprogram, the individual operation subprograms of an information-hiding module must be functionally cohesive. The operation subprograms of an information-hiding package must be *loosely coupled* to the software outside the package and rely on parameters rather than direct references to global data. (Internally, context coupling obviously applies, since, by definition, the operation subprograms may access the internal data structure freely.)

4.5.2.2 Justification of pragmatic information-hiding packages

Just as an independent subprogram may be justified if it eliminates the duplication of program text, a pragmatic package may be justified if it has high fan-in. A package has high fan-in if the operation subprograms are frequently used in a given environment, or the package has true potential for reuse in other environments. As for subprograms, *separation of concerns* is a justification for an information-hiding package with fan-in = 1. This justification must be used with care. Unfortunately, just about any decomposition can be justified with a sweeping reference to separate concerns. For this reason we must make very clear what the different concerns are and why they should be separated. Packages introduced for separation of concerns must make the software demonstrably easier to understand or modify.

Like subprogram decomposition, pragmatic packaging poses a risk of fragmentation. Although almost any data structure can be encapsulated, trivial information-hiding packages where the data structure consists of a few single variables or an array are seldom helpful. Once a cohesive, information-hiding package has been defined, it is often counterproductive to decompose it further into smaller packages. The line between pragmatic packages and modeling packages is sometimes fuzzy. For example, a certain problem environment may explicitly require the use of stacks, and in such an environment, the STACK package becomes a modeling package. In any case, if a certain package models an entity in the problem environment, that is an additional justification for its existence.

4.6 CHAPTER SUMMARY

> An object in possession seldom retains the
> same charm it has in pursuit.
> (Nihil aeque gratum est adeptis, quam
> concupiscentibus.)
>
> *Pliny the Younger*

The packaging feature of Ada allows two types of modeling of objects in the reality. A *single, static object* can be modeled by means of an *information-hiding package*, and a *set of similar objects* can be modeled by means of *abstract data type*. The type is defined in an *adt package*, and individual objects are modeled by instantiation of the type. Such instances may be created during execution.

Both information-hiding modules and abstract data types have *secrets* and *interfaces*. The interface is the assumptions that a client may make about the module or the type. If M is a module or an instance of an abstract data type, M is a *model* of an object O in the problem environment if the assumptions that can be made about M could also be made about O.

An information-hiding module or an abstract data type may model an object by hiding its physical interface or by containing a data model representing the object (*data abstraction*). An abstract data type may be a natural extension of the built-in set of types or may be tailor made for a particular application.

The Ada package syntax supports information-hiding and abstract data types, which are implemented by means of private and limited private types. In addition to modeling, packaging is important for such concerns as maintenance, reuse, and configuration. It is also useful in software development, where the idea of the interface as a contract can be used to create separate, self-contained work assignments. Packages play an important role in concurrent programs. The discussion of packages and objects continues in Chapters 7 through 9 based on the introduction of tasks in Chapter 6.

REFERENCES

BLACK, U., *OSI: A Model for Computer Communications Standards*, Prentice Hall, Englewood Cliffs, N.J., 1991.

BOOCH, G., *Object Oriented Design with Applications*, Benjamin-Cummings, Menlo Park, Calif., 1991.

BUHR, R. J. A., *Software Design with Ada*, Prentice Hall, Englewood Cliffs, N.J., 1984.

BUHR, R. J. A., KARAM, G. M., HAYES, C. J., and WOODSIDE, C. M., Software CAD: a revolutionary approach, *IEEE Trans. Software Eng.*, 15:3, March 1989, pp. 235–249.

BUHR, R. J. A., *Practical Visual Techniques in Systems Design with Applications to Ada*, Prentice Hall, Englewood Cliffs, N.J., 1990.

COAD, P., and YOURDON, E., *Object-Oriented Analysis*, Yourdon Press, Englewood Cliffs, N.J., 1990.

COX, B. J., *Object Oriented Programming: An Evolutionary Approach*, Addison-Wesley, Reading, Mass., 1986.

DAHL, O. J., and NYGAARD, K. S., SIMULA: an ALGOL-based simulation language, *Commun. ACM*, 9:9, September 1966, pp. 671–678.

GOLDBERG, A., and ROBSON, D., *Smalltalk-80: The Language and Its Implementation*, Addison-Wesley, Reading, Mass., 1983.

KOFFMAN, E. B., *Problem Solving and Structured Programming in Pascal*, 2nd ed., Addison-Wesley, Reading, Mass., 1985.

LISKOV, B., and GUTTAG, J., *Abstraction and Specification in Program Development*, MIT Press, Cambridge, Mass., 1986.

MEYER, B., *Object-Oriented Software Construction*, Prentice Hall, Englewood Cliffs, N.J., 1988.

PARNAS, D. L., Software engineering principles, *INFOR Can. J. Oper. Res. Inf. Process.*, 22:4, November 1984, pp. 303–316.

RUMBAUGH, J., BLAHA, M., PREMERLANI, W., EDDY, F., and LORENSEN, W., *Object-Oriented Modeling and Design*, Prentice Hall, Englewood Cliffs, N.J., 1991

SMITH, M., and TOCKEY, S., *An Integrated Approach to Software Requirements Definition Using Objects*, Boeing Commercial Airplane Support Division, Seattle, Wash., 1988.

STROUSTRUP, B., *The C++ Programming Language*, 2nd ed., Addison-Wesley, Reading, Mass., 1991.

STROUSTRUP, B., What is object-oriented programming? *IEEE Software*, May 1988, pp. 10–20.

EXERCISES

4.1 Polynomial[3]

A *polynomial* in a single variable, X, may be represented as a linked list where each node contains the coefficient and exponent of a term of the polynomial. For example, the polynomial

$$4*X**5 + X**2 - 5*X + 2$$

would be represented as the following linked list with the terms in decreasing order of the exponent. (The constant 2 is equivalent to $2*X**0$.)

Write a package POL_PAK including the type TERM, the **private** type POLYNOMIAL and the operation subprograms INSERT, "*", and an iterator that returns one term of the polynomial at a time. TERM is a record with a coefficient and an exponent. POLYNOMIAL is the representation of the polynomial as a linked list as described above. There is at most one term for each exponent and the terms are sorted according to the exponent. Any terms with a zero coefficient is eliminated. The procedure INSERT takes a polynomial as an **in out** parameter and a term as an **in** parameter, and inserts the term at its proper place in the polynomial. "*" takes two polynomials as **in** parameters and returns their product as another polynomial. "*" is overloaded on the multiplication operator. Examples:

Poly 1:	X + 1
Poly 2:	−X + 1
Product:	−X**2 + 1

Poly 1:	3*X**2 + 1
Poly 2:	2*X
Product:	6*X**3 + 2*X

Poly 1:	4*X**5 + X**2 − 5*X + 2
Poly 2:	X**2 + X**−1
Product:	4*X**7 + 5*X**4 − 5*X**3 + 2*X**2 + X − 5 + 2*X**−1

The iterator consists of two subprograms, GET_FIRST and GET_NEXT. Each takes a polynomial as an **in** parameter and returns a term. GET_FIRST returns the first term of the polynomial. GET_NEXT returns each of the following terms, one at a time. A term with a zero coefficient is returned when the polynomial has been exhausted.

The main procedure contains a loop where it reads two polynomials and prints them and their product.

Input. Each polynomial is input from the keyboard as a set of terms, and each term as a pair of integers:

---

[3] This exercise is adapted from [Koffman].

coefficient exponent

The terms of a polynomial may be entered in any order, and multiple terms with the same exponent are accepted. A zero coefficient may be used to mark the end of a polynomial. An instance of POLYNOMIAL is created for each input polynomial.

Processing. The product of each pair of polynomials is calculated. The result is an instance of POLYNOMIAL.

Output. Each pair of polynomials and their product are printed. Each polynomial is printed on a separate line in a format similar to the example above. The main program obtains each term of each polynomial by calls to GET_FIRST and GET_NEXT, and formats it appropriately.

4.2 Generic LONG_INT

Make the package LONG in Section 4.3 generic and dependent on a generic parameter defining the maximum number of digits in a long integer.

4.3 Information-hiding and adt packages

In a simplified version of the elevator example, an information-hiding package, REQUESTS, is given that represents a set of requests for elevator service. The requests from floor buttons and elevator buttons are stored in the arrays F_REQUESTS and E_REQUESTS, respectively. Four operation subprograms are included:

E_REQ, to register a new request from an elevator button

F_REQ, to register a new request from a floor button

UP_VISIT, which returns a BOOLEAN indicating whether a certain floor must be visited on the way up

DN_VISIT, which returns a BOOLEAN indicating whether a certain floor must be visited on the way down.

Note that UP_VISIT and DN_VISIT also mark requests for service as served. The bodies of E_REQ and F_REQ are not provided. The package exists within a unit where the types DIR and FLOOR are defined.

```
package REQUESTS is
   procedure E_REQ(F: FLOOR);
   procedure F_REQ(F: FLOOR; D: DIR);
   function UP_VISIT(F: FLOOR) return BOOLEAN;
   function DN_VISIT(F: FLOOR) return BOOLEAN;
end REQUESTS;

package body REQUESTS is
E_REQUESTS: array (FLOOR) of BOOLEAN:=(others=>FALSE);
F_REQUESTS: array (FLOOR, DIR) of BOOLEAN:=(others=>(others=>FALSE));
```

```
procedure E_REQ(F: FLOOR) is .....

procedure F_REQ(F: FLOOR; D: DIR) is .....

function UP_VISIT(F: FLOOR) return BOOLEAN is
begin
   if E_REQUESTS(F) then
      E_REQUESTS(F):=FALSE; return TRUE;
   elsif F_REQUESTS(F, UP) then
      F_REQUESTS(F, UP):=FALSE; return TRUE;
   else return FALSE;
   end if;
end;

function DN_VISIT(F: FLOOR) return BOOLEAN is
begin
   if E_REQUESTS(F) then
      E_REQUESTS(F):=FALSE; return TRUE;
   elsif F_REQUESTS(F, DOWN) then
      F_REQUESTS(F, DOWN):=FALSE; return TRUE;
   else return FALSE;
   end if;
end;
end;
```

Now assume that there are several different sets of requests, served by different elevators. Each set includes floor requests and elevator requests. Convert the package REQUESTS into an *adt package*, with a limited private type REQ_SET representing such a set of requests. Include a private part in the specification and make any other changes that are necessary in the given program text so each operation works on an instance of REQ_SET supplied as a parameter. You need not supply the bodies of the procedures F_REQ and E_REQ.

PROJECT: CRAZY EIGHTS

Crazy Eights is a popular, simple card game. The purpose of this project is to produce a software product that will play a reasonably good game of Crazy Eights against one human component. The product is not an example of embedded software or systems software, but it illustrates object-based software construction and the handling of behavior patterns.

The Crazy Eights game involves a standard 52-card deck of playing cards. The cards are shuffled, and each player is dealt seven cards. The next card on top of the deck is placed face up as the start of the *discard pile*. (If the card is an eight, it is reinserted into the draw pile and the next card in the deck is used.) The remaining cards are placed face down and constitute the *draw pile*. The computer player is the dealer, and the human player goes first. A turn must end with the player laying a card face up on the discard pile, according to the following rules:

1. If the current top of the discard pile is not an eight, the new card must match either the rank or the suit of the current top card.

2. If the current top of the discard pile is an eight, the new card must match the suit specified by the previous player.

3. An eight can be played regardless of the current top card. The player laying the eight may specify which suit must be played next.

If a player possesses no legal card according to these rules, he or she must draw cards from the draw pile, placing them in his or her hand, until a card can be discarded. A player wins upon discarding his or her last card. If the draw pile should become empty before the game has been won, the discard pile except the top card is reshuffled and becomes the new draw pile.

Software requirements. The software maintains all cards and is responsible for shuffling, dealing, and the establishment of a draw pile and a discard pile. When it is the human player's turn, the current top card of the discard pile is displayed as well as the current suit if it differs from the suit of the top card. The software also displays the human player's hand and prompts for a play or a draw. If the human player lays an eight, the computer also prompts for a new suit to be specified by the human player.

The actions of the *computer player* are simulated by the software. The computer player follows the same rules as the human player, and plays fairly. Just as the human player, the computer player may choose to draw even if it has a legal card to discard. You may make the simulated computer player as intelligent as you wish. The computer player must not have access to cards that are hidden to a human player (i.e., it can only see its own hand and the top card on the discard pile).

The computer also identifies and announces the situation when either player has won the game. The human player goes first. When the draw pile has been exhausted, the discard pile except the top card is reshuffled and becomes the draw pile, as described earlier. Display a message on the screen when this occurs.

User interface. The computer displays the human player's hand, the number of cards in the computer's hand, the top of the discard pile, and the current suit. It prompts the human player for an appropriate action. The input must be checked for legality: If the player specifies a card that is not in the human player's hand or wants to make an illegal discard, appropriate error messages must appear and the player must be allowed to try again. (The player is allowed to draw a card even if his or her hand contains a legal card to discard, however.)

Design

Behavior patterns. The rules of the game define a fairly obvious behavior pattern, with the players taking turns. Break down the pattern into two subprograms, HUMAN_TURN and COMPUTER_TURN. Base HUMAN_TURN on the interface with the human player via keyboard and screen. Base the control structure of COMPUTER_TURN on the algorithm followed by the computer player.

Objects. The *draw pile* and the *discard pile* are easily identifiable, single objects with operations such as discard, draw, and inspect-top-card. A combined object, piles, has the advantage that the reshuffling of the discard pile becomes part of its secret. A *player's hand* is a potential abstract data type with operations such as insert, search, and extract.

    Packages. Make a header package exporting the type CARD and any other suitable global types or constants. Make an information-hiding package PILES with the operations DRAW, DISCARD, INSPECT_TOP_CARD, and REINSERT. (REINSERT is used to stop the discard pile from starting on an eight, as mentioned above.) Hide the data structure representing the discard and draw piles in the body of PILES. Make an adt package HANDS with a private type HAND_TYPE and operations such as INSERT, FIND_SUIT, FIND_RANK, FIND_CARD, and REMOVE_CARD. All operations that HUMAN_TURN or COMPUTER_TURN need to carry out on the respective hand must be included as operation subprograms. A hand may be represented in various ways using one or more arrays or linked lists.

5 Finite Automata and Software

obedience,
Bane of all genius, virtue, freedom, truth,
Makes slaves of men, and of the human frame
A mechanized automaton.

Shelley, Queen Mab

5.1 INTRODUCTION

In the preceding chapters we have consistently regarded a program as a subject operating on objects. The subject is represented by the control structure in the main procedure and its independent subprograms, and controls the timing and ordering of events during execution. The objects are either single objects, implemented as information-hiding packages, or instances of abstract data types.

The subject is typically modeled on a data stream or a *behavior pattern* in the reality. In the VDU example, the main procedure is built on the structure of the character stream received by the video display unit. In the elevator example, it is based on the behavior of an elevator moving in a shaft and stopping at the floors of a building. These control structures are based on sequence diagrams describing the character stream and the elevator behavior. Sequence diagrams are usually regular expressions and describe behavior patterns without introducing explicit states or modes. Thus the subjects in the VDU and elevator programs rely on implicit mode representation. As mentioned in Chapter 2, it is also possible to use explicit mode representation by introducing a mode variable. Programs with explicit mode representation are modeled on transition diagrams.

The equivalence of explicit and implicit mode representation relies on a formal *automata theory*. A transition diagram shows a *finite automaton*, also known as a *finite state machine*. A finite automaton accepts a *string* of *input symbols* and may produce a string of *output symbols*. Each output symbol is produced as a result of a certain input symbol and/or the current *state* of the automaton, which may change as the automaton receives input.

A regular expression defines a set of strings directly in terms of sequences, iterations, and selections. A finite automaton does the same thing indirectly, by describing a hypothetical machine that accepts exactly a certain set of strings. Those strings that cause a given finite automaton to transition from its *initial* state to a certain state or group of states can always be described by a regular expression. Conversely, given a regular expression, we can always construct a finite automaton that reaches a given set of states on exactly those input strings described by the regular expression. This means that a transition diagram can be used to define a set of strings, and thus provides an alternative to a regular expression.

In this chapter we discuss the theory of finite automata and its application to software construction. When we implement a finite automaton in software, the inputs are sometimes actual input symbols, such as characters, but more often they will be the signals of *events* occurring in the reality. Thus instead of dealing with strings of symbols, we will be dealing with sequences of events occurring in the problem environment. In the elevator problem, for example, the inputs signal events such as "the elevator has reached floor F" or "the UP button on floor 3 is pressed." Similarly, the output often consists of *actions* taken by the program rather than symbols. Finally, since the set of possible states is often very large in realistic problems, it will often be convenient to deal with *sets of states* rather than individual states. A set of states is referred to as a *mode*.

Once the behavior of an entity in the reality has been captured in a transitions diagram we can model it as a software object, whether an information-hiding package or an instance of an abstract data type. Given a set of entities in a problem, the software designer has the choice of representing each of them as a subject or as an object. In a sequential program, only one entity can be modeled as a subject, but in a concurrent program this restriction is lifted and different subjects can coexist as concurrent tasks in one program. This is the topic of Chapters 6 through 9.

This chapter covers the basic notation for finite automata. A more elaborate notation based on finite automata is *Statecharts* [Harel 87, 90]. Statecharts allows a finite automaton to be decomposed into separate communicating processes. It also allows the hierarchical decomposition of transition diagrams into different levels of abstraction. Finite automata and Statecharts are widely used to capture dynamic behavior in software requirements analysis [Davis]. In the OMT approach to object-oriented analysis, a *dynamic model* based on Statecharts is used as a complement to an *object model*, reflecting the classification and association of objects [Rumbaugh].

5.2 AUTOMATA THEORY _____

In this section we formally define finite automata and discuss their properties based on the definitions. A finite automaton may be regarded as a black box accepting a string of input symbols. It can be categorized based on its output. The simplest kind of finite automaton is a *recognizer*. It produces one output only: a signal indicating that the string input so far has been *accepted*. It produces output exactly when an acceptable string has been received and does not differentiate between different, acceptable strings. It continues to consume input symbols after a string has been accepted and will signal acceptance again as soon as the total input represents an acceptable string.

A recognizer answers only the question, "Is the string S accepted?" and its practical usefulness is fairly limited. In software construction, we usually rely on *general finite automata*. A general finite automaton produces a string of output symbols as input symbols are entered. Nevertheless, recognizers are of theoretical interest and can be used to establish properties of general finite automata. For this reason we devote a section to recognizers. One important property is the equivalence of a recognizer and a regular expression. This is the property that allows us to choose rather freely between implicit and explicit mode representation in software.

To study a finite automaton further, we must open the black box and reveal its internal structure. Each finite automaton has a set of states, of which one is the *initial state*. At the outset the automaton is in the initial state. Each time an input symbol is received, it moves to a new (or the same) state, depending on the symbol. This is referred to as a *state transition*. A recognizer has a set of *final* states, and any input string that makes the recognizer move to one of those states is accepted.

General finite automata are classified according to how the output is produced. There are two types, *Moore machines*, which produce symbols as states are entered, and *Mealy machines*, which produce symbols on state transitions. In software construction we generally use Mealy machines, and the output will often be an *action* rather than a symbol. Moore machines are also useful in software, since it is often convenient to let the current state of the automaton be known outside the black box. This is tantamount to defining an output symbol for each state.

5.2.1 Example of a Finite Automaton: Goat–Wolf–Cabbage Problem

As an example of a finite automaton, consider the following problem. A man, a wolf, a goat, and a head of cabbage are on a river bank. The man must carry the wolf, the goat, and the cabbage over the river in a small boat with room for only one item at a time besides the man himself. Consequently, he must row back and forth over the river several times while leaving one or more items on either river bank. He can leave neither the goat and the cabbage, nor the wolf and the goat alone together, lest one devour the other.

In the transition diagram in Figure 5-1, each *state* is shown as an oval and represents a configuration of items on each shore. For example, the initial state, indicated by *Start*, represents the configuration *MWGC-0*, where the man (*M*), the wolf (*W*), the goat (*G*), and the cabbage (*C*) are on the first shore. The state is changed by the man crossing the river with or without an item in the boat, and thus each crossing is an *event* causing a state transition. We can also say that the man provides *input* by deciding whom to take in the boat. These *state transitions* are shown as arrows between states and are labeled *w*, *g*, and *c* if the wolf, the goat, or the cabbage, respectively, is in the boat together with the man, and *m* if the man crosses the river alone. (In this example, for each transition from a state *A* to a state *B* there is another transition from *B* to *A*. This is a property of this particular problem; it is not the case with all finite automata.)

We can use the finite automaton in Figure 5-1 as a *recognizer* by designating *0-MWGC* the only *final state* (marked with a double border). The transition diagram then defines all possible series of moves that lead from the initial to the final state. Only "safe" states, where the items on either shore will not eat each other, are relevant. If another state were entered, one of the items would be eaten and the final state could never be reached. The recognizer is concerned only with series of events leading to the final state.

We can also argue that the transition diagram in Figure 5-1 shows a *general* finite automaton. We then say that the output consists of symbols representing the different constellation of items on each shore. Thus, output is associated with states, which makes the automaton a Moore machine. Again, we do not show the result of movements leading to unsafe states. Rather than treating those events as errors, we regard them as *invalid* and exclude them from the diagram.

In theory, a finite automaton is in a certain state at each point in time. When an input symbol is received, it instantaneously changes states. In the goat–wolf–cabbage problem, this criterion is not quite met; each state transition involves the journey across the river, which takes a finite time. Nevertheless, the events are atomic in the sense that they cannot interrupt each other. In Section 5.2.2 we discuss recognizers and the equivalence of recognizers and regular expressions. In Section 5.2.3 we return to general finite automata.

5.2.2 Recognizers

A finite automaton can be *deterministic* or *nondeterministic*. In a deterministic recognizer, a symbol *x* accepted in a state *S* always causes a transition to a specific state, *T*. Figure 5-1 shows a deterministic automaton. In a *nondeterministic* recognizer, a symbol *x* accepted in a state *S* may cause different transitions, and the resulting state may be *T*, *U*, or *V*, say. In our software applications, we will

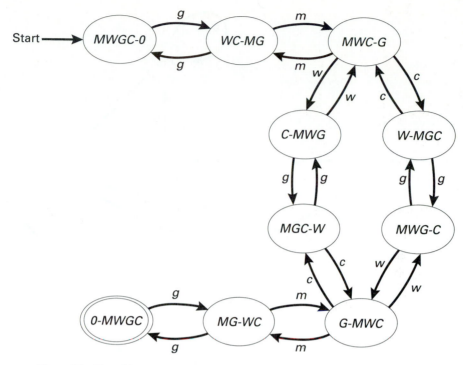

Figure 5-1   Transition diagram for the goat–wolf–cabbage problem. To see what happens, start at "*Start*" and follow the arrows through the different states. Each state represents a configuration of man (*M*), wolf (*W*), goat (*G*), and cabbage (*C*) on each shore. [From J. E. Hopcroft and J. D. Ullman, *Introduction to Automata Theory,* © 1979 by Addison-Wesley 1979. Reprinted with permission of the publisher.]

almost always use deterministic automata, but we will later see that nondeterministic automata are important in order to understand the equivalence of recognizers and regular expressions. Figure 5-2(a) shows a deterministic recognizer, and Figure 5-2(b) shows a nondeterministic recognizer.

5.2.2.1 Deterministic recognizers

Formally, a *deterministic recognizer* is a 5-tuple, (Q,Σ,δ,q_0,F), where

Q is the finite set of states.
Σ is the *input alphabet* (i.e., the set of input symbols).
q_0 is the *initial state*.
F (subset of Q) is the set of *final* (or *accepting*) *states*. (A string x is said to be accepted by a recognizer if the successive symbols in x make the recognizer move from q_0 to a final state.)

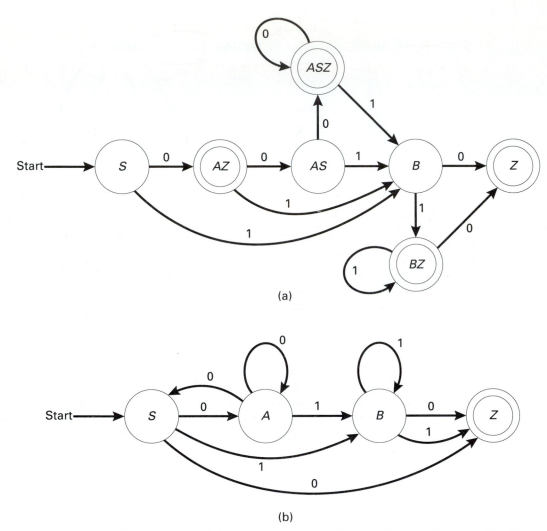

(a)

(b)

Figure 5-2 (a) Deterministic recognizer with the initial state S and the final states Z, AZ, BZ, and ASZ; (b) nondeterministic recognizer with the initial state S and the final state Z. The recognizers in (a) and (b) are equivalent.

δ is the *transition function* mapping $Q \times \Sigma$ onto Q; that is, $\delta(q,a)$ is a state for each state q and input symbol a. We sometimes define δ only for a subset of $Q \times \Sigma$. This is when certain input is *valid* only in certain states. (Another way to deal with this is to include in Q a non-final state *INVALID* and let all transitions that do not lead to meaningful states lead to *INVALID*.)

Figure 5-2(a) is a small formal example. Unlike the goat–wolf–cabbage problem, it does not have any intuitive interpretation. Formal definition:

Q is the set $\{S,AZ,AS,ASZ,B,BZ,Z\}$.

Σ is the set $\{0,1\}$.

$q_0 = S$.

F is the set $\{ASZ,AZ,BZ,Z\}$.

The transition function δ is defined by the diagram. The following is an equivalent definition:

$$\delta(S,0) = AZ$$

$$\delta(S,1) = B$$

$$\delta(AZ,0) = AS$$

$$\delta(AZ,1) = B$$

$$\delta(AS,0) = ASZ$$

$$\delta(AS,1) = B$$

$$\delta(ASZ,0) = ASZ$$

$$\delta(ASZ,1) = B$$

$$\delta(B,0) = Z$$

$$\delta(B,1) = BZ$$

$$\delta(BZ,0) = Z$$

$$\delta(BZ,1) = BZ$$

Some of the strings accepted by the recognizer in Figure 5-2 are

0

Any string of at least three zeros

Any number of zeros followed by 10

Any number of zeros followed by 11, 111, 1111, etc.

Any number of zeros followed by 110, 1110, 11110, etc.

If we treat the transition diagram in Figure 5-1 as a recognizer, the goat–wolf–cabbage problem can be defined as follows:

Q is the set of all the states *MWGC-0*, *WC-MG*, *MWC-G*, etc.

Σ is the set $\{m,g,c,w\}$. Each of these represents a movement of the man and the boat that causes a state transition.

q_0 is the initial state, *MWGC-0*.

F is a subset of Q containing only the state *0-MWGC*.

The function δ is described by the transition diagram itself. It is defined only for that subset of $Q \times \Sigma$ that corresponds to valid state–event combinations. For each pair (q,a), where q is the current state and a is either m, g, w, or c occurring in state q, δ defines the new state. Some examples of the value of $\delta(q,a)$ for different q and a are

$$\delta(MWGC\text{-}0,g) = WC\text{-}MG$$

$$\delta(WC\text{-}MG,g) = MWGC\text{-}0$$

$$\delta(WC\text{-}MG,m) = MWC\text{-}G$$

Seen as a recognizer, the transition diagram in Figure 5-1 defines those series of movements that lead from the initial state *MWGC-0* to the single final state *0-MWGC*. Exactly those strings that correspond to such a series of movements are accepted by the recognizer. Examples of such strings are *gmcgwmg*, *gmwgcmg*, *gmcgwcgwcgwmg*, and *gggmmmcccgggwwwmmmggg*. The latter strings represent inefficient, but valid ways for the man to accomplish his task.

5.2.2.2 Nondeterministic recognizers

As pointed out above, a *nondeterminstic* recognizer is one where an input symbol accepted in a certain state may cause transitions to different states. Thus the result of a certain input cannot be determined beforehand. Formally a *nondeterministic recognizer* is a 5-tuple, (Q,Σ,δ,q_0,F), where:

Q is the finite set of states.

Σ is the input alphabet. It may include a *null* symbol, representing no input.

q_0 is the initial state.

F (subset of Q) is the set of final states.

δ is the transition function mapping $Q \times \Sigma$ to 2^Q. The *power set*, 2^Q, is the set of all subsets of Q. This means that $\delta(q,a)$ is the set of states P such that there is a transition labeled a from q to some state in P. If there is no transition from q labeled a, then $\delta(q,a) = \{\ \}$, where $\{\ \}$ is the empty subset.

A string x, consisting of the series of symbols $x_1 x_2 x_3 \cdots x_n$, is accepted by a nondeterministic recognizer if there is a way to reach a final state by starting at q_0 and making exactly the transitions marked x_1, x_2, x_3, . . . , x_n, in that order. Figure 5-2(b) is an example of a nondeterministic recognizer, which is formally defined as follows:

Q is the set $\{S,A,B,Z\}$.

Σ is the set $\{0,1\}$.

q_0 is the state S.

F is the set $\{Z\}$, a set containing one single element.

2^Q is the set $\{\{\ \}, \{S\}, \{A\}, \{B\}, \{Z\}, \{S,A\}, \{S,B\}, \{S,Z\}, \{A,B\}, \{A,Z\}, \{B,Z\},$ $\{S,A,B\}, \{S,A,Z\}, \{S,B,Z\}, \{A,B,Z\}, \{S,A,B,Z\}\}$, where, for example, $\{S,A,B\}$ is the set consisting of the states S, A, and B.

δ is defined by the diagram in Fig. 5-2(b) and alternatively as follows:

$$\delta(S,0) = \{A,Z\}$$

$$\delta(S,1) = \{B\}$$

$$\delta(A,0) = \{S,A\}$$

$$\delta(A,1) = \{B\}$$

$$\delta(B,0) = \{Z\}$$

$$\delta(B,1) = \{B,Z\}$$

For example, $\delta(S,0)$ yields the set of all states that may be reached when 0 is accepted in state S, namely A and Z.

5.2.2.3 Nondeterministic recognizers with null-moves

Like the deterministic recognizers discussed earlier, the nondeterministic recognizer shown in Figure 5-2(b) makes a state transition only upon acceptance of an input symbol. A nondeterministic recognizer that makes state transitions without input is said to have *null-moves*. In that case the input alphabet contains a *null* symbol. An automaton with *null*-moves makes spontaneous state transitions. Figure 5-3(a) shows such an automaton, formally defined as follows:

Q is the set $\{S,A,B,Z\}$.

Σ is the set $\{0,1,null\}$.

q_0 is the state S.

F is the set $\{Z\}$.

The set 2^Q is the set of subsets $\{\{\ \}, \{S\}, \{A\}, \{B\}, \{Z\}, \{S,A\}, \{S,Z\}, \{S,B\},$ $\{A,B\}, \{A,Z\}, \{B,Z\}, \{S,A,B\}, \{A,B,Z\}, \{S,A,Z\}, \{S,B,Z\}, \{S,A,B,Z\}\}$.

The transition function δ is defined by the diagram in Fig. 5-3(a) or, equivalently, as follows:

$$\delta(S,0) = \{A\}$$

$$\delta(A,1) = \{B\}$$

$$\delta(A, null) = \{Z\}$$

$$\delta(B, 0) = \{A\}$$

$$\delta(q, a) = \{ \}\ \text{for all other } q \text{ in } Q \text{ and } a \text{ in } \Sigma$$

In this particular recognizer, each non-*null* input accepted in a certain state causes a transition to exactly one state. Still, the automaton is nondeterministic, since the transition from *A* to *Z* may occur spontaneously without input. Nondeterministic automata where one and the same input may cause different transitions from a given state are rarely useful in practical software engineering, but we may occasionally use *null*-moves to indicate transitions not caused by external events.

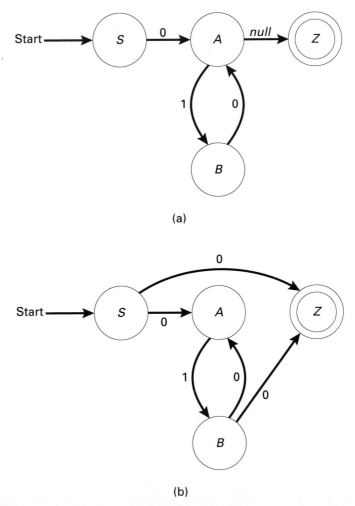

(a)

(b)

Figure 5-3   (a) Recognizer with *null*-move; (b) equivalent recognizer without *null*-move.

5.2.2.4 *Equivalence of deterministic and nondeterministic recognizers*

Deterministic recognizers and nondeterministic recognizers with and without *null*-moves are basically equivalent and can be used to model the same reality. First we note that a deterministic recognizer is a special case of a nondeterministic one, and a nondeterministic recognizer without *null*-moves is a special case of a nondeterministic recognizer with *null*-moves. Furthermore, the following two theorems can be proved:

A. If a string x is accepted by a nondeterministic recognizer with *null*-moves, we can always construct a nondeterministic recognizer *without null*-moves that accepts x.

B. If a string x is accepted by a nondeterministic recognizer *without null*-moves, we can always construct a deterministic recognizer that accepts x.

The recognizer *without null*-moves in Figure 5-3(b) is equivalent to the recognizer *with null*-moves in Figure 5-3(a). Additional moves have been introduced to eliminate the *null*-moves. For example, in Figure 5-3(a), the string 0 followed by *null* leads from the state B to A to Z. In Figure 5-3(b), there is instead a direct transition marked with the symbol 0 from B to Z. The deterministic recognizer in Figure 5-2(a) and the nondeterministic recognizer without *null*-moves in Figure 5-2(b) are equivalent: If a string x is accepted by one, it is also accepted by the other. Note that each state in Figure 5-2(a) corresponds to a *subset* of the states in Figure 5-2(b).

5.2.2.5 *Construction of a deterministic recognizer from a nondeterministic one*

To build a deterministic recognizer from the nondeterministic one in Figure 5-2(b) we successively include states and transitions according to the following algorithm:

1. Include the initial state, S.

2. Find the set of states that can be reached from S on the input 0. This is the set $\{A,Z\}$. Include the state AZ, representing this set, and a transition marked 0 from S to AZ.

3. Find the set of states that can be reached from S on the input 1. This is the set $\{B\}$, so we include the state B and the transition marked 1 from S to B.

4. Investigate each of the newly included states once: For the state AZ, find the set of states in Figure 5-2(b) that can be reached from either A or Z on input 0. This is the set $\{A,S\}$. Then include the set AS and the transition from AZ

to *AS* labeled 0. The set of states that can be reached from either *A* or *Z* on the input 1 is {*B*}, so we include a transition from *AZ* to *B* marked 1.

5. In Figure 5-2(b), *Z* is the only final state. Define the set of final states for the deterministic recognizer as all states representing sets that include the state *Z*. This will be all the states with *Z* in their names, such as *Z*, *AZ*, *BZ*, and *ASZ*.

Continuing this algorithm, we arrive at the determinstic recognizer in Figure 5-2(a). Although the algorithm always ends, the resulting automaton may include a number of states far in excess of the number of states of the original nondeterministic recognizer. (See also [Aho].)

In a nondeterministic recognizer, the set of states that can be reached from a state *X* on the input *I* is sometimes empty. In the deterministic recognizer, this empty set can be represented by the earlier-mentioned state *INVALID*. All transitions from *INVALID* lead back to the state itself, which thus represents a dead end. *INVALID* can be deleted since no input string that causes a transition to it can ever be accepted.

5.2.2.6 *Regular expressions and recognizers*

We have informally discussed regular expressions earlier in the context of sequence diagrams. We now proceed with some formal definitions and then discuss the equivalence of regular expressions and recognizers. A *regular expression* describes a *regular language*, which is a set of strings formed from an alphabet Σ by *concatenation*, *iteration*, or *selection*. The following notation is used:

abc means that the symbols (or strings) *a*, *b*, and *c* are *concatenated* (i.e., they occur in the sequence *a*, *b*, *c*).

*a** means that the string *a* is *iterated* zero or more times.

{*a*,*b*} means that either *a* or *b* is *selected*.

With this notation, the following is a regular expression formed from the alphabet {0,1}:

$$0(10)*$$

It represents a 0 followed by zero or more subexpressions of the form 10. A regular expression can always be equivalently represented as a sequence diagram. Figure 5-4 shows the expression 0(10)*. The advantage of the sequence diagram notation is that it allows subexpressions to be named. In Figure 5-4 the sequence 10 is referred to as *X*, while *A* is the subexpression (10)*.

The following theorems can be proved regarding the equivalence of regular expressions and recognizers:

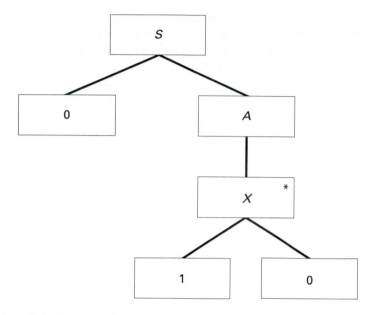

Figure 5-4   Sequence diagram representation of the regular expression 0(10)*. The subsequence X represents the expression 10.

   C. If r is a regular expression, there exists a nondeterministic recognizer with *null*-moves that accepts exactly the strings in r.

   D. If L is a string accepted by a deterministic recognizer, L is described by a regular expression.

The set of strings defined by the regular expression 0(10)* is accepted by the recognizer in Figure 5-3.

5.2.3 General Finite Automata

While a recognizer only lets us know whether the string of input symbols is acceptable, a general finite automaton generates output symbols as it consumes input. This can be done in two ways:

   1. Output can be associated with *state*, so that every time a certain state is entered, a certain output symbol is produced. An automaton working in this way is referred to as a *Moore* machine.

   2. Output can be associated with state *transition*, so that a certain output symbol is produced whenever the automaton makes a certain transition. An automaton working this way is called a *Mealy* machine.

In either case, a deterministic finite automaton is defined as a 6-tuple, where the symbols Q, Σ, δ, and q_0 are the same as for a deterministic recognizer. Thus, a deterministic finite automaton is a 6-tuple, $(Q,\Sigma,\Delta,\delta,\lambda,q_0)$, where

Q is the finite set of states.

Σ is the input alphabet.

Δ is the output alphabet.

δ is the transition function mapping $Q \times \Sigma$ onto Q.

λ is as discussed separately for Moore and Mealy machines in the next two sections.

q_0 is the initial state.

The set F of final states that appears in the formal definition of a recognizer is not used in the definition of a general automaton. A recognizer can be regarded as a Moore machine where all the nonfinal states have *null* output and all final states output the same non-*null* symbol. (See also Section 5.2.3.5.)

5.2.3.1 Moore machines

In a Moore machine, output is associated with each state, and a symbol is output as each state is entered. This means that formally λ is a mapping from Q to Δ, that is, for every q, $\lambda(q)$ yields a symbol d in Δ. If there is no output in a certain state q_1, then $\lambda(q_1) = null$. $\lambda(q_0)$ is the output of the initial state. The machine starts in the initial state and outputs $\lambda(q_0)$ before consuming any input. We can say that the Moore machine produces the output symbol $\lambda(q_0)$ in response to *null* input.

Figure 5-5(a) shows a Moore machine where

Q is the set $\{OFF,UNDEF,ON1, MORE\text{-}ON\}$.

Σ is the set $\{O,C\}$.

Δ is the set $\{T,F\}$.

The initial state is *OFF*.

δ is defined by the diagram and, alternatively, as follows:

$$\delta(OFF,O) = OFF$$

$$\delta(OFF,C) = UNDEF$$

$$\delta(UNDEF,O) = OFF$$

$$\delta(UNDEF,C) = ON1$$

$$\delta(ON1,O) = OFF$$

$$\delta(ON1,C) = MORE\text{-}ON$$

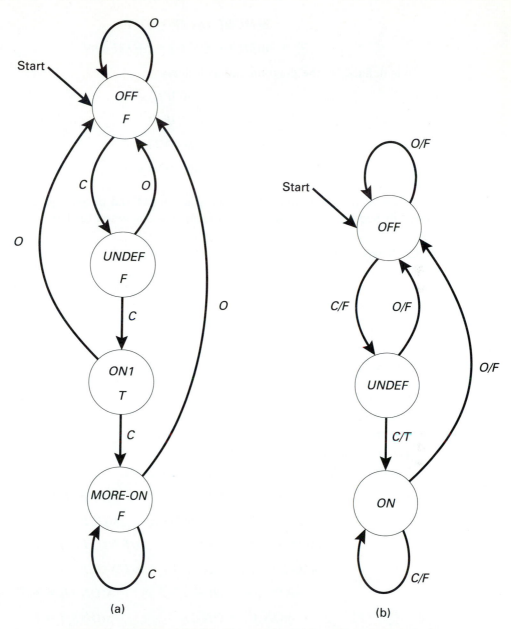

Figure 5-5 (a) Moore machine. The output symbol is shown inside each state bubble. (b) Mealy machine. The two machines are equivalent except for the initial output by the Moore machine.

$$\delta(MORE\text{-}ON,O) = OFF$$

$$\delta(MORE\text{-}ON,C) = MORE\text{-}ON$$

λ is defined by the diagram and as follows:

$$\lambda(OFF) = F$$

$$\lambda(UNDEF) = F$$

$$\lambda(ON1) = T$$

$$\lambda(MORE\text{-}ON) = F$$

These somewhat mysterious state names and input and output symbols are explained in Section 5.2.3.6, where the example is discussed further.

5.2.3.2 Mealy machines

In a Mealy machine, output is associated with state transitions, and a symbol is output as an input symbol is accepted. That way, the transition to a state S can produce different output symbols depending on the input symbol on which the transition takes place. In a Mealy machine, λ is a mapping from $Q \times \Sigma$ to Δ; that is, $\lambda(q,a)$ is the output symbol associated with the transition from q on input a.

Figure 5-5(b) shows a Mealy machine where

Q is the set of states $\{OFF,UNDEF,ON\}$.
Σ is the set $\{O,C\}$, same as in Figure 5-5(a).
Δ is the set $\{T,F\}$, same as in Figure 5-5(a).
The initial state is OFF.
δ and λ are defined by the diagram or as follows:

$$\delta(OFF,O) = OFF \qquad \lambda(OFF,O) = F$$

$$\delta(OFF,C) = UNDEF \qquad \lambda(OFF,C) = F$$

$$\delta(UNDEF,O) = OFF \qquad \lambda(UNDEF,O) = F$$

$$\delta(UNDEF,C) = ON \qquad \lambda(UNDEF,C) = T$$

$$\delta(ON,O) = OFF \qquad \lambda(ON,O) = F$$

$$\delta(ON,C) = ON \qquad \lambda(ON,C) = F$$

5.2.3.3 Equivalence of general finite automata

Two general finite automata are *equivalent* if they represent the same mapping from input strings onto output strings. It is quite possible to construct equivalent but different Mealy machines, that is, different machines that always produce the same output if given the same input. Similarly, it is possible to construct equivalent but different Moore machines.

Moore machines and Mealy machines are equivalent in the sense that for each Mealy machine, it is always possible to construct an equivalent Moore machine. To go the other way and construct a Mealy machine that is equivalent to a given Moore machine, we must consider the output from the Moore machine's initial state. A Moore machine that produces non-*null* output in its initial state can never be equivalent to a Mealy machine, since a Mealy machine requires input in order to produce output. Nonetheless, if the output from the initial state is excluded, an equivalent Mealy machine can always be constructed for any given Moore machine. Figure 5-5 shows equivalent Moore and Mealy machines with the exception of the initial output (F) of the Moore machine. The example is discussed further in Section 5.2.3.6.

In practice we often want to associate output or action with each transition, and thus we tend to use Mealy machines. Nevertheless, it is often convenient to make the current state of the machine known at all times. As mentioned earlier, this is a characteristic of a Moore machine. In practice we sometimes use a machine that is really a hybrid of a Mealy and a Moore machine.

5.2.3.4 Example: Parity checking

Figure 5-6 shows a simple example of a Moore machine. It has two states, *EVEN* and *ODD*, where *EVEN* is the initial state, and the input alphabet {0,1}. At each point in time, the current state of this machine reflects the *parity* of the series of input received so far. (The parity is equal to the number of 1's in the input string.) The output consists of the appropriate parity bit, and thus 0 is output whenever *EVEN* is entered and 1 whenever *ODD* is entered. The automaton stays in *EVEN* until it receives a 1, then moves to *ODD*, where it stays until another 1 is entered. It then moves back to *EVEN*, and so on. In this example, a Moore machine is appropriate since the parity is defined by the current state, no matter how it was entered. As usual, it is quite possible to use a Mealy machine, with the exception that the Mealy machine cannot produce the proper 0 parity bit for input consisting of an empty string.

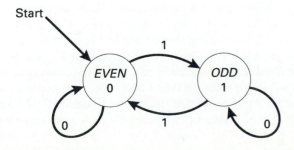

Figure 5-6 Moore machine that outputs 0 or 1 reflecting the even or odd parity of the string input so far.

5.2.3.5 Relationship between general finite automata, recognizers, and regular expressions

In Section 5.2.2 we discussed properties of recognizers. Since, in practice, we will usually rely on general finite automata, it is useful to know to what extent the properties of recognizers extend to general finite automata. First, if we have a recognizer, $R = (Q,\Sigma,\delta,q_0,F)$, we can always define a Moore machine, $M = (Q,\Sigma,\Delta,\delta,\lambda,q_0)$, where Q, Σ, δ, and q_0 are the same, Δ includes one single symbol O and λ is the mapping

$$\lambda(f) = O \qquad \text{for all } f \text{ in } F$$

$$\lambda(x) = null \qquad \text{otherwise}$$

This is a Moore machine that produces output only in those states that are the final states of R. Like a recognizer, it only signals the acceptance of a string. Knowing that the recognizer accepts exactly the strings generated by a certain regular expression, E, we now also know that we can build a Moore machine that outputs O exactly when a string in E has been received.

On the other hand, given a Moore machine, $M = (Q,\Sigma,\Delta,\delta,\lambda,q_0)$ and a subset, F, of Q, we can define a recognizer $R = (Q,\Sigma,\delta,q_0,F)$ that accepts exactly those input strings that bring M to a state in F. In turn, we can make a regular expression generating exactly those strings. Since Mealy and Moore machines are equivalent except for the initial output of the Moore machine, we can say that for practical purposes, explicit mode representation based on general finite automata is equivalent to implicit mode representation based on regular expressions and sequence diagrams.

5.2.3.6 Example of a general finite automaton: Keyboard driver

A *keyboard driver* program regularly senses the state of N contacts, each connected with one keyboard key. Each contact can be *open* or *closed*, depending on whether the key is currently held pressed. The driver must report each new key-in, that is, each situation where a contact is first detected as *open* and then as *closed*. The situation is complicated by a phenomenon known as *contact bounce*: When the contact has been held pressed and is released, it may bounce a number of times, repeatedly closing the contact for a short period ($\ll$ 2 ms, say). A closing of the contact caused by bouncing should not be registered as a new key-in. A real key-in lasts at least 10 to 20 ms. To eliminate errors due to contact bounce, each contact is sensed with a frequency of 2 ms. That way, on a real key-in the contact is detected as *closed* on more than one subsequent sensing, whereas a single reading of *closed* can be ignored due to contact bouncing. The keyboard driver treats each one of the N contacts independently: A new key-in may be reported for one contact while another contact remains depressed. (This is known as *N-key rollover*.) The keyboard driver is discussed further in Section 5.3.3.

To solve this problem, we express the life of each contact as the following regular expression, where *O* stands for *open* and *C* stands for *closed*:

$$(O^*C\{CC^*,O\})^*$$

Figure 5-5 shows two finite automata that accept strings described by this regular expression and identify a new key-in by outputting *T* (true) when the second *C* is received after an *O*. Otherwise, *F* (false) is output. The Mealy machine [Figure 5-5(b)] starts in a state *OFF*, moves to *UNDEF* when a *C* is received, and moves to *ON* and outputs *T* if another *C* is received. It stays in *ON* while additional *C*s are received. Whenever an *O* is received, the machine moves to *OFF*.

In the Mealy machine, outputs *T* and *F* are produced by different transitions to the state *ON*, depending on whether the transition is from *UNDEF* or *ON*. In the Moore machine, different transitions to the same state cannot produce different output. To construct a Moore machine that is equivalent to the Mealy machine in Figure 5-5(b), we must split the state *ON* into two states, *ON1* and *MORE-ON*, where *ON1* produces the output *T* and *MORE-ON* the output *F*. *ON1* is reached exactly when the second *C* in a row is input, while additional *C*s are received in *MORE*-ON, which outputs *F* [Figure 5-5(a)].

5.3 FINITE AUTOMATA IN SOFTWARE

As we have seen, transition diagrams are equivalent to regular expressions in that either notation can be used to define a given finite automaton. We have earlier seen how sequence diagrams, which are basically regular expressions, can be mapped onto control structures. We used this in order to base the control structure on the behavior over time of some entity in the problem environment. Transition diagrams are also useful in practical programming. Like sequence diagrams they are useful for modeling real-world behavior patterns of a certain complexity. We use mostly deterministic Mealy machines, where the output often consists of actions rather than symbols. Such an action is a sequence of program statements executed when an event has occurred. Sometimes the output is irrelevant and not shown in the diagrams.

As discussed in Chapter 1, an entity in the problem environment can be modeled in software either as a *subject* or as an *object*. For our present purposes, a subject corresponds to the main procedure. A sequence diagram describing an external behavior pattern maps nicely onto the control structure of a (main) procedure. In such a procedure the mode is implicitly maintained as execution progresses through the program text (see Section 2.4.3). A behavior captured in the form of a transition diagram can also be used as the basis for a (main) procedure. The states in the diagram remain in the procedure text, and the procedure has *explicit mode representation.* (The difference between states and modes is explained in Section 5.3.1.)

Objects are implemented as information-hiding packages or instances of abstract data types. Each object has a set of operation subprograms and internal variables that remember the state of the object between subprogram calls. The internal variables may include an explicit mode variable. It is convenient to express the mode transitions in a transition diagram. When a transition diagram is used in the analysis of a problem, we routinely encapsulate it in an information-hiding or adt package in the design.

If a sequence diagram is used in the analysis of a behavior pattern in a problem, we can use it as a basis for either a subject or an object in the design. If we want to use it for an object, we must convert the diagram into a form with explicit modes. As we have seen in Section 5.2, a regular expression is always equivalent to a transition diagram, so such a conversion is always possible and quite straightforward. Sections 5.3.1 through 5.3.3 are concerned with objects based on transition diagrams.

Clearly, many objects can be constructed without involving finite automata. The INPUT_STREAM package in Figures 2-23 and 4-2 and the packages REQUESTS and MOTOR in Figure 4-3 are examples. Finite automata are used when the object to be modeled has a complicated set of modes or transitions. This is similar to the situation with main procedures. Although we rely on sequence diagramming to model main procedures on complex behavior patterns, many simple main procedures may be constructed ad hoc.

5.3.1 States, Modes, and Conditions

A state is atomic and indivisible. This means that the number of states necessary to describe even a small and fairly simple entity can be very large. Assume, for example, that we want to describe in state terms a software object such as the package INPUT_STREAM. As shown in Figure 2-23, INPUT_STREAM has two internal variables, the array BUFF and the integer INDEX. The state of INPUT_STREAM that must be remembered between calls includes the value of INDEX and that of every single element in the array BUFF. Thus every time that INDEX is incremented, a transition to a new state occurs. Furthermore, every time a new block of input characters is read into BUFF, a transition occurs. (One might even argue that every possible combination of values in the buffer represents a distinct state.) It is clearly impractical to deal with all those states individually, and furthermore, it is unnecessary. From the point of view of processing, states can be grouped together into *modes*. A mode is a set of states. A transition diagram must include an *exhaustive* set of *disjoint* modes. This means that the automaton must always be in exactly one of the modes. (Two modes *A* and *B* are *disjoint* if the automaton is never in both *A* and *B* at the same time. A set of modes, *A*, *B*, and *C*, is *exhaustive* if the automaton is always in either *A*, *B*, or *C*.)

In the case of INPUT_STREAM, only two modes affect the processing. We can refer to them as NEW_BLOCK and OLD_BLOCK. The OLD_BLOCK mode includes all states where the value of INDEX is within the range of the buffer. In this mode the operation GET returns the next character and increments INDEX. The mode NEW_BLOCK includes all other states. In that mode a block must be read before a character can be returned to the caller.

In INPUT_STREAM, modes are defined by the value of INDEX. In fact, we do not think in terms of modes to develop the INPUT_STREAM package since the deblocking is fairly routine programming. In more complicated examples, where a package is modeled on an object with a complex set of modes and/or mode transitions, we usually introduce an explicit mode variable of an enumerated type, where the enumeration literals each correspond to a mode. The mode variable and the modes are part of the secret of an object. If the object is implemented as an information-hiding package, the mode variable is declared in the package body. If the object is an abstract data type, the type is typically a record, and the mode variable is one of the fields in the record definition (see also Section 2.4.3).

Another example of modes can be found in a variation of the VDU problem. In Chapter 2 we based a main procedure with implicit mode representation on the sequence diagram over FIELDS (procedure VDU in Figure 2-20). A main procedure with the same effect can be based on explicit mode representation. The transition diagram (Figure 5-7) shows the input to the VDU program in the form of a finite automaton with two modes, TEXT and CMND. TEXT is the initial mode, where the automaton remains until a '[' is input, signifying the beginning of a command. It moves from CMND to TEXT when a ']' is input, indicating the end of a command. The figure shows a general finite automaton, where the output consists of actions prompted by each input. For example, when a normal text character is input, it is displayed on the VDU screen. This is indicated by PUT. When the ']' symbol is input, the action is the execution of the command.

So far, we have not taken error input into account. The occurrence of an error character in a text string presents no difficulty; the corresponding action is ABT, signifying the signaling of an abort situation, and the automaton remains in

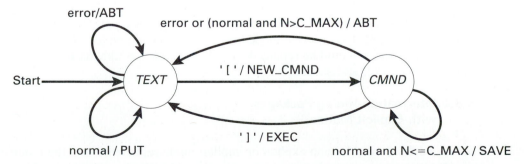

Figure 5-7   Transition diagram showing the input to the VDU program. A normal character and an error character are indicated as "normal" and "error", respectively.

TEXT. An error encountered inside a command string also triggers the action ABT and causes a transition from CMND to TEXT. On the other hand, the error situation where the maximum number of command string characters is exceeded relies on state information that is not captured in the transition diagram in Figure 5-7, since it is dependent on the number, N, say, of command characters already input. To handle this in state terms, we must realize that the mode CMND is a set of states with varying values of N. We could show this by breaking CMND into a set of modes, CMND0, CMND1, CMND2, and so on, where each mode name includes the current value of N. Clearly, such a diagram is impractical. Instead, we let the mode transitions depend on combinations of inputs and *conditions*. Thus a transition takes place on some input provided that a condition also holds. For example, the event normal and N<=C_MAX means that the input is a normal character and that the condition N<=C_MAX holds.

The procedure VDU_EXPL in Figure 5-8 is a typical implementation of the main VDU procedure based on explicit mode representation. MODE is an enumerated type with the literals TEXT and CMND, and M is the explicit mode variable. In addition, the mode transitions depend on the value of the integer N, which is not considered a mode variable. The body of VDU_EXPL contains a loop with a **case** statement over the different modes. In this example, TEXT and CMND are the two **case** statement alternatives. Within each alternative, the various inputs and conditions occurring in each mode are handled.

We will use one single explicit mode variable to reflect the current mode of each object unless there is a strong reason for doing otherwise. The variable is usually of an enumerated type, and all the different modes will appear neatly in the type declaration. If more than one explicit mode variable is used for some reason, the modes of the object are defined as all possible combinations of mode variable values. Suppose that we have two mode variables of two enumerated types as follows:

```
type XMODE is (X1,X2,X3);
type YMODE is (Y1,Y2);
X: XMODE;
Y: YMODE;
```

In this situation, each of the six combinations (X1,Y1), (X1,Y2), (X2,Y1), (X2,Y2), (X3,Y1), and (X3,Y2) is a different mode that must be accounted for. For simplicity and safety, X and Y should be replaced by a single mode variable XY that takes the values X1Y1, X1Y2, and so on.

5.3.2 Information-Hiding Packages with Explicit Modes

While a subject may rely on explicit or implicit mode representation, the mode of an object must be remembered in an explicit mode variable. If a single object is appropriate, it can be implemented as an information-hiding package with the

```
   with INPUT_STREAM; use INPUT_STREAM;
   with SCREEN; use SCREEN;
procedure VDU_EXPL is
-- Main procedure VDU with explicit mode control
C: CHARACTER;
subtype NORMAL is CHARACTER range 'A'..'Z';
C_BUFF: CMND_BUFF;
N: INTEGER range 1..C_MAX+1;
type MODE is (TEXT, CMND);
M: MODE:=TEXT;
begin
   loop
      GET(C);
      case M is
         when TEXT =>
            case C is
               when NORMAL =>
                  PUT(C);
               when '[' =>
                  -- Prepare for command.
                  N:=1;
                  C_BUFF:=NULL_CMND;
                  M:=CMND;
               when others => ABT;
            end case;
         when CMND =>
            if C in NORMAL and N<=C_MAX then
               C_BUFF(N):=C; N:=N+1;
            elsif C = ']' then
               EXEC(C_BUFF);
               M:=TEXT;
            else   -- Error situation
               ABT;
               M:=TEXT;
            end if;
      end case;
   end loop;
end VDU_EXPL;
```

Figure 5-8 VDU program based on explicit mode control. The variable M of type MODE takes the value TEXT when a text string is being processed, and CMND when a command is being processed.

mode variable (and any other persistent data) hidden in the body. For example, the procedure VDU_EXPL in Figure 5-8 can easily be changed into an operation subprogram that is successively called with the character C as a parameter. Figure 5-9 shows an information-hiding package LOGICAL_SCREEN with a procedure PUT_CHAR declared in the package specification. The mode variable M is declared in the body.

This solution requires that we turn the subject–object relationship between the program based on the FIELD structure and that based on the BLOCKS structure

```
package LOGICAL_SCREEN is
   procedure PUT_CHAR(C: CHARACTER);
   ABT_COND: exception;
end LOGICAL_SCREEN;


   with SCREEN; use SCREEN;
package body LOGICAL_SCREEN is
subtype NORMAL is CHARACTER range 'A'..'Z';
C_BUFF: CMND_BUFF;
N: INTEGER range 1..C_MAX+1;
type MODE is (TEXT, CMND);
M: MODE:=TEXT;
procedure PUT_CHAR(C: CHARACTER) is
begin
   case M is
      when TEXT =>
         case C is
            when NORMAL =>
               PUT(C);
            when '[' =>
               -- Prepare for command.
               N:=1; C_BUFF:=NULL_CMND; M:=CMND;
            when others => raise ABT_COND;
         end case;
      when CMND =>
         if C in NORMAL and N<=C_MAX then
            C_BUFF(N):=C; N:=N+1;
         elsif C = ']' then
            EXEC(C_BUFF); M:=TEXT;
         else    -- Error situation
            raise ABT_COND;
            M:=TEXT;
         end if;
   end case;
end PUT_CHAR;
end LOGICAL_SCREEN;
```

Figure 5-9 Package LOGICAL_SCREEN with the operation subprogram PUT_CHAR. LOGICAL_SCREEN maintains the mode of the screen and handles each text character and command character according to the current mode.

around. The deblocking procedure becomes the main procedure (subject). It calls the procedure PUT_CHAR in the object LOGICAL_SCREEN once for each character. We can say that the screen, which used to be the subject, has now been *objectified*. The example is elaborated on in Section 5.4.2.

5.3.3 Abstract Data Types with Explicit Modes

The information-hiding package LOGICAL_SCREEN represents a single object, the VDU screen. As we have seen in Chapter 4, abstract data types allow us to generalize to multiple objects answering to the same general description. In the case of the VDU program, it is possible to think of multiple screens, or more precisely, multiple windows on one screen. This example is discussed in Section 5.4.2. First we discuss abstract data types with explicit modes in the keyboard driver example introduced in Section 5.2.3.6.

In the keyboard driver problem, multiple keyboard keys are sampled with a certain frequency to detect any new key-ins. A new key-in is detected when two subsequent samples of the contact associated with a key are *closed*. In the transition diagrams describing the life of a key (Figure 5-5), the events are *closed* (C) and *open* (O), referring to the two possible values of a key sample. The life of a key could also be described as a regular expression or sequence diagram (Exercise 5.3).

Whether we describe the life of the key by means of a transition diagram or a sequence diagram, we can represent the key as either a subject or an object, at least in principle. If we want to model each key as a subject, we model a control structure on either the regular expression or the transition diagram that describes its life. In the first case, the resulting procedure will have implicit mode representation, and in the second case, it will have explicit mode representation. We cannot have a separate main procedure for each key, however. (A separate task per key is a possibility but not a very practical one.) Instead, we settle for a representation of each key as an object, and since there are several key objects, we define an abstract data type. Figure 5-10 shows an adt package BOUNCE_PAC that exports a private type KEY_TYPE and an operation procedure NEW_REQ. NEW_REQ takes an object of KEY_TYPE and a reading, OPEN or CLOSED, as input and returns a Boolean indicating whether a new request has been detected. KEY_TYPE is the name of our abstract data type, and SAMPLE_TYPE is an interface type. In the private part, KEY_TYPE is declared as a record with a single field of MODE_TYPE, where MODE_TYPE takes the values OFF, UNDEFINED, and ON. We have thus followed the earlier-stated convention to model an abstract data type as a record, but since it has only one field, this is really unnecessary, and the declarations

```
type MODE_TYPE is (OFF, UNDEFINED, ON);
type KEY_TYPE is record
   MODE: MODE_TYPE;
end record;
```

could be simplified to

```
type KEY_TYPE is (OFF, UNDEFINED, ON);
```

The package KEYBOARD hides the physical interface to the keyboard key contacts. While BOUNCE_PAC knows about the interpretation of the series of samples of a key contact, KEYBOARD knows about the makeup of the keyboard as a whole. The specification includes an enumerated type KEY_ID with a literal for each keyboard key. This particular specification of KEYBOARD reflects the stan-

```
package KEYBOARD is
   type KEY_ID is ('0','1','2','3','4','5','6','7','8','9','*','#');
   function CLOSED(K_NO: KEY_ID) return BOOLEAN;
end KEYBOARD;

package BOUNCE_PAC is
   type SAMPLE_TYPE is (OPEN, CLOSED);
   type KEY_TYPE is private;
   procedure NEW_REQ(KEY: in out KEY_TYPE; S: SAMPLE_TYPE; NEW_KEY_IN: out BOOLEAN);
private
   type MODE_TYPE is (OFF, UNDEFINED, ON);
   type KEY_TYPE is record
      MODE: MODE_TYPE:=OFF;
   end record;
end BOUNCE_PAC;

package body BOUNCE_PAC is
   procedure NEW_REQ(KEY: in out KEY_TYPE;
      S: SAMPLE_TYPE; NEW_KEY_IN: out BOOLEAN) is
   begin
      if S=OPEN then
         KEY.MODE:=OFF;
         NEW_KEY_IN:=FALSE;
      else    -- S = CLOSED
         case KEY.MODE is
            when OFF => KEY.MODE:=UNDEFINED; NEW_KEY_IN:=FALSE;
            when UNDEFINED => KEY.MODE:=ON; NEW_KEY_IN:=TRUE;
            when ON => KEY.MODE:=ON; NEW_KEY_IN:=FALSE;
         end case;
      end if;
   end NEW_REQ;
end BOUNCE_PAC;

   with BOUNCE_PAC; use BOUNCE_PAC;
   with KEYBOARD; use KEYBOARD;
procedure P is
A: array (KEY_ID) of KEY_TYPE;
SAMPLE: SAMPLE_TYPE;
NEW_KEY_IN: Boolean;
begin
   loop
      for K in KEY_ID loop
         if CLOSED(K) then SAMPLE:=CLOSED;
         else SAMPLE:=OPEN;
         end if;
         NEW_REQ(A(K), SAMPLE, NEW_KEY_IN);
         if NEW_KEY_IN then
            null;    -- Place holder for actions on new key-in.
         end if;
      end loop;
      delay 0.002; -- Suspend execution for 2 ms.
   end loop;
end P;
```

dard keys on a telephone keyboard. (The body of KEYBOARD is hardware dependent and is not shown in the figure.)

The procedure P in Figure 5-10 is a simple client program *withing* BOUNCE_PAC and KEYBOARD. An array A of KEY_TYPE is declared with one element for each key. This declaration is based on the type KEY_ID from KEYBOARD and the type KEY_TYPE from BOUNCE_PAC. P regularly senses the key contact by calling the function CLOSED in KEYBOARD and then calling NEW_REQ in BOUNCE_PAC to operate on a KEY_TYPE object. For BOUNCE_PAC to work properly, P must sample each key contact about every 2 ms.

5.4 EXAMPLES OF FINITE AUTOMATA IN SOFTWARE _____

5.4.1 Finite Automata in the Automobile Cruise Control Problem

5.4.1.1 Problem description

The cruise control system of a car will be used as an example of a finite automaton where the number of transitions per mode is such that an implementation with explicit mode representation is preferable over implicit mode representation. The cruise control problem is also discussed in [Mellor], [Brackett], [Gomaa] and [Smith]. The cruise control system is a small embedded system whose primary function is to maintain automatically a *cruising speed* selected by the driver. The system is largely operated by means of a *lever* on the steering column, which has the positions *Off* and *Neutral*. After the lever has been moved from *Off* to *Neutral*, it can be held in one of the positions *Const* and *Resume*, and springs back to *Neutral* when released.

While the lever is held in *Const*, the car accelerates at a constant rate. When the lever is released, the current speed is memorized and maintained automatically until either the lever is moved to *Off* or the brake is engaged. In either case, the speed can be resumed later by moving the lever to *Resume*.

The cruise control can be activated only when the engine is running with the gearshift in *Drive*, and is disabled when the engine stops or the gearshift is moved to another position. When the gearshift is put in *Drive* with the engine running, the cruise control is enabled in an initial mode without memorized speed, and *Resume* has no effect until a cruising speed has been memorized.

Figure 5-10   Adt package BOUNCE_PAC exporting a type KEY_TYPE modeled on the behavior of a keyboard key. The package KEYBOARD hides the hardware interface to the key contacts. (The body of KEYBOARD is now shown.) The main procedure P regularly samples each key by calling the procedure KEYBOARD.CLOSED. The sampling is spaced by means of the statement **delay** 0.002 that suspends execution for 2 milliseconds.

5.4.1.2 Events, modes, and transitions

By means of the lever and the brake, the driver creates a number of *events* that turn automatic cruising on or off, cause a cruising speed to be memorized, and so on. In addition, the event where the engine stops affects cruising, although it is not always caused by an intentional act by the driver. The events are defined as follows:

CONST	Move lever to *Const*.
UN_CONST	Release lever from *Const*.
RESUME	Move lever to *Resume*, then release it.
OFF	Move lever to *Off*, then release it.
BRAKE	
DRIVE	Put the gear shift in *Drive* with the engine running.
UN_DRIVE	Put the gear shift in a position other than *Drive*.
ENG_ON	Start engine.
ENG_OFF	Stop engine.

Considering the cruise control system as a finite automaton, the events cause transitions between the following modes (Figure 5-11):

NO_ENG	The engine is off.
NO_DRIVE	The engine is running; the gear is not in *Drive*; no cruising speed is memorized.
INIT	The engine is running and the gear is in *Drive*; the lever is in *Neutral*; no speed is memorized.
INIT_ACC	The lever is held in *Const*; the car is accelerating at a fixed rate; no speed is memorized.
CRUISING	The car is maintaining a memorized speed.
PASSIVE	Cruising is suspended; a memorized cruising speed exists.
ACC	The lever is held in *Const*; the car is accelerating at a fixed rate; a memorized cruising speed exists.

The transition diagram in Figure 5-11 shows only those events that actually lead to transitions. All other events leave the mode unchanged and may thus be ignored. For example, all lever movements in the mode NO_DRIVE are ignored as well as the event RESUME in the mode INIT. The diagram includes two cases where a transition is determined by a condition in addition to an event. The condition is

---

Figure 5-11 Finite automation describing the modes of cruising and the transitions upon events mostly caused by the driver.

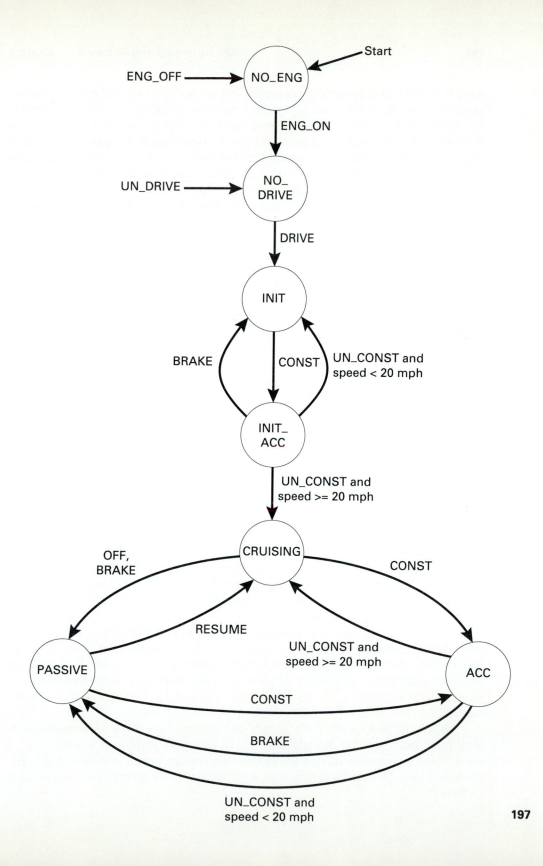

197

used to ensure that automatic cruising is not activated at speeds below a certain minimum speed, in this case 20 mph. Automatic cruising is normally activated when the lever is released from the position *Const* (the event UN_CONST), and at the same time, a new cruising speed is memorized. Thus if the speed is at least 20 mph, the event UN_CONST occurring in either INIT_ACC or ACC causes a transition to CRUISING. If the speed is less than 20 mph, no new speed is memorized, and UN_CONST causes a transition from INIT_ACC to INIT or from ACC to PASSIVE.

The finite automaton is a Mealy machine. Each transition may have an associated action taken by the cruise control system. The actions are listed in Figure 5-12. As mentioned in Section 2.4.3, a transition diagram such as Figure 5-11 is arranged first by mode and then by event. Similarly, Figure 5-12 contains one entry per mode and one subentry per event. Although this tends to be a useful arrangement in most cases, the events UN_DRIVE and ENG_OFF are exceptions. From any mode, the event ENG_OFF leads to the mode NO_ENG, and from any mode but NO_ENG, the event UN_DRIVE causes a transition to NO_DRIVE. For simplicity, the transitions caused by the events UN_DRIVE and ENG_OFF are abbreviated in the transition diagram. Also, they are treated separately and have their own entries in Figure 5-12. Since UN_DRIVE and ENG_OFF cause the same actions and lead to the same new modes regardless of where they occur, they are similar to Ada exceptions that break the normal control structure and cause the transfer of control to an exception handler.

5.4.1.3 Software implementation

In the cruise control software implementation, Figure 5-12 is encoded in a package CRUISE with an operation procedure DRIVER_EVENT that accepts events as input and maintains the mode (Figure 5-13). CRUISE also has the operation functions CONSTANT_ACC, CONSTANT_SPEED, and CRUISE_PERIOD. By calling CONSTANT_ACC and CONSTANT_SPEED, other modules may inquire whether constant speed or constant acceleration has been selected. Similarly, CRUISE_PERIOD returns the current memorized cruising speed in terms of time per N drive shaft revolutions. (It is more convenient to maintain the speed internally this way than in terms of revolutions per unit of time.

The implementation of the operation procedure DRIVER_EVENT is based on a nested **case** statement over modes and events. In the interest of both efficiency and clarity, the transitions caused by the events ENG_OFF and UN_DRIVE are handled separately. As mentioned above, these events may occur in almost any mode, always requiring the same actions, and causing transitions to the same modes.

Since the actions are fairly simple and involve only a few statements each, they have been written directly into the various **case** statement alternatives. If the actions are more complicated, *action subprograms* are sometimes used. Implementations of transition diagrams with action subprograms are discussed in [Allworth].

Current mode	Event and condition	Action	New mode
NO_ENG	ENG_ON	—	NO_DRIVE
NO_DRIVE	DRIVE	—	INIT
INIT	CONST	Activate constant acceleration	INIT_ACC
INIT_ACC	UN_CONST and speed >= 20 mph	Memorize speed, deactivate constant acceleration, activate constant speed	CRUISING
	UN_CONST and speed < 20 mph	Deactivate constant acceleration	INIT
	BRAKE	Deactivate constant acceleration	INIT
CRUISING	CONST	Deactivate constant speed, activate constant acceleration	ACC
	OFF, or BRAKE	Deactivate constant speed	PASSIVE
PASSIVE	CONST	Activate constant acceleration	ACC
	RESUME	Activate constant speed	CRUISING
ACC	UN_CONST and speed >= 20 mph	Memorize speed, deactivate constant acceleration, activate constant speed	CRUISING
	UN_CONST and speed < 20 mph	Deactivate constant acceleration	PASSIVE
	BRAKE	Deactivate constant acceleration	PASSIVE
Any	ENG_OFF	Deactivate constant speed, deactivate constant acceleration	NO_ENG
Any except NO_ENG	UN_DRIVE	Deactivate constant speed, deactivate constant acceleration	NO_DRIVE

Figure 5-12   Actions associated with events and conditions applying in the various modes of the cruise control problem.

```
package CRUISE is
type EVENT_TYPE is (ENG_ON, ENG_OFF, BRAKE, DRIVE, UN_DRIVE, CONST,
UN_CONST, RESUME, OFF, NONE);
function CONSTANT_SPEED return BOOLEAN;
function CONSTANT_ACC return BOOLEAN;
function CRUISE_PERIOD return DURATION;
procedure DRIVER_EVENT(EVENT: EVENT_TYPE);
end CRUISE;
    with SHAFT_PAC; use SHAFT_PAC;
package body CRUISE is
type MODE_TYPE is (NO_ENG, NO_DRIVE, INIT, INIT_ACC, CRUISING, PASSIVE, ACC);
MODE: MODE_TYPE:=NO_ENG;
CONST_SPEED, CONST_ACC: BOOLEAN:=FALSE;
CRU_PERIOD: DURATION:=0.0;
LIMIT: constant DURATION:= 1.0;    -- Cruise period for 20 mph
function CONSTANT_SPEED return BOOLEAN is
begin return CONST_SPEED; end;
function CONSTANT_ACC return BOOLEAN is
begin return CONST_ACC; end;
function CRUISE_PERIOD return DURATION is
begin return CRU_PERIOD; end;
procedure DRIVER_EVENT(EVENT: EVENT_TYPE) is
begin
   if EVENT=ENG_OFF then
      CONST_ACC:=FALSE; CONST_SPEED:=FALSE; MODE:=NO_ENG;
   elsif EVENT=UN_DRIVE and MODE/=NO_ENG then
      CONST_ACC:=FALSE; CONST_SPEED:=FALSE; MODE:=NO_DRIVE;
   else
     case MODE is
       when NO_ENG =>
         case EVENT is
           when ENG_ON => MODE:=NO_DRIVE;
           when others => null;
         end case;
       when NO_DRIVE =>
         case EVENT is
           when DRIVE => MODE:=INIT;
           when others => null;
         end case;
       when INIT =>
         case EVENT is
           when CONST => CONST_ACC:=TRUE; MODE:=INIT_ACC;
           when others => null;
         end case;
```

Figure 5-13 Package CRUISE with the operation procedure DRIVER_EVENT that accepts events as input and maintains the cruising mode. For documentation of DRIVER_EVENT, refer to Figure 5-12. The function SHAFT_PAC.PERIOD returns the current speed in terms of the time for N driveshaft revolutions.

```
        when INIT_ACC =>
          case EVENT is
            when UN_CONST =>
              if PERIOD <= LIMIT then
              -- Real speed >= 20 limit.
                CRU_PERIOD:=PERIOD; CONST_SPEED:=TRUE; CONST_ACC:=FALSE;
                MODE:=CRUISING;
              else -- Real speed < 20 mph.
                CONST_ACC:=FALSE; MODE:=INIT;
              end if;
            when BRAKE => CONST_ACC:=FALSE; MODE:=INIT;
            when others => null;
          end case;
        when CRUISING =>
          case EVENT is
            when CONST => CONST_SPEED:=FALSE; CONST_ACC:=TRUE; MODE:=ACC;
            when OFF | BRAKE => CONST_SPEED:=FALSE; MODE:=PASSIVE;
            when others => null;
          end case;
        when ACC =>
          case EVENT is
            when UN_CONST =>
              if PERIOD <= LIMIT then    -- Real speed >= 20 mph.
                CRU_PERIOD:=PERIOD;
                CONST_SPEED:=TRUE; CONST_ACC:=FALSE; MODE:=CRUISING;
              else -- Real speed < 20 mph.
                CONST_ACC:=FALSE; MODE:=PASSIVE;
              end if;
            when BRAKE =>
                CONST_ACC:=FALSE; MODE:=PASSIVE;
            when others => null;
          end case;
        when PASSIVE =>
          case EVENT is
            when CONST => CONST_ACC:=TRUE; MODE:=ACC;
            when RESUME => CONST_SPEED:=TRUE; MODE:=CRUISING;
            when others => null;
          end case;
        when others => null;
      end case;
    end if;
end DRIVER_EVENT;
end CRUISE;
```

Figure 5-13   (*continued*)

5.4.2 Multiple Windows in the VDU Control Program

In the VDU example discussed earlier, a video display unit is equipped with a microprocessor that executes an embedded control program. The microprocessor receives a stream of characters from a mainframe host to which the unit is connected. The stream of characters arriving from the host consists of text strings to be displayed on the VDU screen interleaved with commands, which are bracketed character sequences. The input stream may also include error characters.

Characters arrive from the host in blocks, and an information-hiding package INPUT_STREAM hides the blocked communication from the VDU procedure behind the operations GET and ABT. Figure 4-2 shows the main procedure VDU, the INPUT_STREAM package, a package HOST_COMM, which represents host communication at a lower level of abstraction than INPUT_STREAM, and the package SCREEN, which represents the VDU screen and is operated on by means of the procedures PUT and EXEC.

In the VDU program, INPUT_STREAM models the mainframe and SCREEN the VDU screen. The choice between information-hiding packages and abstract data types seems clear, since there is no reason to foresee more than one object of each kind. An interesting variation occurs if we want to manage *multiple windows* on the screen. In that variation of the program, each data block is intended for a particular window, and the blocks for different windows are interleaved in the input stream. The program must then deal with an abstract data type WINDOW_TYPE with multiple instances, each of which remembers the mode of one window.

In the one-window case, the structure clash between the input as an iteration of BLOCKS and as an iteration of FIELDS (Figure 2-22) is solved by basing the main procedure on the sequence diagram of FIELDS, and an information-hiding package, INPUT_STREAM, on the sequence diagram of BLOCKS. In the multiwindow case, it is suitable to turn this subject–object relationship around and let the main procedure handle blocks and operate on different window objects, which are instances of WINDOW_TYPE (Figure 5-14).

The package WINDOW is based on the description of a window as a finite automaton discussed in Section 5.3.1 and shown in Figures 5-7 and 5-9. Procedure PUT_CHAR in Figure 5-14 has been supplied with an additional parameter W of WINDOW_TYPE reflecting the current window. Since the deblocking has become the main procedure there is no longer an ABT procedure to be called when an error character is encountered. Instead, the exception ABT_COND is raised in PUT_CHAR.

Figure 5-14 also includes the packages W_SCREEN and W_HOST_COMM, which are the earlier packages SCREEN and HOST_COMM adapted to the multiwindow situation. Without entering into details, we assume that the procedures W_SCREEN.PUT and W_SCREEN.EXEC are capable of addressing a particular window on the screen. Furthermore, W_HOST_COMM.SEND_ABT includes the window identity when signaling an abort condition to the host. Figure 5-15 shows the new

```
package W_SCREEN is
   C_MAX: constant:=5;
   subtype CMND_BUFF is STRING(1..C_MAX);
   NULL_CMND: constant CMND_BUFF:=(others => ' ');
   subtype W_ID_TYPE is CHARACTER range '1'..'9';
   procedure PUT(W: W_ID_TYPE; C: CHARACTER);
   procedure EXEC(W: W_ID_TYPE; CMND: CMND_BUFF);
end W_SCREEN;

   with W_SCREEN; use W_SCREEN;
package W_HOST_COMM is
   MAX: constant:=20;
   procedure GET(C: out CHARACTER);
   procedure SEND_ABT(W: W_ID_TYPE);
   procedure SEND_NAK;
   procedure SEND_ACK;
end W_HOST_COMM;

   with W_SCREEN; use W_SCREEN;
   with W_HOST_COMM; use W_HOST_COMM;
package WINDOW is
   type WINDOW_TYPE is limited private;
   procedure W_INIT(W: out WINDOW_TYPE; I: W_ID_TYPE);
   procedure PUT_CHAR(W: in out WINDOW_TYPE; C: CHARACTER);
   ABT_COND: exception;
private
   type MODE is (TEXT, COMMAND);
   type WINDOW_TYPE is record
      ID: W_ID_TYPE;   -- Window id
      M: MODE:=TEXT;
      C_BUFF: CMND_BUFF:=NULL_CMND;
      INDX: INTEGER;
   end record;
end WINDOW;

package body WINDOW is
subtype NORMAL is CHARACTER range 'A'..'Z';
procedure W_INIT(W: out WINDOW_TYPE; I: W_ID_TYPE) is
-- Provide window object with its identity.
begin W.ID:=I; end;
procedure PUT_CHAR(W: in out WINDOW_TYPE; C: CHARACTER) is
begin
   case W.M is
```

Figure 5-14   Package WINDOW defining the abstract data type WINDOW_TYPE representing a window on the VDU screen. The screen package W_SCREEN and the host communication package W_HOST_COMM have been adapted for multiple windows.

```
        when TEXT =>
          case C is
            when NORMAL =>
              W_SCREEN.PUT(W.ID, C);
            when '[' =>      -- Start of command
              W.INDX:=1; W.C_BUFF:=NULL_CMND; W.M:=COMMAND;
            when others => raise ABT_COND;
          end case;
        when COMMAND =>
          if C in NORMAL and W.INDX <= C_MAX then
            W.C_BUFF(W.INDX):=C; W.INDX:=W.INDX+1;
          elsif C = ']' then
            EXEC(W.ID, W.C_BUFF); W.M := TEXT;
          else -- Error situation
            W.M:=TEXT; raise ABT_COND;
          end if;
      end case;
    end PUT_CHAR;
    end WINDOW;
```

Figure 5-14 (*continued*)

main, deblocking procedure. In an inner loop, each character in a block buffer is transferred in a PUT_CHAR call. When the exception ABT_COND has been raised and handled, the inner loop is abandoned and a new block is accepted from the mainframe.

In the multiwindow case it is not difficult to identify the windows as objects in the problem domain that must be kept track of by the software. The multiwindow solution clearly applies to one single window as a special case, and in hindsight it seems like a good idea to design for multiple windows in the first place. This example illustrates the difficulties of designing for change. Before the idea of multiple windows has occurred, it is not easy to recognize the screen as a potential instance of an abstract type rather than a single object. Instead, the software solution in the one-window case has the one screen as a natural centerpiece with supporting information-hiding modules for deblocking and host communication. Design for change is always limited by the designer's imagination, and we must often be prepared for major redesign when real changes that could not be foreseen occur in the problem environment. Nevertheless, a clear and intuitive software structure modeled on the problem environment is helpful even in the face of extensive redesign. The screen handling, deblocking, and host communication remain the primary subsystems in the modified solution, albeit partly redesigned, and the behavior pattern associated with the screen is conserved in the behavior of each window.

```
with WINDOW; use WINDOW;
with W_HOST_COMM; use W_HOST_COMM;
with W_SCREEN; use W_SCREEN;
procedure W_MAIN is
W: array (W_ID_TYPE) of WINDOW_TYPE;
W_I: W_ID_TYPE;          -- Current window id
type BUFF_TYPE is array (1..MAX) of CHARACTER;
BUFF: BUFF_TYPE;
CHK_SUM: CHARACTER;   -- Checksum
function CHECK return BOOLEAN is separate;
procedure GET_BLOCK is
begin
   GET(W_I);          -- Read window id.
   for I in 1..MAX loop
      GET(BUFF(I));
   end loop;
   GET(CHK_SUM); -- Read check sum.
end GET_BLOCK;
begin
   loop
      begin
         GET_BLOCK;
         while not CHECK loop
            SEND_NAK;
            GET_BLOCK;
         end loop;
         SEND_ACK;
         W_INIT(W(W_I), W_I);  -- Tell window object its id.
         for I in 1..MAX loop
            PUT_CHAR(W(W_I), BUFF(I));
         end loop;
      exception
         when ABT_COND => SEND_ABT(W_I);
      end;
   end loop;
end W_MAIN;
```

Figure 5-15   Main, deblocking procedure in VDU problem adapted to multiple windows on the VDU screen.

5.4.3 Alternative Software Representations of Transition Diagrams

We have opted to implement transition diagrams directly in the control structure usually by means of **case** statements over modes and events. This is an efficient implementation that is often appropriate in reactive software. Alternatively, a transition diagram can be modeled in data. This is appropriate if the transition diagram is large and if efficiency is not an overshadowing concern. Data modeling makes it easier to modify the transition diagram but incurs more overhead than do the kinds of solutions we have used here.

The table in Figure 5-12 may be implemented as a two-dimensional array over modes and events. Such an array will have one element for each theoretically possible mode–event combination. Typically, many of these combinations are invalid, such as the event RESUME in the mode CONST, which is physically impossible due to the construction of the cruise control lever. Such invalid mode–event combinations need not be represented. (Invalid mode–event combinations must be clearly distinguished from *illegal* mode–event combinations that must be detected and cause some error action.) Often the number of valid mode–event combinations is small compared to the number of combinations that are theoretically possible. In that situation, a data representation other than an array may be preferable. A possible representation is a linked structure that allows traversal of all the modes and, within each mode, traversal of all the mode–event combinations for that mode.

Whether a mode–event combination is represented as an array element or as a node in a linked structure, it must describe the associated action and the resulting mode. This new mode can easily be indicated through a reference within the data structure itself. The action subprogram causes more difficulty, since Ada does not allow a subprogram to be referenced from a data structure. (In other languages, such as C, a data structure may contain a pointer to a subprogram. A similar effect can be achieved more elegantly with the *dynamic binding* provided by object-oriented languages.) In Ada we are limited to representing the action subprogram by means of a code such as an enumeration literal. The code must then be interpreted by means of a **case** statement or similar construct. This results in an error-prone manually maintained link between data and control structure.

5.4.4 Alternative Program Structures

When the VDU program is adapted for multiple windows, major redesign is necessary because of the syntactical asymmetry between subjects and objects. Only the main procedure may use the program counter to maintain the mode, while an object must rely entirely on variables. A major part of the redesign is conversion of the main procedure modeling a screen into an object modeling a window, and conversion of INPUT_STREAM object into a subject. There are two ways whereby most of the asymmetry of mode representation can be avoided: to model each entity as an object, and to represent each entity as a subject. These approaches are discussed in the following paragraphs.

One way to avoid redesign of main procedures with implicit mode representation into software objects, and vice versa, is by not using the main procedure for modeling. Instead, a software object with explicit modes is designed for each object or behavior pattern. The main procedure is then reduced to a *scheduler*, which calls the operation subprograms of different objects. Such implementations are discussed in the JSD literature and an *inversion* technique is used to find an adequate set of modes departing from a program sequence diagram [Jackson], [Cameron 86, 89], [Sanden]. (The objects can also be based directly on transition diagrams.) A conceptual disadvantage of such an approach is that the scheduler, which will be a prominent part of the software, is a contraption without counterpart in the problem environment. Another disadvantage is the overhead for the management of the explicit mode variables.

In the scheduler approach, all entities are modeled as objects. It is also possible to model all entities as *subjects* by means of *multitasking*. A multitasking solution of the VDU problem might have a deblocking task and one task per window, where each window task essentially contains the control structure of the original VDU procedure in Figure 2-20. This solution has the advantage that the scheduling is built into the run-time system and hidden from the application program, which can be a pure model of the problem. On the other hand, overhead for task handling and communication is incurred. Multitasking is introduced in Chapter 6.

5.5 CHAPTER SUMMARY

> *Willst du ins Unendliche schreiten*
> *Geh nur im Endlichen nach allen Seiten.*
>
> *Goethe*

In this chapter we have studied the theoretical foundation and the application of mode representation in software. A fundamental equivalence exists between *finite automata*, which we use for explicit mode representation, and *regular expressions*, which we use for implicit mode representation. A finite automaton is a hypothetical machine that moves between different states as it receives input, such as symbols in an input alphabet or signals of events in the reality. A *recognizer* accepts strings of such input symbols by successively moving to a *final state*. The strings accepted by a given automaton can be described by means of a regular expression. The reverse also holds, and we can always construct a finite automaton that accepts exactly those strings defined by a given regular expression.

General finite automata are more useful than recognizers in software construction. A general finite automaton produces an *output* symbol upon each transition. (The symbol may be *null*.) There are two possibilities:

A *Moore machine* outputs a certain symbol whenever a particular state is entered.

A *Mealy machine* outputs a different symbol for each possible state transition.

In software, the output from a finite automaton is often a certain *action* to be taken in association with each transition.

Software, particularly reactive software, frequently deals with the state of various external entities. Often it is more convenient to deal with sets of states—*modes*—than individual states. The behavior of an entity can be captured either in the form of a transition diagram or as a sequence diagram. In principle, these two notations are equivalent. The entity can be modeled in the software either with *implicit or explicit mode representation*. Explicit mode representation is necessary if an entity is modeled as an *object*, such as an information-hiding package or an instance of an adt. An explicit mode variable may be declared in the object. In implicit mode representation, a sequence diagram may be modeled directly in the control structure of a main program or a task.

Explicit and implicit mode representation are equivalent and differ only in terms of efficiency and style. This difference has to do with how easily the external behavior of the program can be deduced from the program text. The regular expression permits more direct modeling, since it is reflected directly in the program structure. Thus the external behavior, seen as a regular expression, can be read directly from the text. This is true even if we depart from the regular grammar and include additional control abstractions, such as exits from loops. They, too, can be interpreted directly as parts of the external behavior.

A transition diagram can be implemented as directly as a sequence diagram, but the program text will contain extraneous elements not reflecting the reality but the technicalities of the model. The mode variable itself is an object that the program manipulates. This makes the program text a less direct description of the external behavior of the software. But explicit mode representation is the only choice if an entity must be modeled as a software object.

REFERENCES

AHO, A. V., and ULLMAN, J. D., *Principles of Compiler Design*, Addison-Wesley, Reading, Mass., 1979.

ALLWORTH, S. T., *Introduction to Real-Time Software Design*, 2nd ed., Springer-Verlag, New York, 1987.

BRACKETT, J. W., *Automobile Cruise Control and Monitoring System Example*, Tech. Rep. TR-87-06, Wang Institute of Graduate Studies, Tyngsboro, MA, 1987.

CAMERON, J. R., An overview of JSD, *IEEE Trans. Software Eng.*, 12:2, February 1986, pp. 222–240.

CAMERON, J. R., *JSP&JSD: The Jackson Approach to Software Development*, 2nd ed., IEEE Computer Society Press, Washington D.C., 1989.

DAVIS, A., *Software Requirements: Analysis and Specification*, Prentice Hall, Englewood Cliffs, N.J., 1990.

GOMAA, H., *Software Design Methods for Concurrent and Real-Time Systems*, Addison-Wesley 1993.

HAREL, D., Statecharts, a visual approach to complex systems, *Sci. Comput. Program.*, 1987.

HAREL, D., LACHOVER, H., NAAMAD, A., PNUELI, A., POLITI, M., SHERMAN, R., SHTULL-TRAURING, A., and TRAKHTENBROT, M., STATEMATE: a working environment for the development of complex reactive systems, *IEEE Trans. Software Eng.*, 16:4, April 1990, pp. 403–414.

JACKSON, M. A., *Principles of Program Design*, Academic Press, New York, 1975.

MELLOR, S. J., and WARD, P. T., *Structured Development for Real-Time Systems, Vol. 3: Implementation Modeling Techniques*, Yourdon Press, Englewood Cliffs, New Jersey, 1986.

RUMBAUGH, J., BLAHA, M., PREMERLANI, W., EDDY, F., and LORENSEN, W., *Object-Oriented Modeling and Design*, Prentice Hall, Englewood Cliffs, N.J., 1991.

SANDEN, B., System programming with JSP: example—a VDU controller, *Commun. ACM* 28:10, October 1985, pp. 1059–1067.

SMITH, S. L., and GERHART, S. L., STATEMATE and cruise control: A case[2] study, *CompSac 88*, IEEE Computer Society, Silver Spring, Md., 1988, pp. 49–56 (also, MCC Tech. Rep. STP-275-88).

EXERCISES

5.1 Equivalence between deterministic and nondeterministic automata

A *nondeterministic* finite automaton contains four states, A, B, C, and D. A is the initial state and D is the only final state. From A, the symbol 0 causes a transition to either B or C. From B, 0 leads back to B and 1 leads to D. From C, the input 0 leads to D. Construct an equivalent *deterministic* finite automaton.

5.2 Rental car

The life of a rental car includes the events: *PURCHASE*, when the car is bought, and *REGISTER*, when it is registered. The car is regularly serviced. This involves two events, *START-SERVICE* and *END-SERVICE*. When the car is not being serviced, there may be zero or more *RENT* events when the car is rented to a customer. After a *RENT* event, there may be zero or more *RENEW* events before the *RETURN* event, when the car is returned by the customer. The final event in a car's life is either *SELL* or *SCRAP*. Show the life of the car in a transition diagram. (Before the car is purchased, let it be in an *INITIAL* mode. Other than that, define modes such as *SERVICED*, or *RENTED*, as necessary.)

5.3 Keyboard driver

Draw a *sequence diagram* of the life of a keyboard key based on the transition diagrams in Figure 5-5.

5.4 Moore machine in the cruise control problem

Figure 5-12 shows the action associated with each mode transition in the finite automaton describing a *driver* behavior. If the actions can be considered an output of the finite automaton, the table defines a Mealy machine. Redefine the driver behavior as a Moore machine. How is the implementation affected?

5.5 Car window

A power car window is manipulated by means of a control lever that can be held in the positions *up* and *down* and springs back to a neutral position when released. Normally, the window moves down while the control is held in the *down* position and moves up when the control is in the *up* position until the window reaches its fully open or fully closed position, respectively. Nevertheless, if the control is held in the down position for more than *S* seconds, the window enters an automatic mode and continues to move down even after the control is released. The following events are caused by the control and by the window reaching its top or bottom position:

DOWN	The control is moved to the *down* position. *Effect*: The window starts moving downward (if possible).
UP	The control is moved to the *up* position. *Effect*: The window starts moving upward (if possible). In *automatic* mode: The window stops at its present position.
UNDOWN	The control is released from the *down* position. *Effect*: The window stops at its present position. In *automatic* mode: No effect.
UNUP	The control is released from the *up* position. *Effect*: The window stops at its present position.
TOP	The window reaches its fully closed position.
BOTTOM	The window reaches its fully open position.
S_SECS	This is the event that the control has been held in the *down* position for exactly *S* seconds. *Effect*: The *automatic* mode is entered.

Draw a transition diagram showing suitable modes and transitions labeled with the events described above.

5.6 Numerical keyboard input

Exercise 2.3 describes the input from a numerical keyboard as a sequence diagram over digits and other characters. Use a *transition diagram* to represent the same input.

5.7 Roman numeral with explicit mode representation

In Exercise 2.8 the input to a program ROMAN is described by means of a sequence diagram. The program determines whether the input represents a correct Roman numeral between 1 and 9 and, if so, determines its value. In Exercise 3.1 the sequence diagram is used to construct a subprogram that recognizes a part of a Roman numeral. The subprogram is based on implicit mode representation.
(a) Describe the same input by means of a transition diagram.
(b) Redesign the subprogram in Exercise 3.1 with explicit mode control based on the transition diagram.

5.8 Cruise control for manual transmission

The cruise control system in a car with manual transmission has two switches, *SET* and *RESUME*, on the steering wheel. The switches can be pushed and held by the driver, and spring back when released. The cruise control system is also affected by the brake and the clutch. The following events occur:

SET	The *SET* switch is pushed.
UNSET	The *SET* switch is released.
RESUME	The *RESUME* switch is pushed.
UNRESUME	The *RESUME* switch is released.
BRAKE	The brake pedal is tapped.
CLUTCH	The clutch pedal is tapped.

The cruise control system has the following modes:

INIT	The car has just been started; no desired speed set.
CRUISING	The desired speed is maintained by the system.
COASTING	The system allows the car to coast.
ACCEL	The system accelerates the car.
PASSIVE	The cruise control is inactive; a desired speed exists.

The switches *SET* and *RESUME* are used primarily to set and resume a cruising speed and start the cruising. This happens when each button is released (i.e., at the events *UNSET* and *UNRESUME*). During cruising, the switches *SET* and *RESUME* can be used to adjust the cruising speed as explained below.

When the engine is started, the cruise control system remains in the *INIT* mode until the driver selects a cruising speed by releasing the *SET* switch. Cruising starts only if the speed is at least25 mph. To start cruising, the cruise control software takes the actions *save speed*, *cruise*, and *on*. (*On* turns on a cruising indicator on the dashboard.)

While the car is cruising, the driver can reduce the speed by pushing the *SET* switch. The action *coast* is then taken, which causes the car to coast. When the driver releases the switch, the car resumes cruising at the current speed, provided that it is at least 25 mph. In that case the actions *save speed* and *cruise* are taken. If the switch is released at a lower speed, the cruise control becomes inactive.

When the car is cruising, the driver can increase the cruising speed by pushing the *RESUME* switch. This causes the action *accelerate*. When the switch is released, the actions *save speed* and *cruise* are taken and the car resumes cruising at the current speed.

Cruise control becomes inactive when the brake or the clutch is tapped. This causes the actions *coast* and *off*. (*Off* turns off the cruising indicator.)

If cruise control is inactive, cruising at the earlier-set cruising speed is resumed when the switch *RESUME* is released provided that the current speed is at least 25 mph. This causes the action *cruise*. (Releasing the *RESUME* switch has no effect at lower speeds.)

Draw a transition diagram with the above-mentioned modes, events, and actions.

5.9 *Garage door*

The door of the basement garage in an apartment building is opened from the outside by means of a magnetic card. From the inside it is opened by a floor sensor tripped by an exiting car. There is also a manual unit with *open*, *close*, and *stop* buttons. Sensors in the door frame are tripped when the door reaches the fully closed and fully opened positions. A warning sign "CAR IN RAMP" flashes whenever the door is not fully closed. A light source in one door post and an optical sensor in the other ensure that the doorway is free from obstacles. Any obstacle will break the light beam and trip the sensor. This stops the door from closing. Refer to the different stimuli as follows:

top:	The door reaches the fully opened position
bottom:	The door reaches the fully closed position
open:	The *open* button is pressed
close:	The *close* button is pressed
stop:	The *stop* button is pressed
card:	A magnetic card with the correct code is inserted in the card reader
floor:	A car trips the floor sensor
break:	An obstacle breaks the light beam
unbreak:	The obstacle is removed from the light beam

The door has the following states:

OPENED:	Fully opened
CLOSED:	Fully closed
MOVING-UP:	Opening
MOVING-DOWN:	Closing
STOPPED:	Stopped in a position other than fully opened or closed.

The actions controlling the warning sign and the door motor are:

on:	turn flashing warning sign on
off:	turn warning sign off
up:	start the motor moving the door up
down:	start the motor moving the door down
halt:	stop the motor

The following conditions exist for the optical sensor in the doorway:

BEAM:	The light beam is unbroken
NO-BEAM:	The light beam is broken

The door is initially fully closed. It opens when either a card is inserted in the reader, or the floor sensor is tripped, or the *open* button is pressed. The *open* button also makes the door move up after it has been stopped. The door becomes fully opened when it hits the top of the door frame. It becomes fully closed when it hits the bottom of the door frame.

The *close* button is used when the door is either stopped or fully opened and causes it to start moving down, but only if the doorway is clear of any obstacles. The *stop* button causes the door to stop moving. The door also stops if it is moving down and the light beam is broken.

When the door has been either fully opened or stopped for 1 minute, it automatically starts moving down, provided there is no obstacle. Refer to this event as *time-out*. In all other state-event combinations, the door remains in the current state.

Draw a transition diagram describing the behavior of the door. Choose a Mealy machine or a Moore machine representation.

6 Concurrent Tasks

Learn to live and live to learn
Ignorance like a fire doth burn,
Little tasks make large return.

Bayard Taylor, To My Daughter

6.1 INTRODUCTION

In the previous chapters we have studied sequential programs where one main procedure (possibly with a set of independent subprograms) is the subject that operates on various objects. Each object is implemented as an information-hiding package or an instance of an abstract data type. We strive to model each software object on one object in the problem environment and to model the control structure of the main procedure on a sequential behavior pattern or thread of events in the reality. Examples of such patterns are the stream of input characters in the VDU problem and the behavior of an elevator in the single-elevator control system (Chapter 2). Another behavior pattern is defined by the periodic sampling necessary in the keyboard driver problem (Chapter 5).

A sequential program may include any number of software objects modeled on distinct objects in the environment, but only one subject. This is sufficient as long as the problem environment contains no *asynchrony*. But many programs, particularly reactive software, must deal with asynchronous behavior patterns. As an introductory example, imagine a video game where a monster with jerky movements appears on the video screen. It flashes its left eye every 1.4 seconds and its right eye every 0.9 second, breathes fire every 3 seconds, lifts its right arm in a menacing gesture every 5 seconds, and lowers it after 2 seconds. The video game monster exhibits four *concurrent*, *asynchronous* behaviors: left-eye flashing, right-eye flashing, fire-breathing, and arm-lifting. We will use the word *concurrent* in the sense of "running in parallel" [Webster]. Thus the behaviors are concurrent since they all continue while the game is being played. The word asynchronous is the opposite of *synchronous*, which we will use in the sense of "recurring or operating at exactly the same periods" [Webster]. The behaviors are asynchronous since the events occur at different intervals in each.

If we were to write a sequential program to create the monster's behavior on the screen, we would have to control all the behaviors from one, combined control structure. Although the problem is simple, this control structure would be non-trivial. A breakdown into objects does not help much since the problem has to do with timing, and we would still be limited to one thread of execution through the objects. To separate the behaviors satisfactorily, we really need four independent subjects each operating according to its own schedule. *Multitasking* allows us to do exactly this. For each behavior we define one *task* with a simple control structure based on that behavior. Together the tasks produce the relatively complex, asynchronous behavior required of the device. The tasks are concurrent in that they run in parallel. We refer to a program that contains concurrent tasks as a *concurrent program*. This is the opposite of a *sequential* program, which has a single thread of control.

Let us assume that we have a subprogram, BREATHE_FIRE, that makes a flame appear on the screen close to the monster's mouth. The task FIRE_BREATHING may then be as follows:

```
task body FIRE_BREATHING is
begin
   loop
      delay 3.0;
      BREATHE_FIRE;
   end loop;
end;
```

The delay statement creates the appropriate spacing of actions in time. It is a built-in Ada feature that causes the execution of the task to be suspended for a given number of seconds.

Assuming that the two subprograms RAISE_ARM and LOWER_ARM cause the monster's arm to move, we can then construct a task ARM_MOVING as follows:

```
task body ARM_MOVING is
begin
   loop
      delay 5.0;
      RAISE_ARM;
      delay 2.0;
      LOWER_ARM;
   end loop;
end;
```

Finally, if the subprogram FLASH(EYE) makes one eye flash on the screen, we can define a *task type* EYE_FLASHING as follows:

```
task body EYE_FLASHING is
N: DURATION;
EYE: EYE_TYPE;
begin.....
   loop
      delay N;
      FLASH(EYE);
   end loop;
end;
```

There are two *instances* of EYE_FLASHING, one with N = 0.9 and EYE = RIGHT_EYE, and another with N = 1.4 and EYE = LEFT_EYE. These values are communicated to each task instance before the loop is entered. (We will later see how this may be done.)

The subprograms BREATHE_FIRE, FLASH, and RAISE_ARM are all operations on an information-hiding package GAME_SCREEN which provides the interface to the video screen (Figure 6-1). This object is *shared* by the tasks. The tasks and the package GAME_SCREEN can all be part of one program controlling the movements of the monster on the screen. Each task is an independent thread of execution of the program text. In a sequential program, there can be only one point of control

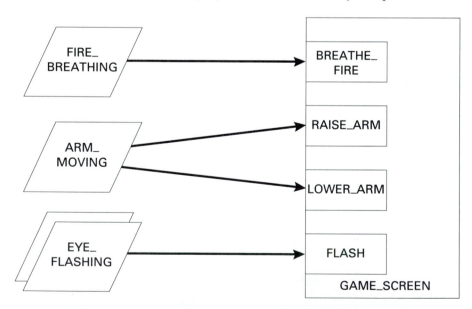

Figure 6-1 Buhrgraph showing the tasks FIRE_BREATHING, ARM_MOVING and instances of the task type EYE_FLASHING operating on the package GAME_SCREEN.

at each point in time. This is represented by the program counter, which indicates which statement in the text to execute next. With multitasking, each task has its own program counter that changes as that task executes. Each task also has its own variables, which are local to the task.

Each of the single tasks FIRE_BREATHING and ARM_MOVING has its own unique task body and appears almost as a separate program. EYE_FLASHING, on the other hand, is a task type, of which there might be several instances. Each instance has its own unique set of task variables—N and EYE in the example—and its own program counter. All instances share the text in the task body. The compiler constructs the code so that it refers to the variables of whatever task instance is executing. That way, multiple instances may execute the text at the same time, each at its own pace. A technical term for program code that can be executed simultaneously by more than one task is *reentrant*. (For further discussion, refer to [Silberschatz].)

Obviously, reactive systems often have much more complex behaviors than the video game has. It is very often helpful to describe such behaviors in terms of concurrent threads of events. Once the external behavior has been analyzed in those terms, it can be modeled by means of multitasking software, with tasks representing the threads of events in the reality. In Ada, tasks are integrated parts of the language. The tasking-related syntax is discussed in Section 6.3. In Section 6.2 we discuss various uses of tasks and forms of parallel and distributed execution. Analysis and design based on threads and multitasking are discussed further in Chapters 7 through 9.

6.2 TASKS AND PROCESSES AS PROGRAMMING ABSTRACTIONS

We regard tasks primarily as programming abstractions that can be used to reflect independent, asynchronous threads of events in the problem environment. This *process* abstraction is used in many kinds of programming. We discuss these uses in the following sections.

6.2.1 Interactive Processes

Parallel processes are familiar to users of most interactive *time-sharing system*s, such as those used for software development or word processing on a mainframe. Individual users access such a system through separate terminals. The system allocates processor time to each user in such a way that ideally, the user has the impression of uninterrupted access to the computer. Furthermore, several users may execute the same software, such as an editor. For this, each user is given a *process* that keeps track of the progress of that user as the software is executed. The system operation whereby a new process or task is given control of the processor is called a *context switch* [Silberschatz].

Process is the term used for a concurrent unit in time-sharing systems (and in much computer science literature). The concurrent units in a reactive system must be designed to allow faster context switching than interactive processes so they can respond to various external events in a timely fashion. For this reason they are sometimes referred to as *lightweight processes*. We use the Ada term *task* for such a lightweight process.

6.2.2 Tasks in Embedded Software

The concept of concurrent processes, each devoted to a time-sharing user, can easily be translated to an embedded, reactive domain. A reactive system often has no human users. Instead, various entities in the problem environment can often be identified, each of which creates a sequential thread of events. A thread of events can then be modeled as a task in the software. Just as an interactive system must give all processes a fair amount of access to the processor, a reactive system must give each task access to the processor as needed in response to external events.

As an example of how a task can be used to reflect an asynchronous thread of events in a reactive environment, take the elevator control system discussed in Chapters 2 and 4. That system can be extended to a *set of elevators* together serving the requests from the buttons on the various floors. In that environment the events

"elevator X arrives at floor W"

and

"elevator Z leaves floor Y"

occur in random order for different elevators. At the same time, the *behavior* or *life* of each elevator can be described sequentially as shown in Figure 2-35.

We have earlier seen how a control structure can be modeled on a sequence diagram. Because of the isomorphism between a thread of events and a task seen as a thread of execution events, we can construct a program with one task per elevator, just as one task is assigned to each time-sharing user. Tasks can thus be used to model the lives of entities such as the elevators. Such *entity-life modeling* tasks in general, and the elevator example in particular, are discussed further in Chapter 8.

6.2.3 Tasks in Nonembedded Reactive Software

While the elevator example is an embedded process control system, many *transaction systems* can be characterized as nonembedded, reactive systems. A transaction system interacts with human operators, but the response-time requirements make it reactive rather than interactive. The operator of a transaction system also has a much more limited repertoire of functions than an interactive computer user has. A checkout clerk operating a software-controlled cash register in a supermarket performs a limited variety of transactions, but requires the system to react as quickly and consistently as a hardware register. The same is true for a teller operating a terminal in a bank office and for a travel agent using the on-line seat reservation system of an airline or a railway company. The software in these systems reacts to events created by human operators, and a task is assigned to each operator either permanently or for the duration of one session or one transaction.

6.2.4 Concurrent Software and Parallel Hardware

It is important not to confuse multitasking with parallel processing on multiple hardware processors. Parallel processors working on the same problem are sometimes used in applications that require massive calculation. For example, an *array processor* allows a calculation to be performed on an entire array at once by operating on all the elements in parallel.

Software intended for parallel hardware must be decomposed into parallel units, somewhat similar to tasks. Nevertheless, we will be concerned primarily with tasks that execute concurrently on one processor. This is sometimes referred to as *virtual* concurrency and is an abstraction used to model concurrent patterns in the problem environment. This abstraction must be supported by a *real-time executive* that schedules the tasks so that they get to utilize the processor one at a time. A real-time executive is part of the Ada library and included automatically when a concurrent Ada program is linked. It is part of the Ada *run-time system*. The run-time system performs execution-time functions such as the allocation of local variables when a block is entered and the dynamic instantiation of record types.

6.2.5 Distributed Systems

A *distributed system* is a set of hardware processors connected by a network. Unlike the parallel processors discussed in Section 6.2.4, which are placed close together in the same hardware unit, distribution usually involves physically separate processors. A supermarket system such as the one mentioned in Section 6.2.3 may have a processor in each cash register. All these processors are connected to a central store computer controlling the price and stock database. The store computers may, in turn, be connected to a central computer for the entire supermarket chain. In Chapter 9 we discuss a distributed flexible manufacturing system (FMS). That system consists of workstations such as lathes or mills. Each worksation is controlled numerically and has its own processor. The workstation processors are, in turn, connected to a central minicomputer that schedules the jobs at different workstations. A small distributed system consisting of a remote temperature sensor (RTS) unit and a host computer is discussed in Section 6.5. Both the FMS and RTS systems rely on *messages* passed between computers. The queueing of such messages is also discussed in an example in Section 7.5.3.

A different kind of distribution involves special-purpose co-processors placed in the same physical cabinet with a main processor. Most computers are actually distributed in this sense, since the hardware boards used as interfaces to disks, printers, and other devices come equipped with their own processors. In addition to this, a *math co-processor* may be used to off-load floating-point calculations from the main processor. Similarly, high-resolution graphics screens usually have dedicated processors with direct access to the display.

6.3 TASK SYNTAX

This section is an overview of important features of the Ada task syntax. It focuses on concepts that will be used for software construction in later chapters. The reader is referred to an Ada primer or *The Ada Language Reference Manual* [LRM] for a complete description of the syntax.

6.3.1 Task Creation and Activation

Tasks need to be specified like other syntactical units. We can declare single tasks and task types. An instance of a task type is created statically or dynamically, much like an instance of a record type. We refer to declaration and instantiation as task *creation*. It is sometimes separate from *activation*, which is when a task starts operating as an independent thread of control. The various forms of creation and activation are explained in the following sections.

6.3.1.1 Declaration of single tasks and task types

A task declaration consists of two parts, the *task specification* and the *task body declaration*. The declaration of the task FIRE_BREATHING mentioned in Section 6.1 is as follows:

```
task FIRE_BREATHING;

task body FIRE_BREATHING is
begin
  loop
     delay 3.0;
     BREATHE_FIRE;
  end loop;
end FIRE_BREATHING;
```

The specification and the body declaration are separate declarative units. Each task must have a specification, which must precede the body declaration.

A task may have *entries* or *entry points* at which it receives *entry calls* from other tasks. How this works is explained in Section 6.3.2. The following is a specification of a task SIMPLE with a single entry SIMPLE_ENTRY without parameters.

```
task SIMPLE is
    entry SIMPLE_ENTRY;
end SIMPLE;
```

An entry may have parameters, specified as follows:

```
entry SIMPLE_ENTRY(P: INTEGER);
```

The use of parameters is discussed in Section 6.3.2.1. A task specification can only contain entry specifications. It cannot be a library unit and must always be encapsulated in a procedure or a package. A task specification may be in a package specification or a package body. A task body cannot reside in a package specification.

A task *type* FURNACE is declared as follows:

```
task type FURNACE is
    entry ALERT(F: FURNACE_NO);
end

task body FURNACE is
MY_F: FURNACE_NO;  -- Permanent task variable
.....
begin
    .....
end FURNACE;
```

The task body may contain variable declarations. MY_F in the example above is a *permanent task variable*. It remains defined as long as the task exists. A task can also have its own *temporary task variables*. These are declared in inner blocks and in subprograms called by the task, and so on. Such temporary variables cease to exist when the task's thread of execution leaves their scope.

6.3.1.2 Instantiation of task types

Once a task type has been specified, individual tasks may be created by instantiation. A single instance of FURNACE is declared as follows:

```
F: FURNACE;
```

Instances can be arranged in data structures. The following declaration, where FURNACE_NO is a discrete range, declares a number of instances and arranges them in an array:

    FARRAY: **array** (FURNACE_NO) **of** FURNACE;

The declarations of F and FARRAY appear in the declaration part of a block and are *static*. Task types can also be instantiated *dynamically*, during execution. This is done by means of access types. An access type F_PTR_TYPE referencing instances of FURNACE is declared as follows:

    type F_PTR_TYPE **is access** FURNACE;

Once F_PTR_TYPE has been declared, variables of the type can be declared as usual. (As with any access type, they have the default initial value **null**.) For example:

    F_PTR: F_PTR_TYPE;

Task instances may be created by means of an *allocator* consisting of the reserved word **new** followed by the task-type identifier. When the following statement is executed, a new instance of the task type FURNACE is created. The new instance can be referenced by means of the access variable F_PTR:

    F_PTR:=**new** FURNACE;

A variable may be assigned an initial value upon declaration. If the variable is of an access type referencing a task type, a task instance is dynamically created as a side effect of the variable declaration. In the following declaration, an instance of FURNACE is created and F_PTR is given the reference to the newly created task instance as its initial value:

    F_PTR: F_PTR_TYPE:= **new** FURNACE;

The task type FURNACE is taken from the remote temperature sensor problem (Section 6.5). As we will see, the question of dynamic task instantiation is academic in that example, where the instances of FURNACE are modeled on the physical furnaces. The FURNACE tasks are persistent entities that are present from the start to the end of the program. Dynamic instantiation of task types is useful if the corresponding entities are short-lived, and may start or cease to exist during program execution.

6.3.1.3 *Task activation*

The program unit where a task is declared or a task type is instantiated is called the *parent unit* of that task or task-type instance. When a task instance or a single task has been declared, it starts executing concurrently with the parent as soon as the parent reaches **begin** after the declaration. A task created by means of an allocator starts executing immediately upon creation. For example, assume that the declarative part of the parent includes the following declarations:

```
task FIRE_BREATHING;
task type FURNACE is
    entry ALERT(F: FURNACE_NO);
end;
type F_PTR_TYPE is access FURNACE;
F_PTR: F_PTR_TYPE:= new FURNACE;
F: FURNACE;
begin
    .....
```

Here the tasks FIRE_BREATHING and F start execution when the parent reaches the **begin** in the excerpt above, while the task referenced by the access variable F_PTR starts immediately after the declaration of F_PTR is complete.

6.3.2 Rendezvous

Once started, each task executes independently, at its own pace. Occasionally, it is necessary to synchronize tasks and force them to take some action together. In Ada, this is referred to as a *rendezvous*. A human rendezvous is when people meet at a given place and a given time. The Ada rendezvous should be thought of as a similar situation where tasks execute a sequence of statements at the same time. Tasks may exchange data only while synchronized in that manner.

A rendezvous basically involves two tasks, a *caller* and a *callee*. (More involved rendezvous are discussed later.) Unlike a human rendezvous, which is symmetric in that each person must show up at the agreed place and time, an Ada rendezvous involves different syntactical constructs in the caller and the callee. Let us first consider the callee. A task can be called at any one of the *entries* designated in its specification. For example, the task type FURNACE has the entry ALERT, and the task SIMPLE has the entry SIMPLE_ENTRY. In the body of the callee, **accept** statements refer to the entries. Calls to SIMPLE_ENTRY and ALERT, respectively, are accepted by the statements

```
accept SIMPLE_ENTRY;
```

and

    accept ALERT (F: FURNACE_NO) **do** MY_F:=F; **end** ALERT;

When the task reaches an **accept** statement, it waits for an entry call from another task if a call is not already outstanding.

    Let us now consider the caller. It makes an *entry call* much like a subprogram call. The following statements would appear in the body of a task calling SIMPLE_ENTRY:

    SIMPLE.SIMPLE_ENTRY;

The following is a call to the entry ALERT of the instance FARRAY(I). The entry parameter is I.

    FARRAY(I).ALERT(I);

When the caller reaches an entry call statement it waits for the callee to arrive at an appropriate **accept** statement if the callee is not already waiting. A rendezvous occurs when a caller executes an entry call statement and a callee executes a corresponding **accept** statement. Note that a task is called at an entry, not at a particular **accept** statement. There may be more than one **accept** statement for any one entry, E. They are placed anywhere in the control structure where it is suitable for the task to handle calls made to E.

    The rendezvous at SIMPLE_ENTRY is a *simple rendezvous*. Once each task has reached the appropriate statement, synchronization has been achieved and the two tasks continue their individual processing. The rendezvous at ALERT is an *extended rendezvous*, which is completed only when the **end** of the **accept** statement has been reached. The statements between **do** and **end** are the *body* of the **accept** statement. They are executed while the two tasks remain synchronized. The simple rendezvous may be regarded as a special case. Thus the statement

    accept SIMPLE_ENTRY;

is shorthand for

    accept SIMPLE_ENTRY **do null**; **end** SIMPLE_ENTRY;

In this case the **null** statement is executed while the caller and callee are synchronized. This has no practical significance, but our reasoning about tasks is sometimes simplified by assuming that every **accept** statement has a body (see also Section 6.3.2.3).

6.3.2.1 *Entry parameters*

The body of an **accept** statement is the only place where the entry parameters may be referenced by the callee. This makes parameter passing between tasks more complicated than parameter passing to a subprograms. (A formal subprogram parameter may be referenced throughout the subprogram body.) Like a procedure, an entry can have **in**, **out**, and **in out** parameters. Of these, **in** parameters are the least difficult. Inside the body of the **accept** statement, the value of an **in** parameter may be assigned to a variable belonging to the callee. That variable may be referenced freely after the rendezvous. In the example

> **accept** ALERT(F: FURNACE_NO) **do** MY_F:=F; **end** ALERT;

the parameter F in the entry ALERT is saved in the permanent task variable MY_F.

A more complicated situation exists if there are **in out** or **out** parameters. The values of these parameters are often based on some of the input parameters and must then be calculated during the rendezvous. This means that the body of the **accept** statement may be a substantial segment of program text. There are no particular syntactical restrictions on the complexity of the body, which may include **accept** statements, entry calls to other tasks, and so on.

6.3.2.2 *Conditional and timed entry calls*

Normally, the task making an entry call is suspended until the callee accepts the entry call. That way, synchronization of the caller and callee is accomplished. Sometimes we do not want the caller to be blocked. It can then make a *conditional* entry call. A conditional entry call to the entry A of a task T has the following syntax:

> **select** T.A; <statements>
> **else** <statements>
> **end select**;

A conditional entry call is effective only if the callee is waiting in a corresponding **accept** statement when the call is made. Otherwise, the statements after **else** are executed. If the entry A has parameters, the conditional entry call transfers data between the tasks when it is effective. When the **else** alternative is selected, no data is exchanged.

The *timed* entry call is a variation of the conditional call, where the caller gives the callee a certain time to accept the call. The timed entry call has the following syntax:

```
select
    T.A;
    <statements_1>
or
    delay D;
    <statements_2>
end select;
```

If the entry call at A is accepted by T within D seconds, the rendezvous is made and <statements_1> are executed. If the entry call is not accepted within D seconds, <statements_2> are executed.

6.3.2.3 *The subject concept*

The body of an accept statement is executed while the caller and callee are synchronized. We will take the view that the caller executes the body while the callee is passive. Thus, during the rendezvous, the callee is an object, operated on by the caller. This definition holds for a rendezvous between exactly two tasks, but the Ada syntax allows rendezvous to be much more complex. We still want to attribute the execution of each statement (in the body of an **accept** statement and elsewhere) to exactly one task, which will be referred to as the executing *subject* of the statement.

The body of an **accept** statement may contain entry calls and **accept** statements, which may themselves have nonempty bodies. This allows more than two tasks to take part in a rendezvous. A nested **accept** statement or an entry call in the body of an **accept** statement each causes a rendezvous involving multiple callers and callees. To account for these cases, we define the *subject* recursively as follows:

1. For any statement executed by only one task, that task is the subject.
2. In a rendezvous between two tasks, the caller is the executing subject of each statement in the body of the **accept** statement. (In the case of a simple rendezvous, the caller executes an imaginary **null** statement.)
3. For each statement in the body of an **accept** statement, the subject is the executing subject of the latest entry call that is still in the process of being accepted.

As an example where rule 3 applies, consider the following excerpt from a task T:

```
accept A do
    <statement_1>
    accept B do <statement_2> end B;
end A;
```

Usually, the executing subject of <statement_1> is the task, S_1, say, that contains the call T.A, and the executing subject of <statement_2> is the task, S_2, that contains the call T.B. Complications occur only if the call T.A or T.B is itself in the body of an **accept** statement. Suppose, for example, that the call T.A appears in the task S_1 as follows:

> **accept** C **do** T.A; **end** C;

Then the executing subject of <statement_1> is no longer S_1 but some other task, S_3, which is the executing subject of T.A.

This defines the subject executing each statement. We will refer to any task that ever executes a statement as a subject as a *subject task*. Tasks that never operate as subjects and execute only when called by other tasks will be referred to as *guardian tasks*. A guardian is typically associated with an object, and the subject tasks rendezvous with the guardian when operating on the object. Subject tasks and guardian tasks are discussed further in Section 6.4.

6.3.3 The select Statement

In a conditional or a timed entry call, a **select** statement is used in the caller. A **select** statement can also be used by a callee and allows it to wait for entry calls at different entries at the same time. This is referred to as *selective wait*. In the following statement, the task accepts a call at A, B, or C, whichever comes first.

```
select
    accept A(..) do .... end A;
    <statements_1>
or
    accept B(..) do .... end B;
    <statements_2>
or
    accept C(..) do .... end C;
    <statements_3>
end select;
```

Once an entry call, A, say, has been served, <statements_1> are executed, and so on. Each time the **select** statement is executed, exactly one call to one of entries A, B, or C is served. For this reason, a **select** statement is normally placed inside a loop.

6.3.3.1 Queues of tasks

For each entry of each task or task-type instance there is an associated *queue* of any waiting tasks whose entry calls cannot be served immediately. When a statement **accept** A is executed, the *entry queue* for A is served in first-in-first-out order. (If the task body contains more than one statement **accept** A, they all serve the same entry queue.) A task containing the **select** statement discussed above has a separate queue for each entry, A, B, and C. Should there be tasks waiting in two or more queues when the **select** statement is entered, one of those queues is selected arbitrarily, and the first task in that queue is served. The selection is not affected by the order in which the **accept** statements appear in the **select** statement.

It is important not to get the impression that the entry queues are normally full of waiting tasks. With few exceptions, where tasks are intentionally kept in queues, it is better to think of the queues as empty. Queueing should be thought of as an exceptional measure used when two entry calls happen to coincide.

6.3.3.2 *Select statement with delay alternative*

A **select** statement in a callee may include a **delay** alternative. The **delay** parameter limits the time the task executing the **select** statement will wait for an entry call. The following construct allows a task to accept an entry call at A or B within N seconds. If no caller is queued when the **select** statement is first entered, and none calls within N seconds, then the wait is timed-out, the statements after the **delay** statement are executed, and the callee proceeds to the statement following the **select** statement.

```
select
    accept A do .... end A;
    <statements>
or
    accept B do .... end B;
    <statements>
or delay N;
    <statements>
end select;
```

If the time-out value is zero, the callee will only serve an entry call that is already queued when the statement is entered. An alternative construct with an **else** clause exists for this case:

```
select
    accept A do .... end A;
    <statements>
or
    accept B do .... end B;
    <statements>
else
    <statements>
end select;
```

6.3.3.3 *Termination of tasks*

A select statement in a callee may contain a **terminate** alternative as follows:

```
select
    accept A;
    <statements>
or
    accept B;
    <statements>
or
    terminate;
end select;
```

This construct is useful in guardian tasks, which execute only in response to entry calls from other tasks (see Section 6.4.2). When the **select** statement in a task T is executed, the **terminate** alternative is taken when no other tasks exist, or when all tasks are in a position to select a **terminate** alternative. Under these conditions, T need expect no more calls and may safely terminate.

6.3.3.4 *Guards*

The **select** statement can be enhanced with *guards*, which are conditions under which the various **accept** statements included in the **select** construct may be executed. A guard is a Boolean expression introduced by means of the reserved word **when** in the following way:

```
when <condition_1> =>
accept A;
```

When a **select** statement with guards is executed, only those **accept** statements with guards evaluating to TRUE are considered for execution. In the following construct, calls to the entry A are accepted only when <condition_1> holds, and calls to B only when <condition_2> holds, whereas calls to C are always accepted.

```
select
    when <condition_1> =>
    accept A(..) do ... end A;
    <statements>
or
    when <condition_2> =>
    accept B(..) do ... end B;
    <statements>
or
    accept C(..) do ... end C;
    <statements>
end select;
```

A guard affects only the ability of a caller to be taken off a queue and served, not its ability to be queued. The caller will remain queued until an **accept** statement without a FALSE guard is executed.

6.3.4 Exceptions in Tasks

Exception handlers may be included in tasks as in other Ada structures. If an exception is raised in a task and not handled inside the task, the task will *die* by executing its final **end**. There is no higher level to which the exception can be propagated. When a task executes its final **end**, the execution thread associated with the task expires. This is usually inconvenient; it means that the software quietly changes its way of operation and often leads to unexpected secondary errors. Consequently, if there is any chance that an exception will be raised in a task, an exception handler should be included to prevent the task from dying.

The body of an **accept** statement can include one or more exception handlers that will handle exceptions raised during the rendezvous. If an exception is raised during a rendezvous and is not handled inside the body of the **accept** statement, it is raised automatically in both the caller and the callee. It must then be handled in each task. (The task that does not handle the exception will die.) If rendezvous are nested, all tasks participating in the rendezvous are affected.

6.3.5 The delay Statement

A fundamental property of a task is its ability to control its own timing by suspending its execution for a given period of time. It does this by rescheduling itself for execution after a specified interval. We touched on this in conjunction with the various monster-related tasks in Section 6.1. A concurrent program typically runs for a very long time—hours, days, even years—and any task spends most of its time waiting. Many tasks, such as FIRE_BREATHING, run on their own internal schedules. After each call to BREATHE_FIRE, it suspends its own processing for 3 seconds. A task may suspend its activity for a specified time X by means of the **delay** statement:

    delay X;

Here X is of the predefined Ada type DURATION. DURATION is a fixed-point type and specifies the delay in seconds. The delay can also be specified as a fixed-point constant. A delay of 3 seconds is thus specified as follows:

    delay 3.0;

A **delay** statement where the parameter is zero or negative is legal. It causes no explicit delay but may cause a context switch, whereby another task that is waiting for execution gets control. We say that the execution of the task is *re-sumed* when the delay interval has expired. (Resumption may be delayed if another task is executing at that time; see Section 6.3.5.1.)

The built-in package CALENDAR provides the type TIME as well as useful time-related subprograms such as

```
function CLOCK return TIME;
```

CLOCK returns the current reading of the system clock in terms of seconds and parts thereof. The difference between two values of type TIME is of type DURATION. (CALENDAR also provides other subprograms, which split the current reading of the clock into date, hours, minutes, etc.) In the following loop, which might be part of a task T, the procedure ACTION is called every 5 minutes:

```
INTERVAL: constant:=300.0;

loop
    delay INTERVAL;
    ACTION;
end loop;
```

6.3.5.1 Cumulative drift

In the example above, we want a task T to call ACTION, wait for 5 minutes, then again call ACTION, and so on. Although it may seem that the loop would accomplish this, the realities of multitasking may be different. After a 5-minute wait, T will indeed be ready for execution. But then another task may be processing that cannot be interrupted immediately. This causes the execution time of T to slip. (The discrepancy will depend on the load on the processor and the structure of the software.) Furthermore, we may well want ACTION to be called every 5 minutes regardless of the time it takes to execute the procedure itself. To a reasonable extent, we can compensate for both the interference of other tasks and the execution time of ACTION. This is done by basing each delay on the difference between the current point in time and the scheduled execution time, as follows:

```
with CALENDAR; use CALENDAR;
declare
    INTERVAL: constant DURATION:=300.0;
    NEXT: TIME:=CLOCK; -- Time for next execution (invariant)
begin
    loop
        ACTION;
        NEXT:=NEXT + INTERVAL;
        delay (NEXT − CLOCK);  -- Delay until next execution time
    end loop;
end;
```

This solution assumes that INTERVAL is much longer than the possible slippage caused by other tasks. We also assume that the execution time of ACTION is always less than INTERVAL. This solution cannot guarantee that T will always be executed exactly on schedule, but at least, the discrepancies will not accumulate. The correct working of a task with a **delay** loop requires that the processor load be low so that whenever a task is ready for execution, the processor is idle or becomes idle within a negligible period of time. Note also that a variable of type TIME is automatically reset to zero when it reaches its maximum value. Although NEXT is repeatedly increased, we do not have to deal explicitly with the NUMERIC_ERROR exception that would normally occur when the maximum value is exceeded.

6.3.5.2 Example of a delay-loop task

The program excerpt in Figure 6-2 contains a task type FURNACE that has been mentioned earlier. It periodically samples the temperature of a furnace by calling the entry

        THERMOMETER.READTEMP(MY_F, TEMP);

It then sends the temperature via a communication line to a host computer by means of the entry call

        OUTPUT.SEND(MY_F, TEMP);

(The tasks THERMOMETER and OUTPUT are discussed later.)

To sample the temperatures of several furnaces at individual frequencies we use multiple instances of a task type FURNACE. The instances are arranged in an array, FARRAY. A parallel array, INTERVAL, contains the sampling interval for each furnace. To provide each FURNACE instance with the number of its associated furnace, the main procedure contains the loop

        for F **in** FARRAY'RANGE **loop**
           FARRAY(F).ALERT(F);
        end loop;

In this loop, each task in FARRAY is called at the entry ALERT with its associated furnace number as a parameter. Before entering its loop, each instance of FURNACE receives the furnace number in the statement

        accept ALERT(F: FURNACE_NO) **do** MY_F:=F; **end**;

By means of this number, each task can access the correct sampling interval in the array INTERVAL.

```
task type FURNACE is
-- Periodically sample the temperature of a furnace.
    entry ALERT(F: FURNACE_NO);
end;


FARRAY:    array (FURNACE_NO) of FURNACE;
INTERVAL: array (FARRAY'RANGE) of DURATION;

task body FURNACE is
-- Sample the temperature of furnace MY_F with the sampling
-- interval given in INTERVAL(MY_F).
MY_F: FURNACE_NO;    -- Furnace number
TEMP: TEMP_TYPE;
NEXT: TIME;                  -- Next sampling time
begin
    accept ALERT(F: FURNACE_NO) do MY_F:=F; end;
    NEXT:=CLOCK;
    loop
      THERMOMETER.READTEMP(MY_F, TEMP);
      NEXT:=NEXT + INTERVAL(MY_F);
      OUTPUT.SEND(MY_F, TEMP);
      delay (NEXT − CLOCK);
    end loop;
end FURNACE;


begin
-- Main procedure: Initialize each instance of FURNACE by means
-- of a call at entry ALERT with a unique furnace number.
    for F in FARRAY'RANGE loop
      FARRAY(F).ALERT(F);
    end loop;
  ....
end;
```

Figure 6-2   Program excerpt: FARRAY is an array of FURNACE tasks. Each gets
its furnace number via an entry call at ALERT, then samples temperatures and
sends data packets at intervals stored in the array INTERVAL.

6.3.6 Modules and Tasks

A module is a program unit. A package, a subprogram, and a task body are
modules. Modularization is used for breaking down the program text. It affects
primarily the source program and has little impact on execution. The module
boundaries, which are prominent in the source text, disappear when the program
is compiled and linked. On the other hand, tasks are important primarily at execution time, and may start and end their existence during execution. The execution
thread of a task always starts at the **begin** statement of the task body. But it is

important not to associate the task strongly with the text of its body. The most important concern of a task is not module boundaries, but the thread of execution through the program text.

With a simple analogy, we can regard the text (or the executable code) of a concurrent program as a piece of land. A module is a subdivision that may be subdivided into smaller modules. Tasks, on the other hand, may be thought of as vehicles moving on a web of roads crisscrossing the land, in and out of modules. For example, a subprogram has one road leading into it and one or more roads leading out. A package with N operation subprograms has N inroads, each of which ultimately leads back out from the package. A task enters the territory of the package to execute an operation subprogram and leaves when control is returned. At execution, concurrent tasks simultaneously travel along the same and different paths through the program text.

With the analogy above, each task (or task type) is associated with a piece of land—the task body—but it is in no way restricted to remaining within its bounds. The following simple program illustrates this independence of the thread of control and the task body:

```
procedure INFINITE is
    task HUEY;
    task LOUIE;

    procedure INFINITE_LOOP (T: STRING; D: DURATION) is
    begin
        loop
            -- Display string.
            delay D;
        end loop;
    end INFINITE_LOOP;

    task body HUEY is
    begin
        INFINITE_LOOP ("HUEY",2.0);
    end HUEY;

    task body LOUIE is
    begin
        INFINITE_LOOP("LOUIE",3.0);
    end LOUIE;

begin -- Main procedure
    null;
end INFINITE;
```

In this example, each of the two tasks HUEY and LOUIE starts its execution at the **begin** in the task body. Each task calls the procedure INFINITE_LOOP, from which there is no return. Thus the thread of control of each task begins in its body, then enters the territory of the independent subprogram INFINITE_LOOP, where it stays forever.

As discussed in Chapters 3 and 4, the interface specification of a subprogram (or a package) includes all information a client programmer needs to invoke the subprogram (or each of the operation subprograms of the package). The interface specification is often stated in the form of pre- and postconditions. In a concurrent environment, the pre- and postconditions reflect the state of the calling *task* before the call and after the return from the call, respectively.

6.3.7 Task Scheduling

The implementation of the task abstraction relies on a run-time system that schedules each task for execution. As mentioned earlier, we are concerned primarily with the situation where the tasks share one common processor. In that situation the tasks never actually execute concurrently, but instead, the processor is allocated to each task in turn. Thus tasks reflect concurrency in the *problem domain* rather than the *execution domain*, and we use them wherever the problem is suitably viewed in terms of concurrent behavior patterns. The video game in Section 6.1 is a good example where a total, somewhat complex display pattern is best regarded as an interleaving of concurrent, simple patterns. It would make no sense to use a separate hardware processor for each behavior of the monster, since the necessary computation for each behavior is minimal compared to the synchronization necessary for the management of the shared resource, the video screen.

6.3.7.1 Priorities

Tasks waiting for access to the hardware processor are usually served in first-come-first-served order, but a different scheme can be enforced by means of *priorities*. Ada allows the programmer to assign a priority to each task by means of the pragma PRIORITY(X), where X is a static expression of the INTEGER subtype PRIORITY. The pragma is used as follows:

```
task A is
   pragma PRIORITY(X);
   entry A_E(...);
   ....
end A;
```

Section 9.8.4 of *The Ada Language Reference Manual* [LRM] reads: ''If two tasks with different priorities are both eligible for execution and could sensibly be executed using the same physical processors and same physical resources, then it cannot be the case that the task with the lower priority is executing while the task with the higher priority is not.'' Multiple tasks waiting for access to the processor (or processors) should not be a normal phenomenon in a reactive system, since the processor must have sufficient capacity to respond in a timely fashion to external events occurring at random points in time. Priorities are honored only when different tasks compete for control of the processor, and are therefore usually of limited value. They do not influence the queueing associated with the rendezvous, and a task cannot use its priority in order to jump ahead in an entry queue. The same applies in a **select** statement such as the following:

```
select accept A;
or    accept B;
end select;
```

Here, if one task TA is sitting on A's queue and another, TB, on B's queue, either TA or TB is chosen for execution at random regardless of priorities. Furthermore, *The Ada Language Reference Manual* allows compiler implementations to restrict priorities rather severely. For example, the implementer may declare the subtype PRIORITY with the range 1..1, and in that case, only one priority can be assigned. All in all, the concurrent designs in Ada should generally not depend on the use of priorities.

A special priority consideration applies to interrupt handling. As described further in Section 6.4.1.3, hardware interrupts look like entry calls to an Ada application. Nevertheless, interrupts are generally not queued, and furthermore, the interrupt signal remains outstanding only for a limited time. In order that no interrupts be lost, the run-time system gives higher priority to an interrupt handler than to a task handling entry calls from other tasks. For more discussion of this issue and of priorities in general, see [Burns].

6.4 TASK APPLICATIONS

6.4.1 Subject Tasks

A *subject task* was defined in Section 6.3.2.3 as any task that ever executes a statement as a subject. Tasks that never do this are called *guardian tasks* and are typically associated with objects. The distinction between subject and guardian tasks is important for the design approach discussed here. In this section we look at some typical examples of subject and guardian tasks.

6.4.1.1 Simple subject tasks based on delay *loops*

Many useful subject tasks build on simple variations of the loop with a **delay** statement, introduced in Section 6.3.5. Such tasks take some action at regular intervals and may be classified according to the nature of that action. The action may be the *sampling* of some external quantity, such as the status of a physical or chemical process. A task whose only purpose is periodic sampling is called a *sampler*. The task type FURNACE discussed in Section 6.3.5.2 is a typical example. Another category consists of *output generators*. These tasks periodically output values that may be accumulated by other tasks or calculated by the output generator itself. For example, the software in a music synthesizer may contain a task METRONOME that gives the beat to other tasks and various connected instruments. All the monster-related tasks discussed in Section 6.1 are output generators. A third category, referred to as *regulators*, is discussed in Section 6.4.1.2.

The classification of delay-loop-based tasks as samplers, regulators, and output generators is not intended to be exhaustive. For example, the periodic action may involve both sampling and output generation. Similarly, one task may sample more than one quantity with the same sampling frequency. It is also easy to construct a task that samples one quantity with an interval I and another with the interval K∗I, where K is an integer. Finally, the delay parameter need not be constant but may be calculated as part of the periodic action. With variations like these, the delay-loop structure is a reusable template for task construction and many concurrent applications can be based on delay-loop tasks and guardian tasks alone.

Each sampler, regulator, and output generator is a *subject task* and operates on its own schedule, independent of other tasks. The schedule, of course, is determined by the repeatedly executed **delay** statement. A concurrent program normally contains more than one such subject. The tasks operate on various objects, which may be unique to an individual task or shared. In case an object is shared, it must usually be protected against simultaneous access by different tasks. *Mutual exclusion* of tasks accessing a shared object is enforced by means of *guardian tasks* as discussed in Section 6.4.2 and further in Chapter 7.

The delay-loop tasks are based on simple, commonly occurring behavior patterns that the software is required to exhibit. As a behavior pattern grows more complex, it is more suitable to tailor a task to the particular pattern. This is referred to as *entity-life modeling* and is discussed at length in Chapter 8. Delay-loop tasks rely entirely on a task's *reschedulability*, that is, its ability to reschedule itself for execution at a specified later time, which may be calculated dynamically. More complex tasks may have other functions, but the need for reschedulability remains an important criterion for introducing a subject task into a design (Chapter 8).

6.4.1.2 Feedback paths and regulator tasks

A *regulator task* takes periodic samples of some quantity and creates output depending on their values. A regulator task is part of a *feedback path*. In the automobile cruise control example mentioned in Section 5.4.1 it is important to keep the speed of a car as close to a desired speed as possible. This can be done by means of a simple regulator that periodically measures the current speed and

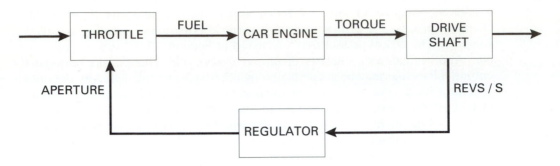

Figure 6-3   Feedback path from the drive shaft via a regulator task to the throttle in the cruise control example.

adjusts the throttle accordingly. That feedback path is illustrated in Figure 6-3 and functions as follows:

> The throttle controls the input to the engine by limiting the amount of fuel.
>
> The engine delivers torque to the drive shaft.
>
> The engine's output in terms of revolutions per unit of time is fed back through the regulator, which adjusts the aperture of the throttle according-ing to the desired speed.

In software, the regulator in Figure 6-3 may be implemented as a task, THROTTLE, based on a delay loop. It samples the speed periodically in terms of drive-shaft revolutions per time unit, compares the current speed to a desired speed, and adjusts the throttle. A *feedback path* passes from the output of the system that must be regulated through the regulator to the system input. In control system terminology, the *output signal* from the system is fed into a *control law* that takes the desired output into account and computes a *control signal* that is fed into the system. In our case the car engine is the system, the number of drive-shaft revolutions is the output signal, and the THROTTLE task in the cruise control software is the regulator. The control law is the algorithm whereby the THROTTLE computes a suitable throttle adjustment based on the number of revolutions and the desired speed. The task adjusts the throttle of the car and thereby sends a control signal to the engine.

In our example we can assume that the control signal at each point in time is dependent only on the output signal at the same point in time. With more complex control laws, the control signal depends on the changing values of the output signal over time. In that case, the software regulator maintains earlier samples of the output signal in memory to use them in the calculation of later control signals.

In the regulator in the cruise control example, the execution time for the control law is probably much shorter than the necessary interval between throttle adjustments. In other software applications, such as avionics, where feedback control is a primary concern, one embedded system may be involved in many feedback paths. The approach with concurrent regulator tasks can be used if the time required for executing each control law is negligible so that the processor is usually idle and available to each task that resumes execution. It is also useful on a multiprocessor architecture, where each regulator is executed on its own processor.

Many reactive systems, such as avionics, are based strongly on feedback paths. Often, such systems are not implemented with concurrent tasks. Instead, the software is divided into *frames* that are executed on a period predetermined basis. Because of the predetermined timing, such *frame-based* systems can be much more efficient than task-based ones. The run-time system used in a frame-based system, called a *cyclic executive*, is considerably simpler than the run-time system needed to support multitasking. A cyclic executive does not support dynamic rescheduling. Frame-based systems are outside the scope of this book; we concentrate on systems where such dynamic rescheduling is necessary.

6.4.1.3 Interrupt handling

A sampler such as FURNACE obtains information about the problem environment by sensing a hardware unit such as a thermometer. The information is gathered on the initiative of the software and obtained at intervals defined by the program. In other situations it is necessary to bring the occurrence of some event in the problem environment to the immediate attention of the software. This is done by means of *interrupts*.

An interrupt is a hardware signal that causes the CPU to discontinue its current execution, save the current program counter and other volatile data (such as the contents of the CPU registers), and start executing an *interrupt handler*. In general, an interrupt handler is a segment of code located at a particular hardware address and designed to handle one particular interrupt. Different interrupts have different handlers at different locations. In Ada, the hardware address of an interrupt handler is associated with an entry point, E, of a task, T. An interrupt is handled the same as an entry call. T executes the statement

> **accept** E;

and is suspended until the interrupt occurs. The execution of T is resumed when the interrupt occurs. As usual, the statement **accept** E may be included in a **select** construct.

An entry is associated with a hardware interrupt address by means of an *address clause* as follows:

> **for** E **use at** 8#45#;

Here, 8#45# is an example of an octal address. A simple interrupt handler task for one interrupt may have the following basic structure:

```
task EHANDLER is
    entry E;
    for E use at 8#45#;
end EHANDLER;

task body EHANDLER is
begin
    loop
        accept E;
        -- (Take appropriate action upon interrupt E)
    end loop;
end EHANDLER;
```

Note that a loop is required to allow EHANDLER to handle a series of interrupts of type E. The action indicated may involve updating some data structure and/or making a rendezvous with another task. An interrupt handler is a subject, like an output generator, sampler, or regulator. It works on a schedule set by the external entity that creates the interrupts.

6.4.2 Guardian Tasks

The purpose of tasking is to allow independent execution threads to proceed simultaneously. Ideally, each task is a subject proceeding at its own pace, totally independent of the others. In reality, tasks usually have to share resources such as a hardware device or a data structure that can be used by at most one task at a time. Each task must have exclusive access to the device in the interval between command and response. Similarly, if a task is accessing a data structure, confusion results if the same data is simultaneously updated by another task.

In Ada, *mutual exclusion* of different tasks accessing shared resources (as well as all other task synchronization) is handled by means of rendezvous. In addition to the subject tasks, an Ada implementation usually includes *guardian* tasks whose sole purpose is the synchronization of other tasks and the control of such resources. A guardian task contains only **select** and **accept** statements enclosed in a loop. A guardian is not a subject. It does all of its processing while locked in a rendezvous with another task. Thus the guardian operates on a schedule set entirely by other tasks. Unlike the subject tasks, a guardian does not add concurrency to a program but rather limits it by forcing task synchronization. The mutual exclusion of tasks accessing shared resources is the subject of Chapter 7.

6.4.2.1 Example of a guardian task

The task FURNACE discussed in Section 6.3.5.2 calls the guardian task THERMOMETER. All FURNACE tasks share one physical thermometer, which is thus a critical resource. Figure 6-4 is an outline of the THERMOMETER task text.

```
task THERMOMETER is
-- Guardian task allowing one FURNACE instance at a time access
-- to the thermometer
    entry READTEMP(F: FURNACE_NO; TEMP: out TEMP_TYPE);
    entry T_INTRPT(PHYS_TEMP: TEMP_TYPE);
    for T_INTRPT use at 8#100#;
end;

task body THERMOMETER is
-- Repeatedly accept an entry call at READTEMP and return a
-- temperature for a certain furnace.
begin
    loop
        accept READTEMP(F: FURNACE_NO; TEMP: out TEMP_TYPE) do
            -- Issue command to physical thermometer.
            -- Wait for interrupt:
            accept T_INTRPT(PHYS_TEMP: TEMP_TYPE) do TEMP:=PHYS_TEMP; end T_INTRPT;
        end READTEMP;
    end loop;
end THERMOMETER;
```

Figure 6-4   The guardian task THERMOMETER accepts an entry call at READTEMP, returns a temperature, and loops back to accept another call. To obtain each temperature, it sends a command to the physical thermometer, then waits for an interrupt at T_INTRPT which corresponds to the octal hardware interrupt address 100 (for example).

The rendezvous mechanism ensures mutual exclusion of FURNACE tasks so that only one at a time can execute the extended rendezvous, where it is locked up by THERMOMETER until a temperature has been obtained. If another task attempts a rendezvous in the meantime, it is queued until the first caller has been served.

The structure of THERMOMETER is based on an **accept** statement in an infinite loop. There need be no delay, since the timing is totally dependent on the calling tasks. THERMOMETER serves callers of the entry READTEMP in a first-come-first-served manner. READTEMP is an extended rendezvous which lasts until the **out** parameter TEMP has been given a value. THERMOMETER is somewhat similar to a subprogram called by the FURNACE tasks. It is important to note that it is a task with its own execution thread. For this reason the loop in the THERMOMETER task is important. If the THERMOMETER task does not explicitly loop back to accept another entry call after one has been served but instead, continues through its final end, the task dies. In that case, further calls at THERMOMETER.READTEMP result in TASKING_ERROR, since they will be attempts at rendezvous with a nonexisting task.

As mentioned in Section 6.4.1.3, external events are often signaled to embedded software by means of *interrupts*. In the RTS, the THERMOMETER task sends a command to the physical thermometer, then accepts an interrupt when the temperature has been obtained. Even though it handles an interrupt,

THERMOMETER is a guardian and not an interrupt handler as defined in Section 6.4.1. It receives the interrupt during a rendezvous with another task and as a response to a specific command. An interrupt handler task handles spontaneous, unsolicited interrupts.

6.4.3 Programs with Multiple Tasks

In addition to calling THERMOMETER, FURNACE sends a temperature in a message to the host by calling

    OUTPUT.SEND(MY_F, TEMP);

Figure 6-5 is a buhrgraph showing the interaction between the tasks FURNACE, THERMOMETER, and OUTPUT. It shows single tasks as parallelograms and the multiple instances of FURNACE by means of shadowing. INITIAL TASK refers to the processing done before any tasks have been explicitly created. The entry points ALERT, READTEMP, and SEND are shown as "sockets" in each task. Entry calls are shown as arrows from calling task to entry point. The interrupt at T_INTRPT is shown as an arrow from nowhere. Parameters transferred with each entry call are indicated by means of little arrows with rings on their tails in the style of structured design (compare Section 4.2.1). All the tasks have been enclosed in a big box representing the procedure RTS, where they are declared.

Figure 6-6 contains the program text. For simplicity, all the tasks are declared in the procedure RTS. The main procedure initializes each FURNACE task by supplying it with the corresponding furnace number. (The initialization of the array INTERVAL is merely indicated by a comment in the main procedure.) The system shown in Figure 6-6 is a simplified version of the remote temperature sensor system discussed in Section 6.5. Like the simple example in Figure 6-6, many concurrent programs can be constructed entirely from delay-loop tasks, interrupt handlers, and guardian tasks. We see examples of that in this and the following chapters.

6.4.4 Debugging and Test of Concurrent Software

This section introduces briefly some issues to do with the testing and debugging[1] of concurrent software. Testing and debugging usually require that we build *scaffolding* software to simulate the behavior of the concurrent software's ultimate

---

[1] The words *bug* and *debug* both predate computers and software. According to the Oxford English Dictionary, *bug* in the sense of a "defect or fault in a machine, plan, or the like" [Oxford] can be traced back to a quote from T. A. Edison in 1889. The dictionary traces the word *debug* in the sense "to remove faults from [a machine, system, etc.]" back to 1945.

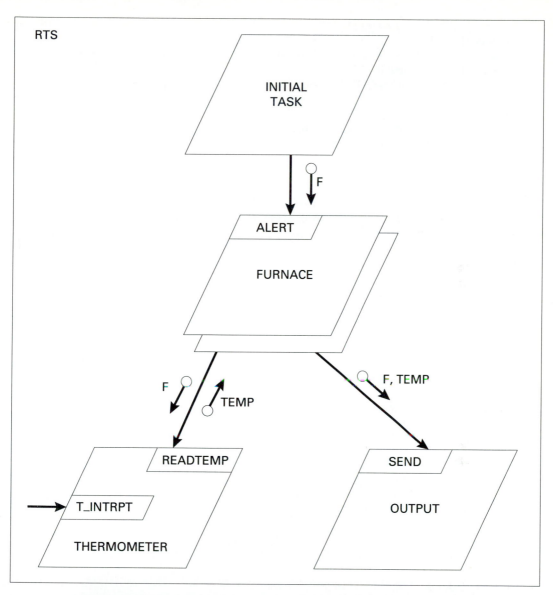

Figure 6-5 Buhrgraph of the RTS program. (A parallelogram indicates a task or a task-type instance.)

working environment. This means that the scaffolding software is modeled on the environment in the sense generally used in this book. Before discussing scaffolding we touch on other issues to do with the monitoring of concurrent programs in progress.

```
    with CALENDAR; use CALENDAR;
procedure RTS is
-- Sampling of 16 furnaces at individual intervals
type TEMP_TYPE is new INTEGER;
subtype FURNACE_NO is INTEGER range 0..15;

task type FURNACE is
-- Sample the temperature of a furnace periodically.
    entry ALERT(F: FURNACE_NO);
end;

task OUTPUT is
-- Allow one FURNACE instance at a time to send a message to the host.
    entry SEND(F: FURNACE_NO; TEMP: TEMP_TYPE);
end;

task THERMOMETER is
-- Guardian task allowing one FURNACE instance at a time
-- access to the thermometer
    entry READTEMP(F: FURNACE_NO; TEMP: out TEMP_TYPE);
    entry T_INTRPT(PHYS_TEMP: TEMP_TYPE);
    for T_INTRPT use at 8#100#;
end;


FARRAY: array (FURNACE_NO) of FURNACE;
INTERVAL: array (FARRAY'RANGE) of DURATION;

task body FURNACE is
-- Sample the temperature of furnace MY_F with the sampling
-- interval given in INTERVAL(MY_F).
MY_F: FURNACE_NO;    -- Furnace number
TEMP: TEMP_TYPE;
NEXT: TIME;               -- Next sampling time
begin
    accept ALERT(F: FURNACE_NO) do MY_F:=F; end;
    NEXT:=CLOCK;
    loop
        THERMOMETER.READTEMP(MY_F,TEMP);
        NEXT:=NEXT + INTERVAL(MY_F);
        OUTPUT.SEND(MY_F,TEMP);
        delay (NEXT − CLOCK);
    end loop;
end FURNACE;
```

Figure 6-6   Procedure RTS with the tasks FURNACE, OUTPUT, and THERMOMETER.

```
task body OUTPUT is
-- Repeatedly accept an entry call at SEND. Send a message
-- to the host and await acknowledgment.
OUTPUT_F: FURNACE_NO;
OUTPUT_TEMP: TEMP_TYPE;
begin
   loop
      accept SEND(F: FURNACE_NO; TEMP: TEMP_TYPE) do
         OUTPUT_F:=F; OUTPUT_TEMP:=TEMP;
      end;
      -- Format and send message to host.
      -- Wait for acknowledgment.
   end loop;
end OUTPUT;


task body THERMOMETER is
-- Repeatedly accept an entry call at READTEMP and return a
-- temperature for a certain furnace.
begin
   loop
      accept READTEMP(F: FURNACE_NO; TEMP: out TEMP_TYPE) do
         -- Issue command to physical thermometer.
         -- Wait for interrupt:
         accept T_INTRPT(PHYS_TEMP: TEMP_TYPE) do TEMP:=PHYS_TEMP; end T_INTRPT;
      end READTEMP;
   end loop;
end THERMOMETER;


begin
-- Main procedure. Initialize FURNACE tasks with unique
-- furnace numbers.
   -- Initialize INTERVAL.....
   --
   for F in FARRAY'RANGE loop
      FARRAY(F).ALERT(F);
   end loop;
end RTS;
```

Figure 6-6   *(continued)*

6.4.4.1 Execution monitoring

A major issue in debugging is to monitor the progress of the software as it is executed. In an interactive environment, with an ongoing dialogue between operator and software, the application output is often an important indicator of the progress of execution. If it is insufficient, the dialogue can often easily be supplemented with additional diagnostic output. Embedded systems, on the other hand, often do not reveal their progress of execution to an operator. A particular problem occurs in concurrent software, where multiple tasks proceed independently. In that environment, the progress of each task must usually be monitored separately.

A *debugger* is a tool included in most software development systems. It provides an artificial, controlled execution environment where a program may be stopped at a given *breakpoint* during execution. The debugger allows the programmer to associate a breakpoint with any program statement. Some debuggers also allow breakpointing by data reference, so that the execution is interrupted as soon as a certain data item is read and/or updated. When execution is interrupted, the programmer may inquire about the current value of program variables.

A debugger allows the programmer to trace a program through successive breakpointing. This is particularly useful if execution derails somewhere in the program text. To find the point of derailment, the programmer first breakpoints a certain statement early in the program. When the break occurs, the programmer knows that execution has progressed correctly so far. Another breakpoint is then set further on in the text, and so on. If a breakpoint is not reached, the programmer knows that execution has derailed after the previous breakpointed statement. Tracing through successive breakpointing is most convenient in a sequential program or in those parts of a concurrent program executed by a single task. If multiple tasks execute the same program text, each task executing a breakpointed instruction causes execution to stop. Some debuggers may allow the programmer to specify that execution may stop only when the breakpoint is reached by a particular task.

6.4.4.2 Scaffolding

Reactive software such as that in the remote temperature sensor is embedded in a larger system. That system may include hardware devices as well as other software modules with which the program will interact. Usually, the software must be developed to some degree without access to its intended working environment, which must then be simulated in software for debugging and testing purposes. Such a simulated environment is called a *test harness* or *scaffolding*.

In concurrent software, the scaffolding typically includes extra tasks that simulate aspects of the environment. We refer to them as *scaffolding tasks*. In general, scaffolding tasks must produce the stimuli that the software normally gets from its working environment. If the software is interrupt driven, a scaffolding task may simulate interrupts by means of rendezvous. Other scaffolding tasks must accept the output produced by the software, and convert it to a form that allows the programmer or tester to monitor the progress of program execution via a terminal.

6.4.4.3 Simulated output

In the development of embedded software, the scaffolding can often be used to produce output that allows the programmer to monitor the progress of program execution. While the intended output may be in the form of hardware signals, the scaffolding may convert it and direct it to a terminal screen. If the system includes a supervisor screen as a permanent part, the simulated output may be directed to that screen. Otherwise, a screen may be connected for debugging purposes only.

Output from multiple tasks, which normally operate on different hardware devices, may have to be channeled to one debugging terminal. In that situation the terminal screen becomes a shared resource. Mutual exclusion is discussed further in Chapter 7. Scaffolding is discussed further in connection with the remote temperature sensor problem in Section 6.5 and in connection with the buoy problem in Chapter 8.

6.5 EXAMPLE:
REMOTE TEMPERATURE SENSOR PROBLEM

In this section the software in a remote temperature sensor (RTS) is presented as a case study in concurrent software design. It illustrates the importance of concurrent tasks as basic software building blocks and their direct relation to concurrent patterns in the problem environment. It also illustrates several aspects of the task syntax. The program in Figure 6-6 is a simplified version of the RTS software, and pieces of the software, including the FURNACE, THERMOMETER, and OUTPUT tasks, were used as examples in the preceding section. The remote temperature sensor example was originally suggested by Young [Young]. It was modified by Nielsen and Shumate [Nielsen], whose software design based on structured analysis is fundamentally different from the one presented here. The differences are discussed in [Sanden]. The example is also discussed in [Cherry], [Carter], and [Howes].

6.5.1 Problem Description

The remote temperature sensor (RTS) (Figure 6-7) is an autonomous software-driven hardware device that uses a digital thermometer to obtain temperature readings from a number of furnaces and reports the temperature values to a host computer. The host sends *control packets* (*CP*) to the remote sensor, each including a furnace number (0..15) and a reading interval (10..99 seconds). The remote sensor acknowledges each CP with a *CP-Ack* (*CP-Nak* if the packet is incorrect). When a correct control packet for a certain furnace has been received, the sensor

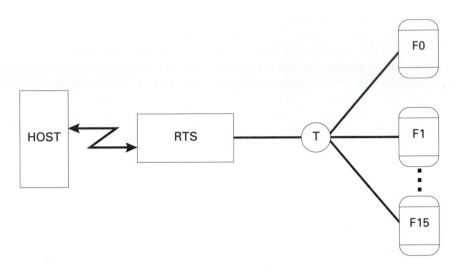

Figure 6-7 The remote temperature sensor (RTS) is connected to a host computer and a thermometer, T. The thermometer is connected to 16 furnaces, F0 .. F15.

reads the temperature of that furnace periodically at the interval given in the packet. The sensor manages up to 16 such simultaneous reading series for different furnaces.

The RTS sends every temperature reading to the host in a data packet (DP), then waits for either a DP-Ack or a DP-Nak from the host. A DP-Nak signifies that the DP has been received incorrectly by the host, and causes the RTS to resend it. If neither a DP-Ack nor a DP-Nak arrives within 2 seconds, it is assumed that a transmission error has occurred, and the DP is resent. The RTS is equipped with one thermometer, which, upon request from the software, stores the temperature of a specified furnace in a designated hardware buffer, then creates an interrupt. At most one thermometer request can be outstanding at any time.

To avoid dealing with the hardware-dependent details, we assume that a simple communication package, RTS_COMM, is available that sends and receives data packets, control packets, and acknowledgments. We will be concerned with a package REMOTE that *withs* RTS_COMM.

6.5.2 Subject and Guardian Tasks

To design the software, we first analyze the problem environment. We are particularly interested in identifying *threads of events* in the reality. The threads of events are captured as subject tasks in the software. As in earlier chapters, we are also interested in *objects* in the reality on which packages in the software may be based. For example, the package RTS_COMM is modeled on the communication line, which is an object in the reality. When identifying threads of events, we try to capture as much of the complexity of the problem as possible in as few threads as possible. In general, the more complexity that can be captured in a single, sequential thread, the better.

The following concurrent threads of events can be identified in the RTS problem environment:

> *The reading series for each furnace*, each with its own periodicity. The reading interval for each furnace is kept in an array INTERVAL. Normally, each reading is followed immediately by the transmission of a DP and the reception of a DP-Ack. There are up to 16 concurrent readings series, which are modeled by the array FARRAY of FURNACE, where FURNACE is a task type.
>
> *The sequence of control packets* arriving at the sensor, each answered by a CP-Ack or a CP-Nak. A task INPUT is necessary and creates the CP-Acks and CP-Naks.

The tasks modeled on these threads of events share resources such as the thermometer and the communication line. In addition to the subject tasks, we will need three *guardian* tasks to enforce mutual exclusion of tasks accessing these shared objects:

> THERMOMETER serializes the accesses to the thermometer.
>
> OUTPUT sends one DP at a time and awaits a DP-Ack, a DP-Nak, or a time-out before sending the next.
>
> CONTROL_INTERVAL serializes the accesses to the array INTERVAL.

6.5.3 Description of the RTS Software

The package REMOTE is shown in the buhrgraph in Figure 6-8. The interface of the package RTS_COMM is also shown, but not the internal structure of the package. Note that bent-back arrows indicate conditional entry calls. In the following sections we describe the various tasks and packages. Figure 6-9 is the program text.

a. Task INPUT

INPUT performs the following loop: Accept an entry call at RECEIVE and receive a CP for a furnace F. If the interval in the CP is out of bounds, send a CP-Nak. Otherwise, send a CP-Ack and call the procedure FPACK.NEW_INT with F and the new temperature-reading interval as parameters. The call to NEW_INT changes the reading interval for furnace F. The subprogram is discussed in the following.

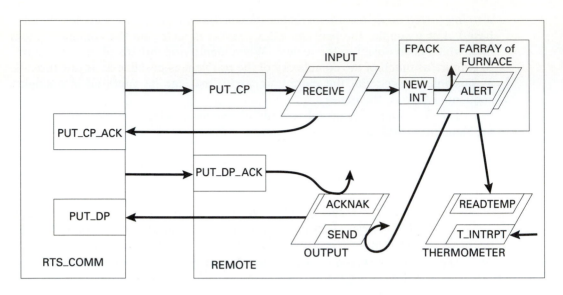

Figure 6-8   Buhrgraph of the complete RTS software. (The guardian CONTROL_INTERVAL is not shown.)

```
package REMOTE is
-- The software in a remote temperature sensor.
   type TEMP_TYPE is new INTEGER;
   subtype FURNACE_NO is INTEGER range 0..15;
   type ACK_OR_NAK is (ACK, NAK);
   procedure PUT_CP(F: FURNACE_NO; INT: DURATION);
   procedure PUT_DP_ACK(AN: ACK_OR_NAK);
end REMOTE;


with REMOTE; use REMOTE;
package RTS_COMM is
-- Procedures for communication with host
   procedure PUT_DP(FNUM: FURNACE_NO; TEMP: TEMP_TYPE);
   procedure PUT_CP_ACK(AN: ACK_OR_NAK);
end RTS_COMM;


   with RTS_COMM; use RTS_COMM;
   with CALENDAR; use CALENDAR;
package body REMOTE is
-- Sample 16 furnaces at individual intervals. Send each
-- sample to the host. Accept control packets with new
```

Figure 6-9   Package REMOTE containing the package FPACK and the tasks INPUT, OUTPUT, and THERMOMETER. The package RTS_COMM contains the communication-line interface. Its body is not shown.

```
-- sampling intervals at any time.
F:      FURNACE_NO;
INT:  DURATION;
MIN:  constant DURATION:=10.0;
MAX:  constant DURATION:=99.0;

task INPUT is
-- Receive control packets
    entry RECEIVE(F:FURNACE_NO; INT:DURATION);
end INPUT;

task OUTPUT is
-- Allow one FURNACE instance at a time to send a message to the host.
    entry SEND(FNUMBER: FURNACE_NO; TEMP: TEMP_TYPE);
    entry ACKNAK(AN: ACK_OR_NAK);
end OUTPUT;

task THERMOMETER is
-- Guardian task allowing one FURNACE instance at a time
-- access to the thermometer
    entry READTEMP(FNUMBER: FURNACE_NO; TEMP: out TEMP_TYPE);
    entry T_INTRPT(PHYS_TEMP: TEMP_TYPE);
    for T_INTRPT use at 8#100#;
end THERMOMETER;

procedure PUT_CP(F: FURNACE_NO; INT: DURATION) is
-- Operation procedure accepting a control packet from the host
begin
    INPUT.RECEIVE(F, INT);
end PUT_CP;

procedure PUT_DP_ACK(AN: ACK_OR_NAK) is
-- Operation procedure accepting a DP-ACK from the host.
-- ACK is dropped if OUTPUT is no longer waiting.
begin
    select OUTPUT.ACKNAK(AN);
    else null;
    end select;
end PUT_DP_ACK;

package F_PACK is
-- Periodic sampling of several furnaces.
    procedure NEW_INT(F: FURNACE_NO; INTVAL: DURATION);
end F_PACK;
```

Figure 6-9   *(continued)*

```
task body INPUT is
-- Repeatedly accept a control packet from the host.
MY_F: FURNACE_NO; IINT: DURATION;
begin
   loop
      accept RECEIVE(F:FURNACE_NO;INT:DURATION) do
         MY_F:=F; IINT:=INT; end;
      -- Make sure that interval is reasonable.
      if IINT >= MIN and IINT <= MAX then
         F_PACK.NEW_INT(MY_F, IINT);
         RTS_COMM.PUT_CP_ACK(ACK);
      else RTS_COMM.PUT_CP_ACK(NAK);
      end if;
   end loop;
end INPUT;


task body OUTPUT is
-- Repeatedly accept an entry call at SEND. Send a message
-- to the host and await acknowledgment.
FFNUMBER: FURNACE_NO;
TTEMP:       TEMP_TYPE;
MY_AN:       ACK_OR_NAK;
PER:         constant DURATION:=2.0;
begin
   loop
      accept SEND(FNUMBER: FURNACE_NO; TEMP: TEMP_TYPE) do
      FFNUMBER:=FNUMBER; TTEMP:=TEMP; end;
      loop
         RTS_COMM.PUT_DP(FFNUMBER, TTEMP);
         select
            accept ACKNAK(AN: ACK_OR_NAK) do
               MY_AN:=AN; end ACKNAK;
               exit when MY_AN = ACK;
         or
            delay PER;  -- Time out acknowledgment
         end select;
      end loop;
   end loop;
end OUTPUT;


task body THERMOMETER is
-- Repeatedly accept an entry call at READTEMP and return a
-- temperature for a certain furnace
begin
   loop
      accept READTEMP(FNUMBER: FURNACE_NO; TEMP: out TEMP_TYPE) do
```

Figure 6-9   (*continued*)

```
      -- Issue command to physical thermometer.
      -- Wait for interrupt:
      accept T_INTRPT(PHYS_TEMP: TEMP_TYPE) do
          TEMP:=PHYS_TEMP;
      end T_INTRPT;
    end READTEMP;
  end loop;
end THERMOMETER;


package body F_PACK is
-- Package containing FURNACE task type and its instances

task type FURNACE is
-- Sample the temperature of a furnace periodically.
    entry ALERT(F: FURNACE_NO);
end FURNACE;

task CONTROL_INTERVAL is
-- Guardian task protecting array of sampling intervals
    entry SET_INT(F: FURNACE_NO; INTVAL: DURATION);
    entry GET_INT(F: FURNACE_NO; INTVAL: out DURATION);
end CONTROL_INTERVAL;

FARRAY: array(FURNACE_NO) of FURNACE;

procedure NEW_INT(F: FURNACE_NO; INTVAL: DURATION) is
-- Operation procedure allowing change of interval
begin
    CONTROL_INTERVAL.SET_INT(F, INTVAL); -- Change interval
                                         -- for furnace F.
    select FARRAY(F).ALERT(F);
    else null;
    end select;
end NEW_INT;


task body FURNACE is
-- Sample the temperature of furnace MY_F with the sampling
-- interval given in INTERVAL(MY_F).
MY_F:   FURNACE_NO;   -- Furnace number, 0..15
TEMP:   TEMP_TYPE;
NEXT:   TIME;               -- Next sampling time
INTVAL: DURATION;
begin
    accept ALERT(F: FURNACE_NO) do MY_F:=F; end;
    NEXT:=CLOCK;
```

Figure 6-9 (*continued*)

```
    loop
        THERMOMETER.READTEMP(MY_F,TEMP);
        CONTROL_INTERVAL.GET_INT(F, INTVAL);
        NEXT:=NEXT + INTVAL;
        select OUTPUT.SEND(MY_F,TEMP);
        or delay (NEXT − CLOCK);
        end select;
        select accept ALERT(F: FURNACE_NO); NEXT:=CLOCK;
        or delay (NEXT − CLOCK);
        end select;
    end loop;
end FURNACE;


task body CONTROL_INTERVAL is
-- Repeatedly accept calls to change or read sampling interval.
INTERVAL: array(FURNACE_NO) of DURATION:=(others => MAX);
begin
    loop
        select
            accept SET_INT(F: FURNACE_NO; INTVAL: DURATION) do
                INTERVAL(F):=INTVAL; end;
        or
            accept GET_INT(F: FURNACE_NO; INTVAL: out DURATION) do
                INTVAL:=INTERVAL(F); end;
        end select;
    end loop;
end CONTROL_INTERVAL;
end F_PACK;
end REMOTE;
```

Figure 6-9   *(continued)*

b. Package F_PACK

For separation of concerns, the FURNACE tasks together with the array INTERVAL are encapsulated in a package F_PACK with an operation procedure NEW_INT(F, INTVAL) which changes the reading interval for furnace F. From the point of view of INPUT, F_PACK is an object with the operation NEW_INT. INPUT calls NEW_INT with the parameters F and I, where F is a furnace number and I is the new reading interval. In NEW_INT, the array element INTERVAL(F) is updated with I, and the following conditional entry call is made to the task-type instance FARRAY(F) that corresponds to furnace F:

```
    select FARRAY(F).ALERT(F);
    else null;
    end select;
```

As discussed in Section 6.3.2.2, a conditional entry call is effective only if the callee is waiting in the corresponding **accept** statement when the call is made. Otherwise, the statement after **else** is executed. In the present case, if the instance FARRAY(F) is waiting at the **accept** ALERT statement, it is resumed by the rendezvous call. If it is already executing, the call has no effect.

A conditional entry call transfers data between the tasks by means of the entry parameters only when the rendezvous actually occurs. This is adequate in the present case. The furnace number (parameter F) need be transferred only once to each task. The new reading interval is not transferred in the entry call. Instead, the FURNACE task always gets it from the array INTERVAL by a call to CONTROL_INTERVAL.GET_INT.

An unconditional entry call to ALERT would be inconvenient since the caller INPUT would be blocked until the callee accepted the call. With the conditional call this is never the case. If the call is not accepted immediately, it is voided and control is returned from NEW_INT to the task body of INPUT.

c. Task Type FURNACE

Each instance of FURNACE performs as follows: Accept an initial rendezvous at ALERT, store the furnace number in the local variable MY_F and the current time in NEXT, then perform the following loop:

Call THERMOMETER.READTEMP and obtain a temperature value.

Call CONTROL_INTERVAL.GET_INT and obtain the current sampling interval.

Call OUTPUT.SEND with a time-out limiting the wait to the next reading time.

Delay until the next reading time or until ALERT is called, signaling a change of reading interval. If a change is made, update NEXT.

This loop contains a timed entry call and a selective wait. As discussed in Section 6.3.2.2, a timed entry call limits the time the task will wait for an entry call to be accepted. The construct is as follows:

```
select
    OUTPUT.SEND(MY_F, TEMP);
or
    delay (NEXT − CLOCK);
end select;
```

With this construct, the call to OUTPUT is timed out after NEXT − CLOCK seconds. This is in case there is a communication problem with the host so that a DP is not transmitted by the time the temperature of a furnace must again be read. In that situation the call is voided and the FURNACE task instance goes back to read the temperature, then makes another call to OUTPUT. That way when communication is resumed, no obsolete temperature readings will be transmitted.

The selective wait construct is as follows:

```
select
    accept ALERT(F: FURNACE_NO);
    NEXT:=CLOCK;
or
    delay (NEXT − CLOCK);
end select;
```

As discussed in Section 6.3.3, this construct allows a task to wait for one of two things: an entry call or the expiration of a time limit, whichever comes first. In the FURNACE task, the **delay** alternative will most often be used. The delay expires when it is time to read a temperature. The **accept** alternative provides for a change of the reading interval. While a task is suspended, a control packet for the corresponding furnace may arrive from the host. The execution of the suspended FURNACE task instance is then immediately resumed. To see the importance of this, consider an extreme case. Suppose that a certain furnace is currently sampled every hour. Suddenly, shortly after a temperature has been read and a data packet sent, the host wants to change the interval to 10 seconds. If **accept** ALERT is executed after the delay has expired, the task must wait until the end of the hour before being made aware of the new interval. The selective wait allows the task to accept an ALERT call while it is waiting for the next, scheduled reading time.

d. Task CONTROL_INTERVAL
The task CONTROL_INTERVAL is a guardian that operates as follows: Repeatedly accept either SET_INT or GET_INT and update or retrieve the value of an entry in the array INTERVAL. (For simplicity, CONTROL_INTERVAL is not shown in Figure 6-8.)

e. Task THERMOMETER
THERMOMETER operates as follows: Repeatedly, accept an entry call (from a FURNACE task) at READTEMP, issue a read request to the digital thermometer for the appropriate furnace, wait for the interrupt at T_INTRPT, and release the caller with the temperature value.

f. Task OUTPUT
OUTPUT performs the following loop:

Accept a rendezvous at SEND (from a FURNACE task). Receive a furnace number and a temperature value. Release the caller.

Send a DP.

Wait for a call at ACKNAK. If a DP-Nak is received, or no call comes within 2 seconds, resend the message, and again wait for a rendezvous at ACKNAK for up to 2 seconds.

Like THERMOMETER, OUTPUT consists of an **accept** statement inside an infinite loop. There is no **out** parameter, and the extended rendezvous only includes the transfer of **in** parameter values to task variables. This simplifies the program text by removing a level of nesting and has no affect on the exclusive access to the line. The task loops back to accept another entry call at SEND only when the first message has been sent and acknowledged. As in THERMOMETER, the loop is essential in order to keep the task alive.

Strictly speaking, OUTPUT is not a guardian task. It introduces concurrency by formatting and sending the message and waiting for the acknowledgment when the caller has already been released from the rendezvous. In principle, the FURNACE task instance can take another temperature sample while the first message is still being sent. (OUTPUT can be made into a guardian task; see Exercise 6.5.)

6.5.4 Efficiency

The execution efficiency of a concurrent program has much to do with the execution time necessary for the rendezvous and for the context switch, the operation necessary to give a new task access to the processor. It is usually safe to assume that both the context switch and the rendezvous are relatively costly operations. Therefore, a program should have no unnecessary rendezvous and context switches. In the RTS problem, the regular sampling of furnace temperatures and transmission of data packets is most interesting from the point of view of efficiency. It is thus important to see how many entry calls are made in the temperature reading–DP–transmission cycle, which is repeatedly executed for each furnace (compare Figure 6-8). The following rendezvous occur:

FURNACE calls THERMOMETER.READTEMP (guardian)

FURNACE calls CONTROL_INTERVAL.GET_INT (guardian)

FURNACE calls DP_OUTPUT.SEND

INPUT calls DP_INPUT.ACKNAK

With a compiler that provides passive tasks, the efficiency of the solution could be improved by making DP_OUTPUT a guardian task, as explained in Section 6.5.4.1.

6.5.4.1 Passive tasks

The time for the rendezvous and the context switch is implementation dependent. In particular, the implementation of guardian tasks, which execute exclusively in rendezvous with other tasks, can readily be optimized. With some Ada compilers, a **pragma** PASSIVE can be used to indicate that a task is to be implemented without a separate control thread. This is possible only for guardian tasks that operate exclusively while in rendezvous with other tasks (Section 6.4.2) and for interrupt handlers (Section 6.4.1.3). The following additional restriction for passive guardian tasks are quoted from the manual for VADS, the Verdix Ada Development System [Verdix]:

> "In a passive task body, you cannot nest **accept** statements."
>
> "Declare blocks are prohibited inside a passive task."
>
> "Except within the body of an **accept** statement, passive tasks should not execute **delay** statements or make entry calls."
>
> "A **delay** alternative is not permitted as a select alternative in a passive task."
>
> "The priority of a passive task is always the same as the priority of the rendezvousing task."

Passive interrupt handlers are subject to similar restrictions.

6.5.5 Scaffolding in the RTS Example

The RTS software (Figure 6-8) contains a package REMOTE, which relies on another package, RTS_COMM, for communication with the host. We can debug and test REMOTE by replacing RTS_COMM with a scaffolding package that simulates the host communication. That is discussed in the next paragraph. We must also simulate the physical thermometer. This can be done either by replacing the task THERMOMETER with a scaffolding task, or by leaving THERMOMETER intact and including an additional scaffolding task that accepts commands to read a temperature and returns simulated temperature data after a delay.

The scaffolding RTS_COMM models the behavior of the host as seen from the remote sensor. It contains two scaffolding tasks, CP_SENDER and DP_RECEIVER, which work as follows:

> CP_SENDER models the activity in the host that occasionally generates control packets. It has one entry, CP_ACK. CP_SENDER calls REMOTE. PUT_CP at irregular intervals. It then waits for a CP-Ack at CP_ACK. CP_ACK is called from the subprogram PUT_CP_ACK, which is shown in Figure 6-8. CP_SENDER occasionally sends an incorrect control packet and then expects a CP-Nak rather than a CP-Ack.
>
> DP_RECEIVER models the activity within the mainframe that receives data packets and sends DP-Acks. It has one entry, DP, which is called from within PUT_DP. After receiving a DP and after a delay to simulate the time elapsed during data transmission, DP_RECEIVER normally sends a DP_Ack via a call to REMOTE.PUT_DP_ACK. It occasionally simulates a break of communication by not sending a DP_Ack within 2 seconds, and then expects retransmission of a data packet.

To facilitate debugging, CP_SENDER and DP_RECEIVER display each message as it is sent or received. Each message is supplied with a time stamp based on the function SECONDS(CLOCK).

6.5.6 RTS Example: Conclusion

In summary, the RTS is an example of a fairly straightforward system based largely on the built-in facilities of Ada and sampler tasks. The difficulties are localized in two areas: the change of reading intervals through control packets and the behavior of the system in the face of a communication breakdown. As mentioned earlier, the design presented here is based on a problem statement stemming from 1982. If the problem were restated today, less emphasis might have been given to optimizing the amount of transmitted data. The time of the temperature reading could then be included in each data packet, which would simplify the communication problem. The design here reflects the original problem statement, which simplifies comparison with the other solutions mentioned in the introduction. The solution relies on a package RTS_COMM for the communication between remote sensor and host. The internals of RTS_COMM are not elaborated here. The reader is referred to Section 7.5.3, where the design of a more complex communications package is discussed in detail.

6.6 CHAPTER SUMMARY _____

> *But now my task is smoothly done,*
> *I can fly or I can run.*
>
> *Milton,* Comus

Multitasking allows us to separate timing concerns within a program. Different *subject tasks* with incompatible schedules may coexist in one program and share resources as necessary. Tasks are useful abstractions both in interactive systems and in embedded and nonembedded reactive systems. We are concerned primarily with tasks sharing one hardware processor where the task structure reflects the concurrent nature of the problem environment, but the model also applies to parallel processors sharing memory.

Each task has a set of *permanent task variables*, *temporary variables*, and a *program counter*. In Ada, single tasks and task types can be declared, where a single task can be regarded as one instantiation of an anonymous task type. A task may reschedule itself for execution at a later time by means of the **delay** statement. A simple task such as a *sampler*, *reporter*, or *regulator* is based on a loop with a **delay** statement.

Task communication in Ada is based on the *rendezvous* as both a synchronization and data-passing construct. A task S can make a (conditional or unconditional) *call* to another task T at T's explicitly defined *entry points*. T waits for and receives calls at a specified entry point by executing an **accept** statement. The **select** construct allows T to wait for calls simultaneously at different entry points, and to limit the wait by means of a time-out value.

In principle, each task is modeled on an asynchronous behavior pattern in the problem environment. Ada's syntax also requires nonconcurrent, *guardian* tasks executing entirely in rendezvous with other tasks. Guardian tasks are used largely for the *mutual exclusion* of subject tasks accessing shared objects. Mutual exclusion is the topic of Chapter 7. Chapter 8 is devoted to the construction of concurrent software based on the mechanics of concurrency control discussed in this and the following chapters. Chapter 9 is a major case study of a concurrent software system.

REFERENCES

BURNS, A., *Concurrent Programming in Ada*, Cambridge University Press, Cambridge 1987.

CARTER, J. R., MMAIM: a software development method for Ada, *Ada Lett.*, VIII:3, May/June 1988, pp. 107–114, and VIII:4, August/September 1988, pp. 47–60.

CHERRY, G., *PAMELA Designer's Handbook*, The Analytic Sciences Corp., Reston, VA, 1986.

CHERRY, G., *PAMELA Designer's Handbook*, The Analytic Sciences Corp., 1986.

HOWES, N. R., Toward a real-time Ada design methodology, *ACM Tri-Ada Conference*, Baltimore, Md., December 1990, pp. 189–203.

LRM, *The Ada Language Reference Manual*, MIL-STD-1815A, U.S. Government Printing Office, Washington, D.C., 1983.

NIELSEN, K. W., and SHUMATE, K., Designing large real-time systems with Ada, *Commun. ACM*, 30:8, August 1987, pp. 695–715; corrected in *Commun. ACM*, 30:12, December 1987, p. 1073.

The Oxford English Dictionary, 2nd ed., Clarendon Press, Oxford, 1989.

SANDEN, B., Entity-life modeling and structured analysis in real-time software design: a comparison, *Commun. ACM*, 32:12, December 1989, pp. 1458–1466.

SILBERSCHATZ, A., PETERSON, J., and GALVIN, P., *Operating System Concepts*, 3rd ed., Addison-Wesley, Reading, Mass., 1991.

Verdix, *VADS Verdix Ada Development System, Programmer's Guide*, Verdix Corporation, Chantilly, VA, 1990.

Webster's Ninth New Collegiate Dictionary, Merriam-Webster, Springfield, Mass., 1986.

YOUNG, S. J., *Real Time Languages: Design and Development*, Ellis Horwood, Chichester, West Sussex, England, 1982.

EXERCISES

6.1 Nonsense

This exercise is intended to demonstrate the effect of multiple concurrent tasks by letting them write to the screen one at a time. Declare a task WRITER with one entry point, DISPLAY, which repeatedly accepts an entry call from another task with a string as a parameter, writes the string on the screen, then goes back to accept another call. Declare a task type NONSENSE with one entry point, INIT. NONSENSE accepts a rendezvous at INIT and receives a string and a value D of type DURATION as parameters. In a loop it then (1) delays D seconds, and (2) calls WRITER.DISPLAY to write the string on the screen. The loop is repeated a constant number of times, say 25.

In the main procedure, create at least three instances of type NONSENSE. Let it call the entry point INIT of each instance and supply a different string and delay interval to each one. The result will be a sequence of strings displayed on the screen. On a PC you will be able to see a string of each type appear with the associated delay interval. On a time-shared mainframe you will only be able to see that the mix of strings reflects the relation between the delay intervals. (For example, if "AAA" is displayed every 20 seconds and "BBB" every 10 seconds, "BBB" will appear twice as often as "AAA".)

Use a **terminate** alternative in WRITER so that WRITER terminates when the NONSENSE tasks have all finished processing.

6.2 Modified nonsense

As a variation of Exercise 6.1, rather than supplying each task with a fixed string, modify each NONSENSE task to prompt the terminal operator for a string of a given length and a value of type DURATION. To support this, define a new entry point GET_STRING for the WRITER task. NONSENSE calls GET_STRING once. GET_STRING prompts the user for a string and a delay, which are returned to NONSENSE. NONSENSE then displays that string repeatedly. WRITER must now have a select statement accepting either a call to GET_STRING or to DISPLAY, which displays the string on the screen. Use *guards* (Section 6.3.3.4) to ensure that no strings are displayed on the screen until all the tasks have obtained a string and an interval from the user. Make WRITER count the number of calls to GET_STRING and not accept calls to DISPLAY until all NONSENSE tasks have called GET_STRING. (This is a fairly inelegant arrangement intended only as an exercise in using guards.)

6.3 Independence of thread of control and the task body

In yet another variation of Exercise 6.1, write a procedure INFINITE_LOOP(T: TXT; D: DURATION) containing a loop with a call to WRITER.WRITE and a delay statement. The type TXT is a string of suitable length. D is the interval used in the delay statement. Then write three tasks, HUEY, LOUIE, and DEWEY, each containing only a call to INFINITE_LOOP. Each task passes its own string and interval. Modify WRITER to output a number with each string. Use this to enumerate the strings output by each task. For example, if HUEY outputs the string "HUEY ", LOUIE the string "LOUIE", and so on, the beginning of the output might look like this:

LOUIE 1   HUEY 1   DEWEY 1   HUEY 2   HUEY 3   DEWEY 2   HUEY 4   LOUIE 2 .....

(Refer to Section 6.3.6).

6.4 Sequence diagrams in the RTS problem

Make a sequence diagram of the life of a furnace, indicating the repeated reading of a temperature, transmission of a message or time-out, and delay. Make an input data sequence diagram of THERMOMETER showing the reception of commands and interrupts from the physical thermometer.

6.5 OUTPUT as a guardian task

Make OUTPUT into a guardian task by including all processing necessary to send a data packet and receive an acknowledgment in the body of the statement "**accept** SEND(...)." Refer to Section 6.5.3.f and Figure 6-9.

6.6 Identification of subjects

The program excerpt below includes three PUT_LINE statements. For each such statement, identify the executing subject.

```
task body A is
begin
   C.X;
end A;

task body B is
begin
   C.Y;
end B;

task body C is
begin
   accept Y do
      accept X do
         PUT_LINE("C.X");
         D.Z;
      end X;
      E.V;
   end Y;
end C;
```

```
task body D is
begin
   accept Z do PUT_LINE("D.Z"); end Z;
end D;

task body E is
begin
   accept V do PUT_LINE("E.V"); end V;
end E;
```

7 Resource Sharing

Friends share all things.

Pythagoras

7.1 INTRODUCTION

In a concurrent program, the subject tasks are independent threads of execution, each processing at its individual speed and operating on various objects. Some of these objects are *shared*; that is, they are operated on by more than one task. We are interested here in objects to which each task needs *exclusive access* for some period of time. In the RTS problem in Chapter 6, for example, tasks need exclusive access to the thermometer, to the array INTERVAL, which is updated by one task and read by others, and to the communication line on which data packets are sent to the host. Each of these objects must be *protected* against *conflicting access* by more than one task at a time.

Subject tasks and software objects are modeled on concurrent threads of events and objects in the problem environment. (This is explored further in Chapter 8.) A program with subject tasks competing for access to shared objects can then be a model of a real-world queueing situation where entities in the reality vie for exclusive access to shared resources. Such a program can be used to manage the queues and give the real-world entities access to the resources in an orderly fashion. In the flexible manufacturing system (FMS), for example, different jobs contend for workstations and other devices. This is controlled in software by means of job tasks contending for software objects representing the devices.

264

The software control of queueing in the reality is facilitated by an important property in Ada tasks that we will call *queueability*. (It is the counterpart of the reschedulability property discussed in Chapter 6.) Typically, we let a guardian task represent a shared resource, while the entities contending for that resource are modeled as subject tasks. Each entry has an associated entry queue of callers. The entry queues of the guardian then represent queues of real-world entities waiting for that resource. In the FMS problem, queueability is one criterion for the choice of the jobs as subjects.

In this chapter we discuss resource sharing in the reality and its software implementation. Section 7.2 deals with issues that apply both to real-world queueing situations and to the software. We discuss the concepts of *granularity* and *extent*, which have to do with the size of a resource that is held exclusively and how long it is held. Section 7.2 also deals with the important issue of *simultaneous, exclusive access* to different resources. This occurs in the FMS, where, for example, a job needs exclusive access to a workstation and an automated vehicle at the same time. For this, the job must gain access to one resource while exclusively holding another. This raises the possibility of *deadlock*, where two or more entities cannot proceed since each holds onto a resource needed by another.

The remainder of the chapter deals with exclusive access in software. In Section 7.3 we discuss the representation of shared resources as software modules. Resource sharing complicates the interfaces between modules since a task executing a subprogram may return with exclusive access to additional resources, which must later be released. Sections 7.4 and 7.5 deal with the implementation of *mutual exclusion*. Mutual exclusion is a way to enforce exclusive access to an object by making sure that only one task at a time may execute the code operating on the object. In Ada, mutual exclusion is always accomplished by means of tasking. Section 7.4 is devoted to the protection of single resources represented by information-hiding packages. In Section 7.5 we discuss the special problems associated with resource types, represented by abstract data types. Shared adts raise a granularity issue since either each instance or the set of all instances may be accessed exclusively.

Adts are used to model similar but distinct resources. For example, a communication system may include a set of message queues, each associated with a particular address. All the message queues have the same structure, but an application task needs to access a particular one to retrieve its own messages. This is different from a *pool* of identical, anonymous resources, where each task may use any one. In the FMS, for example, a pool of automated guided vehicles (AGVs) is shared by all the jobs. Section 7.6 deals with such *pooled resources* as well as *collective resources*, such as memory space and file space, where each task gets a share for its exclusive use.

In this chapter we discuss both the essential principles of resource sharing and exclusive access and the technicalities of how they are implemented. Such technicalities are necessary for our discussion of the examples in Chapters 8 and

9. They serve a similar purpose to the details of Ada tasking given in Chapter 6 and allow us to show the practicality of various designs by demonstrating how they are implemented. The chapter is intended to give the designer of reactive software a rather pragmatic view of resource sharing. The topic is the subject of much computer science research. For an exhaustive discussion, the reader is referred to the literature on concurrency and languages [Andrews], [Burns], [Feldman], [Hoare 74, 85], [Holt 82], operating systems [Deitel], [Silberschatz], [Tanenbaum], and database systems [Korth], [Pratt], [Bernstein].

7.2 ISSUES IN RESOURCE SHARING

In this section we discuss general issues that have to do with the sharing of resources in the real world or in software. In Sections 7.2.1 through 7.2.3 we introduce the concepts of *granularity* and *extent* of exclusive access. The system designer is concerned with the choice of proper granularity taking into account the extent of time a certain resource must be exclusively held. In Sections 7.2.4 through 7.2.6 we discuss *simultaneous exclusive access*, *deadlock*, and *deadlock prevention*.

7.2.1 Granularity

Granularity has to do with how we delimit individually protected resources. Each entity gets exclusive access to one *granule* of the resource at a time. Assume, for example, that multiple tasks need exclusive access to the data in an array. We may then choose to give one task at a time exclusive access to each individual element. This is an example of *fine* granularity. We may also choose to give each task exclusive access to the entire array. This is an example of *coarse* granularity. We say that granularity is either at the *level* of the individual element or at the level of the entire array. The granularity concept is known from database systems. When the database is processed in batch mode, the granule is often one or more entire files. In transaction processing, each transaction may instead keep one or more records locked, putting granularity at the record level [Korth], [Bernstein].

The finest possible granularity in software is at the level of single variables such as integers or Booleans. Exclusive access to such a variable is typically enforced by the hardware. The hardware accesses data in memory with a certain granularity, say 16 bits at a time. In that case the reading (or writing) of a 16-bit value is an *atomic* operation: It cannot be interrupted, even in a configuration where the memory is shared by multiple processors. We say that the hardware *serializes* the accesses to the variable. If, for example, an integer type is always stored and fetched in one piece, it is referred to as an *atomic integer*.

As long as atomicity can be guaranteed, atomic variables often provide a convenient and simple means of data exchange between tasks. On the other hand, many variables cannot be assumed to be atomic. If, for example, the variable S takes two memory accesses, and a task B reads it while another task, A, is writing a new value V_2 over the old value, V_1, then B may gain a *wild* (undefined) value, perhaps consisting of the most significant half of V_1 and the least significant half of V_2. This is obviously unacceptable, and in this case, mutual exclusion of the two tasks must be enforced by software.

In the case of the array INTERVAL in the RTS problem, the finest meaningful granularity is at the level of the individual array elements, since each call to SET_INT or GET_INT changes or retrieves the value of exactly one element. In the solution in Chapter 6, the granularity is actually coarser since each caller has exclusive access to the entire array. That way, the array can be protected by means of a single semaphore or special-purpose guardian task (see Section 7.4). Granularity at the level of the individual array element would require an array of guardian tasks, equal in size to the array INTERVAL itself.

7.2.2 Extent

In the RTS problem, the array INTERVAL is held with exclusive access for the duration of a single operation. In the FMS problem, an AGV is held for several minutes. The time a task is held up waiting for INTERVAL to be released is negligible, whereas the time a job is kept waiting for an AGV is significant. To distinguish between the two cases, we will say that the exclusive access to INTERVAL has *short extent* and the exclusive access to an AGV has *long extent*. The extent is a rough measure of the length of time that a resource is being exclusively held by an entity.

An exclusive access to a resource is of *short extent* if the time an entity has to wait for the resource is negligible. The resource is typically a shared data structure. Short extent is typically in the millisecond or microsecond range. If the extent is short, it is unlikely that two tasks will try to operate on the shared resource at the same time. This unlikely event must nevertheless be accounted for, but queueing is not an issue in the case of a short extent, and the delay involved is not externally noticeable.

The extent of an exclusive access to a resource is *long* if it has a significant effect in the problem environment. A long extent may be in the range of seconds or minutes. The shared resource is typically an object in the problem environment, and the queueing is externally visible. In the FMS system, a job needs exclusive access to an AGV in order to move a part between stands. In this case the extent of the exclusive access is a few minutes. It is orders of magnitude longer than in the example with the array INTERVAL. In the software, queued job tasks represent real jobs waiting for access to an AGV.

Extent is a relative measure. For an operating system giving user tasks access to some external storage device, a disk access is of long extent. But in the FMS problem, a disk access in the millisecond range is negligible compared to the extent of exclusive access to an AGV. Furthermore, a task may hold exclusive access to a program variable for the duration of a lengthy computation. While the computation is carried out at electronic speed, it may still cause a significant delay for other tasks.

7.2.3 Choice of Granularity

The extent of exclusive access affects the required granularity. Long extent typically requires the finest possible granularity, while short extent allows coarser granularity. In the case of INTERVAL, it is reasonable to treat the entire array as one granule because of the short extent of SET_INT and GET_INT. In contrast, in the FMS example, protection at a granularity level of the entire pool of AGVs is ludicrous, since it would give one job at a time exclusive access to all the vehicles although it can use only one.

The processor hardware affects the reasoning about extent and granularity. We said earlier that operations on variables in primary storage usually have short extent. This holds if the software is executed on a single processor, as in the RTS example. In that case a task needs control of the processor for as long as it maintains exclusive access to INTERVAL. Nothing is gained if we change the granularity and allow another task to perform the same computation on another element simultaneously. On a multiprocessor with shared memory, we could make the individual array elements granules and allow different tasks to perform computations on different elements on different processors.

It is unfortunate that the choice of granularity depends on the hardware configuration since it affects software portability between systems with one and more processors. If we develop a system on a single processor, for example, we may choose an unnecessarily fine granularity level in case the system is ported to a system with parallel hardware. On the other hand, simplicity speaks in favor of coarser granularity.

It is a common mistake to make the granularity too fine. Suppose, for example, that while a task is performing a computation on one of the elements of INTERVAL, it also needs to access another element of the array. This poses no difficulty if the granule of protection is the entire array. But if the elements are individually protected, it amounts to simultaneous exclusive access to different resources and poses the danger of *deadlock*. Deadlock is discussed in the following sections. In addition to the extent of exclusive access, the *probability* of conflicting access also influences the choice of granularity. If a resource is heavily used by different entities, it may become a bottleneck even if the extent of each exclusive access is short. In that case a minimum level of granularity should be chosen.

7.2.4 Simultaneous Exclusive Access; Deadlock

Simultaneous exclusive access is when an entity needs to use two (or more) different shared resources at the same time. In that case it must gain exclusive access first to one resource and then to another. Simultaneous exclusive access is interesting since it poses the danger of deadlock. Suppose that an entity E_1 has gained exclusive access to one resource, B, and then needs exclusive access to a second resource, C. If another entity, E_2, already holds C and also wants B, a *circular wait* situation exists, with E_1 waiting for E_2 to release C and E_2 waiting for E_1 to release B. In the general case, circular wait involves a set of entities, $\{E_1, E_2, \ldots, E_n\}$, where E_k is waiting for a resource held by E_{k+1} for $k = 1, 2, \ldots,$ $n - 1$ and E_n is waiting for a resource held by E_1. If no entity is giving up its resource, *deadlock* exists, preventing all entities from continuing [Silberschatz].

Figure 7-1 illustrates a typical deadlock in an Ada program. The example includes two information-hiding packages, B and C. There are two operation procedures in each package, B_OP1, B_OP2, C_OP1, and C_OP2. Each package uses a *semaphore* to enforce mutual exclusion. The semaphores are called B_SEMA and C_SEMA and are instantiations of a task type, SEMAPHORE. The implementation of semaphores in Ada is discussed in Section 7.4.2. For now, suffice it to note that the sections of program text bracketed by B_SEMA.ACQUIRE and B_SEMA.RELEASE are *critical sections*. Only one task at a time can *enter* either section. The same holds for the sections bracketed by C_SEMA.ACQUIRE and C_SEMA.RELEASE. C_OP1 is called from within procedure B_OP1. Because C_OP1 is called from within B_OP1 and B_OP2 is called from within C_OP2, this example contains a potential deadlock. Consider the following sequence of events:

A task T_1 calls B_OP1 and acquires B_SEMA.

Before T_1 reaches the call C.C_OP1, another task T_2 calls C_OP2 and acquires C_SEMA.

When T_1 calls C.C_OP1 and executes C_SEMA.ACQUIRE, it is queued, since the resource is occupied by T_2.

When T_2 calls B.B_OP2 from within C_OP2 and executes B_SEMA.ACQUIRE, it is queued, since the resource is occupied by T_1.

T_1 and T_2 are now deadlocked since one task holds B_SEMA and waits for C_SEMA to be released, while the other task holds C_SEMA and waits for B_SEMA to be released.

7.2.5 Deadlock Prevention

One way to eliminate deadlocks is to avoid simultaneous exclusive access. Sometimes, a coarser granularity can be chosen, so that, in the examples in Section 7.2.4, B and C become a single resource. When simultaneous exclusive access

```
package B is
   procedure B_OP1(...);
   procedure B_OP2(...);
end B;

package C is
   procedure C_OP1(...);
   procedure C_OP2(...);
end C;

   with SEMA_PAC; use SEMA_PAC;
package body B is
B_SEMA: SEMAPHORE;
   procedure B_OP1(...) is
   begin
      B_SEMA.ACQUIRE;

      .....
      C.C_OP1(...);

      ....
      B_SEMA.RELEASE;
   end B_OP1;

   procedure B_OP2 is
   begin
      B_SEMA.ACQUIRE;

      .....
      B_SEMA.RELEASE;
   end B_OP2;
end B;

package body C is
C_SEMA: SEMAPHORE;
   procedure C_OP1(...) is
   begin
      C_SEMA.ACQUIRE;

      ....
      C_SEMA.RELEASE;
   end C_OP1;

   procedure C_OP2(...) is
   begin
      C_SEMA.ACQUIRE;
      B.B_OP2(...);
      C_SEMA.RELEASE;
   end C_OP2;
end C;
```

Figure 7-1 Example of deadlock between Ada tasks. One task may hold B_SEMA, execute C.C_OP1, and try to acquire C_SEMA. At the same time, another task may hold C_SEMA, execute B.B_OP2, and try to acquire B_SEMA.

cannot be avoided, it is sometimes possible to prevent deadlocks by means of a simple design convention. This works if the resources of contention are well-defined objects as B and C. We will refer to the following convention as the *order rule*:

> An *ordering relation*, "$\leq$", is defined for all resources that are ever held with simultaneous exclusive access by any task. If R and S are such resources, either $R \leq S$ or $S \leq R$.[1]
>
> An entity may not wait for exclusive access to a resource R if it already has exclusive access to a resource S such that $R \leq S$.

In simple terms this means that resources that are going to be held simultaneously must always be acquired in a specified order. If $R_1 \leq R_2 \leq R_3 \leq R_4$, an entity with exclusive access to R_2 may also attempt to acquire R_3 or R_4 but not R_1. Once an entity has exclusive access to R_3, the only additional resource it may acquire is R_4. The rule applies only to the resources actually held at any one time, so if the entity has exclusive access to R_1 and R_3 and releases R_3, it may then acquire R_2. Furthermore, the rule only prohibits an entity from *waiting* for exclusive access to a resource R. The entity is allowed to gain access if R is immediately available.

In the example in Figure 7-1, we may order the packages B and C alphabetically,

$$B \leq C$$

A task that already has exclusive access to B may then gain simultaneous, exclusive access to C, but a task holding exclusive access to C may not attempt to gain access to B. This convention allows the call to C_OP1 from within B_OP1 but not the call to B_OP2 from within C_OP2 and thus prevents the deadlock between the tasks T_1 and T_2 in the example.

A classic example of deadlock is the *dining philosophers' problem*. It may be stated as follows: N philosophers are seated around a circular table. On the table, between each pair of philosophers, there is a chopstick. To eat, each philosopher needs both the chopstick on his right and that on his left. Each philosopher must first seize one chopstick and then the other. Assume, for example, that each philosopher seizes the chopstick on his right. Deadlock then occurs when they attempt to seize the chopstick on their left, which is already occupied by another philosopher [Dijkstra].

In the dining philosophers' problem, we can number the chopsticks $C_1 \cdots C_N$ and impose the ordering

---

[1] "$\leq$" is a *partial order*. It is:
    Reflexive: $R \leq R$.
    Antisymmetric: If $R \leq S$ and $S \leq R$, then $R = S$.
    Transitive: If $R \leq S$ and $S \leq T$, then $R \leq T$.

$$C_1 \leq C_2 \leq \cdots \leq C_N$$

Under the order rule, the philosopher facing chopsticks C_N and C_k for some k must seize C_k before C_N. Consequently, one philosopher can seize C_N as his second chopstick, and start eating. This prevents deadlock and allows the philosophers to dine in turn.[2] (The mathematically inclined reader may want to prove this formally by induction.)

Clearly, the order rule provides a solution to the dining philosophers' problem only under the assumption that no philosopher violates the established order, whether out of malice or carelessness. In software development the rule applies if the entire software is under the designer's control. This is the case for the reactive systems we generally discuss in this book. It does not necessarily apply to an operating system or a database system, where application programs outside the system designer's control may cause deadlock by violating any established rule.

7.2.6 Deadlocks and the Ada Task Syntax

The Ada task syntax affords rich possibilities for deadlocks between tasks even without competition for real shared resources. Consider, for example, the task bodies X and Y below:

```
task body X is
begin
    Y.Y1;
    accept X1;
end X;

task body Y is
begin
    X.X1;
    accept Y1;
end Y;
```

Here X is waiting for Y to accept X's entry call and Y is waiting for X to respond to Y's entry call. This obvious deadlock will be detected by the Ada run-time system. More complicated circular wait situations involving several tasks can easily be constructed. In a design with hierarchical subject–object structures, circular entry calling is discouraged since one task is seen as the subject while the other task is regarded as an object. The subject is then the caller. Circular entry calls do not occur accidentally in such a design but only when subject–object structures

---

[2] The rule is intended to prevent deadlock only. It does not prevent *starvation*, which may occur quite literally if a philosopher holds on to the chopsticks forever, stopping others from eating.

are deliberately superimposed. (Subject–object structures are further discussed in Chapter 8.)

In the following example, unnecessarily complicated task interactions lead to a deadlock situation that can easily be avoided [Helmbold]. A system of Ada tasks is used to simulate the workings of a gas station. The *customer* starts by prepaying an amount to the *operator*, then uses the *pump*, and finally waits for change. The CUSTOMER task simulates this in the following sequence[3]:

```
OPERATOR.PRE_PAY(....);
PUMP.START;
PUMP.FINISH;
accept CHANGE(....);
```

The PUMP task accepts the START and FINISH entry calls from CUSTOMER. When FINISH is called, PUMP charges the cost of the pumped gas by calling the OPERATOR task:

```
loop
   accept START;
   accept FINISH do OPERATOR.CHARGE(....); end;
end loop;
```

The OPERATOR task contains the following loop:

```
loop
   select      accept PRE_PAY (....) do .... end PRE_PAY;
   or          accept CHARGE(....) do ....
                  CUSTOMER.CHANGE(....);
               end CHARGE;
   end select;
end loop;
```

This solution contains a fairly obvious deadlock. CUSTOMER calls PUMP.FINISH. While holding CUSTOMER in a rendezvous, PUMP calls OPERATOR.CHARGE. In the body of **accept** CHARGE, OPERATOR calls CUSTOMER.CHANGE. Clearly, CUSTOMER cannot accept the CHANGE call until it has returned from the rendezvous at FINISH. The deadlock results from unnecessarily complicated logic. Particularly, the situations where more then one task is locked in a rendezvous can easily be avoided by moving the statements OPERATOR.CHARGE and CUSTOMER.CHANGE out of the extended rendezvous.

---

[3] Ada excerpts from D. Helmbold, and D. Luckham, Debugging Ada tasking programs, *IEEE Software*, March 1985, pp. 47–57. Copyright © 1985 by IEEE.

7.3 SOFTWARE REPRESENTATION OF SHARED RESOURCES

This and the following sections deal with the representation of shared resources in software. In this section we discuss the representation of resources as software modules. A shared resource or a set of such resources is often modeled as a package or, sometimes, as a guardian task. In this section we are interested in the interface between such a module and its client modules. The client module may be the body of a subject task that operates on the resource or some other module through which the subject's thread of control passes during execution. This section deals with module interfaces. Sections 7.4 through 7.6 deal with the implementation of each module.

We have earlier established *information-hiding* and *modeling* as important modularization goals. These goals apply to the module representation of shared resources. For information hiding, we attempt to localize the accesses to a shared resource in a module and minimize its impact on the module interfaces. When a shared resource is handled entirely within a module, exclusive access is *hidden*. This is in keeping with the modeling goal, where we attempt to pattern each module on an object in the reality. Hidden exclusive access is discussed in Section 7.3.1. In Section 7.3.2 we discuss situations where resources cannot be modeled as modules and exclusive access cannot be hidden. We refer to this case as *explicit resource acquisition*.

For this discussion, recall the distinction made in Section 6.3.6 between modules and tasks. While each task starts executing in a task body, its thread of control may pass through any number of modules. Each module is a piece of source program text. When we discuss information hiding, we are concerned with the information encoded in each module and what a programmer of a module needs to know about another module, M, in order to use it. This is M's *interface*, while any other information encoded in M is its *secret*. A subject task is not a module. It has no secrets and no interfaces. It executes the various modules and acquires and releases resources. A mentioned earlier, the task body is a module, however.

7.3.1 Hidden Exclusive Access

Hidden exclusive access is when a subject task has exclusive access to a resource only while it is executing within a module, M, other than the task body. The exclusive access is then hidden inside M. The subject task's thread of execution enters M through a subprogram or entry call. The state of the subject task with regard to exclusively held resources is left unchanged by the call; that is, it holds no more and no less resources under exclusive access when it returns than it did at the time of the call. It holds additional resources only while executing within M.

In the simplest case, M represents a single resource, R. R is held with exclusive access only for the duration of each operation, which is modeled as one of M's operation subprograms.[4] M may be a package or a guardian task. The RTS example in Chapter 6 includes several examples of shared resources modeled as guardians. Thus exclusive access by the tasks INPUT and FURNACE to the array INTERVAL is enforced by means of CONTROL_INTERVAL, while exclusive access to the thermometer is enforced by means of THERMOMETER.

If a shared resource is modeled as a guardian task, exclusive access is enforced by the task syntax, which serializes the calls. A single, shared resource with hidden exclusive access can also be modeled as a package. In that case, mutual exclusion is enforced inside each operation subprogram, as necessary. Such a package offers the designer more flexibility than a guardian task, and mutual exclusion need only be enforced when, for example, a shared data structure inside the package is actually referenced. In the elevator example (discussed in Chapter 8) the *set of outstanding requests* for elevator service is shared by subject tasks representing elevators and modeled as a package.

It is sometimes appropriate to model a resource type with multiple instances rather than a single resource. We may represent such a type by means of an adt package. As with single resources, exclusive access can be hidden in the adt package if it is required for the duration of each operation only. Mutual exclusion for such operations is discussed in Section 7.5. In the communications example in Section 7.5.3, the shared resources are message queues, holding messages from other computers. There are multiple queues, and a task needs exclusive access to a particular queue long enough to place or retrieve a message. There is also a data structure over all the queues, which is updated whenever a new queue is created. Tasks reference this data structure to find the queue associated with a particular address and need exclusive access to the structure for the duration of that operation.

7.3.2 Explicit Resource Acquisition

Some shared resources cannot be represented as modules, and exclusive access cannot be hidden. This is when a task needs exclusive access to a resource for an extended period of time and particularly if it needs simultaneous, exclusive access to several, different resources. In this case, resource acquisition affects the interface between modules, and a task may return from a subprogram or entry call with exclusive access to a different set of resources than those held before the call. The maker of the client module (often the subject task body) must be aware of

---

[4] A module that enforces mutual exclusion on callers is included in the syntax of some languages. Such a module is called *monitor*. The concept was introduced by Hoare [Hoare 74] and is included in concurrent languages such as Mesa [Lampson], Concurrent Euclid [Holt 82], and Turing [Holt 88].

what resources are currently held by the task and is responsible for releasing them. We refer to this situation as *explicit acquisition* of shared resources.

Explicit acquisition is necessary in the flexible manufacturing system (FMS), where a job must gain simultaneous, exclusive access to a forklift, a workstation stand, and an automated guided vehicle (AGV). The *record locking* used in transaction systems operating on databases is another good example. Typically, a database transaction affects a number of different records, which must all be held with exclusive access until the entire transaction is complete. With explicit acquisition, the *set* of resources is usually represented by a module, and a subject task gains exclusive access to a resource in an operation such as *acquire*, operates on it freely and exclusively, and finally *releases* it. The set itself is a shared resource with short extent, compared to the extent of the exclusive access to a record.

Explicit acquisition is common for *collective* or *pooled* resources. A *collective* resource is one where each task gets a piece, such as memory or file space. There is no contention over any particular piece. A resource *pool* is a set of equal resources, such as the workstations or the AGVs in the FMS. Each task acquires one single resource out of the pool. Unlike the message queues in the communications example, pooled resources such as the AGVs are anonymous and a task is content with exclusive access to any one. The set of free file records, the AGV pool, and the pool of identical workstations are usually represented by packages. That set of collective or pooled resources is itself a shared resource in that only one task at a time may perform an *acquire* or *release* operation on it. The representation of such sets of resources is discussed in Section 7.6.

7.4 MUTUAL EXCLUSION

To ensure exclusive access to a resource, we can identify those segments of program code where the resource is operated on and ensure that only one task can execute such a segment at each point in time. This is referred to as *mutual exclusion*. The code segments that are thus protected are known as *critical sections*. For example, we may identify the set, S, of all critical sections where a certain, shared data structure, D, is referenced. By enforcing mutual exclusion on S we ensure exclusive access to D to one task at a time. Mutual exclusion is useful when exclusive access is only necessary for the duration of each such critical section. This usually means that the exclusive access is hidden.

This section deals with the mutual exclusion of subject tasks operating on a single, shared resource. (Resource types represented as adts are discussed in Section 7.5.) In Ada all mutual exclusion is enforced by means of guardian tasks. We distinguish between special-purpose guardians and general-purpose guardians, or semaphore tasks. As discussed in Section 7.3, the module representing the single resource can either be an information-hiding package encapsulating guardian tasks or a guardian task alone.

```
package INT_PAC is
    subtype FURNACE_NO is INTEGER range 0..15;
    procedure SET_INT(F: FURNACE_NO; INTVAL: DURATION);
    function GET_INT(F: FURNACE_NO) return DURATION;
end INT_PAC;


-- Body 1 of INT_PAC
package body INT_PAC is
task CONTROL_INTERVAL is
    entry SET_INT(F: FURNACE_NO; INTVAL: DURATION);
    entry GET_INT(F: FURNACE_NO; INTVAL: out DURATION);
end CONTROL_INTERVAL;


procedure SET_INT(F: FURNACE_NO; INTVAL: DURATION) is
begin
    CONTROL_INTERVAL.SET_INT(F, INTVAL); -- Change interval
                                         -- for furnace F.
end SET_INT;


function GET_INT(F: FURNACE_NO) return DURATION is
INTVAL: DURATION;
begin
    CONTROL_INTERVAL.GET_INT(F, INTVAL);
    return INTVAL;
end GET_INT;


task body CONTROL_INTERVAL is
INTERVAL: array (FURNACE_NO) of DURATION:=(others => 99.0);
begin
    loop
      select
        accept SET_INT(F: FURNACE_NO; INTVAL: DURATION) do
            INTERVAL(F):=INTVAL; end;
      or
        accept GET_INT(F: FURNACE_NO; INTVAL: out DURATION) do
            INTVAL:=INTERVAL(F); end;
      end select;
    end loop;
end CONTROL_INTERVAL;
end INT_PAC;
```

Figure 7-2   The package INT_PAC hides an array INTERVAL behind the operation subprograms SET_INT and GET_INT. In the body shown here (Body 1), mutual exclusion is enforced by the special-purpose guardian task CONTROL_INTERVAL.

7.4.1 Special-Purpose Guardian Tasks

A special-purpose guardian is tailored to a specific resource. Its entry points correspond to the different operations on the resource. Each **accept** statement body is a critical section operating on the resource. The guardian enforces the mutual exclusion of tasks executing these critical sections by accepting one entry call at a time. In the RTS problem, the array INTERVAL has to be protected from conflicting access. In Figure 7-2 the array and the special-purpose guardian task, CONTROL_INTERVAL, are hidden in an information-hiding package, INT_PAC. The operation subprogram INT_PAC.SET_INT calls the entry CONTROL_INTERVAL.SET_INT, while INT_PAC.GET_INT calls CONTROL_INTERVAL.GET_INT. The bodies of the **accept** statements contain the following critical sections, each consisting of a single statement:

        INTERVAL(F):=INTVAL;

and

        INTVAL:=INTERVAL(F);

By only accepting one entry call at a time, CONTROL_INTERVAL gives one caller at a time access to the array, which is declared in the task body.

7.4.2 Semaphores and Semaphore Tasks

The use of semaphores is a classic technique for process synchronization. The concept is borrowed from railway engineering, where the purpose of a semaphore is to stop two trains from entering the same track segment at the same time. Translating this to software, we use the trains as metaphors for tasks wishing to execute the same critical section. We stretch the metaphor somewhat by using the same semaphore to protect different critical sections operating on one and the same resource. Thus a software semaphore stops tasks from operating on the same resource at the same time even if the tasks are trying to enter different critical sections.

A semaphore is itself a shared object with the operations *acquire* and *release*. It can be implemented as a simple Ada task with the entries ACQUIRE and RELEASE as follows:

```
task SEMAPHORE is
    entry ACQUIRE;
    entry RELEASE;
end SEMAPHORE;
```

```
task body SEMAPHORE is
begin
    loop
        accept ACQUIRE;
        accept RELEASE;
    end loop;
end SEMAPHORE;
```

Repeatedly, SEMAPHORE accepts a call at the ACQUIRE entry and then waits for a RELEASE call before accepting another ACQUIRE call. That way, any sequence of statements bracketed by the entry calls SEMAPHORE.ACQUIRE and SEMAPHORE.RELEASE is executed exclusively by one task at a time.

In Section 7.4.1, mutual exclusion in the package INT_PAC was enforced with a special-purpose guardian task. To implement INT_PAC with a semaphore instead, we bracket each critical section as follows:

```
SEMAPHORE.ACQUIRE;
INTERVAL(F):=INTVAL;
SEMAPHORE.RELEASE;
```

and

```
SEMAPHORE.ACQUIRE;
INTVAL:=INTERVAL(F);
SEMAPHORE.RELEASE;
```

These are the only calls to the SEMAPHORE entries ACQUIRE and RELEASE. They ensure exclusive access to the array INTERVAL by one caller, T, say, at a time. Should another task, S, try to enter either critical section after T has called ACQUIRE and before it calls RELEASE, then S is queued on the ACQUIRE entry.

Since a semaphore is reusable, it makes sense to introduce a semaphore task type. Figure 7-3 shows a package, SEMA_PAC, containing the declaration of the task type SEMAPHORE. A **select** statement with a **terminate** alternative has been included to allow the semaphore task to expire when it is no longer needed. Figure 7-4 shows an implementation of the body of INT_PAC where mutual exclusion is enforced by means of a semaphore task. The body of INT_PAC *withs* SEMA_PAC and includes one instantiation, INT_SEMA, of the SEMAPHORE task type.

There are many variations of the basic semaphore discussed above. One such variation is useful in the *readers and writers* problem, which can be stated as follows: Assume that a certain data structure is shared by some tasks that only *read* the structure and other tasks (the *writers*) that update it. We can then construct a semaphore that allows either a single writer or multiple readers access to the data structure at each point in time (see Exercise 7.3).

```
package SEMA_PAC is
task type SEMAPHORE is
    entry ACQUIRE;
    entry RELEASE;
end SEMAPHORE;
end SEMA_PAC;

package body SEMA_PAC is
task body SEMAPHORE is
begin
    loop
        select
            accept ACQUIRE;
            accept RELEASE;
        or terminate;
        end select;
    end loop;
end SEMAPHORE;
end SEMA_PAC;
```

Figure 7-3 Package SEMA_PAC containing a reusable semaphore task type, SEMAPHORE. The **accept** statements are enclosed in a **select** statement with a **terminate** alternative to allow the task to expire when it is no longer needed.

```
-- Body 2 of INT_PAC
    with SEMA_PAC; use SEMA_PAC;
package body INT_PAC is
INT_SEMA: SEMAPHORE;
INTERVAL: array (FURNACE_NO) of DURATION:=(others => 99.0);

procedure SET_INT(F: FURNACE_NO; INTVAL: DURATION) is
begin
    INT_SEMA.ACQUIRE;
    INTERVAL(F):=INTVAL;  -- Change interval for furnace F.
    INT_SEMA.RELEASE;
end SET_INT;

function GET_INT(F: FURNACE_NO) return DURATION is
INTVAL: DURATION;
begin
    INT_SEMA.ACQUIRE;
    INTVAL:=INTERVAL(F);
    INT_SEMA.RELEASE;
    return INTVAL;
end GET_INT;
end INT_PAC;
```

Figure 7-4 In this implementation of the body of INT_PAC (Body 2), mutual exclusion is enforced by means of a semaphore task (compare Figure 7-2).

7.4.3 Choice Between Special-Purpose Guardians
and Semaphores

The choice between special-purpose guardian and semaphore tasks is often a trade-off between simplicity and safety, where semaphores tend to provide a simpler solution but require more programmer discipline. The implementation of INT_PAC with a semaphore task (Figure 7-4) is shorter and simpler than the implementation relying on a special-purpose guardian (Figure 7-2). This is partly because of the reusable package SEMA_PAC. On the other hand, the solution relies on the correct placement of semaphore calls in the operation subprograms. It is quite possible to commit a serious error by omitting a necessary ACQUIRE-RELEASE bracket altogether. Note also the placement of RELEASE in the function GET_INT in Figure 7-4:

```
INT_SEMA.ACQUIRE;
INTVAL:=INTERVAL(F);
INT_SEMA.RELEASE;
return INTVAL;
```

Since the semaphore must be released before the **return** statement, the variable INTVAL is necessary to carry the value of INTERVAL(F) out of the critical section. In subprograms with multiple **return** statements, the semaphore must be released before each return. It is particularly important to handle correctly any exception that may be raised inside the critical section, since an unhandled exception may be propagated to an exception handler in the calling unit. (Compare subsection 2.7.1.3). Furthermore, the SEMAPHORE task does not ensure that the same task calls first ACQUIRE and then RELEASE. If a semaphore is acquired by one task and released by another, the result is unpredictable. Again, the correct functioning of the semaphore relies on programming discipline.

The association of a semaphore with a shared resource is by convention only. The programmer must make sure that all operations on the resource are bracketed by calls that acquire and release the same semaphore. This is best enforced by means of consistent packaging such that all the software dealing with the resource is encapsulated in a module together with the associated semaphore. One can then ensure by inspection that all critical sections are correctly protected.

The solution with special-purpose guardian tasks leaves less room for programmer errors but instead, tends to be somewhat cumbersome. As shown in Figure 7-2, each operation subprogram calls a corresponding entry point in the guardian task. Generally, the guardian task must have an entry for each operation and may become large and incohesive. Furthermore, the actual operations on the shared resource are often factored out of the guardian as subprograms. This may be a reasonable separation of concerns since the operations are logically distinct and collected in the guardian for mutual exclusion only. In INT_PAC we might place the critical sections in two subprograms, PERFORM_SET_INT and PERFORM_GET_INT, called from the body of each **accept** statement in CONTROL_INTERVAL as follows:

> **accept** SET_INT(F: FURNACE_NO; INTVAL: DURATION) **do**
>   PERFORM_SET_INT(F, INTVAL); **end**

and

> **accept** GET_INT(F: FURNACE_NO; INTVAL: **out** DURATION) **do**
>   INTVAL:= PERFORM_GET_INT(F); **end**;

Such a breakdown results in three syntactical units for each operation. For example, SET_INT would correspond to the operation subprogram INT_PAC.SET_INT, the entry CONTROL_INTERVAL.SET_INT, and the subprogram PERFORM_SET_INT. This situation is both confusing and somewhat costly in terms of overhead incurred for parameter passing.

We use a special-purpose guardian task instead of a semaphore construct if a task that is required for other reasons may also be used to enforce mutual exclusion. This is the case in the RTS problem, where THERMOMETER receives the interrupts from the physical thermometer. At the same time, it gives one FURNACE task at a time access to the thermometer. Things have also been simplified by letting the task itself rather than a package model the thermometer. This is often possible with special-purpose guardians and makes them less cumbersome.

7.5 MUTUAL EXCLUSION FOR ABSTRACT DATA TYPES

Just as a single, shared resource is modeled by means of an information-hiding module, a resource that exists in multiple instances can be modeled as an abstract data type. If the granularity of exclusive access is at the level of the individual instance, such an adt can be implemented as a special-purpose guardian task type. Whenever possible, the entire set of instances should be a single granule, since this is simpler and more economical. In the following we use a hypothetical example to illustrate mutual exclusion at each of the two granularity levels.

7.5.1 Mutual Exclusion for Individual Adt Instances

If the individual instances of an adt must be accessed exclusively, it is often convenient to implement the type as a special-purpose guardian task type.[5] As an example, consider an adt package RESOURCE_PAC that exports a private type RESOURCE_TYPE and an operation subprogram RESOURCE_OP. The package specification is as follows:

```
package RESOURCE_PAC is
   type RESOURCE_TYPE is private;
   procedure RESOURCE_OP(INST: in out RESOURCE_TYPE);
   .......                    -- Other operations
private
   type RESOURCE_GUARD;
   type RESOURCE_TYPE is access RESOURCE_GUARD;
end RESOURCE_PAC;
```

Here RESOURCE_GUARD is a guardian task type whose complete declaration appears in the body of RESOURCE_PAC. Each instance of the adt RESOURCE_TYPE is a pointer to an instance of RESOURCE_GUARD. Only one operation, RESOURCE_OP, on the abstract data type is included. As usual, it has a parameter indicating a particular instance, INST, of the abstract data type.

The body of RESOURCE_PAC, is shown below. Inside the body, it is known that the parameter INST refers to a task, and the procedure RESOURCE_OP contains an entry call to INST. As usual, the body of the guardian task RESOURCE_GUARD is a loop with a **select** statement. Each part of the **select** statement corresponds to one operation on the abstract data type.

```
package body RESOURCE_PAC is
task type RESOURCE_GUARD is
   entry OP_ENTRY(...);
   .....                           -- Other entries
end RESOURCE_GUARD;

procedure RESOURCE_OP(INST: in out RESOURCE_TYPE) is
begin
   INST.OP_ENTRY(....);
end RESOURCE_OP;

task body RESOURCE_GUARD is
....                               -- Shared data
begin
   loop
     select
        accept OP_ENTRY(...) ...
     or ......                     -- Accept other entry calls
     end select;
   end loop;
end RESOURCE_GUARD;
```

---

[5] Semaphores can be used to protect individual adt instances but do not offer a simpler solution than special-purpose guardian tasks. For a discussion of certain pitfalls associated with a semaphore solution, see [Gonzalez 90].

Mutual exclusion for individual adt instances may create a large number of task instances, each of which occupies a certain amount of memory space. For this reason, protection of individual instances of an abstract data type should be used only when operations on the resource have a long extent. Otherwise, the granule of protection should instead be the entire set of instances. This is discussed in the next section.

7.5.2 Mutual Exclusion
for an Entire Abstract Data Type

The adt package RESOURCE_PAC in the previous section can be provided with one single semaphore or special-purpose guardian task that gives one task at a time exclusive access to *all* the instances of RESOURCE_TYPE. If a semaphore is used, the specification and body of RESOURCE_PAC are as follows:

```
package RESOURCE_PAC is
   type RESOURCE_TYPE is private;
   procedure RESOURCE_OP(INST: in out RESOURCE_TYPE);
   .......                  -- Other operations
private
   type RESOURCE_TYPE is record
      .....
   end record;
end RESOURCE_PAC;

   with SEMA_PAC; use SEMA_PAC;
package body RESOURCE_PAC is
   RESOURCE_SEMA: SEMAPHORE;
   ......                   -- Other declarations
   procedure RESOURCE_OP(INST: in out RESOURCE_TYPE) is
   begin
      RESOURCE_SEMA.ACQUIRE;
      ....
      RESOURCE_SEMA.RELEASE;
   end RESOURCE_OP;
   ....
end RESOURCE_PAC;
```

Here mutual exclusion is enforced by RESOURCE_SEMA, which is declared in the body of the package RESOURCE_PAC. In this solution only one task at a time can operate on any instance of RESOURCE_TYPE, while in the previous solution, any number of tasks can simultaneously operate on different instances. The granule of protection is now the set, S, of all instances of RESOURCE_TYPE. In this implementation, RESOURCE_PAC is no longer a pure adt package but also an information-hiding package, representing the set S.[6] Mutual exclusion can be implemented either with a semaphore or with a special-purpose guardian as discussed in Section 7.4. The example in the next section illustrates mutual exclusion at both granularity levels: individual instances and the set of all instances.

7.5.3 Example: Message Queues

A communications example will be used to illustrate the exclusive access to adt instances. The problem has the following background: A distributed system is a set of computers connected via a communication network. The computers are referred to as *physical nodes*. The communication between the application software units (*logical nodes*) in the different computers is usually accomplished by means of a layered software architecture. In the example here, the top layer is a package MSG_COMM that allows message communication between logical nodes regardless of their physical locations. The lower layers are represented by the package NETWORK, which sends messages between physical nodes. There is one copy of MSG_COMM and one of NETWORK in each computer.

MSG_COMM is shown in the buhrgraph in Figure 7-5. Figure 7-6 is the program text. The package NETWORK has the operation subprogram SEND by which a message is sent on the network to another physical node. Two kinds of addresses are involved:

> Each logical node in the entire system has a unique *logical address*. The interface between application and MSG_COMM is based on logical addresses.
>
> Each physical node has a unique *network address*. The interface between MSG_COMM and NETWORK is based on network addresses.

For the purposes of this example, we make the following simplifying assumptions:

> All logical addresses are in the range 1..100.
>
> Each message is of MSG_TYPE and consists of the logical addresses of the sender and receiver and a string of characters. MSG_TYPE is declared in the package HEADER.

The main purpose of MSG_COMM is to provide the application with an abstract interface to the network of logical nodes. MSG_COMM has two operation subprograms, SEND and RECEIVE, intended for application tasks, and one operation subprogram, SUBMIT, intended for tasks in NETWORK. (These tasks are not shown in the figure.) RECEIVE is a *blocking* operation in that MSG_COMM queues RECEIVE

---

[6] Such *hybrid* packages are also discussed in Section 4.4.1.

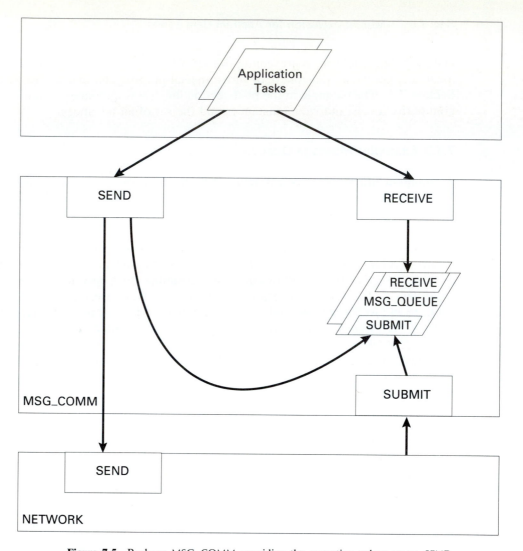

Figure 7-5 Package MSG_COMM providing the operation subprograms SEND and RECEIVE to application tasks. Each application task belongs to a logical node. Each physical node in the distributed network may consist of one or more addressable logical nodes.

callers until a message arrives. Thus, the application task is blocked while waiting for a message.

Each physical node has its own instance of MSG_COMM, which contains one message queue for each logical node in that physical node. Each message queue is implemented as an instance of the guardian task type MSG_QUEUE, which ensures exclusive access to the queue. MSG_QUEUE has two entries, SUBMIT and RECEIVE. SUBMIT adds a message to the end of the queue, and RECEIVE removes the first message in the queue and returns it to the caller. Calls to the entry RECEIVE are accepted only when there are messages in the queue.

```
package HEADER is
   subtype ADDR_TYPE is INTEGER range 1..100;
   type MSG_TYPE is record
      S, R: ADDR_TYPE;  -- Sender and receiver addresses
      X: STRING(1..10);
   end record;
end HEADER;

   with HEADER; use HEADER;
package NETWORK is
   subtype NET_ADDR_TYPE is INTEGER range 1..100;
   procedure SEND(S_MSG: MSG_TYPE; NET_R: NET_ADDR_TYPE);
      -- MSG_COMM sends
end NETWORK;

   with HEADER; use HEADER;
   with NETWORK; use NETWORK;
package MSG_COMM is
-- Message communication package
   procedure SEND(S_MSG: MSG_TYPE);
   -- Application sends.
   procedure RECEIVE(R_MSG: out MSG_TYPE; R: ADDR_TYPE);
   -- Application receives.
   procedure SUBMIT(R_MSG: MSG_TYPE);
   -- Network submits received message.
   procedure NEW_Q(ADDR: ADDR_TYPE);
   NO_SUCH_Q: exception;
end MSG_COMM;

   with UNCHECKED_DEALLOCATION;
   with SEMA_PAC; use SEMA_PAC;
package body MSG_COMM is
-- Record describing one message
type MSG_REC;
type MSG_LINK is access MSG_REC;
type MSG_REC is record
   MSG: MSG_TYPE;
   NEXT: MSG_LINK;
end record;

procedure DELETE_MSG_REC is new
   UNCHECKED_DEALLOCATION(MSG_REC, MSG_LINK);

task type MSG_QUEUE is
   entry RECEIVE(R_MSG: out MSG_TYPE);
      -- Application receives.
```

Figure 7-6 Package MSG_COMM hiding a set of message queues. MSG_COMM *withs* HEADER and NETWORK. The body of NETWORK is not shown.

```
      entry SUBMIT(R_MSG: MSG_TYPE);
        -- NETWORK submits received message
        -- or application submits local message.
   end MSG_QUEUE;

   type MSG_QUEUE_PTR is access MSG_QUEUE;

   -- Record describing a message queue
   type Q_REC;
   type Q_LINK is access Q_REC;
   type Q_REC is record
      ADDR: ADDR_TYPE;
      MQ:   MSG_QUEUE_PTR;    -- Guardian task
      NEXT: Q_LINK;
   end record;

   Q_LIST: Q_LINK;                 -- Linked list of queues
   Q_SEMA: SEMAPHORE;              -- Guardian of set of queues

   function NET_ADDR(A: ADDR_TYPE) return NET_ADDR_TYPE
      is separate;

   function FIND_Q(ADDR: ADDR_TYPE) return MSG_QUEUE_PTR is
   PTR: Q_LINK:=Q_LIST;
   begin
      Q_SEMA.ACQUIRE;
      while PTR/=null and then PTR.ADDR/=ADDR loop
         PTR:=PTR.NEXT;
      end loop;
      Q_SEMA.RELEASE;
      if PTR/=null then return PTR.MQ;
      else return null;
      end if;
   end FIND_Q;

   procedure NEW_Q(ADDR: ADDR_TYPE) is
   begin
      Q_SEMA.ACQUIRE;
      Q_LIST:=new Q_REC'(ADDR, new MSG_QUEUE, Q_LIST);
      Q_SEMA.RELEASE;
   end NEW_Q;

   procedure SEND(S_MSG: MSG_TYPE) is
   -- Application sends.
   Q: MSG_QUEUE_PTR:=FIND_Q(S_MSG.R);  -- Local destination?
```

Figure 7-6   *(continued)*

```
begin
    if Q/=null then
    -- Local message: queue message for S_MSG.R
    Q.SUBMIT(S_MSG);
  else
    -- Convert S_MSG.R to network address and send.
    NETWORK.SEND(S_MSG, NET_ADDR(S_MSG.R));
  end if;
end SEND;


procedure RECEIVE(R_MSG: out MSG_TYPE; R: ADDR_TYPE) is
-- Application receives
Q: MSG_QUEUE_PTR:=FIND_Q(R);
begin
  if Q = null then raise NO_SUCH_Q; end if;
  Q.RECEIVE(R_MSG);
end RECEIVE;


procedure SUBMIT(R_MSG: MSG_TYPE) is
-- Network submits received message.
Q: MSG_QUEUE_PTR:=FIND_Q(R_MSG.R);
begin
  if Q/=null then
    Q.SUBMIT(R_MSG);
  else raise NO_SUCH_Q;
  end if;
end SUBMIT;


task body MSG_QUEUE is
FIRST, LAST:      MSG_LINK;     -- First and last in queue
TEMP_MSG_PTR: MSG_LINK;     -- Temporary variable
begin
  loop
    select
      accept SUBMIT(R_MSG: MSG_TYPE) do
        TEMP_MSG_PTR:=new MSG_REC'(R_MSG, null); end;
      if LAST/=null then
        LAST.NEXT:=TEMP_MSG_PTR;
        LAST:=LAST.NEXT;
      else
        FIRST:=TEMP_MSG_PTR;
        LAST:=FIRST;
      end if;
    or
```

Figure 7-6 (*continued*)

```
        when FIRST/=null =>
        accept RECEIVE(R_MSG: out MSG_TYPE) do
           R_MSG:=FIRST.MSG;
        end;
        TEMP_MSG_PTR:=FIRST;
        FIRST:=FIRST.NEXT;
        DELETE_MSG_REC(TEMP_MSG_PTR);
        if FIRST=null then LAST:=null; end if;
     or terminate;
     end select;
   end loop;
 end MSG_QUEUE;
 end MSG_COMM;
```

Figure 7-6   (*continued*)

The operation subprograms of MSG_COMM function as follows:

SEND determines whether the receiving logical node, *r*, is local or remote. If it is remote, the function NET_ADDR is called to compute the appropriate network address. (NET_ADDR is not shown.) Then NETWORK.SEND is called. If the receiver is local, the entry Q.SUBMIT is called, where Q is the instance of MSG_QUEUE belonging to *r*.

RECEIVE(*r*) is used for retrieving a message addressed to a given logical unit, *r*. RECEIVE calls Q.RECEIVE. The caller is queued at that entry until a message can be returned.

SUBMIT calls the entry Q.SUBMIT, where Q is the MSG_QUEUE instance of the receiving logical node.

MSG_COMM contains a semaphore task, Q_SEMA, protecting the internal data structure, which consists primarily of the linked list, Q_LIST, of message queues. MSG_QUEUE is an abstract data type modeled on a message queue. For simplicity, there is no separate adt package, and the task type MSG_QUEUE is declared in the body of MSG_COMM (see Exer. 7.6).[7]

7.6 REPRESENTATION OF COLLECTIVE AND POOLED RESOURCES

In the preceding sections we discussed the mutual exclusion of tasks accessing a shared resource. The resource could be single, such as the array INTERVAL, or one of many, as in the case of the message queues in Section 7.5.3. In either case the

---

[7] Note that the implementation in Figure 7-6 does not limit the number of queued messages. A realistic implementation must enforce an upper bound either for the messages in each queue or for the total number of messages, and reject SUBMIT and SEND calls when the limit has been reached.

tasks contend for a specific resource. A common, similar case is when tasks contend for one out of a *pool* of equivalent resources or a share of a *collective* resource. In this case the resources are anonymous in the sense that the caller needs exclusive access to any one. Collective and pooled resources are often explicitly acquired and released.

As mentioned earlier, memory space and disk space are typical examples of collective resources. In Chapter 4 we discussed a space-allocation module, DISK_SPACE, with two operation procedures, ALLOCATE and RELEASE. By means of ALLOCATE, a client obtains a piece of a common space resource, such as a disk. It uses RELEASE to relinquish space that it has obtained earlier. If the clients are concurrent tasks, the package DISK_SPACE must enforce mutual exclusion, allowing only one task at a time to execute either ALLOCATE or RELEASE. This preserves the integrity of the data structure representing free and allocated space. We are then dealing with two types of shared resources: The data structure, which is held exclusively with short extent, and the space itself, which may be allocated for a considerable amount of time.

In the version of DISK_SPACE shown in Figure 4-8, the operation subprograms are declared as follows:

```
procedure ALLOCATE(SIZE: INTEGER; ADDRESS: out INTEGER; GRANTED:
    out BOOLEAN);

procedure RELEASE(ADDRESS: INTEGER);
```

Internally, the package DISK_SPACE maintains a linked list of BLOCK records representing allocated space. Each BLOCK record contains the starting address and size of each allocated module.

The implementation above relies on the clients to call RELEASE correctly and not try to release a space belonging to another task. A common practice is to store the identity of the client task in the BLOCK record and allow a task to release only its own space. Ada does not support the automatic identification of a calling task, but an imperfect enforcement could be achieved by changing the operation subprograms as follows:

```
procedure ALLOCATE(T: T_ID; SIZE: INTEGER; ADDRESS: out INTEGER:
    GRANTED: out BOOLEAN);

procedure RELEASE(T: T_ID; ADDRESS: INTEGER);
```

In this solution, each task is assumed to have an identity of type T_ID. In yet another solution, a unique number could be returned by ALLOCATE. RELEASE would require that the same number be returned upon release. If this is not the case, an exception is raised.

In the flexible manufacturing system, shared resources exist in the real-world environment, and an important purpose of the software is the allocation of such resources to different jobs in an orderly manner. The FMS software includes subject tasks of type JOB_TASK, each representing a job. A job is elaborated at various workstations. In addition to the workstations, resources needed by a job include *automated guided vehicles (AGVs)* used to transport a part from one workstation to another. Parts are staged in an *automated storage and retrieval system (ASRS)*. They are transported to and from the ASRS by AGVs, which leave and pick up the part on one of several *ASRS stands*. Both the AGVs and the ASRS stands are *pooled* resources. Thus when a job needs an AGV it can do with any one of a number of similar vehicles. When it needs an ASRS stand, any free stand will do. AGVs and ASRS stands are managed as follows:

AGVS.   Each job needs an AGV only to carry it from one point to another, whereupon the AGV is released. This means that we can provide a package AGVS with an operation subprogram

    MOVE(O_STAND, I_STAND: STAND_TYPE);

Exclusive access to an AGV can be hidden in the body of AGVS. Each AGV is represented by an instance of a task type, AGV_TASK, which contains the necessary steps to transport a part from O_STAND to I_STAND. Since each AGV is represented by a task, the allocation of AGVs to jobs can rely entirely on Ada task queuing. The queue of jobs waiting for AGVs and the queue of AGVs waiting for a job are managed by the guardian AGV_CONTROL. Jobs in need of an AGV are queued on the entry ACQUIRE, while idle AGV tasks are queued on the entry GET_PART. Callers are selected pairwise in a loop that is essentially as follows (the program text in Figure 7-7 also includes **terminate** alternatives):

```
loop
    accept GET_PART(A: AGV_ID_TYPE) do AA:=A; end;
    accept ACQUIRE(AP: out AGV_PTR_TYPE) do AP:=OWNER(AA); end;
end loop;
```

When an AGV is available, its identity is stored in AA, and an ACQUIRE call is accepted. The calling JOB_TASK is given a pointer to the corresponding AGV_TASK. [If AA contains an AGV id, OWNER(AA) is a pointer to the corresponding AGV_TASK instance.]

ASRS stands.   The access to ASRS stands cannot be handled entirely inside a package in a way similar to the AGVs. The reason has to do with simultaneous, exclusive access to multiple resources: A job in the ASRS must obtain a stand and then gain access to a forklift that transports the part from ASRS bin to the stand, then release the truck and acquire an AGV. The stand is released only when the part has been picked up by the AGV. Explicit resource acquisition is used.

```
package AGVS is
-- Package representing the set of AGVs
subtype STAND_TYPE is INTEGER;
procedure MOVE(O_STAND, I_STAND: STAND_TYPE);
-- Move part from O_STAND to I_STAND.
end AGVS;


   with ASRS_STANDS; use ASRS_STANDS;
   with JOBS; use JOBS;
package body AGVS is
-- Task AGV_CONTROL allocates AGVs to jobs.
-- Task type AGV_TASK models a single AGV.
MAX_AGV: constant:=4;
subtype AGV_ID_TYPE is INTEGER range 1..MAX_AGV;
type AGV_TASK;
type AGV_PTR_TYPE is access AGV_TASK;
type AGV_ARRAY is array (AGV_ID_TYPE) of AGV_PTR_TYPE;
OWNER: AGV_ARRAY:=(others => null); -- AGV task corresponding
                                    -- to each AGV id


task type AGV_TASK is
   entry INIT(AA: AGV_ID_TYPE);
   entry MOVE(O_STAND, I_STAND: STAND_TYPE);
end;


task AGV_CONTROL is
   entry ACQUIRE(AP: out  AGV_PTR_TYPE);
   entry GET_PART(A: AGV_ID_TYPE);
end;


procedure MOVE(O_STAND, I_STAND: STAND_TYPE) is
A: AGV_PTR_TYPE;
begin
   AGV_CONTROL.ACQUIRE(A);
   A.MOVE(O_STAND, I_STAND);
end;


task body AGV_TASK is
-- Behavior of one AGV
MY_AGV_ID: AGV_ID_TYPE;
begin
   accept INIT(AA: AGV_ID_TYPE) do MY_AGV_ID:=AA; end;
   loop
      AGV_CONTROL.GET_PART(MY_AGV_ID);
      select
```

Figure 7-7 Simplified package AGVS showing the allocation of AGVs to instances of JOB_TASK.

```
            accept MOVE(O_STAND, I_STAND: STAND_TYPE) do
                -- Perform the move by sending commands to the
                -- vehicle and receiving completion interrupts.
                end MOVE;
            or terminate;
            end select;
        end loop;
end AGV_TASK;


task body AGV_CONTROL is
-- Matching of idle AGVs and jobs in need of transport
AA: AGV_ID_TYPE;
begin
    loop
        select -- Call from idle AGV_TASK:.
            accept GET_PART(A: AGV_ID_TYPE) do
            AA:=A; end;  -- AA is id of first available vehicle.
        or terminate;
        end select;

        select  -- Call from JOB_TASK:.
            accept ACQUIRE(AP: out AGV_PTR_TYPE) do
            -- Return pointer to task of available vehicle.
            AP:=OWNER(AA); end;
        or terminate;
        end select;
    end loop;
end AGV_CONTROL;


begin
    -- Create and initialize AGV tasks.
    for A in OWNER'RANGE loop
        OWNER(A):=new AGV_TASK;
        OWNER(A).INIT(A);
    end loop;
end AGVS;
```

Figure 7-7   (*continued*)

Figure 7-8 shows a package ASRS_STANDS, whose specification contains a task, STANDS_CONTROL, with two entries, ACQUIRE and RELEASE. (As an alternative, the task could also have been hidden in the package body with an operation subprogram for each entry ACQUIRE and RELEASE.) The entries are declared as follows:

```
entry ACQUIRE(S: out ASRS_STAND_TYPE);
entry RELEASE(S: ASRS_STAND_TYPE);
```

```
      with AGVS; use AGVS;
    package ASRS_STANDS is
    -- Package representing the set of ASRS stands
    -- ACQUIRE and RELEASE are operations on the set performed
    -- under exclusive access hidden inside the package.
    MAX_ASRS_STANDS: constant:=4;
    subtype ASRS_STAND_TYPE is STAND_TYPE range 1..MAX_ASRS_STANDS;
    task STANDS_CONTROL is
        entry ACQUIRE(S: out ASRS_STAND_TYPE);
        entry RELEASE(S: ASRS_STAND_TYPE);
    end;
    end ASRS_STANDS;


    package body ASRS_STANDS is
    -- Mutual exclusion enforced by special-
    -- purpose guardian task STANDS_CONTROL
    -- The array FREE represents acquired and free stands.
    task body STANDS_CONTROL is
    type FREE_ARRAY is array (ASRS_STAND_TYPE) of BOOLEAN;
    FREE: FREE_ARRAY:=(others => TRUE);
    NONE: constant FREE_ARRAY:=(others => FALSE); -- No free stand
    begin
        loop
          select
            accept RELEASE(S:ASRS_STAND_TYPE) do FREE(S):=TRUE; end;
          or
            when FREE/=NONE =>
            accept ACQUIRE(S: out ASRS_STAND_TYPE) do
              L: for SS in ASRS_STAND_TYPE loop
                if FREE(SS) then
                  FREE(SS):=FALSE;
                  S:=SS;
                  exit L;
                end if;
              end loop L;
            end;
          or terminate;
          end select;
        end loop;
    end STANDS_CONTROL;
    end ASRS_STANDS;
```

Figure 7-8 Package ASRS_STANDS represents the set of ASRS stands. The guardian task STANDS_CONTROL appears in the package specification. JOB_TASK instances call the entries ACQUIRE and RELEASE.

The variable S represents an ASRS stand. The task body STANDS_CONTROL uses a guard to accept a call to ACQUIRE only when a stand is free, whereas RELEASE is accepted anytime. The array FREE indicates whether each stand is currently free.

The array FREE is an example of data structure reflecting the status of the resource pool. (In DISK_SPACE, a linked list of BLOCK records and a bit map are used for a similar purpose.) FREE is a shared resource, which makes simultaneous, exclusive access necessary. A task, T_1, that needs a stand must first obtain access to the data structure FREE. (FREE is protected by STANDS_CONTROL.) While T_1 has exclusive access to the data structure, it also gains access to one of the stands if one is available. We cannot allow T_1 to maintain exclusive access to FREE while it is waiting for a stand to become available, since this would result in an obvious deadlock. The reason is that another task, T_2, wishing to release a stand must gain exclusive access to FREE in order to do so. The guard

```
when FREE/=NONE =>
```

solves this problem by allowing T_1 exclusive access to FREE only when a stand is actually available. As a footnote on the order rule introduced in Section 7.2.5, note that no universal ordering of the resources "stand" and FREE is possible. T_1 needs to gain access to FREE and then to a stand. T_2 has a stand and needs simultaneous, exclusive access to FREE.

7.7 CHAPTER SUMMARY

> *Not till the sun excludes you*
> *do I exclude you.*
>
> *Whitman*

The problem environment of a reactive system often includes entities that compete for *exclusive access* to *shared resources*. In Ada, such entities may be modeled as subject tasks, and the shared resources may be represented by packages or guardian tasks. The task syntax ensures exclusive access by *serializing* the entry calls to each task and queueing any additional callers. We say that Ada tasks have a *queueability* property since this queuing is supported by the run-time system.

Resource sharing occurs in the reality as well as in software. The choice of *granularity* is an issue in either case. Each entity gets access to one *granule* of a resource at a time. With *fine* granularity, we minimize the waiting by giving each entity access to a minimum resource at a time. On the other hand, this may cause *simultaneous*, *exclusive access* to two or more different resources. This can sometimes be prevented by choosing a *coarser* granularity, which on the other hand increases the probability of access conflict between different entities. The length in time (*extent*) of each exclusive access affects our choice of granularity, since a coarse granularity may be acceptable if the exclusive access has short extent.

Simultaneous, exclusive access raises the issue of *deadlock*. This is when each of two or more entities are waiting for a resource that is being held by another. In a controlled environment such as a self-contained software system, deadlock can often be prevented by means of an *order rule* requiring that all resources always be acquired in a certain, globally defined order. The order rule applies when well-defined entities contend for well-defined resources. Ada's task syntax provides many possibilities for deadlocks where this is not the case. These occur when the distinction between subject and object is unclear, and tasks engage in circular entry calls.

The representation of shared resources raises issues of modeling and information hiding. It is desirable to hide the sharing of a resource inside a module so that a caller enters and exits the module with the same exclusively held resources. This is referred to as *hidden exclusive access*. The simplest example is when a module (a package or a guardian task) represents a single, shared resource, and exclusive access is necessary only for the duration of each operation.

Explicit resource acquisition is when the exclusive access to some resource cannot be hidden inside a module but affects its interface. Typically, the interface contains the operations *acquire* and *release*, where exclusive access to the resource is gained and relinquished, respectively. These operations are usually performed on a package (or guardian task) representing a *set* of resources. The set itself is a shared resource, since only one task can perform acquire or release.

Within a module representing a shared resource, exclusive access is usually enforced by means of *mutual exclusion*. All those *critical sections* of code where the resource is actually operated on are identified. Only one caller at a time is allowed to execute a critical section. Mutual exclusion can be implemented in Ada by means of *special-purpose guardian tasks* or *semaphore tasks*. In a special-purpose guardian, each critical section is placed in the body of an **accept** statement. By serializing the calls, the task syntax ensures that only one critical section is executed at a time.

A semaphore task is a general-purpose guardian task with the entries ACQUIRE and RELEASE. It accepts calls to each entry in an alternating manner. Each critical section in the text of operation subprograms is bracketed by an ACQUIRE call and a RELEASE call. Only one caller at a time can execute within such a bracket, while additional callers are held on the ACQUIRE entry queue. Sometimes, more than one caller may be allowed in a critical section. For example, any number of tasks may be allowed to *read* a data structure, but a task that *updates* the structure requires exclusive access. This can be accomplished by means of a modified semaphore.

Semaphores and special-purpose guardians can be used for a single shared resource and for the *set of instances* of an adt. If the instances of an adt need individual protection, it is most convenient to implement the abstract data type itself as a guardian task type. An example of this is a communication problem with multiple message queues. Each queue is an instance of a task type with the entries SEND, RECEIVE, and SUBMIT.

A *collective* resource is one where each entity gets a share for its exclusive use. Memory and disk space are examples. A *pool* is a set of identical, anonymous resources where an entity gets any one. A set of collective or pooled resource may be modeled as a package or guardian with an ACQUIRE and a RELEASE operation.

REFERENCES

ANDREWS, G. R., *Concurrent Programming: Principles and Practice*, Benjamin-Cummings, Menlo Park, Calif., 1991.

BERNSTEIN, P. A., HADZILACOS, V., and GOODMAN, N., *Concurrency Control and Recovery in Database Systems*, Addison-Wesley, Reading, Mass., 1987.

BURNS, A., *Concurrent Programming in Ada*, Cambridge University Press, Cambridge, 1987.

DEITEL, H. M., *Operating Systems*, 2nd ed., Addison-Wesley, Reading, Mass., 1990.

DIJKSTRA, E., Notes on structured programming, in *Structured Programming*, Academic Press, New York, 1972.

FELDMAN, M. B., *Language and System Support for Concurrent Programming*, Curriculum Module SEI-CM-25, Software Engineering Institute, Pittsburgh, PA, 1990.

GONZALEZ, D. W., Multitasking software components, *Ada Letters* X:1 (Jan/Feb 1990) 92–96.

HELMBOLD, D., and LUCKHAM, D., Debugging Ada tasking programs, *IEEE Software*, March 1985, pp. 47–57.

HOARE, C. A. R., Monitors: an operating system structuring concept, *Commun. ACM*, 17:10, October 1974, pp. 549–557.

HOARE, C. A. R., *Communicating Sequential Processes*, Prentice-Hall International, Hemel Hempstead, Hertfordshire, England, 1985.

HOLT, R. C., and WORTMAN, D. B., A model for implementing Euclid modules and prototypes, *ACM TOPLAS*, 4:4, October, 1982, pp. 552–562.

HOLT, R. C., MATTHEWS, P. A., ROSSELET, J. A., and CORDY, J. R., *The Turing Programming Language: Design and Definition*, Prentice Hall, Englewood Cliffs, N.J., 1988.

KORTH, H. F., and SILBERSCHATZ, A., *Database System Concepts*, 2nd ed., McGraw-Hill, New York, 1991.

LAMPSON, B. W., and REDELL, D. D., Experience with processes and monitors in Mesa, *Commun. ACM*, 23:2, February 1980, pp. 105–117.

PRATT, P. J., and ADAMSKI, J. J., *Database Systems: Management and Design*, 2nd ed., Boyd & Fraser, Boston, 1991.

SILBERSCHATZ, A., PETERSON, J., and GALVIN, P., *Operating System Concepts*, 3rd ed., Addison-Wesley, Reading, Mass., 1991.

TANENBAUM, A. S., *Modern Operating Systems*, Prentice Hall, Englewood Cliffs, N.J., 1992.

EXERCISES

7.1 Semaphore as a finite automaton

Illustrate the behavior of a semaphore task by means of:
- **(a)** A sequence diagram.
- **(b)** A transition diagram.

7.2 Semaphore and special-purpose guardian

The specification and body of a package P are as follows:

```
package P is
   procedure INCR_X;
   function SEE_X return INTEGER;
end P;

package body P is
task PT is
   entry INCR_X;
   entry SEE_X(I: out INTEGER);
end PT;

procedure INCR_X is
begin
   PT.INCR_X;
end;

function SEE_X return INTEGER is
I: INTEGER;
begin
   PT.SEE_X(I);
   return I;
end;

task body PT is
X: INTEGER:=1;
begin
   loop
      select accept INCR_X; X:=X+1;
      or accept SEE_X(I: out INTEGER) do I:=X; end;
      end select;
   end loop;
end PT;
end P;
```

The shared resource X is protected from conflicting accesses by means of a special-purpose guardian task, PT. Write a modified package body, where X is instead protected by means of a semaphore task.

7.3 Readers and writers

"Readers and writers" is a classic mutual-exclusion problem. Several tasks share a data structure, D. Some tasks (the readers) need only read access to D, while other tasks (the writers) update it. Many readers may access D at the same time, but each writer needs exclusive access. While a writer is updating D, no other writer or reader is allowed to access D. If the reading and the writing are of short extent and executed on a single processor, we can solve the problem by allowing exactly one reader or writer at a time. A more interesting situation exists if the accesses are of long extent or if the readers and writers execute on parallel processors with shared memory. In that situation it makes sense to allow more than one reader at a time.

Use guards to design a semaphore task, RWSEMA, such that the reading can be bracketed by

        RWSEMA.START_READ;

and

        RWSEMA.END_READ;

and the writing by

        RWSEMA.START_WRITE;

and

        RWSEMA.END_WRITE;

As long as there is no queue for the START_WRITE entry, any number of START_READ calls are accepted. If there is a queue for START_WRITE or if a writer is active, no calls to START_READ are accepted. A START_WRITE call is accepted only when the number of readers is zero and no other writer is active.

7.4 Deadlock with special-purpose guardian tasks

Figure 7-1 illustrates a potential deadlock situation where mutual exclusion is enforced by means of semaphore tasks. Illustrate the same situation by means of special-purpose guardian tasks.

7.5 *Automatic queuing system for a bank office*

Many bank offices with multiple teller positions maintain one central waiting line of customers rather than one line per teller position. An automatic ticketing machine is sometimes used. A customer entering the office presses a button on the machine, which then issues a ticket with a queue number. The next number to be served is displayed on an overhead display together with the number of an available teller position.

Construct a task WAIT_LINE that might run in such an automatic queueing system. The task has two entries, GET_TICKET and GET_CUSTOMER, and contains a loop with a **select** statement as follows:

```
select
    accept GET_TICKET ......
or
    accept GET_CUSTOMER .....
end select;
```

The task WAIT_LINE must keep track of the number, A, of *arrived* customers and the number, S, of *served* customers.

> When the entry GET_TICKET is called, A is incremented and printed on a ticket.
>
> Calls to the entry GET_CUSTOMER are only accepted when there are unserved customers. When a call is accepted, WAIT_LINE increments and displays S and the number of the available teller.

To test WAIT_LINE, write a scaffolding task type TELLER to simulate the behavior of a teller. It includes a loop with a call to WAIT_LINE.GET_CUSTOMER and a delay. Instantiate TELLER for a suitable number of tellers with different delay intervals. Also, write a scaffolding task CUSTOMERS representing the arrival of customers. It includes a loop with a call to WAIT_LINE.GET_TICKET followed by a delay. Arrange for a suitable varying delay. Include diagnostic output in WAIT_LINE by displaying each number given to an arriving customer and each number displayed on the overhead display. You may arrange for orderly termination of the system in the following way: Include a third entry, CLOSE_OFFICE in WAIT_LINE. The task CUSTOMERS calls CLOSE_OFFICE after the last customer of the day has received a ticket. When a call to CLOSE_OFFICE is received, WAIT_LINE changes the value of an internal variable. This should cause any waiting calls to GET_CUSTOMER to be accepted. A closing status is returned to TELLER tasks, which then exit their loops and terminate.

7.6 *Modifications of MSG_COMM*

In the communications example in Section 7.5.3, a guardian task type MSG_QUEUE represents a queue of incoming messages. For simplicity, no explicit adt package is used, but the task type is declared inside the package MSG_COMM. Modify the design by introducing an adt package QUEUE_PAC with a specification along the following lines:

```
package QUEUE_PAC is
    type MSG_QUEUE_TYPE is private;
    procedure SUBMIT(MQ: MSG_QUEUE_TYPE; R_MSG: MSG_TYPE)
    function RECEIVE(MQ: MSG_QUEUE_TYPE) return MSG_TYPE;
    function NEW_QUEUE(MAX_MSG: NATURAL) return MSG_QUEUE_TYPE;
    NO_QUEUE: constant MSG_QUEUE_TYPE;
private
    type MSG_QUEUE;
    type MSG_QUEUE_TYPE is access MSG_QUEUE;
    NO_QUEUE: constant MSG_QUEUE_TYPE:=null;
end QUEUE_PAC;
```

Prevent queue overflow by limiting the number of messages in each queue. (The parameter MAX_MSG is passed when a new queue is created by means of the function NEW_QUEUE.) Declare a suitable exception to be raised when a message is submitted to a queue that is full.

For testing purposes, write suitable scaffolding to simulate application tasks sending and receiving messages. Implement a scaffolding version of the package NETWORK with tasks submitting messages to the queues in MSG_COMM.

7.7 Order rule

In a certain system, any subject task may gain exclusive access to any number of the shared resources $R_1 - R_3$. The resources are always acquired according to the order rule with the ordering

$$R_1 \leqslant R_2 \leqslant R_3$$

Each subject task frequently writes a diagnostic message on a shared computer screen, S. Such diagnostic messages are inserted at various places in the task body. Each subject task needs exclusive access to S while it is writing a message only. For this reason, S is acquired before each message and released immediately afterward. Include S in a workable ordering of all the shared resources in the system.

7.8 Guards in the RTS problem

This is a somewhat unrealistic modification of the RTS problem in Section 6.5. Suppose that there are three thermometers, any one of which may be used to read the temperature of any furnace. This requires three separate THERMOMETER tasks, THERMO1, THERMO2, and THERMO3, each with an entry T_INTRPT mapped to the interrupt location for a physical thermometer. Design a package THERMO_PAC encapsulating these three tasks together with a guardian task, THERMO_CONTROL, that controls access to the thermometers. THERMO_PAC has the operation function GET_TEMP(F: FURNACE_NO). GET_TEMP includes the sequence

THERMO_CONTROL.ACQUIRE(T);
-- Read temperature of furnace F using thermometer T.
THERMO_CONTROL.RELEASE(T);

The entry call THERMO_CONTROL.ACQUIRE acquires a thermometer if one is available. THERMO_CONTROL.RELEASE releases a thermometer. THERMO_CONTROL must include a guarded select statement that accepts an ACQUIRE call when at least one thermometer is free, and a RELEASE call at any time. Include scaffolding tasks that regularly call THERMO_PAC.GET_TEMP and scaffolding tasks PHYSICAL1, PHYSICAL2 and PHYSICAL3 that simulate the behavior of physical thermometers. PHYSICAL1 accepts a suitable entry call from THERMO1, delays and then simulates an interrupt by making an entry call to THERMO1.T_INTRPT. PHYSICAL2 and PHYSICAL3 behave analogously.

8 Entity-Life Modeling

Where entity and quiddity
The ghosts of defunct bodies, fly

Butler, Hudibras

8.1 INTRODUCTION

In earlier chapters we used the means of expression available in sequential programs—primarily control structuring and modularization—to represent real-world structures, such as threads of events and objects. We will now see how the means to express concurrency enhances our representation of the problem environment. Most important, subject tasks can represent asynchronous, sequential threads of events in the reality. It is often intuitive to think of such a sequential thread as the "life" of some real-world entity, and for this reason, the approach to concurrent software construction presented here is referred to as *entity-life modeling*. An *entity* is a real-world thing, whether concrete or abstract, that exhibits a sequential behavior. Given a sequential behavior, the entity is that which behaves. In entity-life modeling, a behavior pattern is identified first. An entity is then defined that exhibits the pattern. The term *entity-life modeling* particularly refers to the representation of such entities as tasks, but it is also used for the entire approach to the construction of concurrent software presented here, including the modeling of subsystems and objects as packages and abstract data types.

Existing analysis and design approaches dealing with objects and processes tend to give preference to one over the other. In the *object paradigm* of computing, objects are the first concern. Once the objects are identified, the life of

304

individual objects may be regarded as processes [Rumbaugh], [Coad]. The object paradigm captures sequential patterns that fit neatly into single objects but may miss patterns extending beyond objects. There is also a *process paradigm* of computing [Jackson], where the emphasis is on concurrent, communicating processes. The process paradigm deals well with sequential patterns but has difficulties with simple but useful objects that do not change in interesting ways over time. Entity-life modeling combines the object and process paradigms by giving equal weight to objects and behavior patterns [Sanden 89a, 89c].

Entity-life modeling produces software structures where tasks modeled on external threads of events operate on objects. Each task moves the action forward while it progresses at its own pace. In Ada, we must distinguish such *subject tasks* from guardian tasks. A guardian task does not move the action forward on its own but operates only during rendezvous with subject tasks. The term *subject* is used in the grammatical sense as in the sentence "Adam eats the apple," where Adam is the subject operating on the object, the apple.[1] One subject and any objects it operates on is referred to as a *subject–object structure*. A concurrent program generally consists of superimposed subject–object structures where subjects may share objects, and an object may contain a subject. For example, a subject task may be declared in the body of an information-hiding package. Such a subject may operate on objects outside the body of the package.

In entity-life modeling, we first identify suitable *threads* (or *sequences*) *of events* in the reality. Regarding each thread as the *behavior pattern* (or *behavior*) of some *entity* sometimes helps our reasoning.[2] If, for example, a thread is described by a regular expression, the entity is a finite automaton with modes and transitions. In the elevator problem, for example, we can talk about a thread of such events as "arrive at floor x" and "leave floor y" in terms of the behavior of an elevator entity with modes such as "stopped at floor x" and "traveling upward." To capture the behavior of the elevator we must describe all possible, valid ways in which these events may occur over time. In Chapter 6 we discussed simple behavior patterns that map directly onto delay-loop tasks such as samplers. In the RTS problem, we associated the sampling behavior with a furnace entity. Since the sampling emanates from the remote sensor device rather than the furnaces, the analyst may prefer to say that the device consists of 16 furnace–sampler entities. The choice is relevant only from an intuitive point of view; the entity has no properties other than its behavior and no physical location.

In the analysis of the problem environment, the identification of threads, objects, and subsystems are equally important, although the choice of threads

---

[1] Note that the term *subject* is used by other authors in an entirely different sense [Coad]. In an environment other than Ada, the subject concept may be redundant, and *subject* and *subject task* may be replaced by *process*. In such an environment, it is appropriate to talk about *process-object structures*.

[2] Some practitioners of entity-life modeling dispense of the term *entity* and instead use the term *behavior* in sentences such as "the behavior is in the mode traveling upward."

often determines what objects are necessary. The goal is a compelling description of the problem environment in terms of subject–object structures. Entities that are suitable to play the role of subjects in this context are referred to as *subject candidates*. A subject–object structure in the reality consists of a *subject entity* and the real-world objects of which it operates. Different choices of subjects lead to different descriptions, and we choose the most compelling one. This often means that some of the subject candidates are reduced to objects. The analysis results in a description of the problem environment that is directly representable in software.

In Section 8.2 we study the anatomy of a concurrent program in terms of subject–object structures. In Section 8.3 we discuss problem analysis in terms that lead to such software designs, using the buoy problem as an example. Section 8.4 is a case study of the elevator problem. In that problem, the chosen solution includes the elevator itself as a subject. We compare this solution to another, where the elevator is instead an object operated on by sampler entities.

8.2 PROPERTIES OF A CONCURRENT PROGRAM

A concurrent program contains multiple subject tasks. In this section we discuss the structure of such a program in terms of subjects and objects. In later sections we see how we can analyze a problem in terms that map directly onto such a structure.

8.2.1 Subject–Object Structures

A sequential program has one single task, which we will call the *initial* (or *default*) *task*. (A concurrent Ada program also has one initial task executing alone until other tasks have explicitly been declared and activated.) The main procedure can be regarded as the body of the initial task, which is the only *subject task* in a sequential program. We can represent the sequential program as one hierarchical *subject–object structure* as in Figure 8-1. The figure shows the initial task directly operating on objects X, Y, and Z. Z is also operated on from within Y, while W is operated on only from within Y. Calls to the operation procedures in X, Y, and Z appear in the main procedure or in independent subprograms called from it. Y contains operation subprogram calls to Z and W. Regardless of the textual place of these calls, all operations on X, Y, Z, and W are executed by the initial task, which is the only subject and the only thread of control in the program.

A concurrent program has more than one subject task and more than one subject–object structure. Each subject–object structure is similar to a sequential program and includes one subject task and zero or more objects. Since some of the objects are shared by different tasks, the subject–object structures overlap.

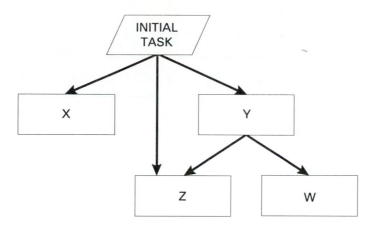

Figure 8-1   Buhrgraph showing the subject–object structure of a sequential program.

Furthermore, an object, operated on by one task S, may contain a task T declared in its body. T is not visible to S and has its own subject–object structure. A concurrent program consists of several, *superimposed* subject–object structures.

Figure 8-2 is a buhrgraph of a small hypothetical concurrent Ada program. There are three tasks, A, B, and C, declared in the packages P, Q, and R, respectively. C is a guardian task, while A and B are both subject tasks. (C is called from within each of the operation procedures R1 and R2.)

Task A operates on package Q by means of the operation Q1 and on package R by means of R1. Consequently, A is a subject task whose subject–object structure includes Q and R. Task A regards the packages Q and R as objects and ignores the existence of tasks B and C.

Task B operates on package P by means of the operation P1 and on R by means of R1. B's subject–object structure contains P and R. B regards P and R as objects and ignores the existence of tasks A and C.

The guardian task C inside package R protects any data structure in R from conflicting access by A and B. Mutual exclusion of A and B while they operate on R is part of the secret of the package R.

In Figure 8-2, task A operates on the package Q by means of Q1, and Q1 may include an entry call to task B. The rendezvous between tasks A and B is hidden inside the object Q. We will often let tasks interact that way, but for simplicity tasks also rendezvous directly, without the extra layer provided by a package. In that situation, the called task is regarded as an object in the subject–object structure of the caller. In Figure 8-3 the subject–object structure of G contains the package V and the task H. If the package X is operated on during the rendezvous

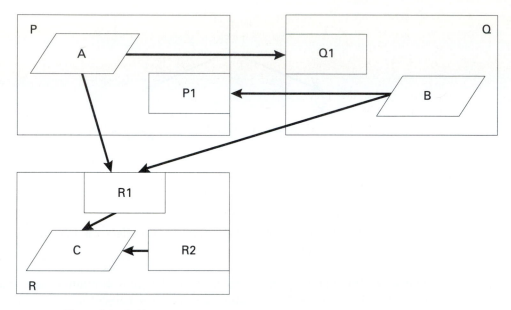

Figure 8-2 Subject task A operates on the packages Q and R and ignores the existence of tasks B and C. Subject task B operates on packages P and R and ignores the existence of tasks A and C. A and B both operate on C, but the operations are hidden inside R.

between G and H, it is part of the G's subject–object structure. If H operates on X outside the rendezvous with G, then H is a subject task with its own subject–object structure, which includes X.

We saw an example of superimposed subject–object structures in the RTS solution in Figure 6-8. F_PACK is an object representing the set of furnaces. It is operated on by means of the subprogram NEW_INT. At the same time, each

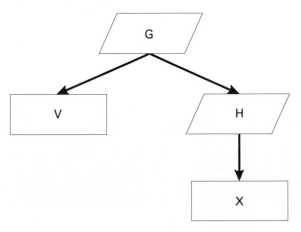

Figure 8-3 G's subject–object structure includes the package V and the task H. The subject operating on X may be either G or H.

FURNACE task, declared in the body of F_PACK, operates on the objects THERMOMETER and OUTPUT. For simplicity, THERMOMETER and OUTPUT are not encapsulated in individual packages.

It is important to remember that we use buhrgraphs as simplified pictures of the software. They are not intended to define the design but only to illustrate it. In the buhrgraph, subjects and objects appear as discrete pieces, where a subject is placed outside the objects it operates on. In reality, the subject is a thread of execution that passes through the objects as the operation subprograms are executed. The buhrgraph must be complemented with a description of this thread. (This may be a program sequence diagram or the text of the task body.) The subjects in the buhrgraph should not be seen as black boxes to be refined in some later stage. Instead, the sequential structure of each subject is as important as the buhrgraph.

8.2.2 Subject Packages

It is often useful to encapsulate tasks in a package even if the package is not operated on by any subject task. Such a package has an empty specification and must contain at least one subject task to be meaningful. A package with an empty specification that contains one or more tasks in its body is called a *subject package*. Figure 8-4 shows three tasks, D, E, and F, declared in the packages S, T, and U, respectively. Package U is an object with an operation subprogram U1. F is a

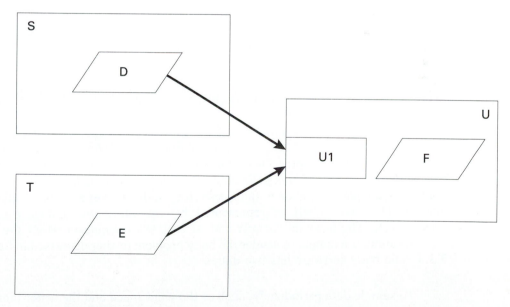

Figure 8-4   Tasks D and E are subjects operating on the object U. F is a guardian task. S and T are subject packages.

guardian task. S and T are both subject packages. (Note that a subject package is not itself a subject. Instead, it is a package containing one or more subject tasks.)

A subject package is a degenerate information-hiding package that has no operations. Ada favors a software structure where a program consists of a network of library units that are independently developed and compiled. This makes subject packages particularly useful since a task on its own cannot be a library unit but must always exist within a package or a procedure. A subject package offers the usual advantages of modularization and may serve as a work assignment and as a unit for reuse and reconfiguration (Chapter 4).

Subject packages also offer conceptual advantages, since they allow *subsystems* to be represented in the software. A subsystem is a self-contained, cohesive part of the problem environment. It is not operated on like an object. It maps onto a subject package in the software. A subsystem is a degenerate object that has no operations. If a subsystem is given an operation so that it can be operated on, it becomes an object. As a matter of analysis it is not necessary to make a firm distinction between subsystems and objects, since one may change into the other during analysis.

As an example, consider the automobile cruise control system, which was discussed briefly in Chapter 5. The cruise control system has two subsystems:

> The *primary function*, which is to maintain a cruising speed set by the driver. This involves the driver-operated devices (lever, brake, gearshift) and an regulator entity that maintains the desired speed.
>
> The *secondary function*, which is to display various values, such as the average fuel consumption, on a unit mounted on the dashboard. This consists of a sampler and an output-generator entity.

The example also contains a *drive-shaft* object that keeps track of speed and distance traveled. Subjects within each subsystem operate on an object package representing the drive shaft.

The software is shown in Figure 8-5. A subject package, PRIMARY, contains an interrupt handler, DRIVER, and a regulator task, THROTTLE. (The package CRUISE discussed in Chapter 5 is part of PRIMARY. THROTTLE is discussed further in Section 6.4.1.2 and DRIVER in Section 8.2.3.2.) Another package, SECONDARY, contains a sampler, S, and an output-generator, G, that makes periodic displays as needed. The drive shaft is represented by an information-hiding package, SHAFT_PACK. The tasks in PRIMARY and SECONDARY operate on SHAFT_PACK.

As another example, consider the buoy problem further discussed in Section 8.3.3. The buoy software has two duties:

> To sample data periodically, such as the wind speed and the water temperature
>
> To transmit the data via radio to passing ships

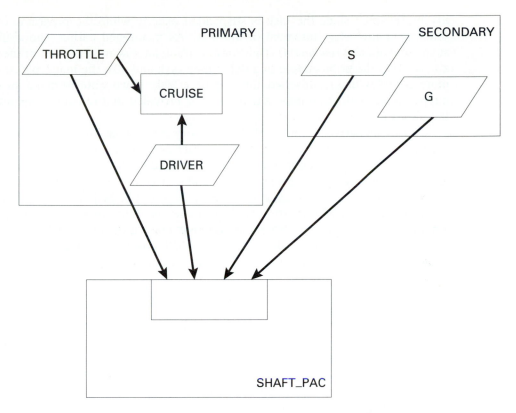

Figure 8-5   The cruise control system with the subject packages PRIMARY and SECONDARY and the information-hiding package SHAFT_PAC. The subject tasks THROTTLE, DRIVER, S, and G all operate on SHAFT_PAC. An information-hiding package, CRUISE, declared in the body of PRIMARY is operated on by THROTTLE and DRIVER.

The sampling and the transmission are different subsystems represented as subject packages. Subjects within each subsystem operate on a *database* of samples that must be maintained for a certain period of time to permit comprehensive, history broadcasts. The software representation of the database object is an information-hiding package operated on by tasks in each subject package.

8.2.3 Mode Representation in Concurrent Software

In Chapter 2 we introduced the concept of implicit mode representation where the mode of a sequential program (or a task) is reflected by its progress through the program text rather than by the values of any explicit mode variables. Some implicit mode representation is built into the syntax. For example, the **delay** statement causes the executing task to be suspended. The suspended mode is implicitly represented since the task is suspended exactly while the program counter remains at the **delay** statement in the text. As mentioned earlier, the ability to suspend itself and *reschedule* itself for execution later is an important property of a task. It is the primary role of a delay-loop task and also the main role of some more complex tasks. Rescheduling ties up a task: If we want to make an event happen X seconds from now, a task must be provided that remains suspended in the interim.

Like the **delay** statement, the *rendezvous* may cause implicit suspension of the tasks involved. Typically, either the caller or the callee is suspended until the other party enters the rendezvous. The suspended mode ends when the tasks are allowed to proceed in the program text, and consequently, the mode representation is implicit. As mentioned in Chapter 7, the ability to be put on an entry queue is an important task property. We use this *queueability* to represent situations where an entity in the problem environment must wait for access to some resource. As mentioned in Chapter 7, the FMS problem contains several such situations. At each point in time, there may be a queue of jobs waiting for access to the forklift truck. In the software, this situation is modeled by JOB_TASK instances sitting on the queue of the entries STAND_TO_BIN and BIN_TO_STAND of the guardian task, FORK.

Reschedulability and queueability are central issues when it comes to deciding how to implement a subject candidate in software. In general, an additional task is needed only if the entity needs to be either queued or rescheduled. Otherwise, it can often be objectified. This is discussed further in Sections 8.2.3.2 and 8.3.2. Some entities are both queued and rescheduled during their lifetime, and an entity-life modeling task may be both queueable and reschedulable.

8.2.3.1 Choice of mode representation

Since rescheduling and queueing are represented implicitly in the task syntax, it is often suitable to base the design of a task entirely on implicit mode representation. Sequence diagrams may then be used as a basis for programming, as in the case of the REPORTER task (Chapter 2) and the ELEVATOR task (Chapter 2 and Section 8.4). **Delay** and **accept** statements are inserted right into the program text, in the proper mode contexts. That way, timing concerns are naturally integrated in the program. This often adds to the resilience of the design in the face of changing requirements. For example, if it becomes necessary to make a **delay** in a certain mode, it is simply placed in the program text at the proper place. An example of this is discussed in conjunction with the elevator problem in Section 8.4.4.

Many designers find it easier to capture a behavior pattern in a transition diagram than in a sequence diagram. A transition-diagram representation leads naturally to explicit mode representation. It is sometimes possible and suitable to separate the timing-related parts of a task where the language forces implicit mode representation from the representation of the mode of an entity. An example of this is the task KEY_SAMPLER and the package BOUNCE_PAC. The circumstances around this example are discussed in Chapter 5 and briefly recapitulated here.

KEY_SAMPLER periodically senses the contacts associated with each key on a keyboard and determines whether it is *open* or *closed*. Each key is modeled as an instance of an abstract data type, KEY_TYPE, which reflects the current mode of the key. Due to the *contact bounce* phenomenon, each key has three modes, OPEN, CLOSED, or UNDEFINED. The UNDEFINED mode is entered after the key has been sensed as CLOSED once and it is still to be determined whether this is due to a true key-in or just a contact bounce. A true key-in is detected if the contact remains closed for a comparatively long period of time, say 10 to 20 ms. As shown in Figure 8-6, KEY_TYPE is declared in an adt package BOUNCE_PAC, and KEY_SAMPLER submits the value OPEN or CLOSED in the parameter SAMPLE to the operation subprogram BOUNCE_PAC.NEW_REQ.

With the solution in Figure 8-6, the life of each key is expressed with explicit mode representation in an instance of an abstract data type. At the same time, the correct modeling of the key behavior is directly dependent on the design of the task KEY_SAMPLER. The KEY_TYPE instance reflects the correct mode of the key only if the key is sampled with sufficient frequency. That way, the life of a key is modeled by the adt package in conjunction with the task. (Since all the keys are sampled at the same rate, there is only one KEY_SAMPLER task rather than one per key.)

One drawback with explicit mode representation becomes apparent when additional modes are introduced during implementation. This results in a mixed-mode representation. In KEY_SAMPLER, this happens because of the sampling. In addition to the modes OFF, UNDEFINED, and ON, each key has a mode UNDETECTED where it has been pressed, but the pressing has yet to be detected. The key is in UNDETECTED when MODE = OFF and the program counter is at the **delay** statement. UNDETECTED reflects the program's finite response time to external events. This time is unimportant in KEY_SAMPLER, where the other modes reflect communication with a human operator and have much greater extent. In a program communicating at electronic speed, UNDETECTED may be an externally visible mode, caused by a **delay** statement or the wait for a shared resource.

8.2.3.2 Objectification

The relationship between an object, such as an information-hiding package or an adt, and the task or tasks operating on it, is often much simpler than in the case of KEY_SAMPLER. The object often correctly reflects the mode of an entity on the sole precondition that an operation subprogram is called every time a mode-changing event occurs in the reality. This is the case when the mode transition depends entirely on the combination of current mode and event, without additional timing restrictions. In this case it is possible to *objectify* an entity by modeling it as a package or adt instance without its own task.

```
package KEYBOARD is
   -- Interface to physical keyboard
   type KEY_ID is ('0','1','2','3','4','5','6','7','8','9','*','#');
   function CLOSED(K_NO: KEY_ID) return BOOLEAN;
end KEYBOARD;


   with KEYBOARD; use KEYBOARD;
package NEW_HOST_COMM is
   -- Communications interface to host computer
   procedure PUT(K: KEY_ID);
end NEW_HOST_COMM;


package BOUNCE_PAC is
   -- The adt KEY_TYPE is a data model of a keyboard key.
   -- NEW_REQ must be called periodically with samples of
   -- current contact status (open or closed). Out parameter
   -- NEW_KEY_IN is true iff a new key-in is detected.
   type SAMPLE_TYPE is (OPEN, CLOSED);
   type KEY_TYPE is private;
   procedure NEW_REQ(KEY: in out KEY_TYPE; S: SAMPLE_TYPE;
   NEW_KEY_IN: out BOOLEAN);
private
   type MODE_TYPE is (OFF, UNDEFINED, ON);
   -- Because of contact bounce, the key is in UNDEFINED
   -- when the contact has been reported closed once.
   type KEY_TYPE is record
      MODE: MODE_TYPE:=OFF;
   end record;
end BOUNCE_PAC;


package body BOUNCE_PAC is
   -- NEW_REQ updates mode of the key and returns
   -- NEW_KEY_IN when the mode first transitions to ON
   procedure NEW_REQ(KEY: in out KEY_TYPE; S: SAMPLE_TYPE;
   NEW_KEY_IN: out BOOLEAN) is
   begin
      if S=OPEN then
         KEY.MODE:=OFF; NEW_KEY_IN:=FALSE;
      else   -- S = CLOSED
         case KEY.MODE is
            when OFF => KEY.MODE:=UNDEFINED; NEW_KEY_IN:=FALSE;
            when UNDEFINED => KEY.MODE:=ON; NEW_KEY_IN:=TRUE;
            when ON => KEY.MODE:=ON; NEW_KEY_IN:=FALSE;
         end case;
```

Figure 8-6   Procedure VDU_UNIT with the task KEY_SAMPLER. KEY_SAMPLER samples each keyboard key every 2 ms. The mode of each key is maintained in an instance of the abstract data type KEY_TYPE declared in BOUNCE_PAC.

```
      end if;
   end NEW_REQ;
end BOUNCE_PAC;

   with NEW_HOST_COMM;
   with BOUNCE_PAC; use BOUNCE_PAC;
   with KEYBOARD; use KEYBOARD;
procedure VDU_UNIT is

task KEY_SAMPLER;

task body KEY_SAMPLER is
-- KEY_SAMPLER contains an instance of KEY_TYPE
-- for each keyboard key and periodically calls
-- NEW_REQ, reporting any new key-in to the host.
A: array (KEY_ID) of KEY_TYPE;
INTVAL: constant DURATION:=0.002;
SAMPLE: SAMPLE_TYPE;
NEW_KEY_IN: BOOLEAN;
begin
   loop
      for K in KEY_ID loop
         if CLOSED(K) then SAMPLE:=CLOSED;
         else SAMPLE:=OPEN;
         end if;
         NEW_REQ(A(K), SAMPLE, NEW_KEY_IN);
         if NEW_KEY_IN then
             NEW_HOST_COMM.PUT(K); -- Report key-in.
         end if;
      end loop;
      delay INTVAL; -- Suspend execution for INTVAL s.
   end loop;
end KEY_SAMPLER;

begin
   null;
end VDU_UNIT;
```

Figure 8-6   (*continued*)

The cruise control problem was mentioned earlier and illustrated in Figure 8-5. As discussed in Chapter 5, the driver behavior is represented as an object CRUISE that reflects the cruising mode as a function of the events that are reported to it, regardless of when they are reported. The driver behavior is described by means of a transition diagram (Figure 5-11) and implemented as an information-hiding package CRUISE (Figure 5-13). In a concurrent implementation, the interrupts from the lever, the brake and the gearshift are handled by a task DRIVER which calls CRUISE.DRIVER_EVENT with the appropriate event literals. DRIVER repeatedly executes a loop of the following general description:

```
loop
   select
      accept lever interrupt
      DRIVER_EVENT.... -- Report event.
   or
      accept brake interrupt
      DRIVER_EVENT(BRAKE);
   or
      accept gear interrupt
      DRIVER_EVENT....
   end select;
end loop;
```

The separation of the task DRIVER and the package CRUISE is possible because of the separation of timing concerns and modes. Regardless of the current mode, DRIVER always accepts the interrupts from gearshift, brakes, and lever. On the other hand, the package CRUISE is independent of the timing in DRIVER and will remain in any mode indefinitely unless DRIVER_EVENT is called.

If explicit mode representation is suitable, and it can be separated from any timing concerns, objectification as in the cruise control problem may afford a simple solution. It decouples the model of the entity from the tasks, and the package modeling the entity can be operated on by any subject task. The decoupling must be based on a determination that mode representation and timing concerns are separable, even if requirements change in the future. If new requirements may make sampling and interrupt handling dependent on the explicit mode, objectification is not a good solution. In the cruise control problem, such a change would seriously complicate the interface between the CRUISE package and the DRIVER task. This issue is discussed further in connection with the elevator problem in Section 8.4.4.

Note that the term *objectification* refers to the case where the behavior of an entity is captured in a transition diagram, which in turn can be represented by means of a mode variable. Such an entity may be said to be *passive*, while an entity with its own task is *active*. The passive entity is driven by other tasks. This should be distinguished from the situation where a subject task is hidden in a package, which is operated on by other tasks. This is discussed in Section 8.2.1. In Figure 8-2, tasks A and B are encapsulated in packages P and Q, respectively. This is an example of superimposed subject–object structures and not an example of objectification.

8.3 CONSTRUCTION OF CONCURRENT SOFTWARE _____

As described above, a concurrent program consists of asynchronously executing subject tasks operating on software objects. We will let the program structure represent the structure of the problem environment. Thus we model the subject tasks on asynchronously operating entities and model the software objects on real-world objects (whether concrete or abstract). For this reason, entity-life modeling starts with an analysis of the problem environment, where we must:

Identify *behavior patterns* (*threads of events*) in the reality. These patterns are the *subjects* in our model of the reality. For each behavior pattern, we define an *entity* that exhibits that behavior.

Identify *objects* in the reality. The objects are part of the subject–object structure associated with each subject. During its life, a subject operates on objects. For this reason, the identification of objects is dependent on the identification of behavior patterns.

Identify *subsystems* in the problem environment. Subsystems serve to break the problem into manageable parts. The interfaces between subsystems should contain a minimum of information. A subsystem contains one or more subjects. It is not operated on by a subject.

Most of this section is concerned with the first issue above, the capturing of behavior patterns. This focuses on the *time dimension* of a problem, that is, the ordering of events in the reality. For this purpose we regard the problem environment in terms of threads of events, each of which is sequential. Any asynchrony exists between threads, not within any one thread. We associate each thread with some intuitive entity in the reality, with which the software must interact. There are two related issues:

We want to find a sufficient set of threads of events to describe the problem. Each relevant event in the problem environment must belong to one thread. For conceptual economy, we look for a minimum number of different threads. For this reason, threads with long extension in time are desirable. Such threads often (but not necessarily) exist as long as the system as a whole.

We must suitably define the sequence of events within each behavior pattern. For this we can rely on implicit or explicit mode representation as discussed in Chapters 2 and 5.

The analysis of the reality in terms of subjects and objects is logically followed by synthesis, where a software model of the reality is designed and implemented. In practice, the analysis and the synthesis are not necessarily separate, consecutive phases. Instead, the analysis of a part of the problem may be followed by a partial design before the rest of the problem is analyzed. Normally, a real-world subject is represented as a task, while each real-world object becomes an information-hiding package or an instance of an abstract data type.

As an example, consider the FMS example studied in detail in Chapter 9. The FMS is an automated factory where the software controls the movements of *parts* that are elaborated at various *workstations* in a series of manufacturing steps, defined for each part in its *process plan*. The parts are moved between workstations by a set of *automated guided vehicles*. A human *supervisor* oversees the operation and defines new jobs and process plans. The supervisor may also inquire into the status of the system and find out how many parts are queued for a certain type of workstation, and so on.

Most events in the FMS problem are associated with specific jobs. They have to do with part movements, the assignment of jobs to workstations, and the operations on a part at each workstation. We can capture these events by identifying each *job* as an entity. Most additional events are captured in a thread associated with the supervisor. Each job comes into contact with workstations and automated guided vehicles. By making the job a subject, we take the view that these devices are *objects* on which the job operates. These objects are parts of the subject–object structure of a job. The subject–object structure of the supervisor contains process plans as objects. In the software, there is a JOB_TASK type and a SUPERVISOR task. SUPERVISOR is modeled on the dialogue between the human being and the software. Such *user tasks* are discussed in Section 8.3.4.

8.3.1 Problem Analysis

This section focuses on the identification of behavior patterns and objects in the problem environment. We must find a sufficient set of threads of events to describe the problem so that each relevant event belongs to a thread. Each suitable thread is a *subject candidate*. It may not end up as a subject in the description of a given problem since different descriptions with different subjects are often possible. The choice of subjects influences the choice of objects in that subjects and objects together are taken into account in choosing the most elegant and effective problem description.

8.3.1.1 Choice of subjects

To find an effective model of our problem we need to capture all of the events in the problem environment in as few sequential threads as possible. Otherwise put, we want to express the problem in terms of as few entities as possible. We have earlier discussed criteria for the identification of such simple entities as samplers and regulators. These criteria still hold and will not be repeated here. The following are additional criteria used to identify other subject candidates. The first two criteria have to do with reschedulability and queueability, which were earlier identified as important task properties. Since entities in the analysis are intended to map onto tasks in the software, we endow entities with the same properties:

A *reschedulable* entity is a subject candidate. Such an entity captures a requirement that certain actions must be taken at a certain time or with a certain interval.

In a system where entities queue for resources, a *queueable* entity is a subject candidate. A queueable entity is the user of various shared resources.

Reschedulability and queueability have a direct impact on the representation of the entities in software and will be discussed further in Section 8.3.2. The following criteria define desirable properties in subject candidates and may be used as heuristic guidelines by the analyst:

A subject candidate should contribute to describing the *time dimension* of a problem by defining the ordering of events in the problem environment.

An entity representing a thread through a *variety of events* in a system is a subject candidate. Some systems include *mobile* entities that physically or figuratively move through the system and visit stationary entities. Often, a mobile entity has more variety and is a more useful subject candidate than a *stationary* entity.

A *long-lived* entity whose behavior pattern has long extension in time is usually preferred over a more short-lived entity. It is desirable that the life of an entity be as long as that of the system itself.

Time dimension, variety, and longevity are discussed further in the following subsections. The cruise control, elevator, and FMS examples are used to illustrate the concepts. While conceptual economy dictates that there should be as few different behavior patterns as possible, *multiple instances* of the same pattern are encouraged. This corresponds to a class of entities. In the multiple-elevator problem, for example, all the elevator entities exhibit the same behavior pattern.

a. Time Dimension

An entity contributes to describing the *time dimension* of a problem if it defines the *order* in which events in the problem environment occur. An entity that does this is a subject candidate. It is usually a better subject than one that does not reflect important ordering relationships between events.

The driver in the cruise control problem defines the state of cruising as a function of the series of inputs received from the brake, the lever, and so on. It describes relevant sequences of such events and the related states of cruising. A sequence of events could also be associated with an individual device, such as the lever, but even if such a sequence is included for each device, taken together they would not capture the time dimension of the problem. The state of cruising is not simply the sum of the states of the devices.

The elevator reflects the time relationship between such events as arrival at a floor, door opening, door closing, and departure, and also reflects that the elevator moves up or down one floor at a time.

The job in the FMS system reflects the ordering of several events occurring when the part is transported from the storage to a tool, moved into the tool for processing, and so on.

In Chapter 2 we used an iteration of a selection as an example of a *wide* sequence diagram describing a behavior where events of certain different types may occur in random order. (An equivalent transition diagram has one mode with many transitions leading back to it.) An entity with such a behavior does not contribute to describing the time dimension of a problem. An iteration of a selection imposes no ordering constraint, since the events may occur in any sequence.

b. Variety

Variety means that an entity participates in many different events. Entities with varied lives account for many events and reduce the number of different threads necessary to describe a certain problem environment. The more varied the lives of the entities, the fewer entities are usually necessary to describe a problem.

Often, a set of similar entities accounts for many events. This is true in the FMS system, where most events happen to a job, and in the elevator system, where most events happen to an elevator. Variety speaks in favor of the driver entity in the cruise control as opposed to the brake or other devices that lead fairly monotonous lives. An entity may have a varied life without contributing to the time dimension of the problem. This is the case when it suffers a wide variety of events in random order. Such an entity should normally not be chosen as a subject, if alternative subject candidates exist. On the other hand, samplers and regulators are examples of useful entities *without* variety, where the rescheduling of a simple action is instead emphasized.

Some problems include *mobile* entities that physically move and visit other *stationary* entities. Such entities often have more variety than the stationary entities. In the FMS system, the forklift is a mobile entity. So are the jobs, since they are associated with parts that are moved between workstations. The storage facility and the workstations are stationary entities. In the elevator system, the elevators are mobile while the floors are stationary.

A mobile entity, such as the job, ties together events at different places in one thread and describes the movements between workstations, and so on. This makes it a varied entity. Mobility may also be used in a figurative sense. For example, in the traffic light example in Exercise 2.9, the lanes in different directions and their associated, individual lights are stationary. We can identify an abstract, rotating entity that gives each direction in turn a green light if the traffic warrants it. This entity is a subject candidate somewhat similar to the elevator that moves between floors in a certain pattern, stopping when necessary.

c. Longevity

Longevity refers to how long an entity remains in existence. Long-lived entities are generally more desirable than short-lived ones. Entities that exist as long as the system as a whole are particularly useful. In the remote temperature sensor (RTS), cruise control, and elevator examples, all entities are as long-lived as the system.

In a transaction system, a transaction is often a reasonable, albeit short-lived entity that represents an important behavior pattern. It is often possible to form a longer-lived entity by considering a sequential chain of transactions that must follow one after the other. For example, if each operator enters transactions one at a time, the operator becomes a suitable, longer-lived entity than the individual transaction. If the transactions entered at each terminal follow one after the other and do not overlap in time, a terminal may be an even longer-lived entity than the operator. Sometimes, the terminal configuration is fixed so that the life of a terminal becomes as long as that of the entire system.

Longevity is generally less important than variety and time dimension. In the FMS problem, jobs come into existence during execution as they are defined by the supervisor and end their existence when finished. A job is thus shorter-lived than, for example, a workstation or an AGV. On the other hand, it has more variety and a stronger time dimension. Even though the creation of new jobs causes some overhead, the job entity is more helpful in separating the concerns of concurrency from sequentiality in the problem.

8.3.1.2 Identification of objects

As discussed in Chapter 4, we usually model a real-world object in software either by providing an abstract interface to it or by representing it as a data structure. To identify important objects in the reality we must thus look for objects that the software needs to have an interface to and objects that it must maintain information about. Some objects in a concurrent problem are operated on by a single subject entity and are no different from objects in a sequential environment. Each elevator in a multielevator system has its own motor that it operates on the same as in a single-elevator system. For this reason, this discussion of object identification in a concurrent environment focuses on objects that are in some way shared by different entities.

A simple extension of the situation in a sequential program is when a device is shared between subject entities. This is the case in the cruise control system, where driver and throttle entities as well as the sampler and generator share an object representing the speed of the car and the distance traveled. In the software this object is represented by the package SHAFT_PAC, since speed and distance are calculated based on shaft revolutions. Each entity needs exclusive access to the shaft entity for the duration of a query into the current distance or speed.

If there are collective or pooled resources as discussed in Section 7.6, the pool or the collective itself becomes a resource that needs protection from conflicting access. This identifies it as an object. In the FMS, the set of AGVs is such a pooled resource and is modeled as a package AGVS in the software. A similar situation occurs with objects about which the software must maintain information. In the elevator system, an individual request for elevator service may be an intuitive object. But an elevator must consult a number of outstanding requests in order to decide its further movements and needs exclusive access to the set of all outstanding requests to do so. This identifies the *set* of outstanding requests as an object.

In general, object identification is heavily dependent on the choice of subjects. Certain objects are needed to complement a subject entity in a subject–object structure that describes the reality in a complete and intuitively compelling way. The subject–object structures of existing systems such as the examples worked in this book may serve as guides to the structure of the system being analyzed.

8.3.2 Software Design

The purpose of the analysis discussed in Section 8.3.1 is to identify entities, objects, and subsystems that map directly onto the software structures described in Section 8.2. Some practical software considerations come into play, however, primarily with respect to the implementation of entities as tasks. In principle, each subject entity is implemented as a subject task. Entities that are neither reschedulable nor queueable allow us to reduce the number of tasks by objectification, as described in Section 8.2.3.2.

Each reschedulable entity requires its own task, even if there are multiple instances. This allows each instance to be rescheduled independently. Each queueable entity requires its own task in order to rely on the Ada task queueing mechanism. Many queueing situations in the reality can be modeled by means of Ada task queueing. It is clearly preferable to reuse that mechanism whenever possible. The task queueing mechanism has certain limitations, however, which force us to build our own queues as data structures in the application program. This is discussed further in Chapter 9 in connection with the FMS problem. In the following sections we discuss the representation of short-lived entities and entities with repetitive patterns.

8.3.2.1 *Representation of short-lived entities*

One of the subject criteria recommends that we find long-lived entities that remain in existence as long as the system as a whole. Sometimes, it is suitable to choose entities with shorter lives. Such an entity is typically implemented as a dynamically created instance of a task type. Unless it is well controlled, such dynamic resource allocation poses the risk that the system run out of resources. Such a situation is particularly undesirable in an embedded system operating without possibility of human intervention. Unnecessary allocation and deallocation should therefore be particularly avoided in such systems.

Controlled dynamic allocation is used in the FMS system. The job is a short-lived entity that is created during execution and exists until finished. Each job is assigned one bin in a storage facility. There are N bins, which is also the upper bound for the number of simultaneous jobs. In the FMS software, we create JOB_TASK instances as new jobs are defined and occupy bins in the storage, and let the tasks expire by executing through their final **end** as the jobs finish. No more than N JOB_TASK instances can exist at any one time.

8.3.2.2 *Representation of repetitive behavior patterns*

The control structure modeled on a behavior pattern may contain repeated subsequences that are identical or differ only slightly. For instance, in the elevator example, the upward and downward movements of the elevator are fairly similar. In the sequence diagrams in Figures 2-35 and 2-36, these subsequences are represented by the subtrees UPWARD and DOWNWARD. As discussed in Chapter 3, the well-known technique to deal with such subsequences is to declare a subprogram, which is then called repeatedly, with different parameters if necessary. In principle, this technique is applicable to tasks modeled on behavior patterns by means of implicit mode representation. Unfortunately, the technique cannot always be used with Ada tasks because of a restriction that **accept** statements must appear in the body of the task and not in a subprogram. Two solutions are possible. The first solution is to avoid subprograms and allow repetition in the program text. This is the solution chosen in the elevator problem[3] (see Chapter 2 and Section 8.4).

In the second solution the repeated subpattern is implemented as an extra task, which we refer to here as a *subtask*. This solution saves memory by reducing code duplication but incurs overhead for task communication. Also, the subtask is conceptually unjustified since it is part of the same thread as the original

---

[3] Different operation subprograms are called during the upward and downward motion of the elevator. This makes the introduction of a subprogram or a subtask nontrivial and justifies the duplication of code in this case.

task. The original and the subtask execute one at a time and never concurrently. Subtasks must be used with discretion to avoid program fragmentation into a large number of tasks. Fragmentation defeats the purpose of entity-life modeling by making the software structure unclear. Not unlike a sequential program with too many subprograms, a fragmented concurrent program is difficult to understand and maintain. In addition, the maintainer of the concurrent program runs the risk of inadvertently introducing deadlocks. An example of a subtask in the elevator system is given in Section 8.4.4.3.

8.3.3 Entity-Life Modeling in the Buoy Example[4]

In this section we discuss the complete, multitasking solution of the buoy problem that was partially introduced in Chapters 2 and 4. The problem contains subjects, objects, and two subsystems. There are simple and complex behavior patterns. The software includes subject packages and an information-hiding package DATABASE, which was discussed in Chapter 4. The control structure of the entity-life modeling task REPORTER was used as an example in Chapter 2.

8.3.3.1 Problem description

There exists a collection of free-floating buoys that provide navigation and weather data to air and ship traffic at sea. The buoys have the following properties:

> The buoys collect air and water temperature, wind speed, and location data through a variety of *sensors*. Each buoy may have a different number of wind and temperature sensors and may be modified to support other types of sensors in the future.
>
> Each buoy is also equipped with a *radio transmitter* (to broadcast weather and location information as well as an SOS message) and a *radio receiver* (to receive requests from passing vessels.)
>
> A sailor in distress who reaches the buoy may flip an *emergency switch* on its side to initiate an SOS broadcast.

Software for each buoy must:

> Maintain current wind, temperature, and location information; wind speed readings are taken every 30 seconds, temperature readings every 10 seconds, and location data every 10 seconds.
>
> Broadcast current wind, temperature, and location information every 60 seconds.

---

[4] This problem was suggested by David Weiss and is also discussed in [Sanden 89b]. The description here follows that of Grady Booch [Booch].

Broadcast wind, temperature, and location information from the past 24 hours in response to requests from passing vessels; this takes priority over the periodic broadcast.

Continuously broadcast an SOS signal after a sailor engages the emergency switch; this signal takes priority over all other broadcasts and continues until reset by a passing vessel.

8.3.3.2 Analysis

As described earlier in this section, the analysis of the buoy problem aims at identifying behavior patterns, objects, and subsystems in the problem environment. The behavior patterns must be sequential and may include simple behaviors such as sampling as well as complex patterns that capture the time dimension of the problem. We strive to describe the problem in as few sequential patterns as possible. For this, we look for long-lived and varied patterns that encompass many different events. With these considerations in mind, we identify the following patterns:

Sampling patterns associated with wind speed, water temperature, and location.

A *radio transmission* pattern. This pattern includes both the normal case and the emergency case as follows: The *normal* case is the periodic transmission of wind, temperature, and location data and the transmission of historic data from the last 24 hours. The *emergency* case is triggered by the emergency switch and consists of a transmission of SOS messages until a *reset* message is received.

Each pattern is ascribed to an entity. Thus the buoy consists of sampler entities and a radio-transmission entity. The radio-transmission entity determines the appropriate radio transmission at each point in time based on history requests and the input from the emergency switch. As regards the identification of objects and subsystems, we first realize that a database of wind, temperature, and location information is necessary for the history broadcasts. The identification of subsystems closely follows the division into behavior patterns. There is one *sampling* subsystem and one *reporting* subsystem. The interface between the subsystems is entirely through the database. Thus the sampling subsystem puts values into the database, while the reporting subsystem retrieves values.

8.3.3.3 Software design

Based on the analysis, the software consists of the subject packages SAMPLING and REPORTING and the information-hiding package DATABASE. The sampler entities are represented by a SAMPLER task type declared in the body of SAMPLING.

The radio-transmission entity is represented by the task REPORTER, which is declared in REPORTING. REPORTING also contains the handling of the radio receiver and transmitter and the emergency switch. Further details of each package are given in the following subsections. A buhrgraph is shown in Figure 8-7.

a. Package SAMPLING

The designer has some latitude in designing the tasks for sensor sampling. If two different sensors are sampled with the same frequency (or multiples thereof), they may be handled by one sampler task. With the sampling frequencies given in the problem description, all sampling can be included in one task with an inner loop for air temperature, water temperature, and location, and an outer loop for wind speed. The inner loop has a 10-second delay, and the outer loop is executed once for every three inner loops. But the most flexible solution is probably to assign one sampler to each sensor. Each sampler is then of the basic form discussed in Chapter 6. If a certain sensor exists in more than one copy in each buoy, or may be installed in multiple instances in the future, a task type may be declared and instances created as necessary.

Depending on the hardware, the sampler tasks for different sensors may be similar but not identical. If they are similar enough, it may be advantageous to make them instantiations of a *generic*. Since tasks cannot be generic units, the task-type declaration may be enclosed in a generic package with suitable parameters. That way, a generic task-type declaration is effectively obtained. (Such a solution is discussed in Section 8.3.3.4 and shown in Figure 8-13.)

b. Package REPORTING

The reporting involves the radio receiver, the radio transmitter, and the emergency switch. A sequence diagram of the radio transmission behavior was introduced in Section 2.7.4 and is shown in Figure 8-8. As further explained in Chapter 2, the behavior pattern is an iteration of a *posit-admit* construct called REPORTER_BODY. The construct consists of a normal case, marked *P* for posit, and an exception case, marked *A* for admit. The NORMAL behavior starts with an iteration called PERIODICS. The iterated sequence, PERIODIC, consists of PERIODIC_MSG followed by a delay. The iteration ends when a HISTORY_REQUEST is received. HISTORY_MSG is then iterated. This ends NORMAL and also REPORTER_BODY, and another loop through the top-level iteration REPORTER follows.

The normal pattern is interrupted when the emergency switch is flipped. The triangles below the boxes DELAY and HISTORY_MSG show the points in the pattern where this emergency event may occur. The admit branch of the posit-admit construct is then entered immediately. That branch consists of the se-

---

Figure 8-7 Buhrgraph of the buoy software with the subject packages SAMPLING and REPORTING and the information-hiding package DATABASE.

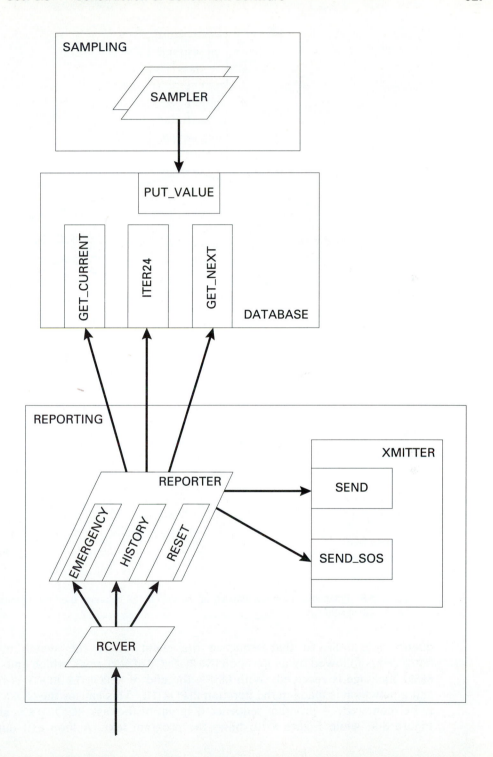

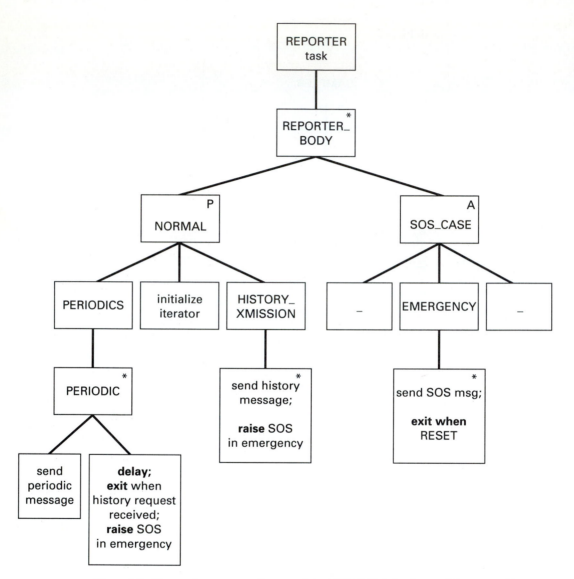

Figure 8-8 Pragmatic sequence diagram of the REPORTER behavior used for a simplified backtracking solution.

quence SOS_CASE. In that sequence the event where the switch is flipped (SWITCH) is followed by an iteration EMERGENCY of SOS_MSG, which ends when a RESET message is received. With RESET, the end of REPORTER_BODY is reached, and a new loop is made in the iteration REPORTER. This causes the NORMAL case to be reentered. A program sequence diagram of the task REPORTER is shown in Figure 8-9, while Figure 8-10 shows the program text. A loop exit out of the

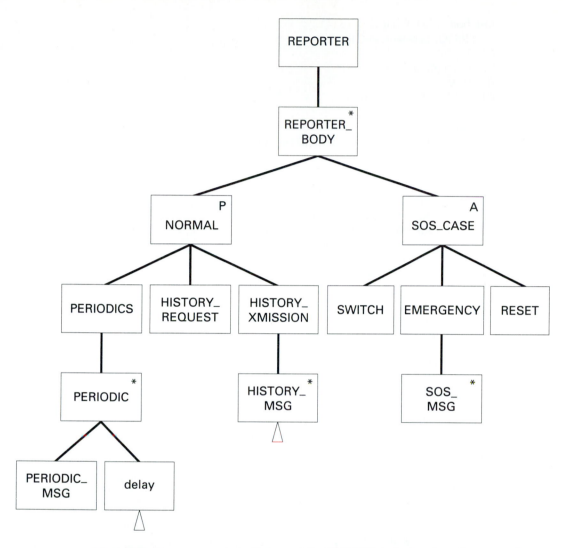

Figure 8-9   Program sequence diagram of the REPORTER task, based on the pragmatic sequence diagram of the reporter behavior in Figure 8-8.

PERIODICS loop is used when a history request is received. The emergency switch causes an exception. The admit branch is implemented as an exception handler within the loop corresponding to the iteration REPORTER_BODY in the sequence diagram.

Without getting involved in the workings of the radio hardware, we assume somewhat summarily that a task RCVER detects the history requests and reset requests and also handles the interrupt caused when the emergency switch is flipped. RCVER calls the respective entry points REPORTER.HISTORY,

```
task body REPORTER is
R_PERIOD: constant:=60.0;
NEXT: TIME;
SOS: exception;
IT: ITEM;
ITER: ITERATOR;
begin
  loop
      -- Posit-admit construct REPORTER_BODY.
      begin
        -- Normal case
        NEXT:=CLOCK;
        PERIODICS: loop
           NEXT:=NEXT+R_PERIOD;
           for E in REAL_ELT loop
              SEND(GET_CURRENT(E));
           end loop;
           select accept EMERGENCY; raise SOS;
           or accept HISTORY; exit;
           or delay NEXT−CLOCK;
           end select;
        end loop PERIODICS;
        -- History transmission
        ITER24(ITER);
        GET_NEXT(ITER, IT);
        while IT.ELEM/=NONE loop
           SEND(IT);
           GET_NEXT(ITER, IT);
           select accept EMERGENCY; raise SOS;
           else null;
           end select;
        end loop;
      exception
        -- SOS case
        when SOS =>
           EMERGENCY: loop
              select accept RESET; exit;
              else SEND_SOS;
              end select;
              end loop EMERGENCY;
      end;
  end loop;
end REPORTER;
```

Figure 8-10 The task REPORTER based on the program sequence diagram in Figure 8-9.

REPORTER.RESET, and REPORTER.EMERGENCY. An information-hiding package, XMITTER, hides the physical interface to the radio transmitter behind an interface consisting of the operation subprograms SEND and SEND_SOS. The task REPORTER uses the operation subprograms GET_CURRENT, ITER24, and GET_NEXT belonging to the package DATABASE, discussed in the next section.

c. Package DATABASE

The need to keep historic data, and the asynchrony between the sampling and reporting patterns, makes a database of samples necessary. (The patterns are asynchronous in that samples are not broadcast at the same rate as they are taken.) This suggests a package, DATABASE, which is shared by the REPORTER task and the samplers. The interface of DATABASE is shown in the buhrgraph in Figure 8-7.

For the purposes of this discussion, we take a very simplistic approach to the design of DATABASE. In the implementation in Figure 8-11, every reading returned from each of the sensors is stored as an integer value in a record in a circular array. The type REAL_ELT contains the elements WIND, AIR, WATER, and LOC (for location), which are used to identify the records. The record type ITEM includes a field ELEM of type ELEMENT, which includes the same enumeration literals as REAL_ELT plus an additional neutral element, NONE. NONE is used as an initial value. Also, a record with the element equal to NONE is used as an end-of-file marker in the interface.

GET_CURRENT and PUT_VALUE are straightforward operation subprograms providing read and write access to the database. GET_CURRENT is used during the periodic broadcast of the most recent reading of each element, and PUT_VALUE is used to add a new reading for a certain element to the database. ITER24 and GET_NEXT together represent an *iterator* operation that allows a user to obtain the data from the last 24 hours, one record at a time in chronological order (see also Section 4.4.3). ITER24 finds the appropriate starting record, and GET_NEXT returns successive records beginning with the starting record and ending with the most current record. After all relevant records have been delivered, GET_NEXT returns a record with ELEM = NONE. The iterator relies on an index stored in an instance of the limited private type ITERATOR.

The REPORTER task and one or more sampler tasks need exclusive access to the DATABASE package. Exclusive access is hidden in the package. As shown in Figure 8-11, mutual exclusion of tasks calling the operation subprograms is enforced by means of a semaphore task. The DATABASE package body *withs* the package SEMA_PAC (see Chapter 7) and contains an instance (SEMA) of the task type SEMAPHORE. Each operation subprogram contains the calls SEMA.ACQUIRE and SEMA.RELEASE, as appropriate. A solution with a special-purpose guardian task is also possible (Exercise 8.1).

Note that we cannot give REPORTER exclusive access to the database for the entire duration of the history transmission. Instead, mutual exclusion is enforced during each call to ITER24 and GET_NEXT. In this example REPORTER is the only one task that iterates over the values in the database. By assigning a unique instance of the type ITERATOR to each caller of ITER24, the solution allows multiple tasks to retrieve historical values independently and asynchronously.

```
        with CALENDAR; use CALENDAR;
    package DATABASE is
        type ITERATOR is limited private;
        type ELEMENT is (WIND, AIR, WATER, LOC, NONE);
        subtype REAL_ELT is ELEMENT range WIND..LOC;
        type ITEM is record
            ELEM: ELEMENT:=NONE;
            TIME_STAMP: TIME:=TIME_OF(1901,1,1);
            VALUE: INTEGER:=0;
            NO: INTEGER:=0;
        end record;
        function   GET_CURRENT(E: ELEMENT) return ITEM;
        procedure PUT_VALUE(T: TIME; E: ELEMENT; V: INTEGER);
        procedure ITER24(ITER: out ITERATOR);
            -- Initialize iterator to return each item starting 24 hours ago.
        procedure GET_NEXT(ITER: in out ITERATOR; IT: out ITEM);
            -- Return next item, provided that iterator has been initialized.
        NO_ITERATOR: exception;    -- Iterator not initialized
    private
        type ITERA is record
            PTR: INTEGER;
        end record;
        type ITERATOR is access ITERA;
    end DATABASE;


        with SEMA_PAC; use SEMA_PAC;
    package body DATABASE is
    MAX:     constant:=.....
    STORE:   array (1..MAX) of ITEM;
    PTR:     INTEGER range 1..MAX+1:=1; -- Where to put next item
    ZERO:    ITEM;
    COUNT: INTEGER:=0;
    WRAP:    BOOLEAN:=FALSE; -- Wraparound of circular buff occurred.
    SEMA:    SEMAPHORE;
    procedure PUT_VALUE(T: TIME; E: ELEMENT; V: INTEGER) is
    -- Store new record for element E.
    begin
        SEMA.ACQUIRE;
        -- If buffer full, wrap around.
        if PTR > MAX then PTR:=1; WRAP:=TRUE; end if;
        STORE(PTR).ELEM:=E;
        STORE(PTR).TIME_STAMP:=T;
        STORE(PTR).VALUE:=V;
        COUNT:=COUNT+1;
        STORE(PTR).NO:=COUNT;
```

Figure 8-11   Implementation of DATABASE with a semaphore task. (The buffer size, MAX, has been left undefined.)

```
            PTR:=PTR+1;
            SEMA.RELEASE;
         end PUT_VALUE;
         function GET_CURRENT(E:ELEMENT) return ITEM is
         -- Find most recently stored record for element E.
         IT: ITEM;
         begin
            SEMA.ACQUIRE;
            for I in reverse 1..PTR−1 loop
               if STORE(I).ELEM = E then
                  IT:=STORE(I);
                  SEMA.RELEASE;
                  return IT;
               end if;
            end loop;
            -- If wraparound has occurred, look at old records.
            if WRAP then
               for I in reverse PTR..MAX loop
                  if STORE(I).ELEM = E then
                     IT:=STORE(I);
                     SEMA.RELEASE; -- Release sema before
                     return IT;         -- returning.
                  end if;
               end loop;
            end if;
            SEMA.RELEASE;
            return ZERO;
         end GET_CURRENT;
         procedure ITER24(ITER: out ITERATOR) is
         -- Locate element stored 24 hours (86,400 seconds) ago.
         -- Create ITERATOR record. Save index in ITER.PTR.
         -- If no such element, ITER = null.
         T: TIME:=CLOCK - 86_400.0;
         begin
            SEMA.ACQUIRE;
            -- Start at current element and search backward.
            for I in reverse 1..PTR−1 loop
               if STORE(I).TIME_STAMP <= T then
                  ITER:=new ITERA; ITER.PTR:=I;
                  SEMA.RELEASE;
                  return;
               end if;
            end loop;
            -- If wrap has occurred, continue with old records.
            if WRAP then
               for I in reverse PTR..MAX loop
```

Figure 8-11   (*continued*)

```
                  if STORE(I).TIME_STAMP <= T then
                      ITER:=new ITERA; ITER.PTR:=I;
                      SEMA.RELEASE;
                      return;
                  end if;
              end loop;
          end if;
          SEMA.RELEASE;              -- Element not found
      end ITER24;
      procedure GET_NEXT(ITER: in out ITERATOR; IT: out ITEM) is
      -- Part of iterator: Return record at ITER.PTR. Increment
      -- ITER_PTR. Return ZERO when no more left.
      -- Raise NO_ITERATOR if none defined.
      begin
          if ITER = null then raise NO_ITERATOR; end if;
          SEMA.ACQUIRE;
          if ITER.PTR=0 or ITER.PTR = PTR then
              IT:=ZERO;
          elsif ITER.PTR > MAX then
              ITER.PTR:=1; IT:=STORE(1);
          else IT:=STORE(ITER.PTR);
              ITER.PTR:=ITER.PTR + 1;
          end if;
          SEMA.RELEASE;
      end GET_NEXT;
  end DATABASE;
```

Figure 8-11   (*continued*)

8.3.3.4 Scaffolding in the buoy example

Referring to the discussion in Section 6.4.4, we now discuss a debugging version of the buoy software running in a simulated, interactive environment. This version includes both diagnostic output statements inserted in the normal tasks, and scaffolding tasks to provide the necessary external stimuli. A debugging version of package REPORTING is shown in Figure 8-12. It uses the DATABASE package discussed above and shown in Figure 8-11. The task REPORTER includes diagnostic output which writes messages such as ''Start of reporting'' and ''Historic transmission'' to the screen. It also accepts entry calls simulating incoming radio messages and activations of the emergency switch. (The actual radio receiver is not included in this simulation.)

To simulate the interrupt-generated input to the task REPORTER, which is hidden inside the package REPORTING, a package TESTING containing the scaffolding tasks SAILOR and SHIP is placed in the body of REPORTING. That way, the scaffolding tasks can make direct entry calls on REPORTER. The scaffolding tasks

```
package REPORTING is
end REPORTING;


    with TEXT_IO; use TEXT_IO;
    with DATABASE; use DATABASE;
    with CALENDAR; use CALENDAR;
package body REPORTING is
-- Debugging version of REPORTING
package IIO is new INTEGER_IO(INTEGER);
package DIO is new FIXED_IO(DAY_DURATION);
package EIO is new ENUMERATION_IO(ELEMENT);
use IIO; use DIO; use EIO;

task REPORTER is
    entry EMERGENCY;
    entry RESET;
    entry HISTORY;
end REPORTER;

package XMITTER is
    procedure SEND(E: ITEM);
    procedure SEND_SOS;
end XMITTER;
use XMITTER;

package TESTING is
end TESTING;

task body REPORTER is
-- Use PUT_LINE to display diagnostic messages.
R_PERIOD: constant:=60.0;
NEXT: TIME;
SOS: exception;
IT: ITEM;
ITER: ITERATOR;
begin
    PUT_LINE("Start of reporting");
    delay R_PERIOD;
    loop
      begin
        NEXT:=CLOCK;
        PERIODIC: loop
          NEXT:=NEXT+R_PERIOD;
          for E in REAL_ELT loop
            SEND(GET_CURRENT(E));
          end loop;
          select accept EMERGENCY; raise SOS;
          or accept HISTORY; exit;
          or delay NEXT-CLOCK;
          end select;
```

Figure 8-12 Debugging version of the package REPORTING with the internal debugging package TESTING. TESTING contains the scaffolding tasks SAILOR and SHIP.

```
                    end loop PERIODIC;
                    PUT_LINE("History transmission");
                    ITER24(ITER);
                    GET_NEXT(ITER, IT);
                    while IT.ELEM/=NONE loop
                        SEND(IT);
                        GET_NEXT(ITER, IT);
                        select accept EMERGENCY; raise SOS;
                        else null;
                        end select;
                    end loop;
                    PUT_LINE("End of history");
                exception
                    when SOS =>
                        NEW_LINE;
                        loop
                            select accept RESET; exit;
                            else SEND_SOS;
                            end select;
                        end loop;
                        NEW_LINE;
                end;
            end loop;
    exception
        when others =>
                PUT_LINE("Error in reporter");
    end REPORTER;

    package body XMITTER is
    -- Debugging version of radio transmitter package
    -- Display each radio message on debugger's screen.
    procedure SEND(E: ITEM) is
    begin
        PUT(E.ELEM,10); PUT(SECONDS(E.TIME_STAMP));
        PUT(E.VALUE); PUT(E.NO); NEW_LINE;
        delay 0.1;
    end SEND;
    procedure SEND_SOS is
    begin
        PUT("SOS ");
        delay 0.05;
    end SEND_SOS;
    end XMITTER;

    package body TESTING is
    -- Scaffolding tasks included in REPORTING package
    task SAILOR;
```

Figure 8-12   (*continued*)

```
task SHIP;
task body SAILOR is
-- Simulate emergency with certain intervals.
begin
   loop
      delay 333.5;
      REPORTER.EMERGENCY;
      delay 41.7;
      REPORTER.RESET;
   end loop;
end SAILOR;
task body SHIP is
-- Request history broadcast with certain intervals.
begin
   loop
      delay 257.7;
      REPORTER.HISTORY;
   end loop;
end SHIP;
end TESTING;
end REPORTING;
```

Figure 8-12   (*continued*)

simulate external activities as follows: SAILOR occasionally activates the emergency switch and, after an interval, simulates a RESET message. It consists of the following loop:

```
loop
   delay X;
   REPORTER.EMERGENCY;
   delay Y;
   REPORTER.RESET;
end loop;
```

For a more thorough simulation, the values of X and Y should be varied in a suitable manner. SHIP simulates a sequence of requests for history broadcast by means of the following loop:

```
loop
   delay Z;
   REPORTER.HISTORY;
end loop;
```

Somewhat despite their names, SAILOR and SHIP are modeled on the behavior of a *series* of sailors in distress and a *series* of ships requiring history broadcasts one after the other. This is based on the assumption that only one ship at a time requests a history broadcast. As discussed earlier in this section, we prefer to model tasks on long-lived entities whenever possible. Should the synchronization of history requests from different ships become an issue, the task SHIP can be replaced by a number of tasks representing different ships, requesting history information independently.

The handling of radio reception and transmission is severely simplified in our version of the buoy software. The package XMITTER can be said to be part of the scaffolding itself. For testing purposes, the radio-transmitter output is simply displayed on the screen. The operation SEND displays the contents of one database entry, including its sequential number.

The debugging version of **package** SAMPLING relies on a generically defined SAMPLER task. Since tasks are not generic units, a package GEN_SAMPLER is declared (Figure 8-13). It *withs* the DATABASE package in Figure 8-11 and takes three generic parameters:

D: the sampling interval (type DURATION)

E: the sampled element (wind, air, water, or location; type ELEMENT)

Function GET_SAMPLE **return** INTEGER: a function returning a sample of a suitable element

The package GEN_SAMPLER contains one sampler task, which calls DATABASE.PUT_VALUE with a sample returned by GET_SAMPLE every D seconds. The debugging version of the package SAMPLING is shown in Figure 8-14. The hardware-dependent sampling functions have been replaced by the dummy func-

```
    with CALENDAR; use CALENDAR;
    with DATABASE; use DATABASE;
generic
    D: DURATION;
    E: ELEMENT;
    with function GET_SAMPLE return INTEGER;
package GEN_SAMPLER is
end GEN_SAMPLER;

package body GEN_SAMPLER is
task SAMPLER;
task body SAMPLER is
NEXT: TIME:=CLOCK;
begin
    loop
        NEXT:=NEXT + D;
        PUT_VALUE(CLOCK, E, GET_SAMPLE);
        delay (NEXT − CLOCK);
    end loop;
end SAMPLER;
end GEN_SAMPLER;
```

Figure 8-13 Generic package GEN_SAMPLER. Each instance of GEN_SAMPLER contains a sampler task. Generic parameters are the sampling interval and the sampled element (wind, air temperature, etc.) The task submits a sample to the sample database.

```
            with GEN_SAMPLER;
            with CALENDAR; use CALENDAR;
            with DATABASE; use DATABASE;
      package SAMPLING is
      end SAMPLING;

      package body SAMPLING is
      -- Debugging version of SAMPLING package
      function SAMPLE_WIND return INTEGER is
      -- Simulate wind sample.
      begin return 1; end SAMPLE_WIND;
      function SAMPLE_AIR return INTEGER is
      -- Simulate air sample.
      begin return 2; end SAMPLE_AIR;
      function SAMPLE_WATER return INTEGER is
      -- Simulate water sample.
      begin return 3; end SAMPLE_WATER;
      function SAMPLE_LOC return INTEGER is
      -- Simulate location sample.
      begin return 4; end SAMPLE_LOC;
      package APAC is new GEN_SAMPLER(10.0, AIR, SAMPLE_AIR);
      package WPAC is new GEN_SAMPLER(10.0, WATER, SAMPLE_WATER);
      package LPAC is new GEN_SAMPLER(10.0, LOC, SAMPLE_LOC);
      package WIPAC is new GEN_SAMPLER(30.0, WIND, SAMPLE_WIND);
      end SAMPLING;
```

Figure 8-14   Debugging version of the package SAMPLING relying on the generic package GEN_SAMPLER to produce four sampler tasks, one per element.

tions SAMPLE_WIND, SAMPLE_AIR, and so on, each returning an integer constant. SAMPLING contains four instantiations of GEN_SAMPLER. The debugging version of the buoy software includes a main procedure *withing* all necessary packages and containing an empty body (a **null** statement).

Like the remote temperature sensor example in Chapter 6, the debugging version of the buoy software is an example where scaffolding is used to simulate the real working environment. The debugging version as shown here does not rely on a general-purpose debugger, but diagnostic output has been inserted into the text of each task. The scaffolding tasks, which simulate the behavior of various entities, are interesting in their own right. They are modeled on the behavior of these entities and provide nice examples of control structures representing behavior patterns.

8.3.4 The User Entity

In any problem environment where a human user sustains some kind of ongoing dialogue with the system, the user is often a good candidate for subject entity. This includes systems such as the FMS, where the supervisor maintains a dialogue via a terminal as well as the cruise control system, where the driver gives a series of commands to the system over time by means of various devices. In the FMS, the system responds in terms of output on a terminal screen, whereas in the cruise control system, various indicators on the dashboard may be turned on or off.

Transaction systems are mentioned in Chapter 6 as examples of non-embedded reactive systems. In such systems, trained operators perform restricted sets of transactions against databases. A teller terminal system used in a bank and an order-entry system for the phone operators of a mail-order company are two examples. Another application is on-line seat reservation for an airline, bus, or railway company. Point-of-sales systems and supermarket checkout systems are similar applications where special-purpose equipment is typically used rather than general-purpose terminals. With its human operators, such a transaction system superficially resembles interactive time sharing, but it is technically closer to a reactive system such as the elevator controller. The transaction system is an optimized, single-purpose application with strict response-time requirements. A tailormade transaction control system can be made much more reliable and responsive than some application run on a general-purpose, time-sharing system.

Various systems providing *automatic services* to the public form a similar category. Examples include automatic teller machines (ATMs), and credit-card-operated telephones, gas pumps, and vending machines. These systems may include some database access, but the dispensing of a service is the function that is most visible to the customer. In these systems the options available to the user are even more limited than in a transaction system, and the customer has the perception of using an automatic machine rather than executing a program.

In all these systems, most events are interactions between the user and the system. The systems can typically be structured around a *user entity* (or a user entity type with several instances) as its primary subject. The user behavior pattern is usually sequential and satisfies the time dimension and variety criteria mentioned earlier. Most of the activity within the system is done on behalf of a user. Different users operate asynchronously. For example, each bank clerk or mail-order operator serves customers at his or her own pace. Background activities such as bookkeeping and database maintenance sometimes constitute additional, concurrent threads of events.

In the software, each user entity is represented as a *user task*. In transaction systems, a task is assigned to each operator either permanently or for the duration of one session or one transaction, depending on the number of tasks that can be accommodated. Sometimes, the user task can be modeled on a series of physical users, operating one after the other. In a transaction system, each terminal often represents such a chain of users that follow each other in time rather than overlap. Such a series is a longer-lived entity than the individual users (Section 8.3.1.1c). Similarly, in automatic service systems, a task can usually be associated with each outlet, such as each gas pump or each ATM, and represent the sequence of users of that outlet.

As an example of a transaction system, consider the teller-terminal program introduced in Chapter 3. It was assumed that each teller in a bank enters customer transactions on a PC. The transactions belong to different subsystems, such as savings and checking, and include deposits, withdrawals, and so on. Instead of a PC, each teller may have a terminal connected to a branch-office computer. The software for all the tellers runs on that computer, and there is one instance of a task type TELLER for each teller position. The control structure of TELLER is similar to the PC program and based on the sequence diagrams over subsystems and transactions shown in Figures 3-19 through 3-22. Each instance of TELLER has its own permanent task data, including a teller identification, totals relevant to this teller, and so on.

8.4 ENTITY-LIFE MODELING IN THE ELEVATOR EXAMPLE

In Chapter 2 we discussed the behavior pattern of a single elevator in terms of a sequence diagram and modeled the control structure of a program on it. In Chapter 4 we introduced suitable information-hiding packages and discussed relevant and irrelevant objects in the elevator problem environment. We now broaden the problem to include multiple elevators serving a common set of requests. These elevators are of the kind common in hotels and apartment buildings. They travel in parallel shafts and together serve the requests made from various floors. The elevator problem in this form was introduced by Jackson [Jackson].

A system of multiple elevators may use different scheduling strategies. A comparison of such strategies is beyond the scope of this book. Instead, the purpose is to establish a general software structure for elevator control and similar systems that is fairly independent of the strategy. We will use a particular scheduling strategy to illustrate the design. In a concluding section (8.4.5) we discuss briefly how the design is affected by a change. Our scheduling strategy is suitable for a medium-sized building of, say, 5 to 15 floors. A taller building may require a different strategy where some elevators serve only certain floors. The strategy used here is also better suited for a hotel or office building with heavy traffic than for a residential building.

8.4.1 Problem Description

A number of elevators, say 3 to 5, travel in parallel shafts, serving all floors in a building. At each floor except the top floor, there is an UP button that users can press to summon an elevator to take them upward; at each floor, except the ground floor, there is a DOWN button for downward travel. Inside each elevator, there are internal buttons marked with the floor numbers. There is a pair of doors for each elevator at each floor and another pair of doors on each elevator itself. Both pairs open and close simultaneously.

The elevators are raised and lowered by cables that are wound and unwound by motors positioned above the top floor. At each floor, in each elevator shaft, there is a mechanical *floor sensor*, operated by a small wheel attached to the elevator: When the elevator is within 15 cm of the *home position* at that floor, the sensor is depressed by the wheel and closes an electrical switch.[5] If required, the elevator then stops when it has reached the position next to the doors (the *home position*) at the floor. *Door sensors* are provided that sense whether the various pairs of doors are in the fully closed position.

The elevator system is equipped with a microcomputer used to schedule the elevators. It is referred to as the *elevator controller*. This example is concerned with designing the elevator controller software. The software schedules the travel of the elevators according to the users' requests for service and produces commands for the motors. The motor commands are as follows:

START	Causes the motor to start
STOP	Causes the motor to stop
SET_UP	Sets the motor polarity for upward travel
SET_DOWN	Sets the motor polarity for downward travel

The software must sample the floor sensors to know when an elevator arrives at a floor. Hardware devices are used to ensure that elevators stop at the home position of a floor if a STOP command has been issued properly. The software must *sample* the button contacts and maintain outstanding requests. The software also controls the *floor lights*. There is an UP and a DOWN light for each elevator at each floor indicating the travel direction of the elevator while it is visiting the floor. (The top and ground floors have only one light each.) The software controls the *doors* by issuing an *open* command and sampling the door sensors to detect the situation when the doors are fully closed. It is assumed that a hardware device closes the doors automatically after a certain interval if they are not obstructed. (A software solution for this is discussed in Section 8.4.4.)

8.4.1.1 Passenger's view of elevator behavior

The elevator scheduling strategy will first be described from the passengers' point of view. When idle, the elevators sit at the ground floor and normally with the doors closed. The doors are opened if a passenger presses the UP button. The passenger may then enter an elevator cabin and press an internal button for a floor F. The elevator then travels to floor F. Whenever the elevator passes a floor G on its way up, it stops for passengers inside the elevator wishing to exit at G and for

---

[5] This is one example of how the floor sensor might work. Other constructions are equally possible. The software design is independent of the workings of the sensor. The distance between the sensor and the home position is dependent on the speed and deceleration of the elevator.

passengers waiting at floor G and wishing to travel upward. When the elevator stops at a floor, the doors open automatically to allow passengers to enter and exit, then close automatically. When they have been completely closed, the elevator continues.

A passenger at a certain floor F, other than the ground floor, who wants to travel up or down presses the UP or DOWN button at that floor to stop the first elevator passing F in the right direction. When entering the cabin, the passenger normally selects a floor G by pressing one of the internal buttons. Assume first that the passenger wants to travel up and stops an elevator moving upward. G is then greater than F. The elevator continues upward, and if necessary, extends its journey to reach G. A passenger at the floor F may also enter an elevator moving in the wrong direction that happens to stop at F. Assume that a passenger wants to travel down to floor G but enters an elevator moving upward. In that case, G is less then F, and the elevator will serve any outstanding requests requiring it to continue up before changing direction in order to reach G.

8.4.1.2 Multiple-elevator strategy

All the elevators help serve the outstanding requests from floor buttons. For example, if a request is outstanding for travel downward from a floor F, the first elevator passing that floor on its way down serves the request. If no elevator is currently scheduled to reach the floor, some elevator must be dispatched from the ground floor or extend a journey to serve the request.

With multiple elevators, more than one elevator might set out to serve the same request. Clearly, only the first arriving elevator actually gets to serve the request. It is important to avoid situations where elevators extend their journeys or set out on new journeys from the ground floor only to arrive too late to serve a request. The avoidance of such *race conditions* is an issue of elevator-systems analysis rather than software design. We skirt it by taking a rather simpleminded approach suggested by Jackson [Jackson]:

> Whenever an elevator sets out to answer a request at a certain floor, it *promises* to serve that request as well as all requests for travel in the proper direction at intermediate floors. For example, if the elevator is about to go from floor 1 to floor 4 in answer to a request made at floor 4, it promises to serve any UP button requests at floors 2 and 3 as well as the request at floor 4. That way, the other elevators need not be activated unnecessarily.
>
> When an elevator has visited or passed a floor in either direction, any outstanding promise issued by that elevator for that floor and direction is erased.
>
> More than one elevator may issue a promise to serve a floor. Only the most recent promise is actually maintained for each floor and direction.

> When an elevator has detected a new request, it checks for outstanding promises before deciding to leave the ground floor or to prolong a travel to serve the request.

Race conditions are discussed further in Section 8.4.3.3.

8.4.1.3 Further problem description

Even with an unsophisticated scheduling strategy, the behavior of several cooperating elevators includes various special cases. Jackson cites some examples observed by "advanced connoisseurs of elevator behavior" [Jackson]. A knowledgeable commissioner of an elevator system might want to include in the problem description a list of *mandated* requirements of elevator behavior such as "a request for service shall be served within X seconds." Such a list would describe the external behavior of the elevator system (i.e., *what* the system is supposed to do without specifying *how* it is to do it) [Davis].

Instead of listing further mandated requirements, we proceed with a *proposed* specification of elevator behavior. This often happens in practice. A proposed specification is written by the maker of the elevator system and submitted to the commissioner for approval. Like the mandated specification, it must describe the external behavior of the elevator system. But the writer of the proposed specification has the advantage that the specification can be cast in such terms as to lead directly to a software design. In our case we accomplish this by basing the problem analysis on behavior patterns, objects, and subsystems.

One further aspect of our basic design of the elevator control software is discussed here. The software is designed so that there is only one *decision point* for each elevator and each floor. This decision point is when the elevator comes within 15 cm of the home position at the floor and triggers the mechanical sensor. At that point it is decided not only whether to stop at the floor, but also whether to change the direction after the floor has been visited. Thus the decision is made before passengers have entered the cabin and have had a chance to press the elevator buttons. Suppose that the elevator is moving upward and stopping at a floor F. If there are outstanding requests for floors above F that this elevator must serve, or if the UP button on floor F has been pressed, the elevator will not change direction. Otherwise, a decision to turn is made. The situation is similar when the elevator is traveling downward. A modification that allows the elevator to better serve the entering passengers is discussed in Section 8.4.4.2.

8.4.2 Analysis

This section focuses on the identification of entities, objects, and subsystems in the elevator problem. Section 8.4.2.1 applies the subject criteria laid out in Section 8.3. Section 8.4.2.2 describes the sequential behavior of the elevator entity.

The problem also includes sampling patterns. These are discussed in Section 8.4.2.3 together with objects and subsystems.

8.4.2.1 Choice of subjects

The elevators have already been mentioned as subject candidates. Possible alternative candidates are the *floors* and *doors* with their sensors, which can be said to operate on the elevators by deciding when they have to stop and start. All these entities are as long-lived as the system as a whole. We also briefly touch on the *elevator passenger* as a possible user entity.

Elevator.   Each elevator has a sequential behavior since it can be at only one place at each point in time. Applying the heuristics for subject choice to the elevator we note the following:

> The elevator has *time dimension* since it ties together the arrivals, stops, and departures at different floors in a sequential thread of events and thus captures much of the elevator scheduling strategy.

> The elevator has sufficient *variety*; together, the elevators account for all events except those having to do with the pressing of the elevator buttons. Also, the elevator entity is *mobile*.

The elevator entity is specified in Section 8.4.2.2. With the requirements discussed so far, it is neither queued nor rescheduled. This means that it can be *objectified*; it needs no task of its own but can be represented as an instance of an abstract data type. This is discussed further in Section 8.4.4.

Floors and doors.   There is a floor sensor and a door sensor per elevator shaft per floor, and the sensors are involved in important events in the system: The floor sensor defines the decision point when it is determined whether the elevator must stop, continue, and so on, and the door sensor indicates when the elevator can restart after visiting a floor. Essentially, the life of each floor sensor can be described as an iteration of the event *arrival*, and the life of the door sensor is an iteration of the event *closed*. Consequently, they are entities with a *weak time dimension* and little *variety*. They capture much less of the timing and ordering requirements of the system than does the elevator entity.

Passenger.   At first glance the elevator passenger might be taken for a typical user entity. Obviously, the elevators exist for the passengers, but the individual's interface to the elevator system is very limited and short-lived. A typical scenario is: press floor button, wait, enter elevator, press elevator button, exit. The main difference between the elevator passenger and the driver of an automobile with cruise control or the operator of a transaction system is that the elevator system serves a collective of passengers simultaneously.

8.4.2.2 The elevator entity

The scheduling strategy requires an elevator behavior that can be described as follows: After waiting at ground for a request, each elevator oscillates up and down while requests are outstanding. Each oscillation consists of an *upward* motion over one or more floors and a *downward* motion over one or more floors. When no requests remain, the downward motion continues to the ground floor.

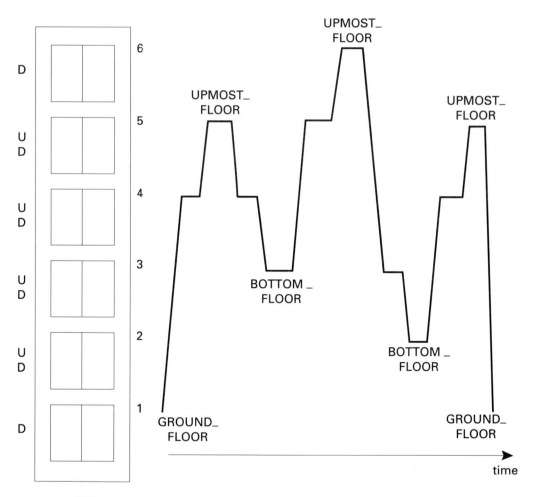

Figure 8-15 Informal diagram showing the position of the elevator cabin as a function of time. In this example, the elevator starts at floor 1 (the GROUND_FLOOR), stops at floor 4, stops and turns at floor 5, stops again at floor 4, stops and turns at floor 3, and so on. The floor where the elevator turns on each journey are indicated as BOTTOM_FLOOR and UPMOST_FLOOR.

This behavior is shown in the informal diagram in Figure 8-15. The sequence diagram in Figure 8-16 shows the inputs governing the elevator behavior: ALERT, ARRIVED, and CLOSED. They have the following meaning:

ALERT signals that a request for elevator service has been received.

ARRIVED signals that the elevator has reached a floor sensor.

CLOSED signals that the doors have been fully closed.

The elevator behavior is an iteration of JOURNEY_GROUP. A JOURNEY_GROUP starts with the elevator sitting idly at GROUND_FLOOR. Once an ALERT signal is received, the iteration OSCILLATE continues as long as there are outstanding requests, servable by this elevator. Then the elevator returns to the ground floor. OSCILLATE is an iteration of JOURNEY_PAIR. A JOURNEY_PAIR is a journey UPWARD followed by a journey DOWNWARD. The UPWARD journey reaches UPMOST_FLOOR, which is the highest floor that must be reached to serve any outstanding, servable request at a given point in time. UPMOST_FLOOR is not necessarily the top floor of the building. The journey DOWNWARD reaches BOTTOM_FLOOR. This is not necessarily GROUND_FLOOR, but if the elevator is idle it returns to GROUND_FLOOR, thus completing a JOURNEY_GROUP.

8.4.2.3 Additional entities, objects, and subsystems

The choice of objects in a single-elevator system is discussed in Chapter 4. One object is the elevator *motor*, which is operated on by means of the commands *start*, *stop*, and so on. Each of the multiple elevators has its own motor, which operates much the same as in the single-elevator case. The motor object will not be discussed further here. In addition to the elevator motor, the single elevator operates on the set of currently outstanding *requests*. The elevator queries the set of requests for reasons to stop, change direction, and so on, and updates it to reflect served requests. Multiple elevators must also operate on the set of requests, but to avoid race conditions we let each elevator operate on the subset *servable requests*. This is the set of requests minus the set of requests being served by other elevators. While the sets of requests and servable requests exist in the problem environment regardless of the software solution, the *set of promises* is an object introduced by the scheme to avoid race conditions discussed in Section 8.4.1.2.

Two sampling behaviors are identified: one for *floor and door sensors* and another for *buttons*. These behavior patterns are asynchronous with the elevator behavior. The button sampling belongs to a subsystem, *buttons*, devoted to the detection of new requests. The sensor sampling belongs to a subsystem *elevators* together with the elevator behaviors.

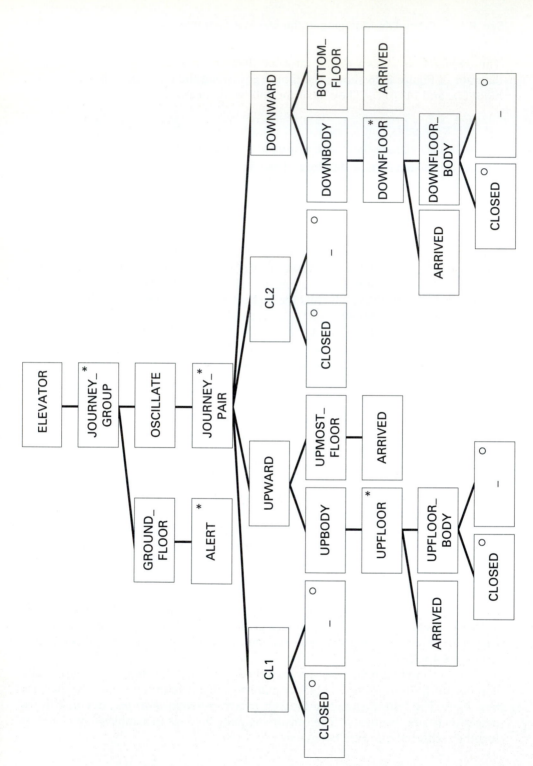

Figure 8-16 Data sequence diagram of elevator inputs: ALERT, signal that a new request for elevator service has been made; ARRIVED, arrival at a floor sensor; CLOSED, signal that the doors are fully closed.

8.4.3 Software Design

Each elevator represents a sequential thread of events such as "leave floor X" and "arrive at floor Y." According to the entity-life modeling principle, each elevator is represented by an instance of a task type ELEVATOR. As before, the sampling behaviors for floor and door sensors and button are mapped onto sampler tasks. In this case one task, E_SAMPLER, samples floor and door sensors, while B_SAMPLER samples buttons.

The objects and subsystems discussed in the preceding section are modeled by information-hiding and subject packages as described below. Packages and tasks are shown in the buhrgraph in Figure 8-17 and discussed in the following sections.

ELE_DEFS: header package containing global constant and type declarations (Figure 8-18).

ELEVATORS: information-hiding package including the declaration and instantiations of the task type ELEVATOR and the task E_SAMPLER (Section 8.4.3.1). E_SAMPLER detects door closings and elevator arrivals at different floors (Section 8.4.3.1b).

REQUESTS: information-hiding package representing the set of outstanding requests for elevator service (Section 8.4.3.2).

PROMISES: information-hiding package used by SERVABLE_REQUESTS. PROMISES represents the set of promises for service made by different elevators (Section 8.4.3.3).

SERVABLE_REQUESTS: information-hiding package *withing* REQUESTS and PROMISES. To each elevator, SERVABLE_REQUESTS represents its set of servable requests. This set is a subset of all the requests since some outstanding requests are already being served by other elevators (Section 8.4.3.4).

BUTTONS: subject package, including the task B_SAMPLER (Section 8.4.3.5). B_SAMPLER samples the floor buttons and internal elevator buttons and detects new requests.

SERVABLE_REQUESTS and REQUESTS represent two layers of abstraction of the set of requests in the reality. As discussed in Section 4.2.2, REQUESTS is hidden below SERVABLE_REQUESTS in that all calls to the operations subprograms in REQUESTS are made from SERVABLE_REQUESTS. The ELEVATOR tasks are the subjects executing all the calls.

8.4.3.1 Package ELEVATORS

The package ELEVATORS is an information-hiding package with two operations, ALERT and ALERT_ANY, used as follows:

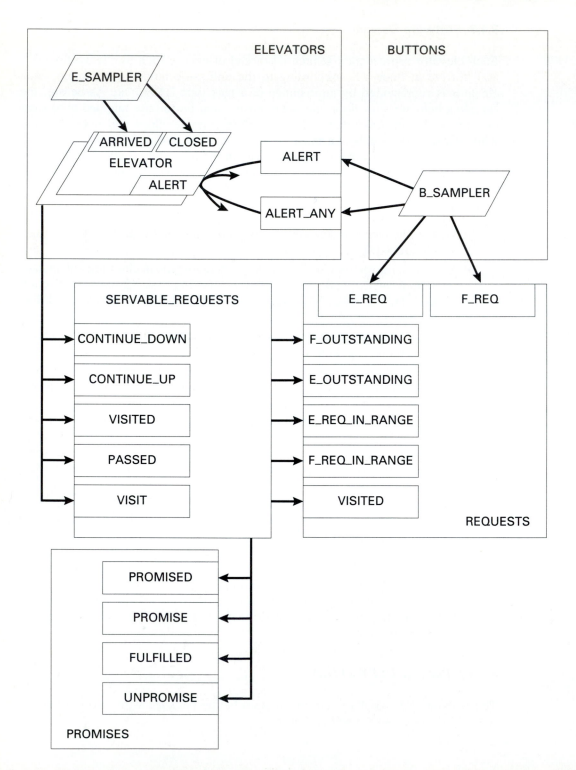

Figure 8-17 Buhrgraph of the elevator control system with the subject package BUTTONS and the information-hiding packages ELEVATORS, SERVABLE_REQUESTS, REQUESTS, and PROMISES.

ALERT activates one specific elevator, in case it is idle at the ground floor.

ALERT_ANY activates one of the elevators that are currently idle at the ground floor, if any.

ALERT and ALERT_ANY are both called by B_SAMPLER and are discussed further in Section 8.4.3.5.

a. Task Type ELEVATOR

The program text of the ELEVATOR task type is included in Figure 8-19. Its structure with nested loops follows that in Figure 8-16. Several details have been added in the program text as explained below.

1. *Operation subprograms used in ELEVATOR.* The iteration and selection conditions in the ELEVATOR text are based on calls to the operation functions of **package** SERVABLE_REQUESTS. Furthermore, operation procedures are called to update SERVABLE_REQUESTS for the benefit of other elevators. To understand the control structure of ELEVATOR, it is necessary to know the meaning of each subprogram. The calls use the following parameters:

E: E_TYPE	Identity of the calling elevator
F: F_TYPE	Floor number
D: D_TYPE	Direction, UP or DOWN

```
package ELE_DEFS is
    -- Directions, up and down:
    type        EXT_D_TYPE is (NO_D, UP, DOWN);
    subtype     D_TYPE is EXT_D_TYPE range UP..DOWN;
    -- Floors:
    GROUND:     constant:=1;
    NO_F:       constant:=GROUND-1;
    TOP:        constant:=8;
    subtype     EXT_F_TYPE is INTEGER range NO_F..TOP+1;
    subtype     F_TYPE is EXT_F_TYPE range GROUND..TOP;
    -- Elevators:
    NO_E:       constant:=0;
    MAX_E:      constant:=5;
    subtype     EXT_E_TYPE is INTEGER range 0..MAX_E;
    subtype     E_TYPE is EXT_E_TYPE range 1..MAX_E;
    -- Button array:
    type        B_ARRAY is array (F_TYPE) of BOOLEAN;
end ELE_DEFS;
```

Figure 8-18 Header package for the elevator program.

```
    with ELE_DEFS; use ELE_DEFS;
package ELEVATORS is
    -- Package represents the set of all elevators.
    procedure ALERT(E: E_TYPE);
    procedure ALERT_ANY;
end ELEVATORS;

    with MOTOR; use MOTOR;
    with SERVABLE_REQUESTS; use SERVABLE_REQUESTS;
package body ELEVATORS is
    -- Package contains ELEVATOR task type with instances.
    task type ELEVATOR is
        entry INIT(E: E_TYPE);
        entry ALERT;
        entry ARRIVED;
        entry CLOSED;
    end;
    ES : array (E_TYPE) of ELEVATOR;
    task E_SAMPLER;
    procedure ALERT(E: E_TYPE) is
    -- Conditionally call ALERT entry. (Call will be
    -- received if elevator is idle.)
    begin
        select ES(E).ALERT;
        or delay 0.01;
        end select;
    end;
    procedure ALERT_ANY is
    -- Alert any one idle elevator.
    begin
        for E in ES'RANGE loop
            select ES(E).ALERT; exit;
            or delay 0.01;
            end select;
        end loop;
    end;
    task body E_SAMPLER is separate;
    procedure LIGHT_ON(E: E_TYPE; F: F_TYPE; D: D_TYPE) is separate;
    -- Turn on light at floor F, direction D.
    procedure LIGHT_OFF(E: E_TYPE; F: F_TYPE) is separate;
    -- Turn off light at floor F.
    procedure OPEN(E: E_TYPE; F: F_TYPE) is separate;
    -- Open doors at floor F.
```

Figure 8-19 Package ELEVATORS with the declaration of the task type ELEVATOR and its instantiations. The body of E_SAMPLER is separate (see Figure 8-21).

```
task body ELEVATOR is
FLOOR: F_TYPE:=GROUND;
MY_E: E_TYPE;
begin
   accept INIT(E: E_TYPE) do MY_E:=E; end;
   LIGHT_ON(MY_E, GROUND, UP);
   ELEV: loop    -- Loop forever.
      -- If no servable request, wait at ground.
      while not CONTINUE_UP(MY_E, GROUND) loop
         accept ALERT;
         -- Open elevator doors on any request.
         if VISIT(MY_E, GROUND, UP) then
            VISITED(MY_E, GROUND, UP);
            OPEN(MY_E, GROUND);    -- Open doors
            accept CLOSED;          -- Wait until closed
         end if;
      end loop;
      -- Oscillate until elevator is back at ground.
      OSCILLATE: loop
         -- Elevator starting upward from bottom floor
         -- Open doors for any UP button/internal button.
         if VISIT(MY_E, FLOOR, UP) then
            OPEN(MY_E, FLOOR);          -- Open doors.
            accept CLOSED;              -- Wait until closed.
            VISITED(MY_E, FLOOR, UP); -- Report visit.
         else PASSED(MY_E, FLOOR, UP);   -- Report pass.
         end if;
         SET_UP(MY_E); START(MY_E);
         LIGHT_OFF(MY_E, FLOOR); FLOOR:=FLOOR + 1;
         accept ARRIVED;
         UPBODY: while CONTINUE_UP(MY_E, FLOOR) loop
            -- Non-upmost floor
            LIGHT_ON(MY_E, FLOOR, UP);
            -- Stop for UP floor button/internal button.
            if VISIT(MY_E, FLOOR, UP) then
               STOP(MY_E);
               OPEN(MY_E, FLOOR);  -- Open and close doors.
               accept CLOSED;         -- Wait until closed.
               START(MY_E);
               VISITED(MY_E, FLOOR, UP); -- Report visit.
            else PASSED(MY_E, FLOOR, UP); -- Report pass.
            end if;
            LIGHT_OFF(MY_E, FLOOR);
            FLOOR:=FLOOR + 1;
            accept ARRIVED;
         end loop UPBODY;
```

Figure 8-19 (*continued*)

```
                    -- Upmost floor: Stop and change direction.
                    LIGHT_ON(MY_E, FLOOR, DOWN);
                    STOP(MY_E);
                    -- Open doors on request from floor DOWN button
                    -- or internal button. Do not serve UP request.
                    if VISIT(MY_E, FLOOR, DOWN) then
                        OPEN(MY_E, FLOOR);  -- Open doors.
                        accept CLOSED;           -- Wait until closed.
                        VISITED(MY_E, FLOOR, DOWN);
                    else PASSED(MY_E, FLOOR, DOWN); -- Stop without opening doors.
                    end if;
                    SET_DOWN(MY_E); START(MY_E);
                    LIGHT_OFF(MY_E, FLOOR);
                    FLOOR:=FLOOR − 1;
                    accept ARRIVED;        -- Wait for elevator to arrive.
                    DOWNBODY: while CONTINUE_DOWN(MY_E, FLOOR) loop
                        -- Nonbottom floor
                        LIGHT_ON(MY_E, FLOOR, DOWN);
                        -- Stop for DOWN floor button/internal button.
                        if VISIT(MY_E, FLOOR, DOWN) then
                            STOP(MY_E);
                            OPEN(MY_E, FLOOR);  -- Open doors.
                            accept CLOSED;           -- Wait until closed.
                            START(MY_E);
                            VISITED(MY_E, FLOOR, DOWN);  -- Report visit.
                        else PASSED(MY_E, FLOOR, DOWN); -- Report pass.
                        end if;
                        LIGHT_OFF(MY_E, FLOOR);
                        FLOOR:=FLOOR − 1;
                        accept ARRIVED;
                    end loop DOWNBODY;
                    -- Stop at bottom floor (including ground).
                    LIGHT_ON(MY_E, FLOOR, UP);
                    STOP(MY_E);
                    exit OSCILLATE when FLOOR = GROUND;
                end loop OSCILLATE;
                -- Ground floor: open doors on internal request.
                if VISIT(MY_E, FLOOR, DOWN) then
                    VISITED(MY_E, FLOOR, DOWN);
                    OPEN(MY_E, FLOOR);
                    accept CLOSED;
                else PASSED(MY_E, FLOOR, DOWN); -- Mark any promise fulfilled.
                end if;
            end loop ELEV;
        end ELEVATOR;
begin -- Initialize all elevator tasks.
    for I in ES'RANGE loop
        ES(I).INIT(I);
    end loop;
end ELEVATORS;
```

Figure 8-19   (*continued*)

The subprograms are as follows:

function CONTINUE_DOWN(E, F) **return** BOOLEAN;

Elevator E reports that it is approaching floor F from above and inquires whether to continue or change direction.

function CONTINUE_UP(E, F) **return** BOOLEAN;

For F/=GROUND, elevator E reports that it is approaching floor F from below and inquires whether to continue or change direction. For F = GROUND, E is sitting idly at the ground floor and inquires whether to start a journey or remain.

function VISIT(E, F, D) **return** BOOLEAN;

Elevator E inquires if it must stop at floor F when moving in direction D.

procedure VISITED(E, F, D);

Elevator E reports a visit to floor F in direction D.

procedure PASSED(E, F, D);

Elevator E reports that it is passing floor F without stopping, in direction D.

The subprograms are also shown in Figure 8-20 and discussed further in Section 8.4.3.4. In addition to the subprograms above, ELEVATOR also calls a subprogram OPEN in order to open and close the elevator doors after a stop at a floor. The body of OPEN is not shown, and we assume that the doors are handled by a mechanical system, independent of the software (see also Section 8.4.4).

```
    with ELE_DEFS; use ELE_DEFS;
package SERVABLE_REQUESTS is
    -- Package represents all requests that must be served
    -- by each elevator.
    function CONTINUE_DOWN(E: E_TYPE; F: F_TYPE) return BOOLEAN;
        -- Elevator E at floor F. Continue down?
    function CONTINUE_UP(E: E_TYPE; F: F_TYPE) return BOOLEAN;
        -- Elevator E at floor F. Continue up?
    function VISIT(E: E_TYPE; F: F_TYPE; D: D_TYPE) return BOOLEAN;
        -- Elevator E at floor F. Must stop?
    procedure VISITED(E: E_TYPE; F: F_TYPE; D: D_TYPE);
        -- Elevator E visited floor F, direction D.
    procedure PASSED(E: E_TYPE; F: F_TYPE; D: D_TYPE);
        -- Elevator E passed floor F, direction D.
end SERVABLE_REQUESTS;
```

Figure 8-20   Package specification SERVABLE_REQUESTS.

Other, fairly trivial subprograms are LIGHT_ON and LIGHT_OFF, which turn the floor light associated with each elevator and direction on and off, and the subprograms START, STOP, SET_DOWN, and SET_UP operating on the elevator motor.

2. *Description of ELEVATOR.* This description follows the text of ELEVATOR in Figure 8-19 from top to bottom. By means of the INIT entry call, each ELEVATOR task is provided with a unique elevator number. It then turns on the UP light on the ground floor. The loop ELEV is the iteration ELEVATOR in the sequence diagram in Figure 8-16. At the top of the iteration, the elevator has just arrived at the ground floor.

The operations associated with the wait at ground are somewhat more complicated than in the single-elevator case discussed in Chapter 2:

```
while not CONTINUE_UP(MY_E, GROUND) loop
    accept ALERT;
    if VISIT(MY_E, GROUND, UP) then
        VISITED(MY_E, GROUND, UP);
        OPEN(MY_E, GROUND);
        accept CLOSED;
    end if;
end loop;
```

In this loop, the elevator first queries SERVABLE_REQUESTS for any reason to start moving. It then waits for a call at ALERT from B_SAMPLER, indicating a new request. VISITED signals that the request has been served. The doors are opened if a request exists at the ground floor, whether from an elevator button or a floor button. The elevator sets out on a journey only when CONTINUE_UP returns the value TRUE. This is done to avoid race conditions, since the request signaled by B_SAMPLER may have been served by an elevator already traveling above the ground floor. In that case, the task goes back to wait for another ALERT call.

At the top of the iteration OSCILLATE, the elevator is at a bottom floor (not necessarily the ground floor). The following sequence, referred to as the *visit selection*, is normally repeated at each floor. (It differs slightly depending on whether the elevator is moving up or down.)

```
    if VISIT(MY_E, FLOOR, UP) then
        OPEN(MY_E, FLOOR);         -- Open and close doors.
        accept CLOSED;             -- Wait until closed.
        VISITED(MY_E, FLOOR, UP);  -- Report visit.
    else
        PASSED(MY_E, FLOOR, UP);   -- Report pass.
    end if;
```

The OPEN command opens the doors unless they are already open. It is followed by **accept** CLOSED, where the task waits for the doors to close completely. VISITED signals the fulfillment of the request to stop, while PASSED removes any outstanding promise to serve the floor. START(MY_E) starts the physical elevator moving. By executing **accept** ARRIVED, the elevator waits for the signal that it is arriving at a floor.

At the top of loop UPBODY, the loop condition CONTINUE_UP is evaluated when the physical elevator has arrived at a floor sensor. The loop is exited if the upmost floor has been reached. Otherwise, the visit selection is executed. The floor lamp and the counter FLOOR are handled as appropriate. When control reaches the statement immediately after **end loop** UPBODY, the elevator is at the upmost floor, where it always stops and then changes direction. The visit selection is executed.

The loop DOWNBODY is analogous to UPBODY. When control reaches the statement immediately after **end loop** DOWNBODY, the elevator is at the bottom floor, where it always stops.

> If the bottom floor is not the ground floor, execution continues at the top of loop OSCILLATE, where the visit selection is executed.

> If the bottom floor is also the ground floor, the loop OSCILLATE is exited. Execution continues with the visit selection immediately after **end loop** OSCILLATE. This is for the benefit of any request from an internal elevator button. (There is no DOWN button at the ground floor.) Execution then continues with the wait at ground at the top of iteration ELEV.

b. Task E_SAMPLER

E_SAMPLER samples the sensors at each floor in each of the parallel elevator shafts and all the door sensors. It maintains the latest sample for each sensor and detects *sensor closings*, defined as situations where a sensor is first detected as open and then as closed. When a floor sensor closing is detected E_SAMPLER calls the entry ARRIVED of the appropriate ELEVATOR task. If a door sensor closing is detected, it instead calls the CLOSED entry. The text of E_SAMPLER is shown in Figure 8-21.

8.4.3.2 Package REQUESTS

REQUESTS is modeled on the set of all outstanding requests. A request is entered in the set when a button is pressed, and deleted from the set when it has been served by an elevator. REQUESTS includes the following operation subprograms (Figure 8-22):

function F_OUTSTANDING (F, D) **return** BOOLEAN;

A floor request is outstanding at floor F, direction D.

```
      separate (ELEVATORS)
  task body E_SAMPLER is
    -- Samples floor sensors to determine arrival
    -- of an elevator at a floor.
    F_S: array (E_TYPE) of B_ARRAY:=(others => (others => FALSE));
        -- Last sample, floor sensors
    DR_S: array (E_TYPE) of B_ARRAY:=(others => (others => FALSE));
        -- Last sample, door sensors
    OLD: BOOLEAN;
  begin
    loop
        -- Compare sensor to value stored in F_S for
        -- each sensor. Report arrival to proper
        -- ELEVATOR task and update F_S.
        for E in E_TYPE loop
        for F in F_TYPE loop
          OLD:=F_S(E)(F);
          F_S(E)(F):=F_SENS(E)(F);
          if F_SENS(E)(F) and not OLD then
             ES(E).ARRIVED;
          end if;
          -- Same for each door sensor. Last sample
          -- value stored in DR_S.
          OLD:=DR_S(E)(F);
          DR_S(E)(F):=DR_SENS(E)(F);
          if DR_SENS(E)(F) and not OLD then
             select                    -- Relevant only
                ES(E).CLOSED;  -- if ELEVATOR
             else null;             -- is waiting.
             end select;
          end if;
        end loop; end loop;
        delay 0.01;
    end loop;
  end E_SAMPLER;
```

Figure 8-21 Task body of E_SAMPLER. E_SAMPLER samples the floor and door sensors. It addresses the sensors directly as the arrays F_SENS and DR_SENS.

function E_OUTSTANDING(E, F) **return** BOOLEAN;

An elevator request is outstanding for elevator E, floor F.

function F_REQ_IN_RANGE(F1, F2) **return** RQST_TYPE;

Return a record R of type RQST_TYPE with a floor field R.F and a direction field R.D. Return R.F=f and R.D=d if a floor request is outstanding for floor f, direction d, in the range F1 through F2. Otherwise, R.F=NO_FLOOR.

```
      with ELE_DEFS; use ELE_DEFS;
package REQUESTS is
   -- Package represents all outstanding requests for elevator service.
   type RQST_TYPE is record
      F: EXT_F_TYPE:=NO_F;
      D: EXT_D_TYPE:=NO_D;
   end record;
   function F_OUTSTANDING(F: F_TYPE; D: D_TYPE) return BOOLEAN;
      -- Any outstanding floor request?
   function E_OUTSTANDING(E: E_TYPE; F: F_TYPE) return BOOLEAN;
      -- Any outstanding elevator-button request?
   function F_REQ_IN_RANGE(F1, F2: F_TYPE) return RQST_TYPE;
      -- Any floor request in floor range?
   function E_REQ_IN_RANGE(E: E_TYPE; F1, F2: F_TYPE) return RQST_TYPE;
      -- Any elevator-button request in floor range?
   procedure VISITED(E: E_TYPE; F: F_TYPE; D: D_TYPE);
      -- Elevator has visited floor.
   procedure E_REQ(E: E_TYPE; F: F_TYPE);
      -- Register new elevator request (from B_SAMPLER).
   procedure F_REQ(F: F_TYPE;  D: D_TYPE);
      -- Register new floor request (from B_SAMPLER).
end REQUESTS;
```

Figure 8-22   Package specification REQUESTS.

function E_REQ_IN_RANGE(E, F1, F2) **return** RQST_TYPE;

If a request from an elevator button is outstanding for a floor f such that

$$F1 \leq f \leq F2,$$

return a record R of RQST_TYPE with R.F=f. Otherwise, return with R.F=NO_FLOOR.

procedure VISITED(E, F, D);

Report an elevator visit to a floor. (There is also an operation SERVABLE_REQUESTS.VISITED, which in turn calls REQUESTS.VISITED.)

procedure E_REQ(E, F);

Report a new request from an elevator button.

procedure F_REQ(F, D);

Report a new request from a floor button.

The calls F_REQ and E_REQ are used by B_SAMPLER and are discussed further in Section 8.4.3.5. REQUESTS is a fairly straightforward information-hiding package that hides a data structure representing the set of all outstanding requests. Mutual exclusion of tasks accessing the requests data structure is maintained by means of an instance of the task type SEMAPHORE. (This structurally insignificant task is not shown in Figure 8-17.)

8.4.3.3 Package PROMISES

The package PROMISES is modeled on the set or promises as discussed in Section 8.4.1.2. Its interface is shown in Figure 8-23. The secret of PROMISES is how the set of promises is represented. There is at most one promise for every floor and direction, and thus a simple implementation is a two-dimensional array over F_TYPE and D_TYPE. The array elements may be of type EXT_E_TYPE, which includes the identity of each elevator and a neutral element, NO_E. That way, each component of the array may contain the identity of the elevator issuing the promise, and the neutral element if no promise has been made. The array may be declared as follows:

    PROMI :array (F_TYPE, D_TYPE) of EXT_E_TYPE:=(others=>(others=>NO_E));

The operation procedures PROMISE, FULFILLED, and UNPROMISE update the array, while the function PROMISED returns TRUE if an elevator other than the caller has already promised to serve a certain request.

8.4.3.4 Package SERVABLE_REQUESTS

SERVABLE_REQUESTS is modeled on the set of servable requests. Its secret is how the set of servable requests is determined at each point in time. For this, it relies on the packages REQUESTS (Section 8.4.3.2) and PROMISES (Section 8.4.3.3). It is irrelevant to its clients that SERVABLE_REQUESTS contains no data structure of

```
    with ELE_DEFS; use ELE_DEFS;
  package PROMISES is
    -- Package represents promises made by elevators to serve certain floors.
  function PROMISED(E: E_TYPE; REQ_F: F_TYPE; REQ_D: D_TYPE) return BOOLEAN;
    -- Any promise made for floor/direction?
  procedure PROMISE(E: E_TYPE; F1, F2: EXT_F_TYPE; REQ_D: D_TYPE);
    -- Promise to serve floors/direction
  procedure FULFILLED (E: E_TYPE; F: F_TYPE; D: D_TYPE);
    -- Promise fulfilled
  procedure UNPROMISE(E: E_TYPE; F1, F2: EXT_F_TYPE);
    -- Revoke promise
  end PROMISES;
```

Figure 8-23 Package specification PROMISES.

servable requests. An ELEVATOR task operates on SERVABLE_REQUESTS by means of the subprograms listed in Section 8.4.3.1 and Figure 8-20. Two or three kinds of information are conveyed between the task and the package in most of the calls:

1. The operation functions return a result to ELEVATOR with both the outstanding requests and the promises of the other elevators factored in.
2. Each operation subprogram call by an ELEVATOR task conveys information regarding the current status of the elevator to SERVABLE_REQUESTS. Each elevator reports to SERVABLE_REQUESTS whenever it approaches, visits, or passes a floor.
3. By calling an operation function, the elevator commits to abide by the returned result. Thus, if CONTINUE_DOWN returns TRUE, the elevator will return down, and so on.

SERVABLE_REQUESTS needs to know the status and committed future behavior of each elevator to keep the set of requests and the set of promises current. Since SERVABLE_REQUESTS is operated on by different tasks, it is necessary to convey information both from task to package and from package to task in each operation. Each operation subprogram call can be regarded as an atomic operation, but immediately after the call from one task, another task may call and change the information in the package.

Synchronization of elevator behavior, promise management, and request management is necessary for the following reason: Whenever an elevator detects a request and sets out to serve it, a promise must be issued before another elevator detects the same request. Similarly, when a floor is visited, any outstanding request and promise must be removed simultaneously. SERVABLE_REQUESTS ensures mutual exclusion and makes the necessary calls to REQUESTS and PROMISES. An instance, SSEMA, of the SEMAPHORE task type is used, and each operation procedure body is bracketed by SSEMA.ACQUIRE and SSEMA.RELEASE. (SSEMA is not shown in Figure 8-17.)

8.4.3.5 Task B_SAMPLER

Each button contact must be sampled at least once during the shortest reasonable time a button is held pressed. We assume that the button contacts can be sampled directly from the software. We assume further that an array F_CONT is mapped to the floor button contacts and E_CONT to the elevator button contacts. That is, the value of F_CONT(D)(F) is the actual, current value of the button contact at floor F, direction D. (The Ada syntax allows such mapping of variable names to fixed hardware addresses. Refer to an Ada text or the LRM.)

Figure 8-24 shows the specification and body of B_SAMPLER. B_SAMPLER scans all floor and elevator button contacts periodically. To keep track of changes in the status of each contact, a Boolean PRESSED contains the latest sample.

```
        with ELEVATORS; use ELEVATORS;
        with REQUESTS; use REQUESTS;
    package body BUTTONS is
        -- Subject package containing the task B_SAMPLER,
        -- which samples buttons to detect new requests.
        task B_SAMPLER;
        task body B_SAMPLER is
            F_B: array (D_TYPE) of B_ARRAY:=(others => (others => FALSE));
                -- Last sample, floor buttons
            E_B: array (E_TYPE) of B_ARRAY:=(others => (others => FALSE));
                -- Last sample, elevator buttons
            OLD: BOOLEAN;
        begin
            loop
                -- Compare sensor to value stored in F_B
                -- for each button. Report new
                -- requests to REQUESTS and update F_B.
                for D in D_TYPE loop
                for F in F_TYPE loop
                    OLD:=F_B(D)(F);
                    F_B(D)(F):=F_CONT(D)(F);
                    if F_B(D)(F) and not OLD then
                        REQUESTS.F_REQ(F, D);
                        ELEVATORS.ALERT_ANY;
                    end if;
                end loop; end loop;
                -- Same for elevator E_B
                for E in E_TYPE loop
                for F in F_TYPE loop
                    OLD:=E_B(E)(F);
                    E_B(E)(F):=E_CONT(E)(F);
                    if E_B(E)(F) and not OLD then
                        REQUESTS.E_REQ(E, F);
                        ELEVATORS.ALERT(E);
                    end if;
                end loop; end loop;
                delay 0.1;
            end loop;
        end;
    end BUTTONS;
```

Figure 8-24   Package body BUTTONS with the specification and body of the task B_SAMPLER.

(PRESSED is TRUE if the button was found pressed when last sampled.) Any detected change in the status of an elevator or floor button is reported to REQUESTS by means of the operation subprograms E_REQ and F_REQ, respectively.

As mentioned, an elevator idling at the ground floor is alerted to the existence of a request for service by means of an entry call at ALERT. This call is made by B_SAMPLER from within either operation ELEVATORS.ALERT or ELEVATORS.ALERT_ANY (Figure 8-19). The ALERT call is relevant only when the elevator is idling, and that is the only situation in which it is accepted by the ELEVATOR task. In principle, this calls for a *conditional* entry call, so that B_SAMPLER is not left hanging if the ELEVATOR task does not immediately accept the call. In reality, the following *timed* entry call is used instead:

```
select ES(E).ALERT(E);
or delay 0.01;
end select;
```

The 0.01-second delay is intended to provide an ample safety margin in case the elevator is idle at the time of the entry call, but the ELEVATOR task has not yet executed the statement **accept** ALERT. ALERT_ANY contains a similar construct. It visits one elevator in turn, and gives each one 0.01 second to reach the **accept** statement.[6]

8.4.4 Mode Representation in the Elevator Example

In this section we discuss the representation of the mode of the elevator with a background of the discussion in Sections 8.2 and 8.3. The solution in Section 8.4.3 uses implicit mode representation based on a sequence diagram. But with the requirements stated so far, which will be referred to as the *basic requirements*, explicit mode representation of the elevator is also possible. This means that the elevator can be objectified. An objectified elevator has no task of its own but is represented as an instance of an abstract data type that is operated on by other subject tasks. We will also see that such a solution has severe limitations as a design for change, in that it falls apart if the software requirements are slightly modified. Objectification is discussed in Section 8.4.4.1 and its limitation in Section 8.4.4.2.

8.4.4.1 Objectification of elevator

Under the basic requirements the life of an elevator can be expressed as a transition diagram (Figure 8-25) with the following modes:

---

[6] ALERT_ANY alerts the first idle elevator it finds, if any. The algorithm in Figure 8-19 is unfair since it always scans the elevators in the same order. If most of the elevators are usually idle, elevator 1 would be activated more often than the others. If necessary, a more elaborate algorithm can easily be devised.

GROUND_FLOOR
UP_MOVING
UP_STOPPING
DOWN_MOVING
DOWN_STOPPING

Transitions are caused by events such as the arrival at a floor plus conditions based on the results returned by the operation functions VISIT, CONTINUE_UP, and so on. The elevator behavior as expressed by the diagram is independent of timing concerns. Thus the elevator remains in each mode until one of the events ALERT, ARRIVED, or CLOSED causes a transition, no matter how long it takes. Consequently, the elevator can be objectified and represented by an abstract data type, ELEVATOR_TYPE. The instances of ELEVATOR_TYPE are operated on by the

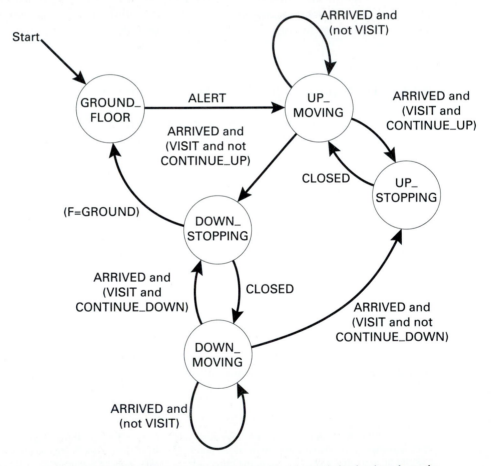

Figure 8-25 Simplified transition diagram of elevator behavior based on the events ALERT, ARRIVED, and CLOSED and conditions expressed in terms of the results returned by the operations on the package SERVABLE_REQUESTS.

two sampler tasks E_SAMPLER and B_SAMPLER. Together, these tasks register all the important events in the system and can perform the necessary operations on relevant elevator objects. Figure 8-26 is a simplified buhrgraph illustrating this. (Operation subprograms and entries are not included.) The instances of ELEVATOR_TYPE are shown as boxes.

ELEVATOR_TYPE is a limited private type implemented as a record where a field MODE of type ELEVATOR_MODE indicates the current mode. An adt package ELEVATOR_ADT may be declared as follows:

```
package ELEVATOR_ADT is
   type ELEVATOR_TYPE is limited private;
   procedure ARRIVED(E: in out ELEVATOR_TYPE);
   procedure ALERT(E: in out ELEVATOR_TYPE);
   procedure CLOSED(E: in out ELEVATOR_TYPE);
private
   type ELEVATOR_MODE is (GROUND_FLOOR, UP_MOVING, UP_STOPPING,
      DN_MOVING, DN_STOPPING);
   type ELEVATOR_TYPE is record
      MODE: ELEVATOR_MODE:=GROUND_FLOOR;
      F: FLOOR_TYPE:=GROUND;
   end record;
end ELEVATOR_ADT;
```

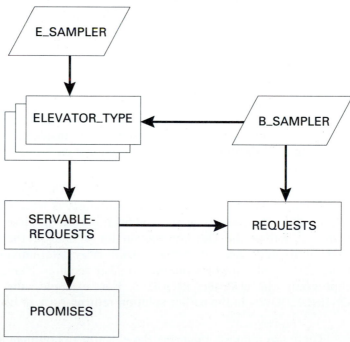

Figure 8-26 Buhrgraph of the elevator system with the elevator modeled as an abstract data type.

The procedures ARRIVED and CLOSED are called by E_SAMPLER whenever an elevator reaches a floor and whenever the doors are fully closed, respectively. ALERT is called by B_SAMPLER when a new request is registered. In turn, the operation procedures of ELEVATOR_ADT call suitable operation subprograms of SERVABLE_REQUESTS. Mutual exclusion must be enforced.

The elevator behavior discussed so far is simplified and it is quite easy to imagine realistic modifications that justify a task based on implicit mode representation. We study such modifications in the next section.

8.4.4.2 Impact of requirements on mode representation

The basic requirements of the elevator system are simplified. Some reasonable modifications to the basic requirements involve timing. When these modifications are taken into account, it will no longer be possible to objectify the elevator entity. Instead, the solution where each elevator is represented by a subject task will be justified. The following are some such requirement modifications:

1. The basic requirements assume that the elevator doors are mostly handled by hardware. The software may be required to handle the doors.
2. With the basic requirements, idle elevators return to the ground floor immediately when no requests remain outstanding. A reasonable change is to let an elevator wait for a while at the floor where it made its last stop, before returning.
3. The software should be required to detect certain abnormal situations and hardware errors.
4. With the basic requirements, the decision to change direction is taken when the elevator arrives at a floor. That way, the desires of entering passengers must be anticipated (see Section 8.4.1.3). Instead, the decision should be made after the doors have been closed and passengers have been given time to press buttons.

Modification 1, door handling by software, is treated in detail in the next section. The other requirements modifications are discussed briefly next. *Modification 2*, letting the elevator remain for a time at the floor of its last request, introduces **select** constructs with **delay** alternatives at suitable points in the ELEVATOR control structure. It also requires changes of the operation subprograms in SERVABLE_REQUESTS. For example, the operation function CONTINUE_DOWN in the earlier solution returns TRUE in two cases:

There are requests requiring the elevator to continue to a lower floor.

There are no requests at all, so the elevator must go on to the ground floor.

With the modification, these two results must be separated. The modification affects SERVABLE_REQUESTS but not REQUESTS.

Modification 3, abnormal situations that can be detected by the ELEVATOR tasks by means of timing, include the case where the doors are obstructed so that the elevator cannot leave a floor. This is discussed in Section 8.4.4.3 in conjunction with door handling.

Another abnormal situation is when an elevator stops between floors. This can be detected automatically by including each **accept** ARRIVED statement in a **select** construct with a **delay** alternative, as follows:

```
select accept ARRIVED;
or delay T;
    -- Take appropriate action.
end select;
```

In regard to *modification 4*, to introduce a decision point after the elevator doors have been closed and the entering passengers have had time to press buttons, the visit selection mentioned in Section 8.4.3.1 can be augmented with a **delay** statement following the statement **accept** CLOSED. After the delay, CONTINUE_UP or CONTINUE_DOWN is called and action is taken as necessary. (Some additional modifications are necessary; see Project 8.2.)

8.4.4.3 Handling the elevator doors by software

In the solution based on the basic requirements, the software gives the command OPEN to open the doors, then waits for an entry call at CLOSED, indicating that the doors are in a fully closed position. The following door-handling rules are implemented:

- The doors open when the elevator has stopped at a floor and there is a request outstanding for that floor, whether from within the elevator or from a floor button.
- The doors are normally closed while the elevator is waiting idly at the ground floor, but they open for any relevant request, whether from within the elevator or from a passenger pressing the UP button at the ground floor.

The basic requirements leave the rest of the door handling to the hardware. But it is not unreasonable to require the software to handle the doors entirely. After the doors have been opened to allow passengers in and out of the elevator cabin, the doors must start to close automatically. This happens after a certain time. There must also be a tolerance for passengers wanting to enter or exit the cabin after the doors have started to close. For this reason, a sensor must detect the presence of an object in the passage through the doors. Based on this, a possible door closing algorithm is the following:

> Once the doors have been opened, they must be closed when the passage through them has been clear for T1 seconds, where T1 is a suitable interval. If the passage is again blocked while the doors are being closed but before they are fully closed, the doors must reopen and remain open for T2 seconds. Then closing begins again. (T2 may be less than T1.) If the doors are obstructed again, they reopen. An alarm sounds if the doors remain open for more than a total of T3 seconds.
>
> There is a button to open the doors in each elevator cabin. If it is pressed while the doors are being closed, the doors reopen. Once the doors are closed completely, the button has no effect. (The button contact is sampled by B_SAMPLER.)

To implement a door-closing strategy, we let the specification of the ELEVATOR task type include the following entries corresponding to door-related events:

OPENED	The doors are fully open.
CLOSED	The doors are fully closed.
OPEN_BUTTON	The button to open the doors is pressed.
OBSTRUCTED	The doors are obstructed.

Assume further that we have an information-hiding package DOORS with the following operation subprograms. (The parameter conventions are defined in Section 8.4.3.1):

procedure OPEN(E: E_TYPE; F: F_TYPE);

Issue a hardware command to open the doors of elevator E at floor F. If the doors are already open, the command has no effect on the doors but gives rise to an OPENED event.

procedure CLOSE(E: E_TYPE; F: F_TYPE);

Issue a hardware command to close the doors of elevator E at floor F. If the doors are already closed, the command has no effect on the doors but gives rise to a CLOSED event.

procedure ALARM_ON;

Sound an alarm indicating that the doors are obstructed.

procedure ALARM_OFF;

Turn off the door obstruction alarm, if it is on.

A door-closing strategy can then be implemented by replacing each occurrence of the statement **accept** CLOSED in the text of ELEVATOR in Figure 8-19 with the following door closing sequence: (MY_E contains the identity of the elevator, and FLOOR contains the current floor number. OPENING_TIME is a variable of type TIME.)

```
-- Door-closing sequence:
OPENING_TIME:=CLOCK;                    -- Note time when doors open.
delay T1;                              -- Minimum open time
loop
    CLOSE(MY_E, FLOOR);                -- Start closing.
    select
        accept CLOSED;                 -- Doors fully closed
        ALARM_OFF;                     -- Turn off alarm, if any
        exit;                          -- Exit loop
    or accept OBSTRUCTED;              -- Doors obstructed
    or accept OPEN_BUTTON;             -- Button pressed
    end select;
    OPEN(MY_E, FLOOR);                 -- Reopen doors.
    if CLOCK − OPENING_TIME > T3 then
        ALARM_ON;                      -- Maximum opening time exceeded
    end if;
    delay T2;                          -- Additional time
end loop;
```

The entry calls to OBSTRUCTED and OPEN_BUTTON are meaningful only when the elevator is actually stopped at a floor. A call occurring at any other time can be regarded as spurious and should be dismissed. To accomplish this, all the calls must be conditional or timed. The door-closing sequence above is executed identically at various places in the ELEVATOR text. To avoid code duplication, we may place the door-closing sequence in a *subtask* as discussed in Section 8.3.2.2. A task type, DOOR_TASK, say, is required, with as many instances as there are elevators. In the ELEVATOR text, an entry call would then replace the door-closing sequence above.

8.4.5 Elevator Example: Conclusion

With the modifications discussed in Section 8.4.4 taken into account, the elevator system is based on *reschedulable* entities that take action after certain time intervals. As mentioned earlier, the **delay** statements fit into a program text based on implicit mode representation. The objects shared by the ELEVATOR tasks represent the common database of outstanding requests for service.

The reschedulability speaks in favor of choosing the elevators as subjects. Furthermore, the elevator entities account for most important events and capture the scheduling strategy. The thread of execution of each elevator passes through the body of the ELEVATOR task and the operation subprograms of SERVABLE_REQUESTS and other packages. This determines the *timing* in the system: Computation is triggered by events in the life of an elevator, such as the arrival at a floor. (Additional, asynchronous computation is associated with button pressings, which are served by their own sampler task.)

The issue of *modularization* is separate from that of timing and has to do with information hiding. The scheduling strategy is represented primarily by two modules, the body of the ELEVATOR task type and the package SERVABLE_REQUESTS. The task body knows only the basic elevator behavior, while elevator coordination is the secret of SERVABLE_REQUESTS. The basic behavior includes everything to do with rescheduling. The elevator task spends time only in the task body, while the time spent in calls to SERVABLE_REQUSTS is negligible. It is also worth noting that the mode of an elevator is not changed in the operation subprograms, which are mere computations returning results based on shared data. (The FMS problem in Chapter 9 contains several examples where the mode of the job entity is changed during its operations on various objects.)

The scheduling strategy implemented in SERVABLE_REQUESTS is executed only when one of the ELEVATOR tasks reports an event (as in a call to VISITED) or must make a decision (such as in a call to CONTINUE_UP or VISIT). Within this limitation, an arbitrarily sophisticated strategy may be built into SERVABLE_REQUESTS. For example, the current position of all elevators as well as all outstanding calls for service may be factored into a decision to let an elevator continue up or down.

8.5 CHAPTER SUMMARY

> *It is circumstance and proper timing that give*
> *an action its character and make it either good or bad.*
>
> *Plutarch*, Lives (Agesilaus)

In this chapter we introduced the entity-life modeling approach to the design of concurrent programs. With entity-life modeling, a program is modeled directly on threads of events, objects, and subsystems identified in the problem environment. A concurrent program is seen in terms of superimposed *subject–object structures*, each containing a subject task and the objects on which it operates. Together, the subject tasks move the action forward by each executing at its own pace. Subject tasks can be delay-loop-based samplers, output generators, and regulators or more complex tasks whose control structures are tailored after behavior patterns in the reality.

Tasking is used basically to model the time dimension of a problem. Each subject task should be modeled on a *thread of events* in the reality. The goal of entity-life modeling is to describe the reality in terms of a minimum number of such concurrent threads. A thread of events is seen as the *behavior pattern* of an *entity* in the problem environment.

Entity-life modeling raises two analysis issues: The identification of suitable entities, called *subject candidates*, and the software representation of the behavior of each entity. Heuristics for the identification are given. A subject candidate must capture the time dimension of a problem by defining the order between different events. It should also be involved in a *variety* of different events and preferably be *long-lived*. It is also important to look for *reschedulable* entities, which need to take action at predetermined times or intervals, and *queueable* entities, which need to compete for resources.

The mode of a subject task can be represented implicitly or explicitly. The control of timing and queueing in Ada is based on implicit mode control where, for example, a task is suspended while it is executing a **delay** statement and is resumed as it proceeds in the text. This often makes it convenient to use implicit mode representation throughout.

Sometimes, the mode of an entity is independent of timing and queueing. It can then be represented *explicitly* by means of a mode variable. In that case, an information-hiding or adt package, which encapsulates the variable, and a suitable task together model the entity. An entity can be *objectified* if it can be modeled as a package or adt instance without requiring that the operation subprograms be called with a particular frequency.

The elevator problem is an example of entity-life modeling where a task type ELEVATOR represents the life of an elevator. Explicit mode representation is possible if the elevator reacts exclusively to events such as its arrival at a floor or the closing of the doors. In that case, the elevator can be objectified. More realistically, the elevator task needs to rely on rescheduling by stipulating various time-out values. Implicit mode representation is used to allow various modifications of the elevator tasks, including the insertion of **delay** statements at suitable points in the control structure. While the elevator task is important as a reschedulable entity, the JOB_TASK in the FMS system is important as a queueable entity. The FMS system is the subject of the next chapter.

REFERENCES

BOOCH, G., Object-oriented development, *IEEE Trans. Software Eng.*, 12:2, February 1986, pp. 211–221.

COAD, P., and YOURDON, E., *Object-Oriented Analysis*, 2nd ed., Yourdon Press, Englewood Cliffs, N.J., 1991.

DAVIS, A., *Software Requirements: Analysis and Specification*, Prentice Hall, Englewood Cliffs, N.J., 1990.

JACKSON, M. A., *System Development*, Prentice-Hall International, Hemel Hempstead, Hertfordshire, England, 1983.

RUMBAUGH, J., BLAHA, M., PREMERLANI, W., EDDY, F., and LORENSEN, W., *Object-Oriented Modeling and Design*, Prentice Hall, Englewood Cliffs, N.J., 1991.

SANDEN, B., An entity-life modeling approach to the design of concurrent software, *Commun. ACM*, 32:3, March 1989, pp. 330–343(a).

SANDEN, B., The case for eclectic design of real-time software, *IEEE Trans. Software Eng.*, 15, March 1989, pp. 360–362(b).

SANDEN, B., Entity-life modeling and structured analysis in real-time software design: a comparison, *Commun. ACM*, 32:12, December 1989, pp. 1458–1466(c).

WARD, P. T., How to integrate object orientation with structured analysis and design, *IEEE Software*, March 1989, pp. 74–82.

EXERCISES

8.1 Special-purpose guardian in the buoy problem

In Section 8.3.3.3, mutual exclusion in the DATABASE package is managed by means of a semaphore task. Design a variation of the package that instead relies on a special-purpose guardian task for mutual exclusion.

8.2 Tank control

A simple software system controls the filling and emptying of a tank by monitoring the liquid level in the tank and by opening and closing an inlet valve and an outlet valve. The inlet valve has two positions: *open* and *closed*. It is always controlled by the system. The outlet valve has the two positions *open* and *closed* and the modes *automatic* and *manual*. It is controllable by the system only when in *automatic*. Otherwise, it is manually controlled [Ward]. The system obtains the current mode by monitoring the valves. We assume that two information-hiding packages, INPUT_VALVE and OUTPUT_VALVE, are provided. INPUT_VALVE has the following operation subprograms:

function CLOSED **return** BOOLEAN;

Return TRUE if the input valve is closed and FALSE if it is open.

procedure CLOSE;

Close the input valve.

procedure OPEN;

Open the input valve.

OUTPUT_VALVE has the following operations:

function CLOSED **return** BOOLEAN:

Return TRUE if the output valve is closed and FALSE if it is open.

function AUTOMATIC **return** BOOLEAN;

Return TRUE if the output valve is in *automatic* and FALSE if it is in *manual*.

procedure CLOSE;

Close the output valve.

procedure OPEN;

Open the output valve.

A package TANK is also provided, with the operation

procedure LEVEL **return** INTEGER;

Return the current level of liquid in the tank.

Design a concurrent program controlling the tank. The program must

Display the maximum fill level for the tank on request.
Accept and store a desired liquid level.
Accept commands to fill the tank to the desired level, and to empty the tank.
Report errors if a desired level greater than the maximum fill level is entered or if a valve fails to respond to a command. After a CLOSE (OPEN) command, the valve should be completely closed (open) after N seconds [Ward].

Hint: Use a transition diagram to show the filling modes of the tank: filling, emptying, and idle. The mode is changed by the events: tank full, tank empty, and the commands to fill or empty the tank. In the software design, consider a regulator task and a user task.

8.3 Explicit mode representation in the buoy problem

In the buoy problem, the REPORTER task can be replaced by a guardian task RPTRGUARD and three additional tasks, PERIODIC_TASK, HISTORY_TASK, and SOS_TASK, which produce periodic messages, history messages, and SOS messages, respectively. The messages are submitted to RPTRGUARD, which sends them over the radio. The specification of RPTRGUARD may be as follows:

```
task RPTRGUARD is
    entry PERI_MSG(MSG: MESSAGE);   -- Periodic message
    entry HIST_MSG(MSG: MESSAGE; EORPT: BOOLEAN); -- History message
        -- EORPT = TRUE marks the end of the history report
    entry SOS_MSG(MSG; MESSAGE);    -- SOS message
    entry HIST_REQ;        -- History request from ship
    entry SWITCH;          -- Emergency switch flipped by sailor
    entry RESET;           -- SOS reset by passing ship
end RPTRGUARD;
```

The body of SOS_TASK is as follows:

```
begin
  loop
    RPTRGUARD.SOS_MSG("SOS");
  end loop;
end;
```

The following table defines a finite automaton with the modes NORMAL, HISTORY, and EMERGENCY. Entry calls define the events causing actions and mode transitions:

Mode	Entry call	Action	New mode
NORMAL	PERI_MSG	SEND(MSG)	NORMAL
	HIST_REQ	HIST_TASK.START	HISTORY
	SWITCH	None	EMERGENCY
	Others	None	NORMAL
HISTORY	HIST_MSG (not EORPT)	SEND(MSG)	HISTORY
	HIST_MSG (EORPT)	None	NORMAL
	SWITCH	None	EMERGENCY
	Others	None	HISTORY
EMERGENCY	RESET	None	NORMAL
	SOS_MSG	SEND(MSG)	EMERGENCY
	Others	None	EMERGENCY

Write the body of RPTRGUARD so that it maintains the current mode of the finite automaton described above with explicit mode representation and repeatedly accepts entry calls and takes action according to the input and the mode.

Hint: The body of RPTRGUARD is a **select** statement in a loop. A call that causes no action in a certain mode can either be accepted and ignored, or not accepted. In the latter case it remains in the entry queue.

8.4 Formal specifications in elevator problem

Formulate invariants and formal specifications with pre- and postconditions for the packages PROMISES and REQUESTS (compare Section 3.3).

PROJECTS

Many examples of systems with user tasks based on human–computer interfaces can be found in everyday life. As an exercise in entity-life modeling, design an appropriate user task based on your experience with one of these systems. Capture the exchange between user and system either in informal structured English or in a sequence diagram and implement it as the control structure of a user task. Examples include:

> *An automated gas station.* The user task reflects an iteration of customers, each going through a series of steps: insert credit/debit card, select gasoline quality, start pump, stop dispensing, receive receipt, and so on.

An automatic teller machine (ATM). A simplified version of an ATM–user interface was discussed in Exercise 2.2. Complete the interface by taking into account situations where the transaction is aborted for various reasons.

A vending machine for a metro transit tickets. Some transit systems issue tickets for repeated use. Each ticket is provided with magnetically registered information that is initialized when the ticket is purchased and updated each time the ticket is used. The vending machine must:

> Accept a used ticket for trade-in
> Accept bills and coins up to a certain maximum amount
> Allow the user to adjust the amount
> Make change, if necessary
> Issue the ticket
> Various error conditions must be accounted for.

The supermarket checkout system described in detail below includes a somewhat complex user task based on the cashier interface.

8.1 Supermarket checkout[7]

The checkout system in a supermarket consists of a *store computer* to which the *cash registers* are connected. Each cash register is equipped with its own processor, a *keypad* with numeric keys and function keys, an electronic *bar-code scanner*, a *scale*, a *receipt printer*, and a *display* where item and price information is shown. The display is visible to both the customer and the cashier. There is also a special *store-coupon printer*. Each register has a holder for a *till* containing cash, checks, coupons, and so on, which is opened automatically at the end of each customer transaction.

We are concerned with the operations of each cash register. As a cashier begins a shift, he or she inserts a till into the cash register, logs onto the register, and waits for approval from the store computer. He or she is then ready to process customer orders. A customer order can be processed only when a till has been locked in the till holder.

As a customer checks out an order, the cashier enters the *identification number* of each item. This is done either by scanning the item over the bar-code scanner or manually from the keypad. In the latter case, the cashier enters the number followed by the function key ITEM_ID. Based on the number, the cash register obtains *product information* from the store computer. The product information contains an *item description* to be displayed and printed on the receipt, *price*, any *age restriction* on the item, and information on whether the item carries a *preferred-customer discount* and whether it triggers a *store coupon* for some related product. In the latter case, such a coupon is immediately printed.

If the quantity is greater than 1, the cashier enters the number of items followed by the QUANTITY button. This sequence must precede the identification number. If two different quantities are entered (such as "2 QUANTITY 3 QUANTITY") the last quantity input overrides any previous quantity. The number of identical items is displayed. On the receipt, one line only is printed for such a group of identical items rather than one line per item.

The price of an item may be based on a discount offer such as "3 for a dollar." In

---

[7] The details of this project were worked out by Dan Buckley and Lisa Jensen.

that case, the cash register program keeps track of the number of similar items checked out, even if the QUANTITY button is not used. The price of each item is displayed separately and printed on a separate line on the receipt. In the "3 for a dollar" example, the first two items are charged at 34 cents each and the third item at 32 cents.

For bulk items, the product information includes a signal that the item must be weighed. The cash register program then activates the scale. The final weight is calculated when the cashier presses the SCALE button. The weight and price are displayed and printed on the receipt.

If an age restriction exists, the cashier is prompted to verify the customer's age. To acknowledge this, the cashier must press either the ACCEPT or the CANCEL function key. Once the prompt has been displayed and acknowledged for one item, it is not done for other items unless a higher age restriction is encountered.

If an item is to be credited, the cashier presses CREDIT before scanning the item or manually entering the identification number.

The cash register program accumulates the total price of the order as it prints the item description and price on the receipt. As items are being checked through, prices and item descriptions appear on the display.

After all the items in the order have been processed, the cashier presses the SUBTOTAL function key. The cash register computes and displays the total price, including tax. The tax and the total are also printed on the receipt. At this point any *discount coupons* are accepted from the customer. For each coupon the cashier either scans the coupon across the bar-code scanner or enters the amount manually and presses the COUPON function key. If the coupon is scanned automatically, the system verifies its expiration date and whether the discounted item has actually been bought. The customer may also present a *preferred-customer card*, which is scanned over the electronic scanner. The card entitles the customer to a discount on certain items. If some such items have been checked out, the total preferred-customer discount is displayed and printed on the receipt. If a customer without a preferred-customer card has bought discounted items, the promotional message "You could have saved X dollars" is printed on the receipt.

After the SUBTOTAL key is pressed but before the TOTAL key is pressed, the customer may cancel some items from the order. The SUBTOTAL button may be pressed more than once for each order. Each time, the current subtotal and tax are displayed and printed. The TOTAL button can be pressed only once for each order. Once TOTAL has been pressed, the order cannot be changed. When the total has been computed, the till is automatically opened.

After the discounted total has been displayed, the cashier accepts payment. The payment amount is entered followed by a payment-type button: CASH, CHECK, FOODSTAMP, or MONEY_ORDER. If a check is used, the cash register program prompts the cashier for the *check-cashing card* number unless a preferred-customer card was presented earlier. The number is verified with the store computer. If the number is not accepted and no other payment is offered, the order is canceled. If the check is accepted, the cashier is prompted to place it in the receipt printer. A line containing date, time, store identity, cashier identity, and order number are printed on the check.

When complete payment has been received, the cash register computes the amount of change, displays it, and prints it on the receipt. Finally, the receipt is fed out of the printer. At this point the cashier must close the till, which is locked in position automatically until the next customer transaction has been completed.

A cashier repeatedly processes customer orders until the end of his or her shift. The cashier then logs off of the cash register. The log-off operation unlocks the till, which is removed by the cashier.

Write a user task based on the cashier interface to the cash register. Declare entries such as the following:

> KEY(F,N), where F is one of a set of possible function keys such as SUBTOTAL, TOTAL, CASH, and so on, and N is an integer entered from the keypad before the function key
>
> SCALE(W), where W is the weight
>
> BAR_CODE(B), where B is an item identification number

Assume that suitable functions are available for communication with the store computer and for manipulating the devices at the checkout position. You may want to capture the behavior of the cashier in a sequence diagram with an iteration over customer orders and an inner iteration over items, and so on.

8.2 Complete elevator system

Implement the elevator system as described in this chapter. Make the elevator task more realistic and resilient by including proper exception handling. Implement the modifications discussed in Section 8.4.4:

> *Modification 1.* Let the software handle the closing of the elevator doors as described in Section 8.4.4.3.
>
> *Modification 2.* Let the elevator remain at the floor of the last request before returning to the ground floor when idle (Section 8.4.4.2).
>
> *Modification 3.* Detect unintentional elevator stops between floors (Section 8.4.4.2).
>
> *Modification 4.* Implement an additional decision point as discussed in Section 8.4.4.2 as follows: After the doors have been shut, the elevator task waits for N seconds to give entering passengers time to press elevator buttons. The task then uses the subprograms CONTINUE_UP and CONTINUE_DOWN to decide whether to change direction.

Implement a RESERVE switch for each elevator. Such a switch is useful in certain situations, as when an elevator is used to move furniture. The switch is operated by means of a special key. The elevator may then be reserved so that it obeys only its own internal elevator buttons. The automatic door closing is also disabled, and the doors are operated by means of the OPEN_DOORS and CLOSE_DOORS buttons in the cabin. The reserved status remains until the special key is removed. Include scaffolding simulating the behavior of the physical elevators in response to the motor commands START, STOP, and so on.

Provide a suitable user interface that allows you to simulate the software from a terminal. Enter test data consisting of simulated requests for elevator service either interactively or from a file. Display a trace of the movements of all the elevators on the terminal or save it on a file for subsequent analysis. Work out suitable test data that allows you to validate the elevator behavior. Verify the behavior against assertions about appropriate behavior.

9 Case Study: Flexible Manufacturing System

A happy and gracious flexibility

Matthew Arnold

9.1 INTRODUCTION

In this chapter, the various aspects of software construction discussed throughout the book come together in one concrete and fairly realistic example, the flexible manufacturing system (FMS). The FMS problem has clearly distinguished subjects and objects. While the system operates on a relatively slow time scale, it is inherently concurrent with multiple simultaneous activities and may serve as a model for systems operating under stricter timing constraints. The FMS example was introduced as a student project at the Wang Institute in 1987 [Gomaa 88, 89] and is also the subject of [Sanden 88].

In this section we introduce the idea of flexible manufacturing and give an informal account of how this particular FMS operates. Section 9.2 contains a detailed problem description, including device interfaces, the job scheduling strategy, and the sharing of resources between jobs. In Sections 9.3 and 9.4 we describe problem analysis and software design. This case study highlights the modeling and packaging aspects of the design of a realistic software system. For reasons of space, the problem has been stylized and limited to what are considered central issues. The handling of errors such as the breakdown of various devices has been omitted. In Project 9.4 we discuss how error handling can be incorporated.

9.1.1 Flexible Manufacturing

Numerically controlled machinery has been used for some time in the manufacturing industry to replace manually operated tools. In a tool such as a lathe, a piece of material is shaped in a series of steps, each requiring adjustments of various controls. In a manual operation, these adjustments are made by a human operator. In a numerically controlled lathe, the steps are instead encoded in a simple program that the tool automatically follows. We refer to such a program as an *NC program*, where the abbreviation *NC* stands for *numerically controlled. Computer-integrated manufacturing (CIM)* attempts to integrate many such tools as well as transportation and storage facilities into automated factories. In *flexible manufacturing*, several individualized *jobs* are elaborated simultaneously.

In the example to be studied here, the FMS controls the *workstations* in a factory. A *job* is concerned with the development of one *part*, which starts out as a piece of raw material and is then milled and lathed in a series of steps at different workstations. The series of such *job steps* is defined in a *process plan* associated with each job. Of those jobs in progress at a given point in time, some may have different process plans and some may share the same plan.

Parts are moved between workstations on *automatic guided vehicles (AGV)*. There may be several, independently traveling AGVs. The system also includes an *automated storage and retrieval system (ASRS)*, an automated warehouse for raw material and finished parts. The warehouse is also used as a staging area for parts that must be taken off the factory floor between job steps.

The flexible manufacturing system in our example may have the factory-floor layout shown in Figure 9-1. The workstations (WS) include *lathes* and *mills*. The mills and lathes are automatic, numerically controlled workstations. Each includes a tool, whether a lathe or a mill; a *robot*, *R*; and two stands, an *input stand*, *IS*, and an *output stand*, *OS*. In addition to the mills and lathes, there are manual *wash stations* and *inspection stations*. The automated warehouse (ASRS) is shown at the bottom of the layout. The ASRS has four stands (*S*) and a *forklift* that moves parts between *storage bins* and stands. (The storage bins are not shown.) The tracks of the automated guided vehicles (AGVs) connect all the stands.

The operation of the FMS is supervised from a *supervisor terminal* not shown in the diagram. From that terminal, a human supervisor defines new jobs by associating the piece of raw material in a certain warehouse bin with a process plan. For this, the supervisor may reuse an already existing process plan or define a new one. Any number of jobs may use the same process plan at the same or different times. The supervisor assigns a priority to the new job and may also change the priority of jobs already in progress. The FMS software runs on a central minicomputer and on distributed microcomputers. Each microcomputer manages a workstation, while the minicomputer provides coordination. The software interacts with the various hardware devices described above.

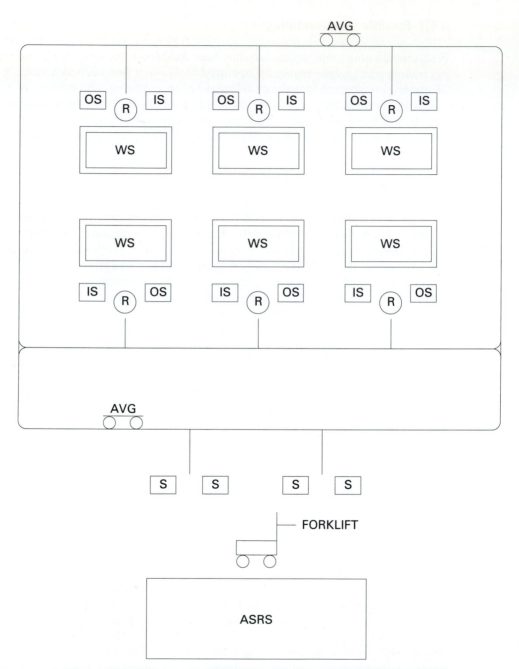

Figure 9-1 Possible factory-floor layout of a flexible manufacturing system. The diagram shows several workstations (WS) with robots and stands. The workstations and the storage facility (ASRS) are connected by AGV tracks.

9.1.2 Operation of the FMS Plant

In our discussion of the flexible manufacturing system, we assume that raw material is stored into the automated warehouse (ASRS) by an external device. Once a raw part is present in one of the storage bins, the supervisor creates a new job, J, by associating the bin with a process plan. The process plan for J may have the following steps:

> Lathe(A)
> Wash
> Inspect
> Mill(B)
> Wash
> Inspect
> Mill(C)
> Wash
> Inspect

Here lathe and mill refer to the two types of numerically controlled workstations. Lathe(A) represents a certain NC program, A, for the lathe. There may be several lathe workstations on the factory floor, and we will assume that the program can be run at any one. Mill(B) and Mill(C) represent two different milling operations, requiring different NC programs, B and C. We assume that all the milling workstations on the factory floor are identical and can execute any program. (There could also be different groups of milling workstations with different program repertories.)

As soon as a job has been created, it is scheduled automatically for the first operation in its process plan. For job J, the first operation is Lathe(A), so the system attempts to assign a lathe to the job. If both lathes are occupied by other jobs, J is queued for a lathe and the part remains in the ASRS until a lathe is released. Assume that J ultimately acquires Lathe 1. The part must then be moved from the warehouse bin to Lathe 1. This is a transport operation in several steps:

> First, the part is taken by the forklift from its storage bin to one of the ASRS stands.
> The part is picked up at an ASRS stand by an automated guided vehicle, AGV, and moved to the input stand of Lathe 1.

When the part is on the input stand of Lathe 1, it still needs to be moved into the tool proper. When the tool is released by the preceding job, the robot at the workstation moves the part into the tool, and the input stand is released to be used by another job. Each numerically controlled workstation is controlled by a micro-processor. As the part is moved from input stand to tool, the appropriate program indicated in the process plan is loaded into the microprocessor. Thus, when the part in our example is moved into Lathe 1, program A is loaded into the controller of that workstation. When the lathing operation is completed, the robot moves the part from the lathe onto the output stand. The tool is then released.

Once the part is on the output stand, the job is scheduled for the next step in its process plan, in this case a wash operation. For this, J must acquire the wash station. If the input stand at the wash station is currently occupied, the part normally stays on the output stand of Lathe 1 until it can be moved to the wash station. Once J has acquired the wash station, it acquires an AGV that moves the part. The wash station is manual, and an operator manually moves the part off the input stand into the wash station proper, and finally onto the output stand.

Ideally, each job can be moved directly from the output stand of one work-station onto the input stand of the next workstation, as described above. But the wait for a workstation may sometimes by considerable, particularly for a low-priority job. For this reason, parts may be *staged* in the ASRS between steps. The part is then moved from the output stand of a workstation to an ASRS stand by means of an AGV, and from the ASRS stand to a storage bin by the forklift. Once a workstation has been acquired, the job is moved in the opposite direc-tion. When a job has been completed according to its process plan, the part is moved to the ASRS one last time. (This also happens if the job is aborted and the part is scrapped.) Finished and scrapped parts are removed from the ASRS by some external device.

At any point in time, a number of jobs at various stages are progressing through the system. The responsibility of the FMS software is to keep track of the progress of each job through its process plan, and to give each job access to workstations and other resources as needed. The FMS system in our example handles this entirely dynamically, by maintaining queues of waiting jobs. Re-sources are allocated based on the priority of each job, and for a given priority, on a first-come-first-served basis. This allows the supervisor to enter new jobs into the system at any time, and to change job priorities. For example, if the priority of a job already in progress is changed to top priority, it will pass all the other jobs in the workstation queues and rush through the system.

9.1.3 Alternative Scheduling

The dynamic scheduling strategy adopted in our flexible manufacturing system may be compared to a more static strategy, where each day's production is planned ahead of time. In such a system, all job data for a day's production is collected, including the expected duration of each operation at each workstation. Based on this, a batch program produces a complete, optimum schedule, which is then followed by a simplified, real-time control program. This control program moves each job to the proper workstation as indicated by the schedule. Such a static system has the advantage that the total use of the machinery can be optimized to avoid idle time. On the other hand, it cannot cope with new, unplanned jobs entering the system or with priority changes.

The FMS software in our example makes no attempt at total optimization. Instead, it assigns each workstation that is released to the first-arrived, highest-priority job waiting for that type of workstation. This scheduling strategy could be improved by means of dynamic optimization. For this, the FMS would have a tentative plan of the day's production. Every time a new job is entered or a priority is changed, the plan would be recalculated to account for the new situation. The software structure discussed in this chapter could be modified to allow such dynamic optimization.

9.2 PROBLEM DESCRIPTION

With the narrative in Section 9.1 as an introduction, we now proceed to a somewhat more detailed problem description. A flexible manufacturing system is to be designed for a factory where parts undergo customized sequences of machining, washing, and inspection operations. Machining is carried out at automatic workstations, each controlled by a microcomputer, while washing and inspection are conducted at manual workstations. The flexible manufacturing system consists of:

> Automated machining workstations (lathes and mills) each controlled by a microprocessor
>
> Manual washing and inspection workstations
>
> An automated storage and retrieval system (ASRS)
>
> Automatic guided vehicles (AGVs)
>
> A minicomputer-based FMS controller with a supervisor terminal

These components are described in detail in the following sections.

9.2.1 Workstation

Each automated workstation has the following components:

> A numerically controlled (NC) machine *tool*
>
> One *input stand* and one *output stand*
>
> A pick-and-place *robot*

A part is delivered to the input stand by an automated guided vehicle (AGV). (AGVs travel on tracks connecting all workstation and ASRS stands.) The part is then moved from the input stand into the tool by the robot. After machining, the part is moved from the tool to the output stand by the same robot. Finally, an AGV removes it from the output stand. The robot has a programmable controller that executes a different *robot program* for each part type. If necessary, a new robot program is loaded before the part is moved from the input stand. (One robot program handles the loading of the part into the tool and its unloading onto the output stand.) Similarly to the robot, the numerically controlled tool may run different NC programs, each corresponding to a certain operation on a certain part type. For simplicity, we will not deal with robot and NC programs separately, but assume that a certain robot program always goes with a given NC program.

Like its automatic counterpart, each *manual workstation* has an input and an output stand. It also has a simple terminal whereby the operator communicates with the FMS software on the minicomputer. That way, the operator may indicate that the input stand is free or that the output stand is needed for a finished part.

9.2.2 Automated Storage and Retrieval System

The automated storage and retrieval system (ASRS) is an automated warehouse used to store raw materials, finished parts ready to be shipped, and scrapped parts ready to be disposed of. It is also used as a staging area for parts in progress waiting for access to different workstations. The ASRS has a number of stands each of which may function as an input or an output stand. An automated *forklift* takes a part from a stand and stores it in a *storage bin*, and vice versa. Parts are moved between stands by means of automatic guided vehicles (AGVs). An AGV picks up a part from a workstation output stand or an ASRS stand, and delivers it to a workstation input stand or an ASRS stand.

9.2.3 FMS Controller and Supervisor Terminal

The workstations, AGVs, and the ASRS are all connected to a minicomputer acting as the FMS controller. The controller maintains system-wide job data such as the job records and the process plans, and handles resource scheduling. As mentioned earlier, the sequence of operations required to manufacture a given part is defined by a process plan. Each operation is defined by a workstation type and the names of the NC and robot programs. The process plans are created by a human supervisor who also defines the jobs. Each job consists of a part and its associated process plan. The supervisor communicates with the system by means of a terminal. In addition to creating jobs and process plans, the supervisor may inspect the status of a job or change job priorities.

The FMS controller software interfaces with the AGVs and the ASRS forklift via commands and interrupts, and with the workstation microprocessors and the supervisor and operator terminals via messages. The interfaces are described in the next two sections.

9.2.4 Interface Between FMS Controller
and AGVs and ASRS

The FMS controller software in the minicomputer interfaces with the AGVs and the ASRS forklift via commands and interrupts. The AGV commands from the minicomputer are as follows:

> Move to stand-id
> Pick
> Place

The forklift commands from the minicomputer are as follows:

> Move to bin-id
> Move to stand-id
> Pick (from stand)
> Place (on stand)
> Get from bin-id
> Put into bin-id

The minicomputer receives completion interrupts from both the AGVs and the forklift. (Status information is transferred with each interrupt but is left outside the scope of this case study.) The interrupts are hard-coded into interrupt-handler tasks (compare Section 6.4.1.3). For example, there is a task FORK that executes the statement **accept** FORK_DONE to wait for the completion interrupt from the forklift.

9.2.5 Interface Between Workstations
and Controller

While the minicomputer has predefined hardware interfaces to the forklift and the AGVs, the message interface to the microcomputer-based workstations may be influenced by the design of the software in the minicomputer and the microcomputers. The guideline is to make the workstations as autonomous as possible by keeping the details of workstation management at each microcomputer. On the other hand, each microcomputer is aware only of its own workstation, while the minicomputer knows about all the workstations as well as overall scheduling and resource management.

   Another goal is to let the minicomputer have the same interface to the manual workstations as to the automated ones at a level of abstraction above the communication software. (As mentioned earlier, the operator of a manual workstation communicates with the minicomputer via an operator terminal.) One message is sent from the minicomputer to a workstation, whether automated or manual:

Job on input stand

The message includes necessary job data defining required robot program, NC program, and so on. Similarly, the messages from workstation to minicomputer are independent of whether the workstation is automatic or manual. They are as follows:

Input stand clear

This message signals that the job on the input stand has been moved into the tool proper

Clear output stand

This message signals that the part currently in the tool needs the output stand.

Job on output stand

This message signals that a job has been moved from the tool proper onto the output stand.

An automatic workstation senses when the output stand has been freed so that the job currently in the tool can be moved. Furthermore, it is assumed that preexisting software modules are used in the minicomputer for communication with the microcomputers and the operator terminals. The design of the microprocessor software running at each automated workstation is also left outside the scope of this study (see Exercise 9.3).

9.2.6 Workstation Allocation

As discussed earlier, the supervisor defines process plans, each of which specifies the sequence of processing steps for a class of jobs. The supervisor also defines *jobs* by specifying a process plan, a part, and a priority. The part is specified by means of its location in the ASRS.

Workstations are dynamically allocated to jobs based on priority. Thus, as soon as a job has been defined, it is queued up for the workstation type of the first job step. As soon as a workstation of that type becomes available, the workstation is acquired by the job and the part is moved to the proper input stand. Until a job acquires a workstation, it may be surpassed in the queue by a later arriving job with higher priority.

A workstation is assigned to a job as soon as its input stand becomes free (i.e., when the preceding job has been moved into the tool). This allocation strategy optimizes workstation utilization since a part will normally be immediately available on the input stand when the previous job has been finished. On the other hand, once a part has been placed on an input stand it will not be removed even if a higher-priority job needs the workstation. (An alternative strategy, which favors rush jobs, is to assign a workstation to a job only when the previous job has been completed.)

When a part, P, has been placed on the output stand of a workstation, W, after processing, it is queued for the next workstation type according to its process plan. If a workstation of that type is not immediately available, the part waits on the output stand. But if P is still on the output stand when the workstation W is nearing completion of the next part, P is *bumped* off and sent to the ASRS for temporary staging.

9.2.7 Resource Sharing

Jobs share system resources such as workstations, AGVs, stands, and so on. A job frequently needs simultaneous exclusive access to several resources. For a discussion of this, it is convenient to distinguish between the following job situations:

>*Outbound job:* job in the ASRS that is assigned a workstation and must be moved from the ASRS to the workstation tool
>
>*Floor job:* job on a workstation output stand that is to be moved to the input stand of another workstation
>
>*Inbound job:* job on a workstation output stand that is to be moved into the ASRS whether it is finished or scrapped or being staged

For an *outbound* job, resources are allocated as follows:

1. Acquire workstation input stand.
2. Acquire ASRS stand. (The part remains in its bin until one of the ASRS stands has been acquired.)
3. Acquire forklift.
4. Release forklift when part on ASRS stand.
5. Acquire AGV.
6. Release ASRS stand when part on AGV.
7. Release AGV when part on workstation input stand.
8. Acquire tool.
9. Release input stand when part moved into tool.
10. Acquire output stand.
11. Release tool.

A *floor job* starts with a workstation output stand. Additional resources are acquired as follows:

1. Acquire workstation input stand.
2. Acquire AGV.
3. Release output stand when part on AGV.

The rest is identical to steps 7 through 11 for an outbound job.

An *inbound* job starts with a workstation output stand. Additional resources are allocated as follows:

1. Acquire ASRS stand.
2. Acquire AGV.
3. Release workstation output stand when part on AGV.
4. Release AGV when part placed on ASRS stand.
5. Acquire forklift.
6. Release ASRS stand when part on forklift.
7. Release forklift when part in bin.

The order rule may be used to prove that the simultaneous exclusive access to these resources does not cause deadlock (see Exercise 9.1).

9.3 ANALYSIS

Based on the problem description in Section 9.2, we now proceed to the analysis of the FMS problem environment in terms of behavior patterns, objects, and subsystems. We want to model the environment in terms of subject entities operating on objects. In the software, this translates into subject–object structures with tasks as subjects. To be a suitable subject candidate, an entity should have time dimension, variety, and preferably longevity. This means that its behavior should be a significant thread of different events extended over a long period of time. In the software, such an entity will be modeled as an entity-life modeling task. The samplers, generators, and regulators discussed in Section 6.4 are also suitable subjects. In addition to the subjects, we may also find other behavior patterns that we choose to represent as software objects.

The software will consist of superimposed subject–object structures, each consisting of a subject task operating on a number of *objects*. These may be single objects, represented by an information-hiding package, or instances of abstract data types. To identify the objects in the software, we look for objects in the problem environment that have sets of well-defined operations, by which they are manipulated. These operations translate into operation subprograms. A degenerate object without operations is referred to as a *subsystem*. It is represented in the software by a subject package, which has no operation subprograms. To be meaningful, such a package must contain one or more subject tasks.

9.3.1 Entities in the FMS Problem Environment

Entities in the FMS problem environment whose behavior patterns can be used as bases for software structures include a *job*, an *AGV*, the *forklift*, a *workstation*, and the *supervisor*. These entities are discussed in the following sections.

9.3.1.1 Job behavior

The transition diagram in Figure 9-2 shows the life of a job in the FMS system. Most transitions are caused by events in the life of the job, such as "job created" or "workstation assigned." The modes, M0, M1, and so on, are characterized as follows:

M0	Initial mode: job not created, no part assigned
M1	Part in ASRS waiting for workstation
M2	Part in ASRS waiting for forklift
M3	Outbound part on forklift
M4	Outbound part on ASRS or output stand waiting for AGV
M5	Part on AGV, en route to workstation
M6	Part on workstation input stand
M7	Part in tool
M8	Part on workstation output stand
M9	Inbound part on output stand waiting for AGV
M10	Inbound part on AGV
M11	Inbound part on ASRS stand, waiting for forklift
M12	Inbound part on forklift
M13	Part in bin
M14	Final mode: part finished or scrapped

Some transitions shown in Figure 9-2 are caused by events in conjunction with conditions. Such a condition further specifies the mode in which the event occurs. (This is discussed in Section 5.3.1.) Moreover, a *null*-move occurs spontaneously, without a causing event (Section 5.2.2.3).

> The transition M8–M9 occurs either if the part is bumped or if the part has been finished or scrapped. In the latter case it occurs on *null* input.

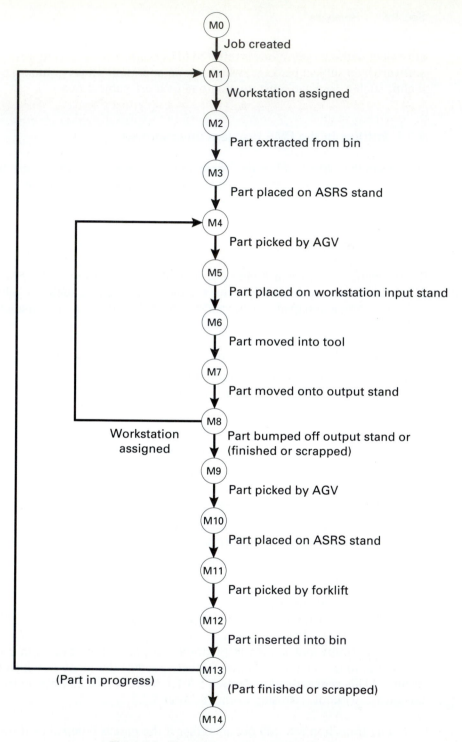

Figure 9-2 Transition diagram of the life of a job.

In mode M13, the *null*-move M13–M1 occurs if the part is in progress. The *null*-move M13–M14 occurs if the part is finished or scrapped.

These *null*-moves are useful since they allow a finished or scrapped part to go through the same steps on its way from an output stand to the ASRS as one that is merely being moved to the warehouse for temporary staging between job steps.

It is evident in Figure 9-2 that the life of a job is fairly straightforward and passes through a series of modes with a few exceptions, where it loops back to an earlier mode. Except for the transitions M8–M4 and M13–M1, each mode is followed by a single transition to the next mode, leading from M0 to M14. This means that the life of a job can easily be rendered as a sequence diagram (see Exercise 9.2).

9.3.1.2 AGV and forklift behaviors

The *AGV* and the *forklift* exhibit rather similar behaviors. The life of an AGV consists of moving different parts between stands and is based on the following loop:

```
loop
    Move to stand
    Pick part
    Move to stand
    Place part
end loop
```

Note that the sequence

```
    Move to stand
    Pick part
    Move to stand
    Place part
```

always refers to one job at a time. Thus it is part of the life of a job as well as that of the AGV.

The life of the forklift is an iteration of a selection between a stand-to-bin move and a bin-to-stand move. The stand-to-bin move consists of the following:

```
    Move to stand
    Pick up part
    Move to bin
    Insert part into bin
```

This sequence always refers to a specific job at a time.

9.3.1.3 Workstation behavior

The life of an automated workstation consists of a loop:

```
loop
    Robot moves part into tool
    Part is elaborated
    Robot moves part onto output stand
end loop
```

This loop is a good basis for entity-life modeling. But the workstation management is delegated to the microcomputer at each workstation, and will not be
further discussed here. The sequence

```
Robot moves part into tool
Part is elaborated
Robot moves part onto output stand
```

always refers to one specific job at a time.

9.3.1.4 Supervisor behavior

The *supervisor* interacting with the system via a terminal is a straightforward user
entity. It has obvious similarities with the user task in a time-sharing system. The
following is a possible outline of the supervisor behavior:

```
loop
    Display menu
    Get user selection
    case <user selection> is
        when <process plan> ⇒
            Prompt for necessary data
        when <job> ⇒
            Prompt for necessary job data
        etc.
    end case;
end loop;
```

9.3.2 Choice of Subjects

The entities are assessed for their suitability as subjects according to the criteria
given in Chapter 8. The intention is to capture as much as possible of the sequen-

tial dependencies of the problem in a minimum set of different subjects. Once we have found a set of subject tasks that account for the timing of all the events in the system, other entities are modeled as objects operated on by the subjects.

Supervisor.   The supervisor is a typical *user entity* representing a sequential human–computer dialogue. It can be modeled by a user task.

Job.   The job is a queueable entity since jobs vie for different resources. A job has a sequential behavior pattern, reflecting the position of the associated part at each point in time. It has time dimension, since the job undergoes long sequential series of operations to do with storage, transportation, elaboration, and so on. It is a mobile entity with substantial variety. All events in the FMS except some events associated with the supervisor happen to a job. The job is not as long-lived as the FMS as a whole, since jobs are created and finished during execution.

Forklift.   A forklift has a sequential behavior pattern: it handles one job at a time and goes through a sequence of motions for each job. It has a weaker time dimension than the job. (All events associated with the forklift are also part of the life of a job. In normal operation, there are no independent events in which no job participates.) The variety of forklift is less than for a job. The forklift is *mobile* and as long-lived as the system. It is not queueable. As in the case of the elevator entity, its reschedulability may be useful for the detection of error situation.

AGV.   The AGV is similar to the forklift. The AGV is queueable, in that idle AGVs queue for jobs.

Workstation.   The workstation has a sequential behavior and reasonable time dimension and variety, reflecting a number of steps taken for each job. Conceivably, the workstation could be regarded as a queueable entity, with idle workstations queueing for jobs. As for the AGV, the reschedulability of the workstation entity could be utilized for detection of breakdowns of the physical workstation.

The thread of events initiated by the supervisor are conveniently accounted for by the supervisor entity. Most of the remaining events in the system can be accounted for by means of *job* entities. We will refer to the solution where the jobs drive the software while operating on devices such as AGVs and the forklift as *Solution 1*. This solution is further explored in the rest of this chapter. With this solution, most of the queueing can be handled by the built-in task queueing mechanism.[1] That the job entity is relatively short-lived is only a minor drawback.

---

[1] As it turns out, the Ada task queueing mechanism is inadequate to handle the queueing of jobs waiting for a workstation (see Section 9.4.5).

Intuitively, Solution 1 means that each job actively pursues its processing plan. It successively acquires resources such as an AGV or a workstation and uses them to transport or elaborate its associated part. The AGV, the workstation, and so on, are objects, or tools that the job operates on. The operations are described in conjunction with each object but carried out by the executing job. With its strong time dimension, the job entity strings together all the events necessary to carry it from creation to completion. As queueable entities, the individual jobs compete for access to the different resources.

As discussed earlier, the allocation of shared resources is a central concern in the FMS. Subjects and objects can be identified by reasoning about resources and resource users. Solution 1 is borne out by this reasoning, since it is natural to think of the job as acquiring and releasing the resources necessary for its completion. Another solution—*Solution 2*—is equally possible, where the workstations drive the software by requesting work. With the workstation allocation policy in Section 9.2.6 we can define an *input-stand* entity that takes action to obtain a part as soon as the previous part has been moved into the tool. To do this, the input stand must identify a suitable job, and, depending on where the part is located, acquire the necessary resources to move it. The life of *input stand* is an iteration of some of the events in the life of a job (Figure 9-2): It takes a job in mode M1 or M8 and leaves it in mode M7.

A job in the workstation tool is subject to a series of actions under the control of a *tool* entity, say, which ultimately places it on the output stand. Once on the output stand (mode M8), the job may be obtained by an instance of *input stand* and moved to another workstation. But this happens only if a workstation wants the job. A different procedure is needed if the job is finished or must be staged in storage. This can be handled by means of an *output-stand* entity that takes a job from mode M8 to either M1 or M14.

In Solution 1, each job is one entity from creation to completion. The downside is that each job needs a thread of control for its entire lifetime, even though it may spend much time in storage. Solution 1 requires N threads for this if there are currently N jobs in the system. Solution 2 requires $M=3*W$ threads of control where W is the number of workstations. (One thread each is needed for the input stand, the tool, and the output stand.) M is typically less than N. On the other hand, the hand-over of jobs between entities is a difficulty in Solution 2. A case in point is when the part is on the output stand of a workstation W1 waiting to be either assigned a workstation W2 or bumped by another job. The part may then become an object of contention between the *output-stand* entity of W1 that must bump it and the *input-stand* entity of W2 that wants to obtain it. Although the workstations drive Solution 2 while the jobs drive Solution 1, the only essential difference is that Solution 2 splits the life of the job in two. The reason for this similarity is that the deadlock-free strategy to acquire and release resources is central to the problem regardless of solution.

9.4 SOFTWARE DESIGN

With the supervisor and job as subjects, the ASRS, AGVs, stands, workstations, and process plans become objects, operated on by the jobs. The detailed behavior of the forklift, the AGV, or a workstation is hidden behind such operations as "move job from stand X to stand Y". Figure 9-3 shows two overlapping subject–object structures, one for the job subject and one for the supervisor subject. The objects accessed by JOB_TASK are:

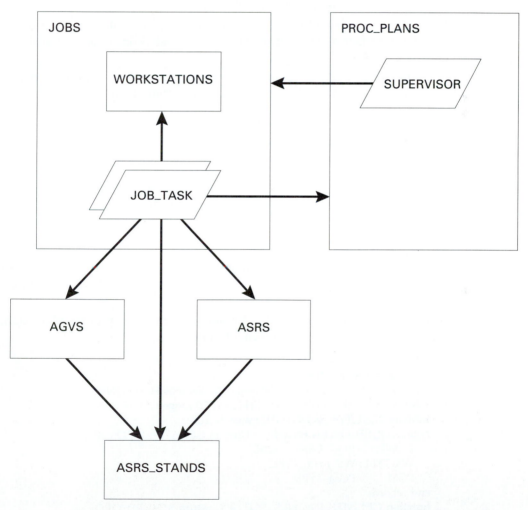

Figure 9-3   Subjects and objects in the FMS software. The JOB_TASK subjects operate on WORKSTATIONS, AGVS, ASRS, ASRS_STANDS, and PROC_PLANS. The SUPERVISOR subject operates on the JOBS object.

ASRS_STANDS, representing the pool of ASRS input/output stands (Section 9.4.2).

ASRS, hiding how parts are stored and retrieved from the automated storage and retrieval system (Section 9.4.3).

AGVS, representing the set of automated guided vehicles in the reality. AGVS hides how parts are transported between two stands by means of AGVs (Section 9.4.4).

WORKSTATIONS, hiding the management of the workstations and workstation queues (Section 9.4.5). This package is modeled on the set of workstations on the FMS factory floor.

PROC_PLANS, hiding information about process plans, job steps, and so on. The interface of PROC_PLANS (Figure 9-4) makes one operation available to JOB_TASK:

GET_STEP_INFO(P, S) returns a *set record* for step S of process plan P indicating workstation type, and NC program identity. (If the process plan has been completed, the step record indicates that the job is done.)

SUPERVISOR is encapsulated in the package PROC_PLANS, which includes all process plan management and is separated from the management of jobs in progress. JOB_TASK is given access to the process plans as described above. On the other hand, the supervisor requires current information about the jobs. For this reason, the JOB_TASK and WORKSTATIONS are encapsulated in a package JOBS. From the point of view of SUPERVISOR, JOBS is an object with the following interface (Figure 9-5):

NEW_JOB creates a new job record and a JOB_TASK instance. The JOB_TASK instance is called at the entry INIT with a link to the job record as a parameter.

GET_JOB_INFO returns such job information as priority, process plan, step, and current status for a given job number.

```
package PROC_PLANS is
type WS_TYPE_TYPE0 is (LATHE,MILL,WASH,INSPECT,NONE);
subtype WS_TYPE_TYPE is WS_TYPE_TYPE0 range LATHE..INSPECT;
subtype PGM_TYPE is INTEGER range 1..100;
type STEP_RECORD is record    -- Used in GET_STEP_INFO call
    DONE:     BOOLEAN:=FALSE;
    WS_TYPE: WS_TYPE_TYPE;
    PGM:      PGM_TYPE;
end record;
function GET_STEP_INFO(P,S: INTEGER) return STEP_RECORD;
end PROC_PLANS;
```

Figure 9-4 Specification of the information-hiding package PROC_PLANS.

```
   with AGVS; use AGVS;
   with PROC_PLANS; use PROC_PLANS;
package JOBS is
type JOB_INFO_RECORD is record   -- Used in GET_JOB_INFO call
   QUE:  WS_TYPE_TYPE0;
   PLAN, STEP, PRI: INTEGER;
   EXISTS, DONE, ABT, IN_ASRS: BOOLEAN:=FALSE;
end record;
procedure NEW_JOB(J_NUM, PLAN, PRI: INTEGER);
procedure REL_OUT_STAND(S: STAND_TYPE);
procedure SET_PRI(J_NUM, PRI: INTEGER);
function GET_JOB_INFO(J_NUM: INTEGER) return JOB_INFO_RECORD;
procedure DELETE_JOB(J_NUM: INTEGER);
end JOBS;
```

Figure 9-5   Specification of the information-hiding package JOBS.

SET_PRI changes the priority of a job in progress and requeues it as appropriate.

DELETE_JOB deletes a finished job. (It is to be used after the finished part has
   been moved out of the ASRS.)

The operation subprograms are explained somewhat further in Section
9.4.7. The interface, which is based on job, process plan, and step numbers, and
hides the actual representation of jobs in progress and process plans, may be
expanded to give the supervisor more information, such as the status of the
workstation queues. The complete, realistic supervisor interface is beyond the
scope of this case study. The package JOBS contains one additional operation
subprogram, REL_OUT_STAND. It is called by an instance of AGV_TASK after a part
has been picked up off an output stand. In the following sections we describe
each subject task and software object.

9.4.1 JOB_TASK

The program text of JOB_TASK, shown in Figure 9-7, is based on the transition
diagram in Figure 9-2. Figure 9-6 includes the declarations of various identifiers
referenced in JOB_TASK. Together with JOB_TASK itself, they are declared in a
package JOBS. Earlier, when basing program text on transition diagrams, we have
usually relied on explicit mode representation and variations on a loop with a case
statement over modes. (See, for example, the program VDU_EXPL in Figure 5-8
and the package CRUISE in Figure 5-13.) In the present case we take advantage of
the straightforward behavior of a job, which makes an explicit mode variable
unnecessary. Instead, we rely on implicit mode representation and map the transition diagram onto a sequential control structure with two loops corresponding to

```
MAX_WS_NO: constant := 5;  -- Maximum workstations per type
subtype WS_NO_TYPE is INTEGER range 0..MAX_WS_NO;
type Q_ELT_TYPE;
type Q_PTR_TYPE is access Q_ELT_TYPE;
type JOB_TASK;
type JOB_PTR_TYPE is access JOB_TASK;
task type JOB_TASK is
    entry INIT(QQ: Q_PTR_TYPE);
    entry ASSIGNED(W_N: WS_NO_TYPE);
    entry ON_OUT_STAND(ABORTED: BOOLEAN);
    entry IN_STAND_CLEAR;
    entry CLEAR_OUT_STAND;
end;
type Q_ELT_TYPE is record                 -- Job record
    TASK_PTR:    JOB_PTR_TYPE:=new JOB_TASK;
    JOB_NO:      INTEGER;                  -- Job number
    IN_ASRS:     BOOLEAN:=TRUE;  -- Job in warehouse
    NEXT:        Q_PTR_TYPE;               -- Next job in queue
    LINK:        Q_PTR_TYPE;               -- Next live job
    PLAN:        INTEGER;                  -- Process plan
    STEP:        INTEGER:=1;               -- Current or next job step
    BIN:         INTEGER;                  -- ASRS bin number
    PRI:         INTEGER;                  -- Priority
    DONE:        BOOLEAN:=FALSE; -- Job done
    ABT:         BOOLEAN:=FALSE; -- Job aborted
    QUEUED_ON: WS_TYPE_TYPE0;      -- Ws type if job queued
end record;
subtype WS_INDX_TYPE is WS_NO_TYPE range 1..MAX_WS_NO;
OUT_STAND, IN_STAND: array (WS_TYPE_TYPE, WS_INDX_TYPE) of
STAND_TYPE; -- Output and input stand number per workstation type and number
LIVE: Q_PTR_TYPE; -- List of job records for all live jobs
```

Figure 9-6 Declaration of task type JOB_TASK and other identifiers relevant to JOB_TASK. (The declarations are in the body of the package JOBS.)

```
task body JOB_TASK is
    Q:         Q_PTR_TYPE;   -- Queueable job record
    I_STAND, O_STAND: STAND_TYPE;
    WS_NO:   WS_NO_TYPE:=0;
    SR:        STEP_RECORD;
begin
    accept INIT(QQ: Q_PTR_TYPE) do Q:=QQ; end;
    SR:=GET_STEP_INFO(Q.PLAN, 1); -- Data for first step
    COMPLETION: loop
        -- Job is in ASRS bin.
        ENQUEUE(SR.WS_TYPE, WS_NO, Q);
```

Figure 9-7 JOB_TASK body modeled on the life of a job.

```
    if WS_NO=0 then
        accept ASSIGNED(W_N: WS_NO_TYPE) do WS_NO:=W_N; end;
    end if;
    -- Workstation has been assigned.
    -- Acquire stand. Move part from bin to stand.
    Q.IN_ASRS:=FALSE;    -- Update job status.
    ASRS.BIN_TO_STAND(O_STAND, Q.BIN);
    FLOOR: loop
        -- Job is on output stand. Move to input stand.
        I_STAND:=IN_STAND(SR.WS_TYPE, WS_NO);
        AGVS.MOVE(O_STAND, I_STAND);
        ON_IN_STAND(SR.WS_TYPE, WS_NO, Q);
        -- Job data sent to ws. Part placed on input stand.
        accept IN_STAND_CLEAR;
        -- Part has been moved to tool.
        REL_IN_STAND(SR.WS_TYPE, WS_NO);
        accept ON_OUT_STAND(ABORTED: BOOLEAN) do Q.ABT:=ABORTED; end;
        -- Part is on output stand; job possibly aborted.
        O_STAND:=OUT_STAND(SR.WS_TYPE, WS_NO);
        exit FLOOR when Q.ABT;    -- Exit upon abortion
        Q.STEP:=Q.STEP+1;          -- Get information for next step.
        SR:=GET_STEP_INFO(Q.PLAN, Q.STEP);
        Q.DONE:=SR.DONE;        -- DONE if job finished.
        exit FLOOR when Q.DONE; -- Exit if job finished.
        ENQUEUE(SR.WS_TYPE, WS_NO, Q);
        if WS_NO = 0 then  -- Ws for next step unavailable.
            select accept ASSIGNED(W_N: WS_NO_TYPE) do WS_NO:=W_N; end;
-- Ws is now assigned.
            or accept CLEAR_OUT_STAND;   -- Job bumped
                DEQUEUE(SR.WS_TYPE,WS_NO,Q); -- Dequeue job
                -- until part is in ASRS. If WS_NO /= 0,
                -- workstation just became available.
                exit FLOOR when WS_NO=0; -- Stage in ASRS
            end select;
        end if;
    end loop FLOOR;
    -- Move job to ASRS.
    STANDS_CONTROL.ACQUIRE(I_STAND); -- Acquire ASRS stand.
    AGVS.MOVE(O_STAND, I_STAND);
    WS_NO:=0;                -- Job is on ASRS stand.
    ASRS.STAND_TO_BIN(I_STAND, Q.BIN); -- Move into bin.
    Q.IN_ASRS:=TRUE;
    if Q.ABT or Q.DONE then -- If job finished or aborted, exit.
        Q.TASK_PTR:=null;
        exit COMPLETION;
    end if;
    end loop COMPLETION;
exception
    when others => null; -- (Placeholder)
end JOB_TASK;
```

Figure 9-7 (*continued*)

the two loops in the transition diagram. We will now proceed to an informal description of the task text where we make references back to the modes in Figure 9-2. Several subprogram calls appearing in the task text are mentioned. More detailed explanations are provided later in the chapter in conjunction with the various packages.

Initially, the job is in mode M0. **Accept** INIT and the GET_STEP_INFO call are part of the creation of a job, and leave the job in mode M1. At the top of the COMPLETION loop, the part is in the ASRS bin, in mode M1. ENQUEUE puts the job on queue for the next workstation type. If a workstation number (WS_NO) other than zero is returned, a workstation has been assigned. Otherwise, the task waits for workstation assignment in the statement **accept** ASSIGNED. When a workstation has been assigned, the job is in mode M2. The subprogram BIN_TO_STAND includes the acquisition of an ASRS stand and the movement from bin to stand. On return, the job is in mode M4. (Mode M3 is internal in BIN_TO_STAND.)

At the top of the FLOOR loop, the part is outbound on an ASRS stand or on a workstation output stand (mode M4). The subprogram AGVS.MOVE moves the part to the input stand of its next workstation. Upon return, the job is in mode M6. (M5 is internal in AGVS.MOVE.) The subprogram ON_IN_STAND transmits job data to the workstation. The task waits in **accept** IN_STAND_CLEAR for the workstation to signal that the part has been moved off the input stand and into the tool. The job is then in mode M7. The input stand is released.

The task now waits in **accept** ON_OUT_STAND for the workstation to finish the present job step and place the part on the output stand. This puts the job in mode M8. If the job step was aborted as indicated by a parameter, the job transitions to mode M9, and the FLOOR loop is exited. If the job is not aborted, GET_STEP_INFO is called to retrieve the next job step information from the process plan. If the job step just completed was the final one, the FLOOR loop is exited (transition to M9). Otherwise, the job is queued for the next workstation type.

If WS_NO/=0 is returned by ENQUEUE, a workstation has been assigned. Otherwise, the task waits in a **select** statement for one of two events, assignment of a workstation or bumping. (This **select** construct is further explained in Section 9.4.6.) Assignment implies a transition to M4, and the task loops back in the FLOOR loop. Bumping implies transition to M9 and causes the FLOOR loop to be exited.

After an exit from the FLOOR loop, the part is on an output stand bound for the ASRS (mode M9). An ASRS stand is acquired, and AGVS.MOVE is called to move the part to the stand. (The call to STANDS_CONTROL is discussed in Section 9.4.3.2.) Upon return from AGVS.MOVE the job is in mode M11. (M10 is internal in AGVS.MOVE.) STAND_TO_BIN moves the part from ASRS stand to bin and leaves the job in mode M13. (M12 is internal in STAND_TO_BIN.) If the job has not been aborted or finished, a transition to M1 occurs, and control returns to the top of the COMPLETION loop. Otherwise, the job transitions to the final mode M14, and the COMPLETION loop is exited.

The text of JOB_TASK is at a fairly high level of abstraction with most of the details hidden in operation subprograms. The handling of the case WS_NO = 0 after the calls to ENQUEUE is the exception, where complicated constructs appear in the JOB_TASK text. This is because Ada does not allow **accept** statements in subprograms, but instead, forces us to include them in-line in the task body.

9.4.2 Package ASRS_STANDS

In the FMS problem environment, the set of ASRS stands is an object with two operations, *acquire stand* and *release stand*. A package ASRS_STANDS, modeled on the set of stands, is shown in Figure 9-8. (It is also included in the buhrgaph in Figure 9-9.) ASRS_STANDS hides how stands are allocated to jobs. The package specification contains the specification of a task STANDS_CONTROL, so clients *withing* the package may call the entries STANDS_CONTROL.ACQUIRE and STANDS_CONTROL.RELEASE directly. STANDS_CONTROL uses a guard, allowing ACQUIRE calls only when stands are available and RELEASE calls at any time. Thus JOB_TASK instances waiting for ASRS stands sit on the ACQUIRE entry queue.

The placement of the task specification of STANDS_CONTROL in the package specification is pragmatic. The task is really a part of the secret of STANDS_CONTROL and could be hidden behind operation subprograms such as STAND_ACQUIRE and STAND_RELEASE, each of which could contain the entry calls to STANDS_CONTROL. Such a solution would be resilient to change but also somewhat lengthy. (Compare also the structure of package ASRS in Section 9.4.3, where the task interface is hidden inside an operation subprogram.)

Although ASRS_STANDS ensures that each stand is allocated to at most one job at a time, it does not influence the strategy involved in stand allocation. For example, ASRS_STANDS cannot enforce the release of a stand after it has been acquired by a job. The initiatives for stand acquisition and release come from JOB_TASK and the packages ASRS and AGVS and are discussed in Section 9.4.3.2. As shown in Figure 9-3, ASRS_STANDS represents an object at a fairly low level of abstraction that is operated on from other objects as well as from the JOB_TASK body. (All operations are executed by the job subject.)

9.4.3 Package ASRS

The ASRS package is modeled on the automated warehouse and hides how warehouse bins are allocated and how the forklift operates. (For the purposes of this case study, bin allocation is greatly simplified, and each job retains its bin throughout its life even while the part is on the factory floor.) In our analysis of the FMS problem environment, a job operates on the ASRS object when the part must be stored in or retrieved from a warehouse bin. In the design, JOB_TASK uses the two operation procedures BIN_TO_STAND and STAND_TO_BIN for this. The buhrgraph

```
      with AGVS; use AGVS;
  package ASRS_STANDS is
  -- Package representing the set of ASRS stands
  -- ACQUIRE and RELEASE are operations on the set performed
  -- under exclusive access hidden inside the package.
  MAX_ASRS_STANDS: constant := 4;
  subtype ASRS_STAND_TYPE is STAND_TYPE range 1..MAX_ASRS_STANDS;
  task STANDS_CONTROL is
      entry ACQUIRE(S: out ASRS_STAND_TYPE);
      entry RELEASE(S: ASRS_STAND_TYPE);
  end;
  end ASRS_STANDS;

  package body ASRS_STANDS is
  -- Mutual exclusion enforced by special-
  -- purpose guardian task STANDS_CONTROL.
  -- The array FREE represents acquired and free stands.
  task body STANDS_CONTROL is
  type FREE_ARRAY is array (ASRS_STAND_TYPE) of BOOLEAN;
  FREE: FREE_ARRAY:=(others => TRUE);
  NONE: constant FREE_ARRAY:=(others => FALSE);  -- No free stand
  begin
     loop
        select
           accept RELEASE(S: ASRS_STAND_TYPE) do FREE(S):=TRUE; end;
        or
           when FREE /= NONE =>
           accept ACQUIRE(S: out ASRS_STAND_TYPE) do
              L: for SS in ASRS_STAND_TYPE loop
                 if FREE(SS) then
                    FREE(SS):=FALSE; S:=SS;
                    exit L;
                 end if;
              end loop L;
           end;
        or terminate;
        end select;
     end loop;
  end STANDS_CONTROL;
  end ASRS_STANDS;
```

Figure 9-8   Information-hiding package ASRS_STANDS.

in Figure 9-9 shows the interaction of JOB_TASK with the packages ASRS and
ASRS_STANDS. The text of ASRS is given in Figure 9-10.

   With the simplified approach to bin allocation, the only secret of the ASRS
package is how a part is transported by the forklift in the two directions from bin-

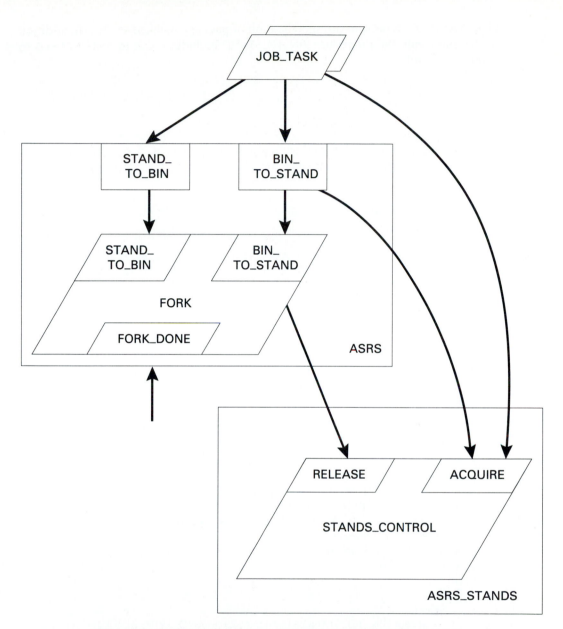

Figure 9-9   Buhrgraph showing JOB_TASK and the packages ASRS and ASRS_STANDS.

to-stand and from stand-to-bin. The sequence of events necessary for this is represented by a task FORK, which has two entries, STAND_TO_BIN and BIN_TO_STAND. Each entry is called from the operation procedure with the same name. (Compare Section 9.4.2, where we instead chose to put the specification of task STANDS_CONTROL in the specification of package ASRS_STANDS.) In addition to the entry call, the procedure BIN_TO_STAND includes a call to ASRS_STANDS to acquire a stand.

```
    with ASRS_STANDS; use ASRS_STANDS;
package ASRS is
procedure BIN_TO_STAND(STAND: out ASRS_STAND_TYPE; BIN: INTEGER);
procedure STAND_TO_BIN(STAND: ASRS_STAND_TYPE; BIN: INTEGER);
end ASRS;

    with TEXT_IO; use TEXT_IO;
package body ASRS is
task FORK is
    entry STAND_TO_BIN(STAND: ASRS_STAND_TYPE; BIN: INTEGER);
    entry BIN_TO_STAND(STAND: ASRS_STAND_TYPE; BIN: INTEGER);
    entry FORK_DONE;
end FORK;
procedure STAND_TO_BIN(STAND: ASRS_STAND_TYPE; BIN: INTEGER) is
begin
    FORK.STAND_TO_BIN(STAND, BIN);
end;
procedure BIN_TO_STAND(STAND: out ASRS_STAND_TYPE; BIN: INTEGER) is
S: ASRS_STAND_TYPE;
begin
    STANDS_CONTROL.ACQUIRE(S);
    FORK.BIN_TO_STAND(S, BIN);
    STAND:=S;
end;
procedure TO_BIN(B: INTEGER) is separate;
procedure BIN_GET(B: INTEGER) is separate;
procedure BIN_PUT(B: INTEGER) is separate;
procedure TO_STAND(S: ASRS_STAND_TYPE) is separate;
procedure PICK is separate;
procedure PLACE is separate;
task body FORK is
begin
    loop
        select
            accept BIN_TO_STAND(STAND: ASRS_STAND_TYPE; BIN: INTEGER) do
                TO_BIN(BIN);
                accept FORK_DONE;
                BIN_GET(BIN);
                accept FORK_DONE;
                TO_STAND(STAND);
```

Figure 9-10   Information-hiding package ASRS.

```
                    accept FORK_DONE;
                    PLACE;
                    accept FORK_DONE;
                end BIN_TO_STAND;
            or
                accept STAND_TO_BIN(STAND: ASRS_STAND_TYPE; BIN: INTEGER) do
                    TO_STAND(STAND);
                    accept FORK_DONE;
                    PICK;
                    accept FORK_DONE;
                    STANDS_CONTROL.RELEASE(STAND);
                    TO_BIN(BIN);
                    accept FORK_DONE;
                    BIN_PUT(BIN);
                    accept FORK_DONE;
                end STAND_TO_BIN;
            or terminate;
            end select;
        end loop;
    end;
    end ASRS;
```

Figure 9-10   (*continued*)

9.4.3.1 *FORK* task

The task FORK has the following schematic structure:

```
        select
            accept STAND_TO_BIN do
                Move forklift to stand
                accept FORK_DONE
                Pick up part
                accept FORK_DONE
                RELEASE(stand)
                Move forklift to bin
                accept FORK_DONE
                Insert part in bin
                accept FORK_DONE
            end STAND_TO_BIN;
        or
                accept BIN_TO_STAND do ......
                end BIN_TO_STAND;
        end select;
```

The program text in Figure 9-10 relies on separate subprograms for hardware commands such as PICK and PLACE. As mentioned earlier, the steps necessary to carry a part between bin and stand are part of the thread of events for the forklift and also part of the life of a job. For this reason, they are executed by the JOB_TASK. As a matter of information hiding, the handling of the forklift belongs in the package ASRS rather than in the body of JOB_TASK. In this regard the task FORK is a subtask of JOB_TASK, as discussed in Section 8.3.2.2. FORK is necessary for two additional reasons:

It serves as a *guardian* of the forklift, which is a shared resource that can only be used by one job at a time.

It serves as the interrupt handler of the completion interrupts from the forklift.

This solution is limited to the case where there is exactly one forklift. A more general solution for a similar problem is used in the package AGVS (Section 9.4.4).

9.4.3.2 Management of ASRS stands

An *outbound* part that is being moved from the storage bin onto the floor is first carried by the forklift to an ASRS stand, from where it is picked up by an AGV. An *inbound* part that is being moved from a workstation output stand to the ASRS is first taken by an AGV to a ASRS stand, where it is picked up by the forklift. To avoid the part being stuck on the forklift or on an AGV when all ASRS stands are occupied, each job reserves an ASRS stand ahead of time. The stand is then released when the part has been moved off of the stand (see also Section 9.2.7).

The policy of releasing ASRS stands as soon as possible leads to asymmetry between outbound jobs and inbound jobs. For an outbound job, JOB_TASK calls STANDS_CONTROL.ACQUIRE from within the procedure BIN_TO_STAND to acquire a stand, which is later released by AGV_TASK. For an inbound job, STANDS_CONTROL.ACQUIRE is called directly from the JOB_TASK body, while STANDS_CONTROL.RELEASE is called by the FORK task. The result is the somewhat complex relation between JOB_TASK, ASRS, and ASRS_STANDS shown in Figure 9-9. The relation between AGVS and ASRS_STANDS is discussed in Section 9.4.4 and shown in Figure 9-11. This is merely a modularization issue. All acquisitions and releases are executed by the JOB_TASK as a subject, regardless of where the ACQUIRE and RELEASE calls occur in the text.

9.4.4 Package AGVS

Just as a job operates on the ASRS object in order to store or retrieve the part from the automated warehouse, it operates on an object representing the set of automated guided vehicles, AGVs, for transportation between stands on the factory floor. The buhrgraph in Figure 9-11 shows the interaction between a JOB_TASK and the package AGVS, which represents the set of vehicles. The text of AGVS is shown in Figure 9-12. The package body contains two tasks, AGV_CONTROL and

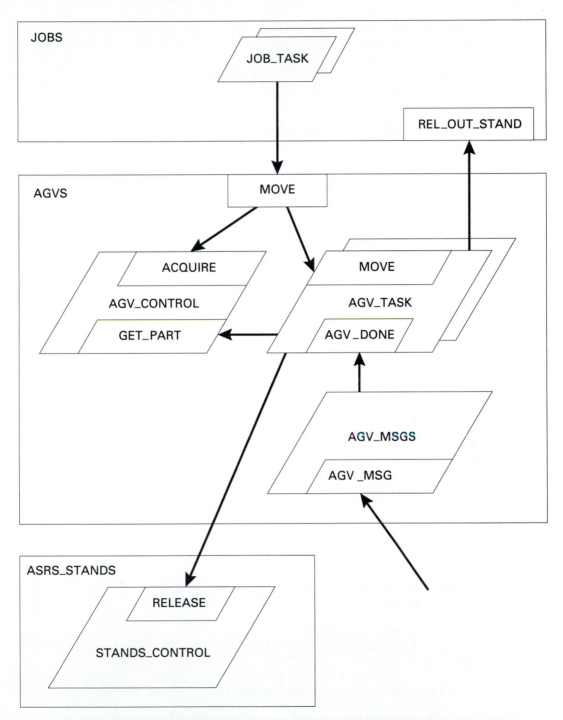

Figure 9-11 Buhrgraph showing the operations by JOB_TASK instances on the packages AGVS and ASRS_STANDS.

```
package AGVS is
-- Package representing the set of AGVs
subtype STAND_TYPE is INTEGER;
procedure MOVE(O_STAND,I_STAND:STAND_TYPE);
-- Move part from O_STAND to I_STAND.
end AGVS;

    with ASRS_STANDS; use ASRS_STANDS;
    with JOBS; use JOBS;
package body AGVS is
-- Exclusive access is enforced by AGV_CONTROL, which also
-- matches requests for transport from jobs with free AGVs.
-- Task type AGV_TASK models a single AGV.
MAX_AGV: constant:= 4;
subtype AGV_ID_TYPE is INTEGER range 1..MAX_AGV;
type AGV_TASK;
type AGV_PTR_TYPE is access AGV_TASK;
type AGV_ARRAY is array (AGV_ID_TYPE) of AGV_PTR_TYPE;
OWNER: AGV_ARRAY:=(others => null);  -- AGV task corresponding to each AGV id
type AGV_MSG_TYPE is record -- Message from vehicle
    AGV_ID: AGV_ID_TYPE;
    ERROR: BOOLEAN:=FALSE;
end record;
task type AGV_TASK is
-- Models one AGV
    entry INIT(AA: AGV_ID_TYPE);
    entry MOVE(O_STAND, I_STAND: STAND_TYPE);
    entry AGV_DONE(ABORTED: BOOLEAN);
end;
task AGV_CONTROL is
-- Guardian task
    entry ACQUIRE(AP: out AGV_PTR_TYPE);
    entry GET_PART(A: AGV_ID_TYPE);
end;
task AGV_MSGS is
-- Handler of interrupts from AGVs
    entry AGV_MSG(MSG: AGV_MSG_TYPE);
end;
procedure MOVE(O_STAND, I_STAND: STAND_TYPE) is
A: AGV_PTR_TYPE;
begin
    AGV_CONTROL.ACQUIRE(A);
    A.MOVE(O_STAND, I_STAND);
end;
```

Figure 9-12 Information-hiding package AGVS containing the task type AGV_TASK. AGV_TASK sends a series of commands to the physical AGV. (This is hardware dependent and here indicated by comments.) After each command, the task waits for an entry call indicating completion.

```
task body AGV_TASK is
-- Behavior of an AGV
A: AGV_ID_TYPE;
M: AGV_MSG_TYPE;
begin
    accept INIT(AA: AGV_ID_TYPE) do A:=AA; end;
    M.AGV_ID:=A;
    loop
        AGV_CONTROL.GET_PART(A);
        select
            accept MOVE(O_STAND, I_STAND: STAND_TYPE) do
                -- Move: Send command to vehicle....
                accept AGV_DONE(ABORTED: BOOLEAN);
                -- Pick: Send command to vehicle....
                accept AGV_DONE(ABORTED: BOOLEAN);
                if O_STAND in ASRS_STAND_TYPE then
                    STANDS_CONTROL.RELEASE(O_STAND);
                else REL_OUT_STAND(O_STAND);
                end if;
                -- Move: Send command to vehicle....
                accept AGV_DONE(ABORTED: BOOLEAN);
                -- Place: Send command to vehicle....
                accept AGV_DONE(ABORTED: BOOLEAN);
            end;
        or terminate;
        end select;
    end loop;
end AGV_TASK;
task body AGV_CONTROL is
-- Matching of idle AGVs and jobs in need of transport
AA: AGV_ID_TYPE;
begin
    loop
        select -- Call from idle AGV_TASK:.
            accept GET_PART(A: AGV_ID_TYPE) do AA:=A; end;
            -- AA is id of first available vehicle.
        or terminate;
        end select;
        select  -- Call from JOB_TASK:.
            accept ACQUIRE(AP: out AGV_PTR_TYPE) do AP:=OWNER(AA); end;
                -- Return pointer to task of available vehicle.
        or terminate;
        end select;
    end loop;
end AGV_CONTROL;
```

Figure 9-12   (*continued*)

```
task body AGV_MSGS is
-- Accept interrupts from AGVs and notify affected tasks.
   M: AGV_MSG_TYPE;
begin
   loop
      select
         accept AGV_MSG(MSG: AGV_MSG_TYPE) do M:=MSG; end;
         OWNER(M.AGV_ID).AGV_DONE(M.ERROR);
      or terminate;
      end select;
   end loop;
end;
begin
   -- Create and initialize AGV tasks.
   for A in OWNER'RANGE loop
      OWNER(A):=new AGV_TASK;
      OWNER(A).INIT(A);
   end loop;
end AGVS;
```

Figure 9-12   *(continued)*

AGV_MSGS, and a task type, AGV_TASK. There is one instance of AGV_TASK for each vehicle.

AGVS has a single operation procedure, MOVE(FROM, TO), where FROM and TO are stand identifiers. MOVE interfaces with the task AGV_CONTROL to obtain a reference, A, to an instance of AGV_TASK, and then calls the entry MOVE of that task as follows:

```
AGV_CONTROL.ACQUIRE(A);
A.MOVE(FROM, TO);
```

The entry call to ACQUIRE assigns an instance A of AGV_TASK to the job. The actual movement of the job by means of the AGV is accomplished through the entry call A.MOVE.

9.4.4.1 Allocation of AGVs

When a call to AGV_CONTROL assigns the instance, A, of AGV_TASK to the calling JOB_TASK instance, the physical vehicle corresponding to A is assigned to the job on the factory floor. The guardian task AGV_CONTROL handles this allocation of AGV_TASK instances in a loop with the following essential structure. The entry GET_PART is called by AGV_TASK instances and ACQUIRE by JOB_TASK instances:

```
loop
    accept GET_PART(A: AGV_ID_TYPE) do AA:=A; end;
    accept ACQUIRE(AP: out AGV_PTR_TYPE) do AP:=OWNER(AA); end;
end loop;
```

Here AA is an AGV identity and OWNER(AA) is a pointer to the corresponding AGV_TASK. With this construct, idle instances of AGV_TASK are queued on the GET_PART entry, while JOB_TASK instances waiting for an AGV are queued on ACQUIRE. (The complete version shown in Figure 9-12 includes **select** statements with **terminate** alternatives so that AGV_CONTROL may expire when its callers have terminated; compare also Section 7.6.)

9.4.4.2 AGV_TASK

The AGV_TASK is modeled on the behavior pattern of an automated guided vehicle. In a loop, it first calls AGV_CONTROL to obtain a part and then performs the series of steps needed to move to a given stand, pick up a part, move to another stand, and place the part. It issues a series of commands to the physical vehicle and awaits its response to each command as follows:

```
loop
    AGV_CONTROL.GET_PART(A);
    accept MOVE(FROM, TO) do
        Issue move command to vehicle
        accept AGV_DONE;
        Issue pick command to vehicle
        accept AGV_DONE;
        Issue move command to vehicle
        accept AGV_DONE;
        Issue place command to vehicle
        accept AGV_DONE;
    end;
end loop;
```

The completion interrupts from the physical AGVs are received by a special interrupt handler, AGV_MSGS, which calls the entry AGV_DONE of the relevant instance of AGV_TASK. AGV_MSGS is necessary because of a limitation in the Ada syntax. Although each instance of AGV_TASK is dedicated to one particular physical vehicle, the syntax does not allow the interrupts from each vehicle to be hardcoded into the corresponding instance.

The body of **accept** MOVE is always executed by a JOB_TASK subject on behalf of a particular job. The events associated with the movement are part of the life of a job, and change its mode. As discussed in Section 9.3.1.1, a job is in mode M5 while the part is being moved to a workstation input stand and in M10 while it is being moved to the ASRS.

As long as the AGV is assigned to a job, AGV_TASK acts as an object, operated on by JOB_TASK instances. (These instances are the subject task executing the body of **accept** MOVE.) In this situation AGV_TASK resembles a guardian that introduces no additional concurrency. It is thus similar to the FORK task. Technically, AGV_TASK is no guardian, however, but a queueable subject task. This is evident only in the statement AGV_CONTROL.GET_PART(A), where the empty AGV queues up for a new job. This statement is executed by the task asynchronously, outside the rendezvous with JOB_TASK.

9.4.5 Package WORKSTATIONS

The package WORKSTATIONS represents the set of workstations and hides the allocation of workstations to jobs. Unlike the forklift and the AGVs, where the exclusive access is hidden in the packages ASRS and AGVS, workstations are explicitly acquired. Furthermore, in the packages ASRS and AGVS, all queuing is based on the built-in Ada task queuing mechanism. For example, JOB_TASK instances waiting for an AGV sit on the entry queue of AGV_CONTROL.ACQUIRE. This queuing mechanism is inadequate for jobs waiting for access to workstations. Instead, the workstation queues are modeled explicitly as data structures. This is necessary for the following reasons:

> The supervisor must be able to change the priority of a queued job and to change its position in a queue accordingly.
>
> A job on an output stand must be able to wait for the first of two events: Either it is assigned a workstation, or it is bumped off the stand.
>
> (A third consideration has to do with Solution 2 discussed in Section 9.3.2. In that solution, jobs in the ASRS do not have threads but must still be queued for workstations.)

The buhrgraph in Figure 9-13 shows the operation subprograms and rendezvous involved in the workstation management. The operation subprograms are explained in Section 9.4.5.1. Figure 9-14 is the program text of WORKSTATIONS. The internal representation of the workstation queues as data structures is discussed in Section 9.4.5.2. Section 9.4.5.3 discusses the interface to the physical workstations.

9.4.5.1 Operation subprograms

As discussed earlier, a workstation is assigned to a job as soon as its input stand is empty. Thus a job acquires a workstation by acquiring its input stand. Workstation acquisition is explicit, but there is no clean-cut *acquire* operation. Instead, ENQUEUE is used for workstation acquisition as described below. The operation REL_IN_STAND is used to release a stand.

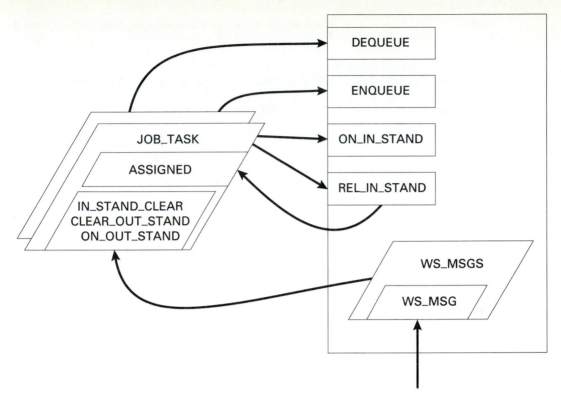

Figure 9-13 Buhrgraph showing the operations by JOB_TASK instances on the package WORKSTATIONS and on other JOB_TASK instances. The operations by WS_MSGS on JOB_TASK instances are also shown.

For workstation acquisition, the operation ENQUEUE is first called and returns a parameter (WS_NO) indicating whether a workstation is immediately available. If this is not the case, the job waits for the entry call ASSIGNED signaling that a workstation has been allocated. (This allows a job to wait for either two events: workstation assignment or bumping; see further Section 9.4.6.)

REL_IN_STAND is the release operation. It is called when a job has been moved from the input stand into the tool proper and allows the input stand to be assigned to another job. REL_IN_STAND makes an entry call to the ASSIGNED entry of the JOB_TASK instance of the first job in the relevant queue.

The following operation procedures are also used by JOB_TASK instances:

DEQUEUE dequeues the calling JOB_TASK. It is used when the job has been bumped off an output stand. (The job is requeued when it has been moved to the ASRS.)

ON_IN_STAND signals to the workstation that a part has been moved to an input stand. Job data is submitted to the workstation.

413

```
package WORKSTATIONS is
procedure DEQUEUE(WS_TYPE: WS_TYPE_TYPE; WS_NO: out WS_NO_TYPE;
Q: Q_PTR_TYPE);
procedure ENQUEUE(WS_TYPE: WS_TYPE_TYPE; WS_NO: out WS_NO_TYPE;
Q: Q_PTR_TYPE);
procedure ON_IN_STAND(WS_TYPE: WS_TYPE_TYPE; WS_NO: WS_NO_TYPE;
Q: Q_PTR_TYPE);
procedure REL_IN_STAND(WS_TYPE: WS_TYPE_TYPE; WS_NO: WS_NO_TYPE);
procedure CHANGE_PRI(Q: Q_PTR_TYPE);
end WORKSTATIONS;


package body WORKSTATIONS is
SEMA: SEMAPHORE; -- Protects WS data structures
type TASK_ARRAY_TYPE is array (WS_TYPE_TYPE, WS_INDX_TYPE) of JOB_PTR_TYPE;
    -- Array of job tasks per workstation type and number
type Q_ARRAY_TYPE is array (WS_TYPE_TYPE) of Q_PTR_TYPE;
    -- Array of job records per workstation type
IN_STAND_TASK, OUT_STAND_TASK, WS_TASK: TASK_ARRAY_TYPE;
    -- IN_STAND_TASK is job task currently occupying input stand.
    -- OUT_STAND_TASK is latest job task occupying output stand.
    -- WS_TASK is job task occupying tool.
FIRST_IN_Q: Q_ARRAY_TYPE:=(others => null);
    -- Queues of job records per workstation type
RESERVED: array (WS_TYPE_TYPE, WS_INDX_TYPE) of INTEGER:=(others =>
    (others => 0));
    -- Job number having input stand reserved, or 0.
    -- Stand is reserved until part is moved into tool.
type EVENT_TYPE is (IN_STAND_CLEAR, CLEAR_OUT_STAND, ON_OUT_STAND);
type WS_MSG_TYPE is record  -- Msg from ws to FMS controller
    EVENT: EVENT_TYPE;
    WS_TYPE: WS_TYPE_TYPE;
    WS_NO: INTEGER;
    ABORTED: BOOLEAN:=FALSE;
end record;
TOTAL_WS: constant array (WS_TYPE_TYPE) of INTEGER:=(others => MAX_WS_NO);
-- Total workstations per type
task WS_MSGS is
    entry WS_MSG(MSG: WS_MSG_TYPE);
    -- This entry is called from the communications
    -- software when a message from the physical workstation
    -- is received. (The communication software is not
    -- shown.)
end;
SHORT: constant DURATION:=1.0;
```

Figure 9-14   Information-hiding package WORKSTATIONS. (WORKSTATIONS is hidden in the body of JOBS.)

```
task body WS_MSGS is
-- Accept messages from workstations and notify job tasks.
   T:JOB_PTR_TYPE;
   M: WS_MSG_TYPE;
begin
   loop
      select
         accept WS_MSG(MSG: WS_MSG_TYPE) do M:=MSG; end;
         SEMA.ACQUIRE;
         case M.EVENT is
            when IN_STAND_CLEAR =>
               T:=IN_STAND_TASK(M.WS_TYPE, M.WS_NO);
               WS_TASK(M.WS_TYPE, M.WS_NO):=T;
               IN_STAND_TASK(M.WS_TYPE, M.WS_NO):=null;
               T.IN_STAND_CLEAR;
            when CLEAR_OUT_STAND =>
               T:=OUT_STAND_TASK(M.WS_TYPE, M.WS_NO);
               if T /= null then
               select T.CLEAR_OUT_STAND;
               or delay SHORT;
               end select;
               end if;
            when ON_OUT_STAND =>
               T:=WS_TASK(M.WS_TYPE, M.WS_NO);
               OUT_STAND_TASK(M.WS_TYPE, M.WS_NO):=T;
               WS_TASK(M.WS_TYPE, M.WS_NO):=null;
               T.ON_OUT_STAND(M.ABORTED);
         end case;
         SEMA.RELEASE;
      or terminate;
      end select;
   end loop;
end;
procedure REMOVE(WS_TYPE: WS_TYPE_TYPE; Q: Q_PTR_TYPE;
   FOUND: out BOOLEAN) is
-- Remove Q element from a queue. Called by DEQUEUE and
-- SET_PRI. Precondition: Caller has acquired SEMA.
F: Q_PTR_TYPE:= FIRST_IN_Q(WS_TYPE);
begin
   FOUND:=FALSE;
   if F=Q then
      FIRST_IN_Q(WS_TYPE):=Q.NEXT;
      FOUND:=TRUE; Q.QUEUED_ON:=NONE;
      return;
   elsif F /= null then
      while F.NEXT/=null loop
         if F.NEXT=Q then
```

Figure 9-14   (*continued*)

```
                F.NEXT:=Q.NEXT;
                FOUND:=TRUE; Q.QUEUED_ON:=NONE;
                return;
            end if;
            F:=F.NEXT;
        end loop;
    end if;
end REMOVE;
procedure DEQUEUE(WS_TYPE: WS_TYPE_TYPE; WS_NO: out WS_NO_TYPE;
Q: Q_PTR_TYPE) is
-- Remove Q from queue. Set WS_NO to 0.
-- If workstation has been assigned, return number in WS_NO.
FOUND: BOOLEAN;
begin
    WS_NO:=0;
    SEMA.ACQUIRE;
    REMOVE(WS_TYPE, Q, FOUND);
    if FOUND then SEMA.RELEASE; return; end if;
    -- Job is not queued. Search owners of input stands.
    for W in 1..TOTAL_WS(WS_TYPE) loop
        if IN_STAND_TASK(WS_TYPE,W)=Q.TASK_PTR then
            WS_NO:=W;
            SEMA.RELEASE;
            return;
        end if;
    end loop;
end;


procedure PLACE_IN_Q(WS_TYPE: WS_TYPE_TYPE; Q: Q_PTR_TYPE) is
-- Used by ENQUEUE and SET_PRI to insert job in workstation queue.
-- Caller has acquired SEMA.
F: Q_PTR_TYPE:=FIRST_IN_Q(WS_TYPE);
begin
    if F=null or else F.PRI<Q.PRI then
        FIRST_IN_Q(WS_TYPE):=Q; Q.NEXT:=F;
    else
        while F.NEXT/=null and then
            F.NEXT.PRI>=Q.PRI loop
            F:=F.NEXT;
        end loop;
        Q.NEXT:=F.NEXT; F.NEXT:=Q;
    end if;
    Q.QUEUED_ON:=WS_TYPE;
end;
```

Figure 9-14   (*continued*)

```
procedure ENQUEUE(WS_TYPE: WS_TYPE_TYPE; WS_NO: out WS_NO_TYPE;
Q: Q_PTR_TYPE) is
-- If workstation free, reserve it, return number in WS_NO.
-- Otherwise, enqueue job for WS_TYPE and set WS_NO to 0.
F: Q_PTR_TYPE;
begin
    SEMA.ACQUIRE;
    for W in 1..TOTAL_WS(WS_TYPE) loop
        if RESERVED(WS_TYPE, W)=0 then
            RESERVED(WS_TYPE, W):=Q.JOB_NO; WS_NO:=W;
            SEMA.RELEASE;
            return;
        end if;
    end loop;
    WS_NO:=0; PLACE_IN_Q(WS_TYPE, Q);
    SEMA.RELEASE;
end;
procedure ON_IN_STAND(WS_TYPE: WS_TYPE_TYPE; WS_NO: WS_NO_TYPE;
Q: Q_PTR_TYPE) is
-- Submit job data to workstation. Part is on input stand.
begin
    SEMA.ACQUIRE;
    IN_STAND_TASK(WS_TYPE, WS_NO):=Q.TASK_PTR;
    SEMA.RELEASE;
    -- Communicate with physical workstation....
end;
procedure REL_IN_STAND(WS_TYPE: WS_TYPE_TYPE; WS_NO: WS_NO_TYPE) is
-- Release input stand. (Part has been moved into tool.)
Q: Q_PTR_TYPF;
begin
    SEMA.ACQUIRE;
    IN_STAND_TASK(WS_TYPE, WS_NO):=null;
    Q:=FIRST_IN_Q(WS_TYPE);
    if Q=null then
        RESERVED(WS_TYPE, WS_NO):=0;
        SEMA.RELEASE;
        return;
    else
        RESERVED(WS_TYPE, WS_NO):=Q.JOB_NO;
        FIRST_IN_Q(WS_TYPE):=Q.NEXT;
        Q.QUEUED_ON:=NONE;
        select Q.TASK_PTR.ASSIGNED(WS_NO);
        or delay SHORT;
        end select;
    end if;
    SEMA.RELEASE;
end;
```

Figure 9-14 (*continued*)

```
procedure CLEAR_OUT_STAND_TASK(WS_TYPE: WS_TYPE_TYPE;
WS_NO: WS_NO_TYPE) is
-- Clear OUT_STAND_TASK entry. Called by REL_OUT_STAND when
-- AGV has removed part from output stand.
begin
    SEMA.ACQUIRE;
    OUT_STAND_TASK(WS_TYPE, WS_NO):=null;
    SEMA.RELEASE;
end;
procedure CHANGE_PRI(Q: Q_PTR_TYPE) is
-- Change priority of a job. Called by SET_PRI.
FOUND: BOOLEAN;
WS_TYPE: WS_TYPE_TYPE0;
begin
    SEMA.ACQUIRE;
    if Q.QUEUED_ON/=NONE then
        WS_TYPE:=Q.QUEUED_ON;
        REMOVE(WS_TYPE, Q, FOUND);
        if FOUND then PLACE_IN_Q(WS_TYPE, Q); end if;
    end if;
    SEMA.RELEASE;
end CHANGE_PRI;
end WORKSTATIONS;
```

Figure 9-14   (*continued*)

The operation subprogram CHANGE_PRI, which is used by SUPERVISOR, is discussed in Section 9.4.7.

9.4.5.2 Representation of workstations and workstation queues

Since internal Ada task queuing cannot be used, the jobs queuing for each type of workstation are represented as linked lists of records of type Q_ELT_TYPE (see Figure 9-6). An array, FIRST_IN_QUEUE, indicates the first job record in queue for each workstation type. In addition, there are three arrays, WS_TASK, IN_STAND_TASK, and OUT_STAND_TASK, for jobs currently occupying each workstation, input stand, and output stand, respectively. The array elements are of type **access** JOB_TASK and are indexed by pairs (T, N), where T is a workstation type and N is a workstation number. Together, T and N uniquely define a workstation. For example, IN_STAND_TASK(T, N) = a, where a points to a certain instance, i, of JOB_TASK, if the part belonging to i is on the input stand of the workstation defined by T and N. Yet another array, RESERVED, represents currently held workstations. Each element RESERVED(T,N) contains the number of any job holding exclusive access to the workstation's input stand.

Each calling task is given exclusive access to the data structures representing workstations and workstation queues while any structure is queried or modified. This exclusive access is hidden in the body of WORKSTATIONS. Mutual exclusion is enforced by means of one instance, SEMA, of the SEMAPHORE task type. The reader may want to inspect Figure 9-14 and ensure that all the critical sections bracketed by SEMA.ACQUIRE and SEMA.RELEASE have short extent and consist entirely of manipulations on data.[2]

9.4.5.3 *Workstation communication*

As discussed in Section 9.2.5, the interface between the workstations and the controller is based on message communication. All messages from workstations are received by a task WS_MSGS, which uses the task arrays described in Section 9.4.5.2 to locate the relevant JOB_TASK instance and makes a rendezvous with it. The following entries are used:

> ON_OUT_STAND when the part has been moved to the output stand
> IN_STAND_CLEAR when the part has been moved off the input stand
> CLEAR_OUT_STAND when the part must be bumped off the output stand (see
>   Section 9.4.6)

WS_MSGS is shown in Figure 9-13. The text is included in Figure 9-14. For simplicity, the details of the communication have been omitted, and WS_MSGS is assumed to receive the messages from the workstations by means of calls to the entry WS_MSG.

9.4.6 Bumping

JOB_TASK as a model of the behavior of a job was discussed in the beginning of the chapter. We now return to an intricate aspect of the JOB_TASK text in the light of the discussion above of the various objects accessed by the task. The situation where a part may be bumped off a workstation output stand by another job was mentioned in Section 9.2.6. This involves three jobs, J1, J2, and J3, and their respective parts and JOB_TASK instances. J1, J2, and J3 have the following status:

---

[2] Note that the internal subprogram REMOVE has a semaphore-related precondition requiring that the calling task acquire SEMA before the call. As a postcondition, the semaphore remains acquired. The reader may verify that the precondition is indeed met. (REMOVE is called from DEQUEUE and SET_PRI.)

J1 is sitting on an output stand of a workstation W waiting for a workstation of a certain type. All workstations of that type are occupied.

J2 is about to release a workstation X of the same type.

J3 is currently occupying the tool of workstation W and is about to be finished.

In this situation, the JOB_TASK instance J1 is waiting for either of two events:

Assignment of the workstation X. This event is caused by J2 when it releases the workstation.

Bumping. This event is caused by J3 when it has finished and needs the output stand.

The selective wait for either event is accomplished by a rather involved use of the rendezvous. JOB_TASK (Figure 9-7) contains the following construct, executed by J1:

```
ENQUEUE(WS_TYPE, WS_NO, Q);
if WS_NO = 0 then
   select accept ASSIGNED(WS_N: WS_NO_TYPE) do
      WS_NO:=WS_N; end
   or accept CLEAR_OUT_STAND;
      DEQUEUE(WS_TYPE, WS_NO, Q);
      exit FLOOR when WS_NO = 0;
   end select;
end if;
```

The **select** statement allows J1 to wait for an entry call at either ASSIGNED or CLEAR_OUT_STAND, whichever comes first.

ASSIGNED is called by the JOB_TASK instance J2 from the subprogram REL_IN_STAND when J2 releases workstation X.

CLEAR_OUT_STAND is called by the task WS_MSGS when J3, which is currently in the tool of workstation W, has been finished.

(The texts of REL_IN_STAND and WS_MSGS are both shown in Figure 9-14.) Different things happen depending on which entry call comes first:

If the call at ASSIGNED comes first, job J1 is moved off the output stand and to the input stand of workstation X.

If the call at CLEAR_OUT_STAND comes first, job J1 is staged in the ASRS.

There is a very small likelihood that the calls are nearly simultaneous. For example, the call to CLEAR_OUT_STAND may occur just after the ASSIGNED call and before the WORKSTATION data structures have been updated to reflect that work-station X has been assigned to J1. The call to CLEAR_OUT_STAND might then become a *dangling rendezvous*, a call that is never served. To avoid a dangling rendezvous, the entry calls to CLEAR_OUT_STAND and ASSIGNED are both *timed*. For example, the entry call in WS_MSGS is as follows:

```
select T.CLEAR_OUT_STAND;
or delay SHORT;
end select;
```

This is a timed entry call with a time-out value of SHORT seconds, where SHORT is a constant of type DURATION equal to, say, 0.2. In this construct, WS_MSGS waits a maximum of 0.2 seconds for the call CLEAR_OUT_STAND to be accepted. After 0.2 seconds, WS_MSGS continues processing after the **select** statement.

In our example, T references the JOB_TASK instance of job J1. If the entry call is not accepted within 0.2 seconds, it is assumed that job J1 has already been assigned a workstation. (The delay interval is designed to cover any reasonable period of time between ENQUEUE and the **accept** statement). REL_IN_STAND contains a similar, timed entry call to ASSIGNED.

There is yet another complication. Assume that job J1 is to be bumped off the output stand. Before it is actually moved, it is taken off the workstation queue by means of a call to DEQUEUE. This is necessary, since a part that is being transported to the ASRS cannot be rerouted to a workstation. (Once the job is in its ASRS bin it is requeued by means of a call to ENQUEUE.)

In DEQUEUE, the slight chance that the job might have been assigned a workstation just after the task received the CLEAR_OUT_STAND entry call is again taken into account. The text of DEQUEUE is shown in Figure 9-14. Once the semaphore, SEMA, has been acquired, IN_STAND_TASK is consulted to see if an assignment has taken place. If so, DEQUEUE returns a nonzero workstation number. As a result, the part is moved to the next workstation rather than the ASRS.

9.4.7 Supervisor Interface

To conclude the description of the FMS software, this section includes a brief discussion of the supervisor interface to the JOBS package. Figure 9-15 shows the relation between the SUPERVISOR task, the package JOBS, and the package WORKSTATIONS, declared inside JOBS. As mentioned in Section 9.4, SUPERVISOR calls the subprograms NEW_JOB, SET_PRI, GET_JOB_INFO, and DELETE_JOB. Each subprogram is outlined below.

> NEW_JOB takes data such as job number, process plan, and priority as input and creates a new job record and a JOB_TASK instance. The JOB_TASK instance is called at the entry INIT with a link to the job record as a parameter.

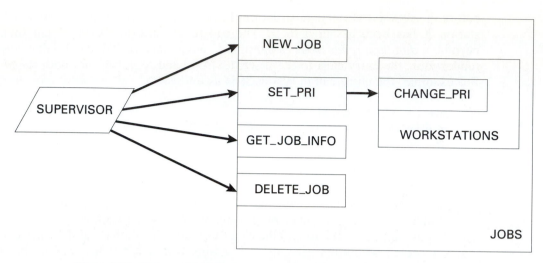

Figure 9-15 Buhrgraph showing the operations by the subject task SUPERVISOR on the package JOBS and the hidden package WORKSTATIONS.

GET_JOB_INFO returns such job information as priority, process plan, step, and current status for a given job number.

SET_PRI changes the priority of a job in progress by calling WORKSTATIONS.CHANGE_PRI (Figure 9-14). CHANGE_PRI investigates whether the job is currently queued for a workstation. If so, it removes the job from the queue and requeues it according to its new priority.

DELETE_JOB deletes a finished job.

9.5 CHAPTER SUMMARY

> *Of making many books there is no end, and much study is a weariness of the flesh.*
>
> *Ecclesiastes*

The analysis and design of the FMS program illustrates the basic principles presented throughout the book applied to a realistic system of reasonable complexity. There is a clear element of modeling both of behavior patterns, represented by tasks, and of objects, represented by packages. There are also examples of data modeling, with the queues of jobs represented as linked data structures. The modeling of data structures on structures in the reality is quite well understood and not a central topic of this book.

In principle, entity-life modeling starts by analyzing the problem environment for entities, objects, and subsystems, which are then modeled in the software. The construction of the FMS software was described as such a straightforward process, leading smoothly to a software solution that nicely reflects the reality. It is not the intention to suggest that a software system can really be developed that way. Clearly, the FMS solution presented here is the polished result of many iterations and false starts. As a summary, it is interesting to use the FMS problem as an illustration of the various analysis and design issues treated throughout the book.

The identification of objects or subsystems in the reality, and the modeling of packages on them, are discussed in Chapters 3 and 4. The theme is revisited for concurrent software in Chapter 8. Some objects in the FMS environment are fairly obvious, such as the ASRS and an AGV or set of AGVs, but it is difficult to arrive at a definite, optimum package structure. In the development of the FMS software, the ASRS_STANDS package was part of the ASRS package before it found its current form. As discussed in Chapter 7, the ASRS stands form a pool of resources shared by different jobs.

In addition to objects, entity-life modeling is also based on identification of behavior patterns in the problem environment. Regardless of approach, analysts of the FMS tend to capture the life of a job at an early stage. Modeling of programs directly on behavior patterns was discussed in Chapter 2, based primarily on sequence diagrams. In Chapters 2 and 5 we introduced finite automata and transition diagrams. Often, software modeled on finite automata exhibit explicit mode representation. In the FMS example, a transition diagram illustrates the life of a job clearly and concisely, but the straightforward behavior pattern is suitable for implicit mode representation.

Tasks based on simple behavior patterns are introduced in Chapter 6 and entity-life modeling tasks in Chapter 8. With this background, the implementation of the job as a task type is natural, leading to the subject–object structure where the JOB_TASK instances move the action forward by operating on objects. An alternative solution with workstations driving the software is also possible. Entity-life modeling is not a narrow method that leads to exactly one solution to each problem. Instead, it is an open-ended principle, whose primary goal is to base each solution on the realities of the problem environment. This can be done in a variety of ways as described throughout the book and summarized in this section.

REFERENCES

DEUTSCH, M. S., Focusing real-time systems analysis on user operations, *IEEE Software*, September 1988, pp. 39–50.

GOMAA, H., *Rapid Prototyping of Real Time Systems*, George Mason University, Fairfax, Va., 1988.

GOMAA, H., A software design method for distributed real-time applications, *J. Systems Software*, 9:2, February 1989, pp. 81–94.

SANDEN, B., *An Example of Concurrent Software Design in Ada*, Tech. Rep. CSSE-88-13, George Mason University, Fairfax, Va., 1988

EXERCISES

9.1 Order rule for FMS resources

Based on the discussion of resource allocation in Section 9.2.7, formulate a workable order rule for the FMS. Include the following resources:

> ASRS stand
> Forklift
> AGV
> Workstation input stand
> Workstation tool
> Workstation output stand

The data structures in WORKSTATIONS are also held exclusively by instances of JOB_TASK. Must this be taken into account when the order rule is applied?

9.2 Sequence diagram of job behavior

Translate the transition diagram in Figure 9-2 into a data sequence diagram.

9.3 Workstation program

The operations at each automated workstation are controlled by a microprocessor. The program running in the microprocessor is built on the life of the workstation as described in Section 9.3.1.3. Design and implement the program.

9.4 JOBS operation subprograms

Based on the specifications in Figures 9-5 and 9-14 and the narrative in Section 9.4.7, supply the details of the operation subprograms NEW_JOB, SET_PRI, GET_JOB_INFO, and DELETE_JOB.

9.5 Handling of raw material

The solution given here excludes the movement of raw material into the ASRS. (It is assumed that a piece of raw material is available in the ASRS when the job is defined.)

Assume instead that the life of a job starts at a *port* with an output stand, much like a workstation, and that the part must be moved from the port to the ASRS by means of an AGV. Redesign the FMS software accordingly. Also consider the case where finished and scrapped parts must be carried to a port to be removed from the system. Treat the output port as a station with one input stand that must be queued for as any workstation.

9.6 "Solution 2"

Redesign the FMS software according to Solution 2 suggested in Section 9.3.2. Focus particularly on the handover of each job between different subjects.

PROJECTS

9.1 Air traffic control game

This project is a computer simulation of air traffic control. The user acts as an air traffic controller and is responsible for the safe departure, direction, and landing of all aircraft in a given airspace. The user views a display screen, which has a radar display and messages indicating the status of each aircraft. The controller enters commands to either direct a specific aircraft or determine its status. The aircraft acknowledges each command with a response in the affirmative or negative, depending on whether it can execute the command.

The controlled airspace is a 15- by 25-mile area from ground level to 9000 feet. There are 10 *entry/exit gateways*, two *airports*, and two navigational beacons (*navaids*) within the airspace (Figure 9-16). A total of 26 aircraft become active in the airspace during the simulation, which can run from 16 to 99 minutes. No aircraft become active in the final 15 minutes. There are two types of aircraft: *Jets*, traveling at 4 miles per minute, and *Props*, traveling at 2 miles per minute. Depending on its origin, each aircraft either becomes ready for takeoff at one of the airports or enters the airspace through a gateway (at 6000 to 9000 feet) with about 1 minute of advance notice. Depending on its destination, each aircraft either leaves the airspace through a gateway (at 5000 feet) or lands at one of the airports. An aircraft may enter and leave the airspace at any angle.

The simulation terminates successfully if all aircraft have safely reached their destination in the allotted time. The simulation is aborted automatically if any of the following occurs:

> The selected simulation time expires before all aircraft have reached their destination.
>
> The controller enters a QUIT command.
>
> An aircraft attempts to exit the airspace at an improper gateway. (An aircraft destined for a gateway can exit the airspace at that gateway only at 5000 feet.) This is called a *boundary error*.
>
> Two aircraft are at the same altitude and less than 3 miles apart. This is called a *conflict error*.
>
> Two aircraft collide or an aircraft reaches zero altitude other than at the proper airport or on an approved landing glide path. This is called a *crash error*.

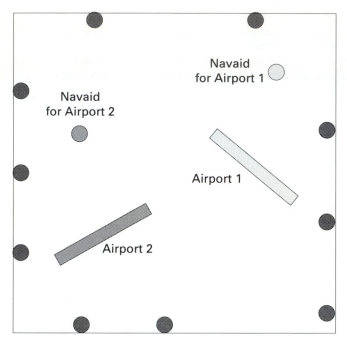

Figure 9-16 Sample airspace with two airports, two navaids and 10 entry/exit gateways.

An aircraft runs out of fuel before reaching its destination. (All aircraft have at least 5 minutes of fuel when they enter the airspace.)

For an aircraft to land at an airport, it needs to be first directed toward the appropriate navaid for that airport. Before the aircraft reaches the navaid, the controller can clear it for approach to the airport or direct it to enter a *holding pattern* at the navaid. The holding pattern consists of a circle through the navaid. The aircraft completes the circle by making eight left turns of 45 degrees each.

The user input consists of two types of commands: *queries* into the aircraft status and *changes* of the status. To query the status of a particular aircraft, the user enters the letter of the alphabet representing that aircraft. The result is displayed in the aircraft status box on the display screen. To change the status of an aircraft, the controller enters the aircraft letter followed by the appropriate letter A, L, or R and a number 0 through 5, as shown in the following table:

	A	L	R
0	Clear to land	Hold at navaid	Continue straight
1	Altitude: 1000 feet	Turn left 45 degrees	Turn right 45 degrees
2	Altitude: 2000 feet	Turn left 90 degrees	Turn right 90 degrees
3	Altitude: 3000 feet	Turn left 135 degrees	Turn right 135 degrees
4	Altitude: 4000 feet	Turn left 180 degrees	Turn right 180 degrees
5	Altitude: 5000 feet	Approach Airport 1	Approach Airport 2

For example, if the controller wanted the aircraft *X* to turn 90 degrees to the right, the proper command would be: *XR2*. An aircraft may turn right or left, ascend or descend any number of times based on the user's commands. The aircraft may be directed to hold at a navaid when it is within one mile from the navaid and headed toward it. It exits the holding pattern when it receives a turn command or an ascend or descend command. For landing, the aircraft must enter the *approach path* for a particular airport. The approach path is a line with its origin at the airport and extending about 8 miles out. It has the same heading as the runway. An aircraft can enter the approach path if a) it is within one mile from it, b) has an altitude of about 3000 feet, and c) has the same heading as the runway. The command is disregarded if the entry conditions are not met. An aircraft aborts its approach if it receives an ascend command. The aircraft must receive a clear-to-land command while it is on the approach path. If the command is not received by the time the aircraft is within 2 miles from the airport, a crash error exists.

The display screen has several sections. There is a *radar scope*, a *communications center*, an *aircraft status window*, and an area where controller commands and time remaining is displayed. The *radar scope* is a rectangle representing a horizontal view of the airspace. One character position on the screen represents a square mile. The object at the highest altitude in each such position is displayed.

Aircraft are displayed as letters from *A* to *Z* with a number following indicating the aircraft altitude in 1000s of feet.

The two *airports* are displayed as % and #, respectively.

Navaids appear as asterisks (*).

Gateways (entry/exit fixes) are indicated by the numbers 0 through 9.

The *communications center* displays all messages. The messages can be from aircraft replying to a command or from the supervisor. The messages are displayed in a scrolling window with the last five displayed at any given time.

The *aircraft status window* shows the status of the active or soon-to-be-active aircraft. This window scrolls if necessary. The status line toward the bottom of the list for a particular aircraft is the most recent but may not be the current status. The controller may request the current status of an aircraft by entering the letter of that aircraft as a command. This will provide the current status in the status box. When an aircraft leaves the airspace, all its status lines are removed. The status information includes: aircraft identity, aircraft type (*J* for jet and *P* for prop), altitude, origin, destination, heading (N, S, E, W, NE, NW, etc.), and plus (+) or minus (−), depending on how much fuel is left. (A plus indicates that more than 5 minutes of fuel remain.) The current actual time and the time remaining in the simulation are both displayed. Commands are displayed as they are entered by the controller and erased once they are processed.

9.2 *Automated vending machine*

The *automated vending machine (AVM)* is a 24-hour facility used to dispense such products as commercial computer programs or videotapes. It provides consistent service while requiring no human employees for normal operations. The AVM has two *front panels*, allowing two customers to purchase items at the same time. Each panel has a *visual display screen* with soft keys, a *keypad*, a *credit card reader*, and a *receipt printer*. The machine has only one *item-dispensing door*. The system contains a database used to keep track of prices and inventory. The system is connected to a credit card verification service and to AVM headquarters via dial-up lines.

A customer selects items from a catalog by responding to menus displayed on the screen. Using the keypad, the customer can browse the catalog. The customer can abort the browsing at any time simply by walking away. If she decides to complete the purchase, she places a major credit card in the card reader. The machine prompts the customer for a personal identification number (PIN) and compares it with the PIN stored on the card's magnetic stripe. If the PINs match, the machine sends a message to a credit card verification service. There are also company-issued credit cards which are instead verified at the AVM headquarters. If the customer does not have adequate credit, she is given the opportunity to reduce the number of items purchased or change the items. If the customer has ample credit, the requested items are delivered through the item-dispensing door one at a time.

Purchased items are taken from internal *carousel bins* by the stocking/delivery mechanism. The bar code on each item is scanned by a *laser scanner* and a field in the item's database entry is decremented before the item is dispensed through the door. A receipt is printed after the customer receives all her items. If a second customer has purchased items simultaneously, she will not begin receiving her items until the first customer receives all her items and her receipt.

After an item is scanned for delivery, the database is checked to determine if the item type is below its reorder point. If so, and the item is not already on order, a *restocking order* is sent to AVM headquarters. The physical restocking is performed by a headquarters employee called the Restocker, who visits each AVM regularly. During restocking, she places each item under the *input scanner*. If the scanner reads the bar code successfully, the proper database entry is incremented, the input conveyor takes the item to the handler, and the handler places the item in the correct bin. Customers can purchase items while restocking is taking place, but the stocking/delivery mechanism can be used by only one customer or the Restocker at each point in time.

Database maintenance, such as addition or deletion of catalog items, is performed by headquarters personnel remotely. These changes to the database, which are delivered in batch mode, cannot occur in parallel with customer browsing, item delivery, or restocking.

The project consists of designing the software operating in each AVM. Feel free to modify the mechanical construction of the AVM.

9.3 Bottling plant[3]

A bottling plant contains a number of *bottle lines* fed by a single *vat* containing the liquid to be bottled. Each line is independently operated by a *line operator*. Each line may fill different-sized bottles at its own pace. An *area supervisor* oversees the operation of several lines connected to one vat. A software program must

> Control the *level* and the *pH* of the liquid in the vat
> Manage the movement and the filling of the bottles on the various bottling lines
> Provide an interface to the line operators and the area supervisor

---

[3] The problem was suggested by M. S. Deutsch. The figure is adapted from [Deutsch].

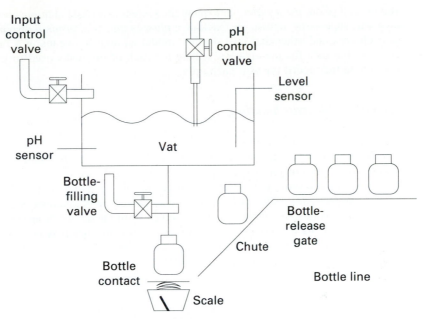

Figure 9-17 Schematic picture of one bottling line. [From M. S. Deutsch, Focusing real-time system analysis on user operations, *IEEE Software*, September 1988, pp. 39–50. Copyright © 1988 IEEE.]

The liquid level in the vat is maintained by means of a *level sensor* and by opening and closing the *input control valve* (see Figure 9-17). The pH of the liquid in the vat is maintained by means of a *pH sensor* and by opening and closing a *pH control valve*. Whenever the pH goes above a given limit, the pH control valve must open automatically to allow a neutralizing liquid into the vat. Bottles move in each line as indicated in Figure 9-17. One bottle at a time is released onto the *chute* through the *bottle release gate*. When the bottle is on the *scale* as indicated by the *bottle contact*, the *output control valve* is opened. The output control valve is closed when the bottle has reached its full weight as indicated by the scale. The system then seals, labels, and finally removes the bottle. A new bottle is then automatically released onto the chute.

The area supervisor can *disable* and *enable* the entire area at any time. If the pH in the vat cannot be kept within limits by means of the pH control valve, the area is disabled automatically. Each line operator can *start* and *stop* an individual line. When the line is stopped, the operator can change the bottle size. The line can be started only when the area is enabled, the bottle contact indicates that no bottle is on the scale, and the output valve is closed. (Any bottle remaining on the scale when the line is stopped must be removed manually before the line can be started.)

The *line operator's terminal* continuously displays the line status (on or off) and the current bottle size. The *area supervisor's terminal* displays the current pH level, the pH limits in effect, the liquid level, the area status (enabled or disabled), the status, and the bottle size of each individual line.

Design and implement the software for the bottling system. Include suitable scaffolding software to simulate the movement of the bottles, the liquid moving through the valves, and so on. As a variation, expand the system to include multiple areas each with its own vat, supervisor, and so on. Include a *plant manager's terminal* displaying the status of each area and other data. To do this, model an area by means of a record type that contains the data for the area and a field for each of the tasks used to model the area. Instantiate the record type for each area.

9.4 FMS with error handling

For simplicity, the treatment of the FMS software in this chapter has ignored the handling of various error situations such as the breakdown of an automated vehicle, workstation, or other device. As a major project, enhance the FMS software with suitable error handling. The following are some of the issues involved in this open-ended project.

Error detection. The FMS software may detect the breakdown of a device in either of two ways: An explicit error signal is received from the device or an operation is timed-out. This happens if a completion interrupt (or similar signal) is not received within a reasonable time from the start of the operation. When an error is detected, the FMS notifies the supervisor, who decides on further action.

Supervisor interface. The supervisor must be allowed to *take down* and *take up* a device such as a workstation, and AGV, or the forklift. By taking down a device, the supervisor takes it out of production so that it will not be scheduled to a job by the software. The supervisor may take down a malfunctioning device or a device in need of preventive maintenance. Furthermore, the supervisor must be able to decide proper recovery action in error situations.

Recovery action. Various actions are possible in response to particular error situations. For example, if an AGV breaks down with a part on it, there are at least three options:

> The part may be left on the AGV until the AGV is repaired. Normal processing then continues. This may be the best solution if the necessary repair is minor.
>
> If the AGV must be taken down for a considerable time, the job may be manually moved to its current destination, where normal processing continues.
>
> The AGV may seriously break down while on its way to pick up a part. In that case, a failure status may be returned to the JOB_TASK, which may then reexecute the MOVE operation. (It will then be assigned another AGV.)

A workstation breakdown may affect jobs occupying the input stand as well as the tool proper. (A part on the output stand is not affected.)

> If a workstation breaks down, a decision must be made whether the part currently in the tool must be scrapped or whether processing can continue once the workstation has been repaired.
>
> If a part is on the input stand of a workstation that breaks down, the simple option is to leave it there and resume processing when the workstation is repaired.
>
> If the job is high priority, it may be necessary to reenqueue the job. The JOB_TASK must then account for a movement of the part from the input stand of the downed workstation to another workstation.

The present design has a single forklift. If the forklift breaks down, the FMS can continue operating in a degraded mode. This means that parts already on the factory floor can continue processing, but no jobs can enter or leave the storage facility (ASRS). The following actions are necessary when the forklift breaks down:

>   If there is an outbound job on the forklift, it should be moved manually to the ASRS stand.
>   Since jobs in the ASRS may have workstations, ASRS stands and/or AGVs reserved, these devices should be released to be used by the jobs on the factory floor.

The redesigned FMS software may be implemented and tested in a simulated environment, such as on a PC. For this it is necessary to provide scaffolding software to simulate the operations of the AGVs, the forklift, and the workstations and their interactions with the FMS software. The scaffolding must simulate breakdowns. Distinguish the scaffolding clearly from the FMS software. As part of the scaffolding, insert PUT statements as appropriate in the FMS software and the scaffolding software so that the progress of each job is reflected on the screen. (Remember that the screen may be a shared resource.)

Allow the user to simulate the breakdown of various devices by means of the supervisor interface. This may be done with specific commands that are propagated to the scaffolding simulating the devices. These commands are part of the scaffolding and must be distinguished clearly from those supervisor commands that would exist in a real system, such as those necessary to take a device up or down and those used for recovery actions.

9.5 *Automated train switchyard*[4]

Freight trains entering a city often have cars bound for destinations that are reached by different tracks leaving the city. Thus a train entering a city may need to be broken up and each of its cars added to a train that is traveling toward that car's final destination. Breakup and reassembly of trains are performed in a train switchyard. Due to the hazardous nature of the working environment, switchyards will be automated to reduce industrial accidents. Here is how such an automated train switchyard might work.

A train is moved into the switchyard when the *switchyard supervisor* determines that the path from the *main line* to the *locomotive siding* is clear. After the train has been parked at the siding, automated equipment is used to break up the train and add its cars to new trains being assembled. The automated equipment identifies cars, locomotives, and switch engines by scanning *bar codes* with which they are marked.

Information about cars and shipments is kept in a *database* in the *switchyard computer*. Destinations are determined by *waybills* describing each *shipment*. Each waybill lists the shipment contents, the consignee, the destination, the route, and the bar codes of the cars carrying the shipment. Each car carries only one shipment, but a shipment can use many cars. A shipment may consist of empty cars being delivered to the location where they will be loaded. In this case, the waybill lists no contents.

---

[4] This project was suggested by Carl Dahlke and Thanh Luu.

Each switchyard is associated with a *freight terminal*. Cars that have reached their destination are deposited at the *freight terminal siding* when the incoming train is disassembled. Once cars are processed at the freight terminal they are either added to outgoing trains (if they are parts of a new shipment) or stored on an *empties siding* (if they have not yet been leased for a new shipment). Cars on the empties siding will eventually be rented to a shipper. When rented, an empty car is either returned to the freight terminal for loading or shipped out empty.

The switchyard computer has a *car manager's terminal* through which new destinations can be assigned to empties. If the destination is "empties siding," the empties are shunted to that siding. A car is brought back from the empties siding to the freight terminal for loading by assigning it the destination "freight terminal." An empty assigned a destination other than "empties siding" or "freight terminal" is picked up at its current location and added to an outbound train.

Figure 9-18 shows a hypothetical switchyard located at Alexandria, Virginia. This particular switchyard has tracks connecting to four other junction cities. A train from any of these junction cities enters the switchyard by approaching the main line and notifying the switchyard supervisor by radio. Once a train has received permission to enter the switchyard, the train engineer drives it to the locomotive siding. From there, the train is broken up and reassembled according to each individual car's destination. The *uncoupling device*, which travels on its own siding parallel to the locomotive siding, first reads the bar code of each car and relays it to the switchyard computer. The computer uses the bar codes to derive the destination of each individual car and commands the uncoupling device to uncouple the train at specific couplers so that contiguous cars with the same next destination are grouped together. We will use the word *car group* to describe one or more contiguous cars with the same next destination. As the incoming train is broken up, the car groups are moved by the switch engines and reassembled at their respective siding for the next waypoint.

Empty cars or locally loaded cars are also reassembled by switch engines under the control of the switchyard computer. The car manager's terminal at the freight terminal is used to enter such data as contents and final destination of locally loaded cars at the freight terminal and empty cars at the empties siding. This information is used by the switchyard computer to reassemble the locally loaded cars or empties to an outbound train.

Outbound trains are allowed to leave when they have more than 90 cars or at least one of the cars is more than 2 days old. The switchyard supervisor clears an outbound train for departure from his terminal. The train crew then boards the train and drives it to the next waypoint.

A *plan* consists of an ordered set of *moves* required to break up a train. A move is defined as travel through the switchyard in one direction. A *forward* move travels away from sidings toward the main line. A *backward* move travels toward a siding. Associated with each move is an ordered set of *switch settings* that define the path the move takes through the switchyard. A *move set* is a complete set of consecutive moves that leaves a car group at a siding. Several move sets can be carried out simultaneously, with different switch engines. The first move in a move set must position the switch engine so that on the second move it can hook up to a set of cars to be moved. There are four move subtypes:

> *Pull.* Move forward (away from a siding) until the car group clears a specified switch.

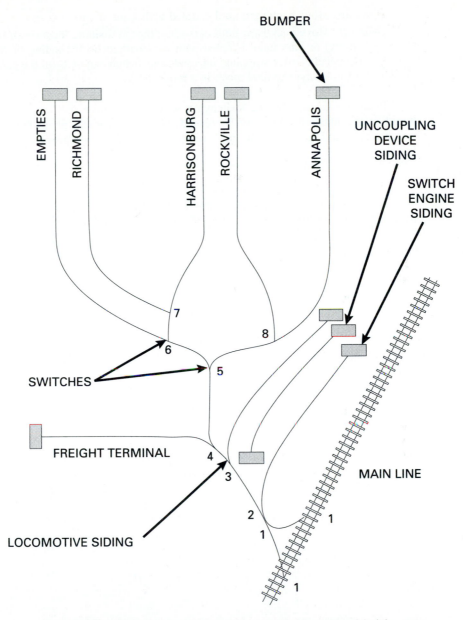

Figure 9-18 Hypothetical switchyard located at Alexandria, Virginia, near Washington, D.C. This particular switchyard has tracks connecting to four other junction cities.

Push. Move backward (toward a siding) until the car group is at a particular siding location. A push move is typically used for parking a switch engine on a siding and has a *siding location* attribute.

Hook up. Move backward until coupled with a set of cars.

Drop off. Move backward until cars are either at a siding location (if the siding is empty) or cars have coupled with cars parked on the siding (if the siding is occupied). After stopping, uncouple the switch engine from the cars. (A drop-off is always the final move in a move set.)

Plans are created by the switchyard supervisor. Move sets and entire plans are stored in the database and may be reused. Here is a sample plan. Train names and switches refer to Figure 9-18. R and L refer to the right and left prong of each switch.

Move	Switch settings
Pull switch engine from switch engine siding; clear switch 2.	2R
Hook up switch engine with car group.	2L, 3R
Pull car group from locomotive siding; clear switch 3.	3R, 2L
Drop off train A at siding.	3L, 4R, 5R, 8R
Pull switch engine clear of switch 3.	8R, 5R, 4R, 3L
Hook up switch engine to car group.	3R
Pull car group from locomotive siding; clear switch 3.	3R, 2L
Drop off car group at siding.	3L, 4R, 5R, 8R

Identify entities, objects, and subsystems in the switchyard problem environment. What are shared resources? Choose suitable subjects. (Consider queueable entities competing for shared resources.) Design the software running in the switchyard computer. Implement the software with appropriate scaffolding allowing you to simulate the environment.

Index